After the crash

DATE DUE

AFTER THE CRASH

AFTER THE CRASH

Financial Crises and
Regulatory Responses

EDITED BY
SHARYN O'HALLORAN
AND THOMAS GROLL

Columbia University Press
New York

Columbia University Press
Publishers Since 1893
New York   Chichester, West Sussex
cup.columbia.edu

Cataloging-in-Publication Data available from the
Library of Congress
ISBN 978-0-231-19284-2 (cloth)
ISBN 978-0-231-54999-8 (electronic)
LCCN 2019000324

Columbia University Press books are printed
on permanent and durable acid-free paper.
Printed in the United States of America

Cover design: Noah Arlow

To my parents,
Sally and James J. O'Halloran ⌒

CONTENTS

FOREWORD

DAVID MADIGAN

The financial contract may be mankind's greatest invention, but it undoubtedly causes all kinds of trouble. The crisis of 2007–2008 had profound consequences across the globe, and so, a decade after the crisis, it is appropriate to pause and take stock of its implications.

The immediate causes of the crisis may be relatively clear: widespread failures in financial regulation, including the Federal Reserve's failure to stem the tide of toxic mortgages; dramatic breakdowns in corporate governance; and an explosive mix of excessive borrowing and risk by households and by Wall Street. Though the causes are simple enough to state, the result in human misery was calamitous.

Over the past 250 years, there have been many similarly calamitous economic and financial crises in the United States and globally: the panic of 1792; the 1825 Latin American crisis; the global crisis of 1857, triggered by railroad stocks and involving runs on major banks; and yet another banking crisis in 1907 involving a run on banks. In 1929, another crisis occurred: commonly referred to as *The Big One*, today it might simply be considered *A Big One*. In short, five particular crises wreaked havoc on the kind of scale seen in 2007–2008. Although no one wants to see a repeat of this crisis, we are still unsure how to prevent such crises in the future. The extraordinary convergence of grave events a decade ago is not the first such incident.

A decade later, therefore, I invite everyone to consider how, through regulation and other means, we can prevent another financial crisis.

PREFACE

SHARYN O'HALLORAN AND THOMAS GROLL

n March 2008, the world was transfixed as it watched the unraveling of Bear Stearns, one of the world's most prestigious investment banks. What ensued was the largest financial and economic crisis since the 1930s Great Depression. The sudden and rapid decline of the financial market that led to a significant contraction in economic activity, coupled with historic levels of unemployment and a double-digit drop in housing prices, placed millions of hard-working Americans and others around the world in an impossible squeeze. Many lost jobs just as the underlying value of their homes fell by as much as 40 percent. The combined impact of lost jobs and declining home values meant that families could not afford to sell their homes. In many cases, the only choice was to take a large loss or enter bankruptcy. For most, the latter was the only option.

In making these statements, we do not absolve individuals of fiduciary responsibility any more than we absolve regulators and bankers of the obligation to fulfill their responsibilities. But it is hard not to see the rise of the populist movement, Trumpism and antiglobalism, as a backlash to the failure to help the average citizen weather the financial turmoil.

The essays contained in this compilation look back to look forward. We examine if the actions and reforms put in place in the aftermath of the financial crisis have made the financial system stronger and better positioned to withstand the next crisis when, not if, it comes.

In short, have we learned the lessons and implemented the necessary policies to mitigate future damaging effects? One common theme that runs through the chapters is the notion of risk and its relation to liquidity in the financial system. Risk takes many forms: market, financial, strategic, and managerial. But in a number of different ways, each chapter addresses whether actions taken during and after the crisis have provided policymakers and market participants with better tools to identify, evaluate, and mitigate these risks when they arise.

Clearly, these were and are risky times for banks, creditors, regulators, and policymakers around the world. The chapter authors are well-known, leading experts in government, business, and academia on various aspects of finance and financial regulation. We hope the chapters shed light on how to think about the risky business that was the financial crisis, how ad hoc policy responses came about often in the depths of uncertainty and surrounded by controversy about effectiveness and fairness, and how we can do better in the future to manage risk and prevent crises that affect so many.

The project was made possible not only by its contributors but also by the support of many who made the conference a success and this volume a reality. Both the conference and the edited volume are a combined Columbia University effort, facilitated by the administrative and financial support of the Columbia Business School (CBS), the Columbia Law School, the School of International and Public Affairs (SIPA) with its Center of Global Economic Governance (CGEG), the Data Science Institute, the Institute for Social and Economic Research and Policy (ISERP), the Graduate School of Arts and Sciences, and the Richard Paul Richman Center.

We would like to thank Maria Cecilia Barcellos-Raible and her team from SIPA's Picker Center, Joe Chartier and his team, JoAnn Crawford, Stephen Francis, Theresa Murphy and her team from CGEG, and Kathleen Rithisorn and her team from the Richard Paul Richman Center for their support. Stephen Wesley from Columbia University Press supported this project from the beginning and, together with Christian Winting, helped us greatly in sharing the expertise of our contributors on this important issue. Numerous students have helped us to organize the conference and review the contributions to this volume: Anthony Cruz, Daniel Eem, Jocelyn Fahlen, Kate Han, Wesley Hu, Antigone Ntagkounakis, and Mateo Tate-Contreras. We would like to thank Geraldine McAllister for her invaluable assistance.

To end where we started: the lessons presented in this volume are not abstract theories and models divorced from reality. Learning the lessons of the financial crisis is important, and getting it right matters deeply for many people. An entire generation has been shaped by the financial crisis and limited by the stranglehold of indebtedness. We owe the next generations more.

AFTER THE CRASH

CHAPTER 1

INTRODUCTION

Overview of the Financial Crisis and Its Impacts

SHARYN O'HALLORAN, THOMAS GROLL, AND GERALDINE McALLISTER

On March 10, 2008, rumors spread that Bear Stearns Companies, Inc., the venerable eighty-five-year-old investment firm, faced default after prices for its subprime mortgage-backed securities plummeted. Despite assurances of the then CEO, Alan Schwartz, that the company had sufficient funds, clients furiously withdrew their deposits. Within forty-eight hours, the bank's precarious liquidity position deteriorated dramatically. Its stock price plunged by 50 percent, dropping from $61.58 to $30.85. Economist William Dudley of the Federal Reserve Bank of New York ominously noted that if "the vicious circle were to continue unabated, the liquidity issues could become solvency issues, and major financial intermediaries could conceivably fail."[1] As Bear Stearns stood at the brink of collapse, financial markets confronted the potential fallout of the Wall Street version of an old-fashioned bank run.

What followed was the unraveling of one of Wall Street's most prestigious institutions. Bear Stearns spiraled from healthy to bankrupt within days. As the drama unfolded, government and industry participants worked frantically to isolate the damage. Yet once the magnitude of Bear Stearns' highly leveraged positions became apparent, government officials proved unable, or perhaps unwilling, to avert its collapse. Regulators feared that their actions would increase *moral hazard*, the specter of firms taking inordinate risks, knowing that they too would be rescued or *bailed out*.[2] Relying on depression era emergency powers, the Federal Reserve authorized a $12.9 billion loan to the troubled bank to forestall bankruptcy. Instead of lending directly to Bear Stearns, however, the Federal Reserve Bank of New York provided bridge funding for up to twenty-eight days through a rival bank, JPMorgan Chase & Co. This left Bear Stearns with two options: find an appropriate buyer or file for bankruptcy.

For many, insolvency was not an alternative. As asset prices fell and bank earnings plunged, stress on the already fragile financial system increased sharply. If Bear Stearns could not meet its obligations, a cascade of margin calls, followed by counterparty failures of interconnected banks in the financial sector, could lead to significant additional disruptions in the already debilitated capital markets. To avert this bleak picture, Timothy Geithner, then president of the Federal Reserve Bank of New York, and then Treasury Secretary Henry Paulson made it clear to Allen Schwartz that he had until Sunday evening to find a buyer for Bear Stearns.

On Friday, March 14, 2008, Bear Stearns turned to JPMorgan Chase to avoid collapse. Initially, JPMorgan Chase offered between $8 and $12 per share. After a long weekend of due diligence revealed significant concerns about the mortgage holdings in Bear Stearns' portfolio, however, CEO Jamie Dimon called off the negotiations.[3] With markets opening in less than twenty-four hours and no buyer in sight, Geithner, Paulson, and then Federal Reserve Chairman Ben Bernanke brokered a deal: JPMorgan Chase agreed to acquire Bear Stearns for $2 per share, with the Federal Reserve promising to absorb $30 billion of potential losses.[4] In what some refer to as the "shotgun wedding heard around the world," JPMorgan Chase acquired Bear Sterns, the first major casualty of the financial crisis.[5]

The above vignette suggests that exorbitant risk-taking by financial institutions inadequately overseen by regulators triggered the financial crisis. The housing market's boom and bust underscores these lessons: permissive regulations allowed banks to offer mortgages with small down payments to buyers who had insufficient income to afford them. Compensation practices at financial firms rewarded volume and short-term performance over long-term sustainable returns. And credit rating agencies, laden with conflicts of interest, gave investment-grade ratings to subprime mortgages made them willing to designate tranches of subprime mortgages as investments-grade assets in exchange for a fee.[6] As the housing bubble burst and prices declined, the underlying value of the mortgages that secured these assets fell into default. The subsequent mortgage crisis led to a liquidity crunch brought on by inadequate price discovery of asset valuations and uncertainty about credit risk. These highly leveraged mortgaged-backed securities, assigned triple-A ratings by credit agencies and with scant regulatory oversight, were exactly the funds that drove Bear Stearns into insolvency.

This story has been told a number of times in a number of ways, but what stands out a decade later is not the horror of watching the demise of a storied investment bank, the suspenseful back-and-forth of whether JPMorgan Chase would rescue Bear Stearns and, if so, at what price and under what conditions, or even what role, if any, the government would play in backstopping the deal. What confounds most is how the excesses of a single firm and its inability, or lack of incentive, to measure, oversee, and manage risk could threaten the stability of the entire financial system.

Yet a decade after the 2007–2009 financial crisis and the ensuing market turmoil, the spillover effects reach well beyond the U.S. financial institutions that propagated the initial shock. Contractions in bank balance sheets prompted substantial reductions in credit to businesses and households; a restructuring of labor markets; dramatic changes to local, state, and federal budgets; unconventional monetary policy; a decline in real gross domestic product (GDP) growth; and a prolonged recovery of the broader economy. The liquidity crisis that began in the United States quickly spread to other countries as the sudden drop in lending and subsequent decline in demand rippled across the global supply chain. In short, the financial crisis contributed immensely to the Great Recession of 2008–2010. As these effects spread globally, they fueled the European Sovereign Debt Crisis that destabilized Portugal, Ireland, Greece, and Spain, as well as eurozone banks holding illiquid, government debt, and the now infamous U.S. mortgage-backed securities. As one domino after another fell, the feedback loop of global capital markets turned negative, with no end in sight. Lingering effects of the crash even reached emerging markets, bringing some of the more fragile economies to the verge of collapse.[7]

This chapter presents a succinct time line of the events from 2007 to 2010 that roiled financial markets. With a series of data trends and charts, we tell the story of how the crisis, and the subsequent market disruptions, deeply affected the broader economy and forever altered the lives of millions in the United States and around the world.[8] The data provide context for the sweeping overhauls of postcrisis global financial markets. Governments introduced regulations to mitigate excessive risk-taking by financial institutions, imposed stringent requirements on how and under what conditions banks set aside capital, and clamped down on tax havens. The following data analysis serves another purpose: it provides a lens through which the subsequent chapters in this book can be viewed. The graphs and charts tell a story of how the financial crisis came about, what actions were taken in its aftermath, and where we stand now.

What Is a Financial Crisis and Why Do They Happen?

A starting point for any retrospective of the financial crisis is to ask why financial crises happen in the first place. Financial institutions perform a special role in the economy through wealth creation. Capital markets transform individual savings into funding for businesses, mortgages, and other investments. Financial intermediaries, such as commercial and investment banks, transfer risk through various financial instruments, such as securities and derivatives, that lower the costs to borrowers and raise the risk-adjusted returns on savings. The financial system supports wealth intermediation in the economy by facilitating payments and clearing, providing liquidity, aiding price discovery, and efficiently allocating credit by mitigating *adverse selection* and *moral hazard*.[9] Deficiencies in any one of these activities can trigger market failures that lead to financial instability.

In particular, three features of the financial system can create unexpected volatility or risk. Shocks to the intermediation process[10] can reduce the supply of liquid assets, high levels of leverage or indebtedness amplify the effects of even a small price decline, and pro-cyclicality magnifies both the upsides and downsides of variations in asset prices. Short-term cyclical pressures that affect borrowing costs influence market fluctuations, including interest rates and available savings, along with long-term trends, such as employment, trade flows, government expenditures, capital investment, and consumption. Misaligned incentives, pricing strategies, and unrealistic expectations, as well as other market imperfections, can further exaggerate swings in asset prices, creating boom and bust cycles.[11] Inevitably, financial markets and, by extension, financial institutions can be inherently unstable.

It is not surprising then that financial crises occur. Reinhart and Rogoff (2009) found that since the 1800s the United States had experienced thirteen banking crises, Great Britain twelve, and France fifteen. Recent U.S. crises include the 1989–1995 Savings and Loan crisis that led the government to liquidate over 1,000 thrifts; the 2000–2001 Dot.com bubble, characterized by speculative investment in technology and internet stocks that caused unrealistic asset prices, a crash in stock prices and, ultimately, a recession; and, most recently, the 2006–2010 U.S. housing crisis that led to nearly ten million home foreclosures and caused 8.7 million workers to lose their jobs.

Time Line of the Financial Crisis: Events and Risk

Why Do Financial Crises Create Risk?

Financial crises happen, and another crisis is likely. But why would reoccurring events create risk? If we define risk as the deviation from expected outcomes (uncertainty), then one way to illustrate the unfolding of the financial crisis and its impact on the larger economy is to correlate the sequence of crisis events with changes of risk in financial markets. The TED-spread is one indicator of uncertainty in the U.S. economy; it measures the price of risk and lending or liquidity in the system. It has two parts: the numerator is the credit risk associated with overnight lending between large depository banks, implied by the London Interbank Offered Rate (LIBOR), and the denominator is a safe alternative, currently U.S. Treasury Bills, both averaged over three months. The ratio measures the perceived likelihood that a borrower will default on a debt obligation against a stable benchmark.

In normal times, the LIBOR approximately equals the U.S. Treasury Bill rate. Large depository banks rarely fail to repay their debts, so the TED-spread is usually close to 1. During crisis times, when the probability of credit default rises (greater risk), the TED-spread increases, reflecting distrust among lending institutions that debt obligations will be repaid, leading to a tightening of credit and a reduction of market liquidity.[12]

The time line in figure 1.1 illustrates the relationship between credit risk and key crisis events. Shown on the chart is the TED-spread from 2006 to 2010, punctuated by decision points: decisions taken by industry, government officials, and the central bank. The graph indicates a positive correlation between adverse crisis events and a rise in the TED-spread. For example, the collapse of Lehman Brothers on September 15, 2007, correlates with a 150 basis point spike in the TED-spread in a single day, rising from 1.7 percentage points to over 3.3 percentage points.

When Did the Financial Crisis Begin?

A second question is when did the crisis begin? Warren Buffett (2002) notes that "you never know who is swimming naked until the tide goes out"; ex ante, it is difficult to realize that a financial crisis has begun until it is plain for all to see. Accordingly, the start date of the financial crisis is a hotly debated topic. Indeed, Lo (2012, 3) asks, "Should we mark its beginning at the crest of the U.S. housing bubble in mid-2006, or with the liquidity crunch in the shadow banking system in late 2007, or with the bankruptcy filing of Lehman Brothers and the 'breaking of the buck' by the Reserve Primary Fund in September 2008?" Focusing solely on the LIBOR, which measures interbank lending rates, Cecchetti and Schoenholtz (2017) make the case for setting the crisis start date in August 2007, when BNP Paribas (2007) halted redemption of mortgage securities because a "complete evaporation of liquidity . . . made it impossible to value certain assets fairly regardless of their quality or credit rating."

As shown in figure 1.1, our analysis instead relies on the TED-spread. Normalizing the LIBOR against a relatively safe benchmark (U.S. Treasury Bills) removes the uncertainty associated with potential rate manipulation and fluctuations that occur simply because the system as a whole is more risky, all else being equal. Looking at the TED-spread, figure 1.1 shows that the antecedents

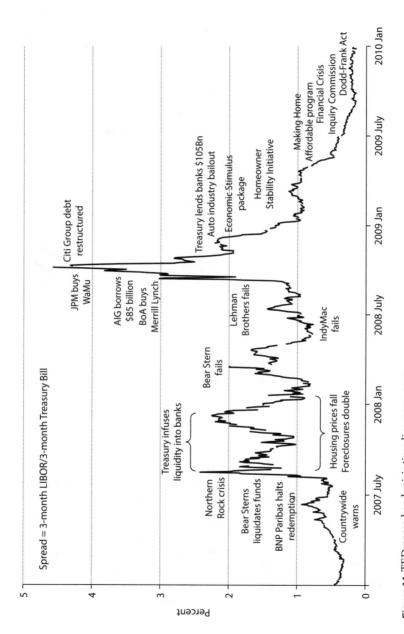

Figure 1.1 TED-spread and crisis time line 2007–2010

Source: Compiled by the authors. Complete list of dates and events can be found in the Appendix and Table 1.1.

of the crisis began in 2006, when the housing bubble started to unravel, crystallized with the liquidity crunch in the late summer of 2007, and came into full bloom in fall of 2008.

By many accounts, then, the start of the crisis dates to September 2008, with the failure of Lehman Brothers investment bank. The demise of Lehman Brothers called into question the creditworthiness of previously thought safe counterparties, leading to demands for collateral and a subsequent tightening of liquidity. Figure 1.1 illustrates the unfolding of this crisis of confidence; successive financial institutions confronting insolvency aligned with a steeply raising TED-spread along with associated increases in uncertainty and market illiquidity. On September 15, 2008, for example, after Henry Paulson said that the government would provide no further Wall Street bailouts, Lehman Brothers filed for bankruptcy. In rapid succession, other firms holding Lehman Brothers debt faced liquidity constraints and proved unable to meet their margin calls. Teetering on the edge of bankruptcy, AIG required an $85 billion loan from the Federal Reserve, Merrill Lynch merged with Bank of America, and JPMorgan Chase acquired Washington Mutual. Not only did investors abandon risky loans like subprime mortgages, they also dumped presumably safe money market funds, leaving banks and businesses with insufficient cash to cover daily operations.

How Did Government Respond?

The government responded tepidly at first in identifying the onset of the crisis, managing its magnitude and mitigating possible long-term consequences. To cool the perceived housing market bubble before the onset of the financial crisis, the Federal Reserve increased the federal funds rate in an effort to reduce market liquidity and curb inflationary pressures.[13] Even though figure 1.2a indicates that core inflation (the percentage change in prices for all items minus volatile food and energy prices) hovered around two percent, figure 1.2b shows that the Federal Open Market Committee (FOMC) raised the federal funds rate in a series of hikes until July 2006, where it stabilized at 5.25 percent. During this same period, mortgage delinquency rates and the number of homes entering into foreclosure began to creep steadily upward. Ultimately, these indicators proved to be early signs of the tide turning on the housing market.

Throughout the summer of 2007, the FOMC maintained the federal funds rate at an average of 5.25 percent. The FOMC stance persisted even after Countrywide Financial Corporation warned of "difficult housing and mortgage market conditions,"[14] Bear Stearns liquidated two hedge funds specializing in mortgage-backed securities, and PNB Paribas halted redemption of

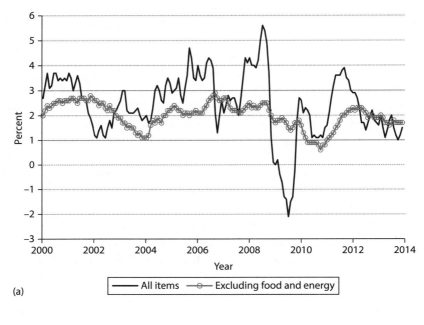

(a)

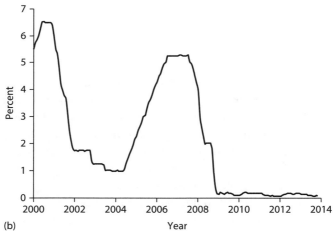

(b)

Figure 1.2 U.S. inflation and Federal Funds Rates, 2000 to 2014; (a) Inflation rate, 2000–2014; (b) Federal Funds Rate, 2000–2014

asset-backed securities because illiquid markets made price discovery impossible. In the FOMC minutes of August 7, 2007, the committee noted that

> although the downside risks to growth have increased somewhat, the Committee's predominant policy concern remains the risk that inflation will fail to moderate as expected. Future policy adjustments will depend on the outlook for both inflation and economic growth, as implied by incoming information.[15]

Credit markets responded to the Federal Reserve's inaction to these growing signs of risk with a notable jump in the TED-spread from below 1 percent, before the August FOMC meeting, to 2.42 percent one week later (see figure 1.1). By September 18, 2007, when the downside risks to economic growth could no longer be denied, the Federal Reserve took a number of steps to calm markets.

Figure 1.2 demonstrates that the Federal Reserve concentrated its efforts on reducing deflationary risks and stabilizing aggregate demand by cutting interest rates. At the September 2007 meeting, the FOMC reduced rates by 50 basis points to 4.5 percent. It approved auction facilities and extended credit to ensure sufficient market liquidity.[16] Figure 1.3 charts the relationship between the effective funds rate, TED-spread, and total borrowing by depository institutions from the Federal Reserve from 2004 to 2010. Once the Federal Reserve

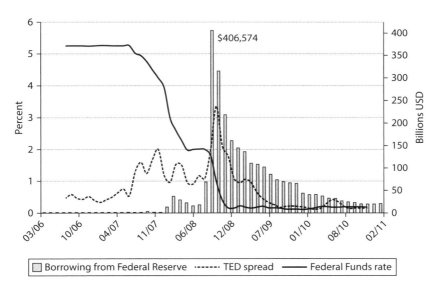

Figure 1.3 Effective funds rate, TED-spread, and total borrowing from Federal Reserve, 2004–2010

Source: Compiled by the authors. Data retrieved from Board of Governors, St. Louis Federal Reserve Bank.

introduced measures to expand access to liquidity by reducing the overnight lending rate and increasing available borrowing facilities, the perceived credit risk in the system declined, thereby lowering the TED-spread.

As soon as the depth of the financial crisis became apparent, government officials expressed concerns that the liquidity crisis would lead to a recession that could turn into a full-blown depression. Recent economic downturns had been associated with price and wage stagnation. But for the first time in the post-World War II era, serious deflationary risks appeared in several segments of the economy. Deflation occurs when households and firms speculate that prices will be lower in the future and delay current purchases, thereby reducing aggregate demand and GDP growth. As economic activity drops and prices fall, the value of holding money becomes greater than the alternatives of lending or spending, thereby leading to a self-fulfilling prophecy of deflationary pressures and creating the vicious cycle witnessed during the Great Depression.

To illustrate the risk of a deflationary cycle, consider the economic indicators during the 2007–2009 market downturn and the associated falling price levels. Figure 1.2a shows the significant drop in U.S. prices in 2008–2009 and supports the fear of decreasing price levels and deflationary risk. To stabilize prices and price expectations, central banks in most countries expanded their money supply by cutting policy rates and increasing open market operations (purchasing assets on the market) to offset deflationary pressures and avoid repeating the monetary policy mistakes of the Great Depression.[17]

With each successive crisis event, the FOMC further reduced the federal funds rate: to 2.25 percent with the Bear Stearns bailout in March 2008 and to 1.5 percent after Lehman Brothers failed and the government bailed out AIG in September 2008. By December 16, 2008, the federal funds rate was effectively zero, pegged at 0.25 percent, the lowest level possible avoiding negative interest rates ("Zero Bound"—and in contrast to measures by the Swedish Riksbank, the European Central Bank, and Bank of Japan, which chose to enact negative rates as unconventional monetary policies). The Federal Reserve kept the rate close to zero between 2008 and 2015, when a gradual increase began.[18]

The most immediate effect of the crisis of confidence on the economy was a credit freeze that placed a stranglehold on liquidity. During the 2008 banking panic, lending to large U.S. corporate borrowers fell 79 percent from its peak during the housing boom. The data also show a 49 percent decline in the fourth quarter of 2008, after the failure of Lehman Brothers. Ivashina and Scharfstein (2010) analyzed these corporate loan data and find that a drop in the supply of credit coupled with an economic recession magnified the impact of the financial crisis on the economy. Without a reduction in lending, loan demand would likely have been attenuated by downward pressure on interest rate spreads. The drop in supply of available loans, however, put upward pressure on interest rates, and thereby deepened the decline in lending. Figure 1.2a shows the basis for these fears. As liquidity dried up and lending contracted, interest rates on thirty-year mortgage rates peaked at 6.8 percent and inflation rose to over 5 percent.

The sequence of events illustrates that the 2007–2009 market crash was more a failure of confidence among the large lending institutions than a liquidity crisis. Once the Treasury infused capital directly into the banks, lending $125 billion to nine banks, restructured Citigroup debt, and took direct ownership of AIG, the perceived credit risk in the system relative to a secure benchmark began to decline. In addition, the U.S. Treasury, Federal Reserve, and Federal Deposit Insurance Corporation (FDIC) committed to a number of facilities to expand liquidity, jump-start the credit markets, and reduce lending risk. These programs included directly purchasing preferred stock, guaranteeing lending between large depository institutions, directly issuing short-term loans to businesses, and lowering the federal funds rate to historic levels. The government also enacted a number of initiatives to offset the impact of the financial crisis on the broader economy, including passing the American Recovery and Reinvestment Act of 2009, the Homeowner Affordability and Stability Plan, and the Making Home Affordable program.

As these monetary, fiscal, and legislative policies took hold, and especially as the Financial Crisis Inquiry Commission issued its report and Congress passed the Dodd-Frank Wall Street Reform and Consumer Protection Act of 2010, the perceived risk in the system declined, and the TED-spread dropped precipitously. Reflecting on the lessons from the financial crisis, William Dudley (2017, 1), Chief Executive Officer of the Federal Reserve Bank of New York, noted that "the evolution of the financial crisis illustrates a number of key issues, including the potential hazards of financial innovation, the pro-cyclicality of the financial system, and the importance of confidence in sustaining effective financial intermediation."

Was the 2007–2009 Financial Crisis Different?

The severity of the financial crisis and the pursuant economic downturn is often compared to the Great Depression. Figure 1.4 places the 2007–2009 financial panic and subsequent recession in context, comparing economic data from 1934 to 2017. Figure 1.4a plots the number of bank failures against the employment rate; figure 1.4b plots GDP growth rates against inflation. The graph shows the validity of this comparison, with two years of negative GDP growth (2007 and 2008), around five hundred bank failures over a six-year period (2008–2013), and an unemployment rate reaching an annual average of 9.6 percent (2010).[19] In addition, from 2007 to 2010, 6.4 million homes entered into foreclosure, and a 2009 estimate found that nearly a quarter of all U.S. homes with mortgages were valued at less than the amount their owners owed the banks holding

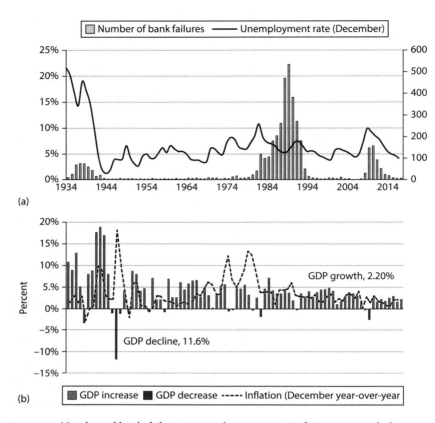

(a)

(b)

Figure 1.4 Number of bank failures, unemployment rate, inflation rate, and changes in GDP, 1934–2017

Source: Compiled by the authors. Data retrieved from the Federal Reserve Bank Economic Data, Federal Reserve Bank of St. Louis. Bank Failure Data, Failures and Assistance Transactions of all Institutions for the United States and Other Areas, Number of Institutions, Annual, Not Seasonally Adjusted; Real Gross Domestic Product, Percent Change from Preceding Period, Annual, Not Seasonally Adjusted; Unemployment Rate, Percent of civilian workforce, annual, seasonally adjusted. Inflation data collected from https://www.thebalance.com/u-s-inflation-rate-history-by-year-and-forecast-3306093. Adapted from fred.stlouisfed.org. See similar analysis in https://www.frbatlanta.org/economy-matters/banking-and-finance/viewpoint/2016/12/06/history-of-bank-regulation.

their loans.[20] In a number of states, including Nevada, this number reached as high as 65 percent.[21] All this transpired in an environment of historically low inflation and stagnant economic growth, making the repayment of mortgages even more difficult for borrowers. By 2010, with the slow economic recovery and sluggish wage rebound, the year-over-year price increase was a negligible 0.06 percent (see figure 1.2b).

In comparison, figure 1.4 shows that the Great Depression witnessed higher levels of unemployment, peaking around 20 percent. The country experienced an 11.6 percent decline in economic activity during the post-World War II recession as the federal government cut military spending. The 1980s Savings and Loans crisis outpaced the number of bank failures by almost 4 to 1, culminating in over 1,900 insolvent banks from 1987 to 1991. Nonetheless, the toll of the 2007–2009 financial crisis was painful and persistent. Despite expansive fiscal and monetary policies, it took almost eight years for unemployment to return to its prerecession rate, and growth rates remained lackluster despite a few good quarters, resulting in record levels of public debt and a ballooning of the Federal Reserve's balance sheet.[22]

The financial crisis of 2007–2009 and the subsequent market turmoil affected segments of the U.S. economy in ways not witnessed since the Great Depression. A distinguishing feature of the crisis was the number of people who lost their homes and employment and who have remained outside of the workforce even as the unemployment rate reached historic lows. Perhaps the most defining characteristic of the postcrisis era is the number of families who can no longer afford a home, even as personal net wealth has recovered. Unlike previous economic expansions, the gains of the recovery have not been widely shared.

The 2007–2009 crisis struck at the fragility of financial intermediaries and the global capital system as a whole. The spillover effects rippled through the basic pillars of economic growth—business activity (investment), the labor and housing markets, and consumer demand. The combination of a banking crisis, liquidity crunch, and a recession impaired financial intermediation and thereby intensified the magnitude of the crisis effects on the rest of the economy, to which we now turn.

Business Activity Downturn

The crisis played out in a number of ways throughout domestic market segments. As lending declined, nonresidential investment, equipment software, and other capital expenditures, as a percent of real GDP, fell abruptly. For example, figure 1.5 shows that during the recession investment in equipment and software as a percentage of GDP plunged by 200 percent. Business spending and investment, which translates directly into business activity, contributed to 1.5 percent of the decline in GDP. Residential investment as a percent of GDP fell from its 2006 peak of 6.75 percent to around 2.5 percent in 2010 and contributed to 1 percent of the decline in GDP growth. Even in 2018 residential investment remained well below its average, adding only around 4 percent of GDP.

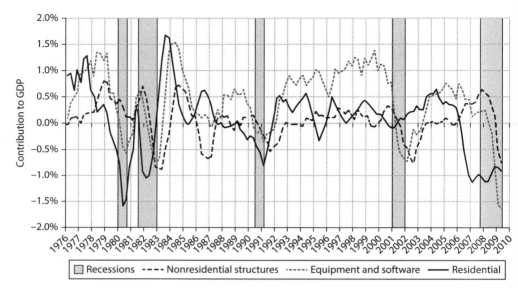

Figure 1.5 Investment contributions as a percentage change in real GDP, 1976–2010

Source: https://www.calculatedriskblog.com/2018/07/q2-gdp-investment.html.

Concurrently, total and single unit housing starts dramatically declined. New construction of U.S. housing units dropped 36.5 percent year-on-year to the lowest level since the 1980s. A decade after the financial crisis, the number of housing starts remains at less than half their precrisis levels. Existing home sales followed a similar pattern: peaking in 2006 with a seasonally adjusted 7,000 units, and dropping by 43 percent to under 4,000 units monthly by the end of 2008.[23]

Employment and Labor Participation Fall

One of the most visible and lasting impacts of the financial crisis is the restructuring of segments of the labor force. With the onset of the crisis, the unemployment rate climbed to 9.5 percent, even touching 10 percent at one point, the highest in twenty-five years. Yet the employment rate also masks underlying trends, some of which have become permanent traits of the U.S. workforce. Figure 1.6 disaggregates this story: figure 1.6a shows the ratio of the number of unemployed persons looking for work per job opening, and figure 1.6b indicates the labor participation rate or the percentage of the population between sixteen and sixty-four that is employed or seeking employment. Prior to the crisis, the ratio of unemployed persons per job opening was 1.9. This ratio peaked at 6.6 in July 2009.

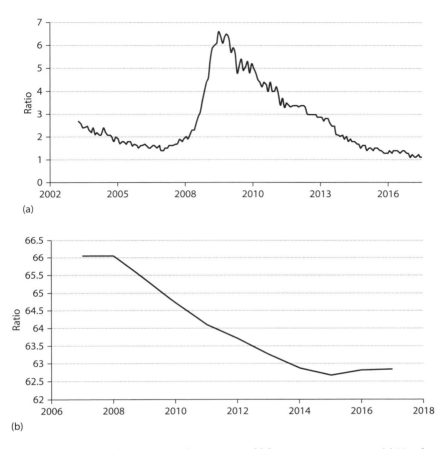

Figure 1.6 Unemployed person per job opening and labor participation rates; (a) Number of unemployed persons per job opening; (b) Labor participation rate

Note: Percent of labor force participation rate, 2007 to 2017, Bureau of Labor Statistics from the Current Population Survey; Labor Force Statistics from the Current Population Survey Original Data Value.

Source: Bureau of Labor Statistics JOLTS Highlights December 10, 2013, https://www.bls.gov/jlt/jlt
_labstatgraphs_december2013.pdf.

In September 2018, ten years after Lehman Brothers filed for bankruptcy, the ratio of unemployed persons per job opening hit 0.9, a series low.[24]

During the same period, the labor force participation rate shown in figure 1.6b indicates a steady downward trend, moving from 68 percent to 62.7 percent, the lowest level of labor participation since 1975. Many employees who lost their jobs during the recession have not reentered the workforce. Instead, they joined the ranks of discouraged workers who became permanently unemployed and face severe challenges to overcome their structural unemployment and reenter the labor market.

The crisis also touched sectors of the economy differently.[25] Figure 1.7 compares the total number and the percent change of workers in the construction, manufacturing and finance sectors from 2005 to 2018. Panel (a) of figure 1.7 shows that the construction industry was most immediately affected by the downturn in the housing market, and the dramatic drop in demand for home renovations and new developments. During the recession, employment shrank by 25 percent. Ten years later, and despite a new housing boom, construction employment remains 5 percent below precrisis levels. Similarly, panel (b) shows that manufacturing, which includes automakers, lost a little over 8 percent of its workforce since 2008. On the other hand, the financial services industry displayed in panel (c) of figure 1.7 gained 5 percent over this period. In relative terms, the severity of the recent recession on the industrial sector was as significant as the oil crisis spurred recession in 1974–1975, but with a longer duration.[26]

Homeownership Declines

Increasing unemployment, the lack of job opportunities as well as the steep and rapid decline in housing prices led to the scenario illustrated in figure 1.8. The rise in delinquency rates, mortgage payments more than ninety days past due, and for many the inevitable foreclosures became a hallmark of the recession. Prior to the housing crisis, less than 2 percent of all mortgages, on average, would fall delinquent. By 2008, delinquencies represented over 10 percent of all outstanding mortgages. In some particularly adversely affected areas, such as Illinois, delinquency rates soared to over 14 percent of all mortgages. These mortgage delinquencies led to a nationwide foreclosure rate of 2.2 percent. During the peak of the recession, each year approximately 2.5 million homes entered foreclosure.

Combined, these forces increased housing inventories, further depressing prices. As shown in figure 1.9, real home prices from 2008 to the end of 2010 declined by an unprecedented 42.4 percent, measured by the Case-Shiller Home Price Index. Indeed, homeownership fell to 63 percent, the lowest level since the Bureau of the Census began tracking this statistics in 1967.

Consumption and Household Wealth Diverge

The uncertainty in interbank lending affected liquidity in the banking system. The unwillingness of banks to make loans is reflected in a corresponding decrease in consumer debt. Figure 1.10a shows data for residential household debt (commonly related to consumer loans and mortgages) as a share of GDP. Figure 1.10b shows the effects on personal consumption and net worth by household.

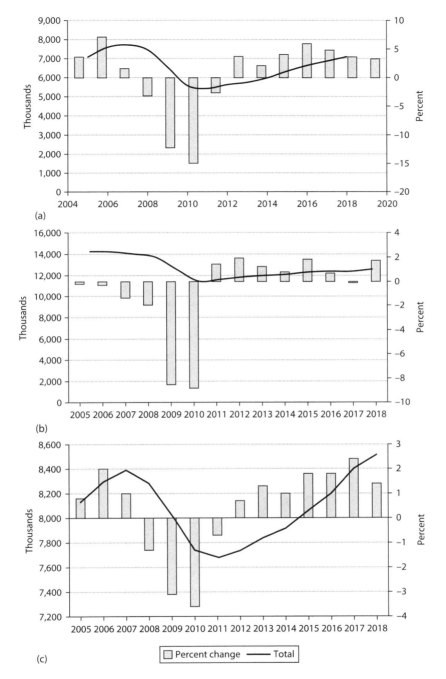

Figure 1.7 Employment by construction, manufacturing, and finance sectors, 2005–2017, total numbers of employees and percent change (thousands, seasonally adjusted); (a) Construction sector; (b) Manufacturing sector; (c) Finance sector

Source: Compiled by authors. Bureau of Labor Statistics Employment, Hours, and Earnings from the Current Employment Statistics survey (National) All Employees (thousands) Seasonally Adjusted, Construction (CES2000000001), Manufacturing (CES3000000001), and Finance Sectors (CES5500000001). Data extracted November 27, 2018.

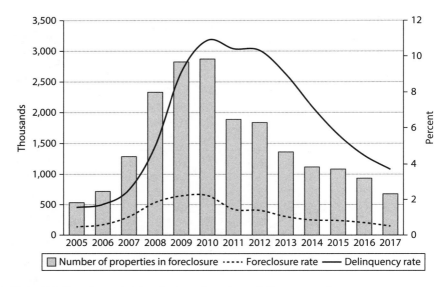

Figure 1.8 Foreclosure total and rate and mortgage delinquency rate

Source: Compiled by the authors. Data retrieved from Board of Governors, St. Louis Federal Reserve Bank; https://fred.stlouisfed.org.

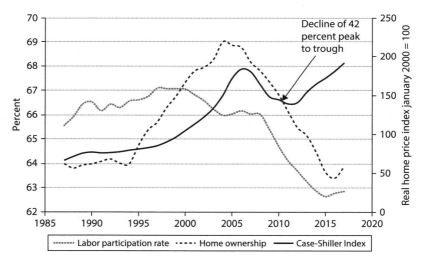

Figure 1.9 Labor participation rate, home ownership, and Case-Shiller Home Price Index, 1987–2017

Source: Compiled by authors. Data: Federal Reserve Economic Data, fred.stlouisfed.org; Case-Shiller Real Home Price Index; January 2000 = 100; U.S. Bureau of the Census, Homeownership Rate for the United States, retrieved from FRED, Federal Reserve Bank of St. Louis; https://fred.stlouisfed.org.

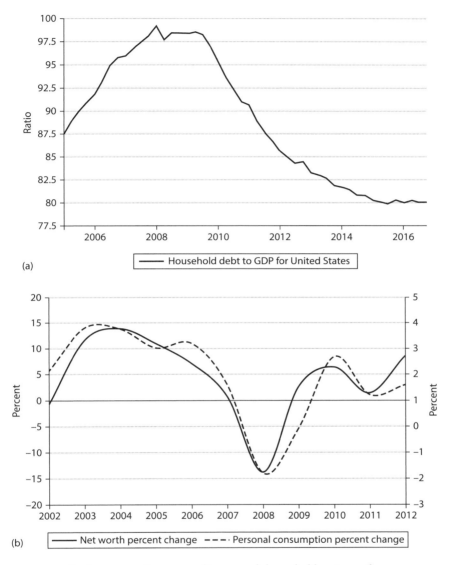

(a)

Household debt to GDP for United States

(b)

—— Net worth percent change   ---- Personal consumption percent change

Figure 1.10 Real consumption expenditures and household net worth, 2002–2012; (a) Household debt to GDP; (b) Consumption expenditures and household net worth

Source: Compiled by the authors. Household Debt to GDP, Personal Consumption Expenditures and Household Net Worth for United States, retrieved from FRED, Federal Reserve Bank of St. Louis; https://fred.stlouisfed.org.

The chart indicates that consumer debt as a share of GDP peaked at the height of the crisis before falling below precrisis levels, where it has remained. As real household wealth plummeted, consumer spending declined, leading to a contraction in individual consumer's spending power, which further eroding the economic climate as exemplified in the 2008 downturn in real GDP.

Economic Growth Stagnates

During the 2007–2010 crisis and recession, real GDP fell at an average annual rate of 7.8 percent in the fourth quarter of 2008 and the first quarter of 2009, the sharpest two-quarter contraction since 1947, when quarterly GDP data was first collected. Figure 1.11 reveals that the percentage change in GDP in the fourth quarter of 2008 was particularly stark, indicating an 8.4 percent reduction.[27]

In short, the economy began to shrink, moving away from its potential productive capacity. This output gap shows the difference between what the economy could produce at full employment and what it did produce with less aggregate demand. Figure 1.11 depicts the steep divergence between real and potential GDP starting in 2008. The graph further projects that it would take

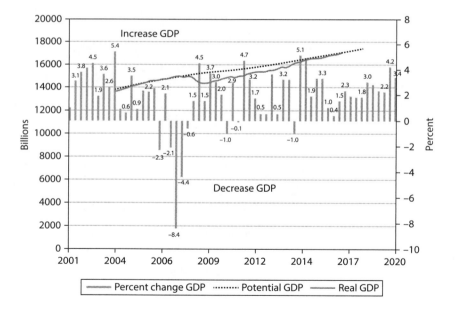

Figure 1.11 Economic growth output gap and real GDP by quarter, 2001 to 2020

Source: Compiled by the authors. Federal Reserve Economic Data; Link: https://fred.stlouisfed.org. Real Potential Gross Domestic Product, Billions of Chained 2009 Dollars, Quarterly, Not Seasonally Adjusted; Real Gross Domestic Product Billions of Chained 2009 Dollars, Quarterly, Seasonally Adjusted Annual Rate.

ten years (not until 2018) for the U.S. economy to finally return to real potential gross domestic product. The costs of the financial crisis were real and have had a lasting impact.

These data trends tell the story of a rapidly evolving scenario, where an increase in perceived market risk (TED-spread) and greater default rates led to the unwillingness and inability of banks to lend (liquidity freeze). In turn, the contraction of liquidity in the economy caused a decrease in residential and capital investment, an increase in unemployment, a decline in consumer spending, a reduction in aggregate economic activity, and a significant drop in net worth. The aggregate impact of these effects is shown in the decline in real GDP growth and the gap between real and potential GDP, had there not been a crisis, and where we are today.

Global Contagion

Warren Buffett identified a distinctive feature of the 2008–2009 financial panic when he reflected that "we're all dominoes and we are all very close together" (Belvedere 2018). The September 2008 collapse of Lehman Brothers resulted from the transmission of risk from individuals to banks to capital markets across the financial system. The default of subprime mortgages, issued to borrowers who were unable to repay these loans, the underlying value of which backed securities sold to investors—and given a triple-A rating by credit agencies—led to the demise of Lehman Brothers and the domino effect of insolvent financial institutions. In this particular financial crisis, the transmission of risk was immediate, far-reaching, and heightened by the previously unknown plethora of cross-border and cross-entity interdependencies.[28] In the decades leading up to the financial crisis, increasingly lax regulation allowed banks, especially in Europe and the United States, to become huge, highly leveraged, and globally interconnected. These micro-institutional features increased risk at the macro-systemic level.

The Size of Financial Institutions

To place the discussion in perspective, financial services firms grew considerably in the decades leading up to the crisis.[29] Between 1990 and 2007, Bair (2013, 16) notes that worldwide total financial assets rose from less than $2.5 trillion to close to $20 trillion. The rate of asset growth was highest among the largest firms, leading to ever-larger firms controlling an ever-greater share of the overall market. The compound annual growth rate (CAGR) for the Top-10 financial services firms was 24 percent for the period 1990–2010. By 2010, these same firms controlled 62 percent of the market. The next Top-30 financial services firms, in comparison, also had a CAGR of 24 percent over this period and controlled 17 percent of the market; and the next Top-50 firms had a CAGR of 14 percent and controlled 6 percent of the market. The remaining financial services firms had a CAGR of 3 percent and controlled 14 percent of the market.

Figure 1.12 illustrates this phenomenal growth in the financial sector. From 2002 to 2015, total assets worldwide increased from \$128 trillion to \$340 trillion. During this time, asset allocation across institution types changed. The size of the shadow banking sector grew from 25 percent to 29 percent of total financial assets worldwide.[30] The insurance sector declined from about 12 percent to 9 percent of the financial services industry. The public finance sector decreased from 8.7 percent to 4.7 percent of total assets, and central banks hold 7.3 percent of total assets, up from 3.7 percent.

The outsized nature of the banking sector is apparent in figure 1.13, which compares domestic banking assets to the size of the overall economy, as measured by gross domestic product (GDP). The graph provides a snapshot of the size of the financial sector relative to the domestic economy. In 2009, at the height of the financial crisis, the domestic banking assets of eighteen developed economies exceeded 100 percent of GDP. Of these economies, fifteen were European, fourteen were EU member states, and eleven were eurozone

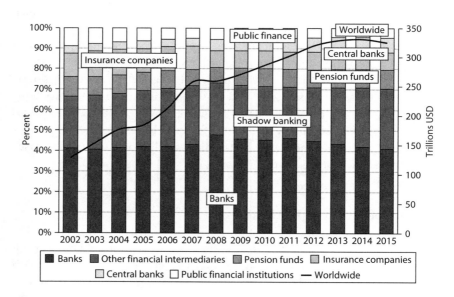

Figure 1.12 Total financial assets by type of financial institution, 2002–2015

Source: Complied by the authors. Data retrieved from Financial Stability Board. Total Assets of Financial Institutions Worldwide from 2002 to 2016, by Institution Type (in trillion U.S. dollars): https://www.statista.com/statistics/421221/global-financial-institutions-assets-by-institution-type/.

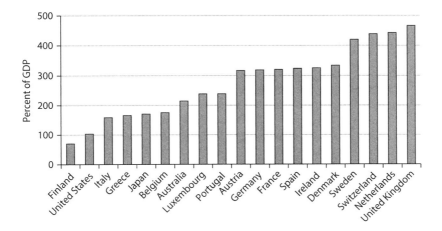

Figure 1.13 Domestic banking assets as a percentage of GDP, consolidated by nationality of headquarters, 2009

Note: The European economies include Finland, Italy, Greece, Belgium, Luxembourg, Portugal, Austria, Germany, France, Spain, Ireland, Denmark, Sweden, Switzerland, Netherlands, and United Kingdom. The EU member states include Finland, Italy, Greece, Belgium, Luxembourg, Portugal, Austria, Germany, France, Spain, Ireland, Denmark, Sweden, Netherlands, and United Kingdom. The eurozone members include Finland, Italy, Greece, Belgium, Luxembourg, Portugal, Austria, Germany, France, Spain, Ireland, and the Netherlands.

Source: Independent Commission on Banking (2011a, 22), using data from ECB, Eurostat, published accounts, national sources, International Monetary Fund, Commission calculations.

members. The banking assets of two EU member states, Luxembourg and Portugal, exceeded 200 percent of GDP. In six others—Austria, Germany, France, Spain, Ireland, and Denmark—they exceeded 300 percent. Three member states—Sweden, The Netherlands, and the United Kingdom—had banking assets in excess of 400 percent of GDP, and in the United Kingdom the figure approached 500 percent. Among EU member states, only Finland had banking assets of less than 100 percent of GDP. By comparison, U.S. domestic banking assets stood at 100 percent of GDP in 2009.[31]

Haldane et al. (2010, 118) analyzed U.S., European, and UK large commercial banks and found that as bank assets as a percentage of GDP increased so too did the share of total assets dedicated to riskier activities such as trading, whereas the share of total assets dedicated to customer loans declined. The banks' role of financial intermediation took a backseat to their proprietary trading activities.

Figure 1.14 displays how banking assets as a percentage of GDP changed over time. The data are divided by country type: Europe, other advanced nations, emerging market economies (EMEs), and important financial hubs, Hong Kong, Singapore, and Luxemburg, which are grouped under (rhs axis).

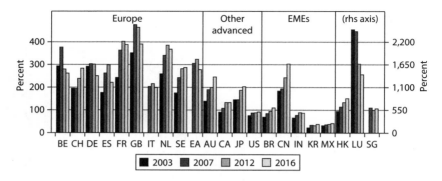

Figure 1.14 Domestic banking assets as a percentage of GDP, consolidated by nationality of headquarters (2003–2016)

Note: Banking system assets are on domestic or resident basis, except for China and Korea, which are on a consolidated basis. The European economies are Finland, Italy, Greece, Belgium, Luxembourg, Portugal, Austria, Germany, France, Spain, Ireland, Denmark, Sweden, Switzerland, Netherlands, and United Kingdom. The EU member states are Finland, Italy, Greece, Belgium, Luxembourg, Portugal, Austria, Germany, France, Spain, Ireland, Denmark, Sweden, Netherlands, and United Kingdom. The eurozone members are Finland, Italy, Greece, Belgium, Luxembourg, Portugal, Austria, Germany, France, Spain, Ireland, and the Netherlands.

Source: Independent Commission on Banking (2011a, 22), including data from ECB, Eurostat, published accounts, national sources, IMF, and Commission calculations. Adopted from the Bank of International Settlements report by Buch and Dages (2018, 12).

All advanced industrial countries witnessed a decline in the share of financial assets as a percentage of the overall economy, with the exceptions of Australia and Japan. In contrast, the emerging market economies either experienced a growth of financial assets as a percentage of economic activity, China and Brazil in particular, or the ratio remained constant.

Leverage

Over the decades leading up to the crisis, not only did banks increase in size and complexity but their leverage ratios, the ratio of assets to shareholders' claims, also increased. As noted in figure 1.15, the leverage ratio of large complex financial institutions (LCFIs) in Europe, which have always acted as universal banks unlike their U.S. counterparts, increased from 30 percent in 2000 to more than 45 percent by 2009, before declining rapidly in the wake of the financial crisis. The leverage ratio of major UK banks followed a similar trend, increasing from over 20 percent in 2000 to more than 30 percent by 2009. In fact, bank leverage in the United Kingdom rose inexorably from the late 1980s onward.

When the financial crisis broke in 2007, UK banks' median leverage ratio approached 50 percent. Leverage ratios for U.S. securities houses, although

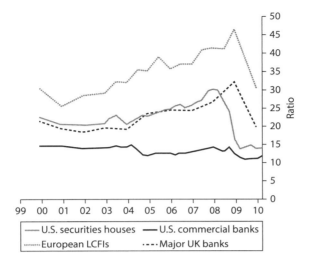

Figure 1.15 Leverage ratio of large complex financial institutions, 2000–2010

Note: Leverage equals assets over total shareholders' equity net of minority interests.

Source: Haldane et al. (2010, 115).

considerably lower than those of their European or UK counterparts, also rose significantly after 2000, from less than 25 percent to over 30 percent in 2008. The 2004 introduction of "Alternative Net Capital Requirements for Broker-Dealers"[32] eliminated minimum capital requirements for investment banks that were part of the Consolidated Supervised Entities Program, which contributed to a dramatic increase in broker-dealer leverage ratios. By 2007, the leverage ratio of Bear Stearns was 33.4 percent, that of Goldman Sachs 22.4 percent, Lehman Brothers 30.7 percent, Merrill Lynch 31.9 percent, and Morgan Stanley 33.4 percent.[33] With the onset of the financial crisis, U.S. securities houses converted to bank holding companies to gain access to the Federal Reserve's lending window, resulting in a fall in their leverage ratios and a rise in the total amount borrowed from the Federal Reserve (see figure 1.4). Beginning in 2004, by contrast, U.S. commercial banks saw their leverage ratios either decline or remain steady.

Interconnectedness

Interconnectedness means that events . . . can be transmitted to domestic economies located far away from the initial source of shock, often at market-speed measured in milliseconds. (William Dudley, 2012)[34]

Former member of the Board of Governors of the United States Federal Reserve Board Tarullo (2011, 1–2) noted that at times of crises interconnectedness exacerbates threats to the financial system through the domino effect, the fire-sale effect, and the essential role certain firms play in financial markets. Over the past two decades, the interconnected nature of global financial markets has increased dramatically. Billio et al. (2012, 543) analyzed U.S., European, and UK LCFIs by graphing the monthly returns (transactions) of the twenty-five largest (in terms of average assets under management) banks, broker-dealers, insurers, and hedge funds from January 1994 to December 1996 and compared the number of transactions over the 2006–2008 time period. Their analysis shows that interconnectedness, as measured by the number of transactions, grew significantly from one time period to the next.

Another way to measure the domino effect and connectivity of financial firms is to compare changes in cross-border claims by foreign counterparties over time. The bar chart in figure 1.16 indicates the stock of foreign claims at each point in time and the percent change line reveals patterns in the flow of claims. Here the data is aggregated by the nationality of the reporting bank. Figure 1.16 shows a rapid increase in the stock of outstanding claims from 2000 to 2008, rising from $10 trillion to $30 trillion in 2008. During the crisis, cross-border claims declined, and only in 2016 did they resume their precrisis trajectory.

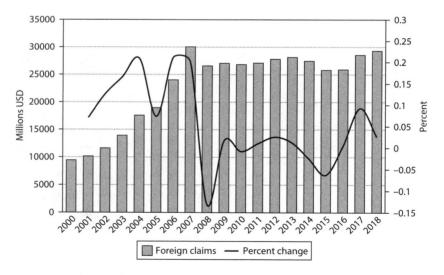

Figure 1.16 Gross cross-border claims by foreign counterparties, 2000–2018

Note: Summary of consolidated statistics, by nationality of reporting bank; amounts outstanding. Stocks reported at end-December for each respective year.

Source: Complied by authors. Bank of International Settlements Statistics Explorer, http://stats.bis.org/statx/.

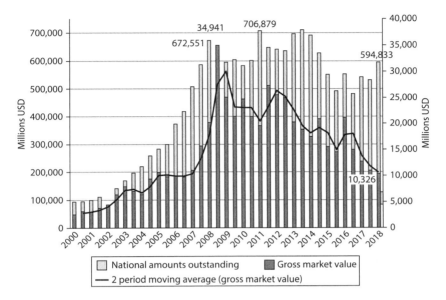

Figure 1.17 Global over-the-counter derivatives market, 2000–2018 (in billions USD)

Source: Compiled by the authors. BIS Statistics Explorer, http://stats.bis.org/statx/.

To mitigate risk, governments encouraged financial firms to issue securities or hedge their liabilities through derivative contracts. In 2008, the notional value of over-the-counter (OTC) derivatives, bilateral contracts between counterparties made outside of an exchange, was $672 trillion, and the gross market valued peaked at $35 trillion. A decade later, even with the introduction of regulations to push derivatives trades to be cleared through central counterparties (CCPs), clearing houses, the notional value of outstanding OTC derivatives increased from $532 trillion at the end of 2017 to $595 trillion by mid-2018.[35]

The gross market value of outstanding derivatives contracts denoted in figure 1.17 represents the current market value of a contract and thereby provides a more accurate measure of amounts at risk.[36] The chart shows that the gross value peaked in 2008 and then has steadily declined, even as the notional value of contracts increased. Ten years later, at the end of the first half of 2018, the gross market value of OTC derivatives reached $10 trillion, its lowest level since 2007.

Organization of the Book

The trends outlined in this chapter set the stage for analyzing the financial crisis a decade after its making. Governments and central banks intervened to stabilize capital markets, increase fiscal spending, pursue expansionary monetary policy, and tighten financial regulation. For the most part, these extraordinary and nonconventional actions worked. But economic recovery has been slow and unevenly shared. Large parts of the workforce face tremendous challenges finding jobs, affording homes, and maintaining their previous standard of living. By contrast, other sectors of the workforce, such as financial services, have benefited from the recovering stock market and growing real wages.

The backlash to these trends is manifested in the worldwide rise of populism and the ascension to power of unconventional leaders such as Donald Trump in the United States, Emmanuel Macron in France, and Eurosceptic parties among the EU nation-states. Although different in style and content, they all attack the basic tenets of globalism, free trade, capital movements, and immigration. In many ways, the cost of saving the financial system was to undermine trust and faith in the very institutions on which it rests.

This book is divided into five sections, addressing key themes highlighted by the financial crisis and the subsequent regulatory responses. Each section is introduced by a renowned scholar or practitioner, followed by chapters written by leading authors that build on the initial framing discussion, and summarized in concluding expert remarks.

Part I places the financial crisis in context. Glenn Hubbard provides a road map for regulatory reform and asks, If it were to happen again, what might we do? Staying with this theme, Antoine Parent extrapolates what the Federal Reserves' policies during the Great Depression tell us about what might work now. Pierre-Charles Pradier looks at regulation and competition in the European financial sector and offers a companion to Groll, O'Halloran, and McAllister in their chapter on trends and challenges in U.S. financial market regulation. Nolan McCarty's discussion emphasizes how political bubbles can interact with financial bubbles to create a financial crisis.

Much of postcrisis global financial regulation focused on getting the incentives for market participants and regulators right. In Part II, former U.S. Secretary of the Treasury Jacob Lew considers the progress made and the challenges remaining. Although clear headway has been made, analysis of the data shows that, in some cases, the regulations have not been evenly applied and the rules that have been applied may have had unintended consequences. Vincent Bouvatier, Gunther Capelle-Blancard, and Anne-Laure Delatte illustrate these patterns in the data involving banks and tax havens. Their analysis shows how regulations can push more financial activity outside the ambit of supervisory oversight. Jeffrey Gordon discusses how postcrisis rules may have created poor incentives for large financial firms. If financial stability is the objective of financial regulation, then what incentives do large significantly important financial institutions have to curb their risk-taking behavior, and who should pay those costs?

Part III focuses on the use and abuse of models in making decisions and predicting financial outcomes. In "Reflections on the Global Financial Crisis Ten Years On," Joseph Stiglitz notes that "banks should be prevented from doing bad things, but they also need to be encouraged to do things that are beneficial to our society and our economy." In the aftermath of the crisis, there should have been far more discussion about what kind of a regulatory system would have created a financial system that actually worked and mitigated risks of systemic failure. Formal models and technology can only go so far, as noted by Emanuel Derman, and Eli Noam goes on to state that the digital age may have fundamentally altered the nature of systemic risk, a factor that regulators have heretofore not considered. O'Halloran and Nikolai Nowaczyk suggest that data science techniques may provide a means to test the impact of regulations on markets *before* enactment. Mark Flood discusses the implications of recent trends in big data, the scalability of processes, and financial stability.

Part IV dives into a discussion on how we should be regulating to avert the impact of the next crisis. Prior to the crash, much of the regulatory debate centered on the Goldilocks syndrome: are financial markets impeded by too much or too little regulation? Paul Tucker discusses the rules-versus-principles approach to financial regulation following the crisis, noting that the response to this question depends on the policy objectives desired. If the purpose of regulation is to enhance capital formation and provision, then a principles-based approach might be best. However, if government's purpose is to provide enhanced supervision of financial institutions to ensure against financial meltdowns, then a rules-based approach may be more appropriate. In practice, regulation is never so simple. Rather, it is a balance between these two objectives. Getting it right is a constant push-and-pull among the key political and economic interests at stake. The tug-of-war among stakeholders is apparent in the individual chapters and lively roundtable discussion provided by Barney Frank, Stephen Cutler, John C. Coffee Jr., and Kathryn Judge.

Part V highlights several growing trends that contain within them the sources of the next financial crisis. Standard Charted CEO William T. Winters, interviewed by Ailsa Röell, provides a candid view of the ways in which financial firms are adapting to new regulations and where the next fault lines may lie. The discussion focuses not on whether there is too much or too little regulation but on whether there is the right regulation and whether postcrisis financial laws and regulations are fit for the purpose.

Experts explore this question through three difference policy areas. Viktoria Baklanova and Joseph Tanega examine U.S. money market funds during the crisis, when values per share fell below $1.00 for the first time, leading to a systemwide liquidity freeze. Their analysis considers the ability of postcrisis regulations to avert similar destabilizing events, stressing the need for data transparency and disclosure. Mark J. Roe and Michael Tröge examine how and why the 2017 Tax Act will incentivize banks to be better capitalized, albeit modestly so. They argue that the taxation of banks can enhance prudential regulation and can do so in a revenue-neutral way. Finally, Agostino Capponi examines the regulations enacted after the crisis that require the trading of standardized derivatives through central clearinghouse exchanges, with the posting of collateral to cover the possibility of default. Capponi analyzes the incentives created at the various stages of the default waterfall structure and explores whether these rules meet the policy objective of mitigating systemic risk.

Appendix

TABLE 1.1 Time Line of Economic Crisis, 2007–2010

Month	Day	Year	Event	Description
2007				
February	27	2007	*Freddie Mac Press Release*	The Federal Home Loan Mortgage Corporation announced that it would no longer buy subprime mortgages/ mortgage-related securities
February		2007	*Home Sales Peak*	Resale single-family home sales peak
March	2	2007	*Bernanke and Poole Forecast Growth*	Counter to Alan Greenspan's statement (February 26, 2017) that a recession would be possibly in 2007
March	6	2007	*Stock Market Rebounds*	After the worst week in years, the stock market rebounded on March 6, 2007; Dow Jones went up by 157 points after dropping more than 600 points, from all time high of 12,786 on February 20, 2007
March		2007	*Housing Slump Spreads to Financial Industry*	Hedge funds had invested an unknown amount in mortgage-backed securities, according to *Business Week*
April	11	2007	*Fed Ignores Warning Signs*	The Federal Reserve was worried about inflation, but investors had been hoping for decrease in the Federal Funds Rate

TABLE 1.1 (*continued*)

Month	Day	Year	Event	Description
April	17	2007	*Fed Encourages Loan Arrangements*	The Federal Reserve encourages federal financial regulatory agencies to work out loan arrangements instead of foreclosure
April	26	2007	*3.4% Increase in Durable Goods Orders*	
June	19	2007	*Home Sales Forecast Revised Down*	National Association of Realtors forecast home sales were projected to total 6.18 million in 2007 and 6.41 million in 2008
July	17	2007	*Bear Stearns Sends Letter to Investors*	Bearn Stearns's High-Grade Structured Credit Fund lost 90 percent of its value
July	31	2007	*Bear Stearns Liquidates Funds*	Bearn Stearns closed two hedge funds based on mortgaged-backed securities
August	7	2007	*Fed FOMC Holds Rate at 5.25%*	The Federal Open Market Committee focused on monetary and financial conditions that will foster price stability.
August	9	2007	*BNP Paribas Suspends Redemption of Asset-Backed Securities*	Evaporation of liquidity in segments of the securitization market prohibited price discovery
August	17	2007	*Fed FOMC Lowers Rate to 4.75%*	Federal Open Market Committee voted to lower Federal Funds Rate from 5.25 to 4.75 percentage points, as opposed to usual adjustments that are only made by a quarter point at a time
September	14	2007	*Northern Rock Crisis*	The bank sought a liquidity support facility from the Bank of England, which led to the first bank run in England in 150 years
September	14	2007	*LIBOR Deviates from Federal Funds Rate*	London Interbank Offered Rate diverges 85 basis points from the Federal Funds Rate

(*continued*)

TABLE 1.1 (*continued*)

Month	Day	Year	Event	Description
October		2007	*Private Equity Deals Drop*	Private equity offers declined to $91 billion in the third quarter of 2007 (down from all time high of $177 billion in the second quarter of 2007)
October	8	2007	*Treasury Lends $125Bn to Banks*	U.S. Treasury infuses liquidity into nine large financial institutions to relieve solvency concerns
October	22	2007	*Fed Governor Warns That Crisis Was Not Over*	Federal Reserve Governor Randall Kroszner announced that recovery would be a "gradual process" for credit markets
November	8	2007	*Treasury Purchases $33Bn in Preferred Stock in Twenty-One Banks*	Capital adds liquidity and aids in the recovery from financial crisis
November	21	2007	*Treasury Creates $75 Billion Superfund*	Citigroup, JPMorgan Chase, and Bank of America set up a $75 billion superfund managed by Blackrock Investments
December	6	2007	*Nationalization of Northern Rock*	Northern Rock was nationalized after two unsuccessful bids did not want to guarantee repayment of public funds
December	21	2007	*Fed Auctions Loans*	Two special auctions made at least $40 billion available to U.S. banks (Swiss National Bank made $24 billion available to European banks)
December		2007	*Foreclosure Rates Double*	December 2007 foreclosure filings were 97% higher than in December 2006; 1% of homes were in foreclosure, compared to 0.58% in 2006
December		2007	*GDP Predicted to Fall in 2008*	

2008

Month	Day	Year	Event	Description
January	22, 30	2008	*Fed FOMC Lowers Rate in Effort to Stop Housing Bust*	Federal funds rate was lowered to 3.5 percentage points on January 22, 2018; then to 3 percentage points on January 30, 2018

TABLE 1.1 *(continued)*

Month	Day	Year	Event	Description
February	13	2008	*Bush Signs Tax Rebate*	Home sales slightly improved (by 2.9%); still remained 24% lower than in 2007
March	7		*Fed Begins Bailouts*	Federal Reserve announced increase of outstanding Term Auction Facility (TAF) amounts to $100 billion—auctions on March 10 and March 24
March	11		*Fed Lends Up to $200 Billion to Bond Holders*	Federal Reserve announced lending of $200 billion in U.S. Treasuries to holders of mortgage-backed securities after secondary market dried up
March	14	2008	*Bear Stearns Takeover*	JPMorgan acquires rival investment bank with backing of the Federal Reserve
March	17	2008	*Fed Continues Bailouts*	On March 17, the Federal Reserve held the first emergency weekend meeting in thirty years
March	19	2008	*Fed FOMC Lowers Rate*	The Federal Open Market Committee lowered the Federal Funds Rate (by 0.75 percentage points) to 2.25 percentage points
April	30	2008	*Fed FOMC Lowers Rate Further*	The Federal Open Market Committee lowered Federal Funds Rate to 2 percentage points
April	7, 21	2008	*Fed Adds Term Auction Facility*	The Federal Reserve added $50 billion each through its Term Auction Facility
May	20	2008	*Fed Expands Auction Facility*	The Federal Reserve auctioned another $150 billion through Term Auction Facility
June	2	2008	*Fed Auctions Total $1.2 Trillion*	Federal Reserve lends another $225 billion to provide liquidity
July	11	2008	*IndyMac Fails*	Failure of one the largest saving and loan associations and the seventh largest mortgage originator was the fourth-largest in U.S. history

(continued)

TABLE 1.1 (*continued*)

Month	Day	Year	Event	Description
July	24	2008	*Housing and Economic Recovery Act*	Congress gave U.S. Treasury ability to guarantee as much as $25 billion in Freddie Mac and Freddie Mae loans; allowed Federal Housing Administration (FHA) to guarantee up to $300 billion in new thirty-year fixed rate mortgages for subprime borrowers; and provide housing tax breaks and grants
September	7	2008	*Government Sponsored Enterprises Placed Under Conservatorship*	Federal Housing Finance Agency took over management control of Freddie Mac and Fannie Mac and backstopped losses
September	14	2008	*Merrill Lynch Sold to Bank of America*	Bank of America bought Merrill Lynch for $50 billion in stocks—paid $29/share after trading for $90/share in January 2007
September	15	2008	*Lehman Brothers Files for Bankruptcy*	U.S. Treasury Secretary Henry Paulson says no to further Wall Street bailouts; Lehman Brothers filed for bankruptcy in response, leading to significant market disruptions
September	16	2008	*Fed Buys AIG for $85 Billion*	AIG received emergency funding from the Federal Reserve
September	17	2008	*Near-Economic Collapse of Mutual Funds*	Investors fled money market mutual funds, which led to banks and businesses having no way of getting money to fund daily operations
September	18	2008	*Paulson and Bernanke Submit Bailout to Congress*	U.S. Treasury Secretary Paulson and Federal Reserve Chair Bernanke asked Congress to approve a $700 billion bailout to buy up mortgage-backed securities at risk of defaulting (Troubled Asset Relief Program [TARP] "bailout")
September	19	2008	*Fed Insures Money Market Accounts*	Bernanke announced that the Fed would lend money to banks and businesses in need so that they would not have to pull from money market funds

TABLE 1.1 (*continued*)

Month	Day	Year	Event	Description
September	22	2008	*Goldman Sachs and Morgan Stanley Apply to Become Commercial Banks*	Investment banks demanded protection for commercial banks from the Federal Reserve
September	23	2008	*Barney Frank Works with Lawmakers to Negotiate a Plan*	With a lower cost that offered more protection for taxpayers, measures which made it into TARP ("bailout bill")
September	26	2008	*WaMu Goes Bankrupt and Is Taken Over by FDIC*	Washington Mutual was taken over by the Federal Deposit Insurance Corporation and sold to JPMorgan for $1.9 billion
September	29	2008	*Stock Market Crashes*	The House of Representatives rejects the TARP bill and the Dow Jones drops by 770 points, most of any single day in history; global markets also went into a panic
October	3	2008	*Congress Passes TARP*	Congress passed Troubled Asset Relief Program and provided $700 billion as public "bailout" to banks
October	6	2008	*Global Stock Markets Collapse*	Central banks restored liquidity in global markets, stock markets around the world plummeted despite bailout approval
October	7	2008	*$1.7 Trillion Loan Program*	The Federal Reserve agreed to directly issue short-term loans, aiming the program to allow businesses to have enough cash flow to stay in business
October	8, 14	2008	*Central Banks Coordinate*	October 8, the Federal Reserve and central banks of the EU, Canada, the UK, Sweden, and Switzerland cut their rates by half a point. October 14, Europe, Japan, and the U.S. coordinate action to spend in order to guarantee bank financing. EU asks that the U.S. increase banking regulation and the role of the IMF in the process

(*continued*)

TABLE 1.1 (*continued*)

Month	Day	Year	Event	Description
October	21	2008	*Fed Lends $540 Billion*	Federal Reserve lent $540 billion to allow money market funds to meet redemptions
November	12	2008	*Fed Creates TALF*	The U.S. Treasury and Federal Reserve partner to use part of TARP to solve the freeze of the consumer credit market by creating the Term Asset-Backed Securities Loan Facility program
November	21	2008	*FDIC Guarantees $1.3 Trillion*	The Federal Deposit Insurance Corporation guaranteed loans between banks of $1.3 trillion
November	25	2008	*Treasury Gives Citigroup $20 Billion*	The U.S. Treasury provided $20 billion in return for $27 billion of preferred shares yielding 8% annual return
December	16	2008	*Fed Hits Zero Bound*	Federal Open Market Committee lowered federal funds rate to between 0.25-0% and discount rate to 0.5%; traditional monetary policy reached its limits
December	19	2008	*Treasury Inserts TARP Funds*	U.S. Treasury inserted $105 billion in TARP funds into eight banks in return for preferred stock; government received 5% and eventual 9% dividend
December	19	2008	*Chrysler, Ford, and GM Ask for Bailout*	Struggling U.S. carmakers ("Big 3") asked for support of $34 billion
2009				
January	12	2009	*Banks Report More Than $1 Trillion Loss*	Banks reported losses accumulated to more than $1 trillion since the beginning of the financial crisis in 2007
January		2009	*Big 3 U.S. Carmakers Receive Bailout*	Chrysler, Ford, and GM receive government funds to stabilize 1 million jobs—Chrysler and GM faced bankruptcy

TABLE 1.1 (*continued*)

Month	Day	Year	Event	Description
February	13	2009	*Congress Approves American Recovery and Reinvestment Act (ARRA)*	Stimulus packages included $288 billion in tax cuts, $224 billion in unemployment benefits, $275 billion for public works, subsidies for education, home purchases, and car purchases; total funds were $787 billion in tax funds
February	18	2009	*Obama Announces Homeowner Stability Initiative*	$75 billion plan, restructured/refinancing mortgages to avoid foreclosures
February	27	2009	*GDP Declines by 6.3%*	U.S. Bureau of Economic Analysis revised its U.S. GDP growth rate for Q4 2008 to −6.3%
March	2	2009	*Freddie Mac Announces Large Losses*	CEO David Moffett resigned after stating that Freddie Mac would need an additional $35 billion to remain solvent
March	4	2009	*Making Homes Affordable Program*	Obama administration launched initiative to help homeowners avoid foreclosure—included Homeowner Affordable Refinance Program (HARP), which fell short (only 810,000 homeowners were helped when the plan was structured to aid up to 2 million), and Home Affordable Modification Program (HAMP)
March	5	2009	*Dow Jones Drops to 6,594.44*	Total decline of 53.4% from its peak of 14,164.43 on October 9, 2007
August		2009	*Foreclosures Peak*	Record foreclosures in July 2009, with banks refusing to make loan modifications in the wake of the crisis; in response, the Obama administration asked banks to double loan modifications by November 1 (Making Homes Affordable program)
October		2009	*Unemployment Hits 10%*	Financial crisis caused economic downturns and Great Recession affects labor markets severely—worst since the recession in 1982

(*continued*)

TABLE 1.1 (*continued*)

Month	Day	Year	Event	Description
December	9	2009	*U.S. Treasury Press Release*	U.S. Treasury Secretary Timothy Geithner sent letter to congressional leaders outlining the exit strategy for TARP, which extended through October 3, 2010
2010				
January	7	2010	*Federal Reserve Releases Advisory*	Advisory reminded depository institutions of supervisory expectations for sound practices in managing interest rate risk
January	13	2010	*First FCIC Hearings*	The Financial Crisis Inquiry Commission (FCIC) held its first public hearing in Washington, D.C.
January	21	2010	*White House Press Release*	President Obama proposed new restrictions on trading activities and market shares of commercial banks
February	18	2010	*Federal Reserve Raises Discount Rate from 0.5% to 0.75%*	Departure from "zero bound" federal funds rate—recovery of conventional monetary policy
May	26	2010	*U.S. Treasury Announces Citigroup Reductions*	U.S. Treasury announced the sale of 1.5 billion shares of its holdings of Citigroup common stock
July	21	2010	*Dodd-Frank Wall Street Reform and Consumer Protection Act*	President Obama signed the Dodd-Frank Wall Street Reform and Consumer Protection Act— overhaul of the regulatory structure governing the U.S. financial service industry
August	10	2010	*FOMC Agrees to Keep the Fed Holdings of Securities Constant*	Federal Open Market Committee reinvested principal payments from agency debt and agency mortgage-backed securities into longer-term U.S. Treasury securities

TABLE 1.1 (*continued*)

Month	Day	Year	Event	Description
October	1	2010	*Financial Stability Oversight Council Starts*	Financial Stability Oversight Council held its inaugural meeting; charged with identifying financial risks, regulating market disciplin, and responding to emerging risks to U.S. financial stability (Dodd-Frank Wall Street Reform Act, Consumer Protection Act)
November	3	2010	*FOMC Expands Security Purchases (QE2)*	The Federal Open Market Committee suggested further measures of unconventional monetary policy and quantitative easing to promote faster economic recovery and ensure inflation is at consistent levels with its mandate; quantitative easing (QE2) was intended to buy $600 billion of U.S. Treasuries by the end of second quarter 2011
December	7	2010	*U.S. Treasury Sells Citigroup Shares*	U.S. Treasury sold its remaining shares of Citigroup common stock

Source: Compiled by the authors. See "Economic Report of the President" 2009, 52. Various FDIC and Federal Reserve Board's press releases.

Notes

1. See Board of Governors of the Federal Reserve System (2008).
2. As we will see throughout the book, the concept of moral hazard, or misaligned incentives toward risk-taking, is a recurring theme both during the crisis and in its aftermath. An example occurs when the government provides financial assistance to ailing firms. Other firms will then be more likely to take risky actions because they believe the government will bail them out too.
3. Bear Stearns specialized in mortgage-backed securities (MBS), a financial instrument that packaged groups or tranches of mortgages of various types and qualities into a single security. Credit rating agencies, which are overseen by the U.S. Securities and Exchange Commission, then assigned these securities a rating or a likelihood of default. In normal liquid markets, asset valuations are set by supply and demand, but in distressed markets, price discovery is not so easy. As firms sold assets at fire-sale prices to meet margin calls, rapidly declining prices created illiquidity in the market for structured finance products, thereby posing difficulties for JPMorgan Chase to ascertain the true value of the original mortgages and the probability of their default.

4. For a sequence of events leading to the demise of Bear Stearns, see https://www.fool .com/investing/general/2013/03/15/a-timeline-of-bear-stearns-downfall.aspx. See also Kelly (2009).

5. Eventually the price would be raised to $8 per share to appease the equity holders who held final approval of any buyout deal. For an analysis of the dynamics around the Bear Stearns takeover decision, see Epstein and O'Halloran (2008).

6. See remarks by Dudley (2017).

7. Bianconi et al. (2013) and Grima and Caruana (2017) show that emerging markets such as Brazil and Russia cannot be segregated from the financial stress emanating from the United States and that they suffered significant spillovers from the financial crisis. Indeed, the Brazilian economy entered its worst economic crisis in 2014–2016 since the 1930s Great Depression.

8. The data mostly focuses on the U.S. economy, but similar trends occurred in Europe. See Gros and Alcidi (2010).

9. Asymmetric information can lead to either moral hazard or adverse selection. Adverse selection arises when lenders cannot distinguish the type of borrower; namely, debtors who are likely to default from those who are not. Moral hazard arises once a loan is granted when a borrower takes risks that were previously undisclosed and jeopardizes a successful repayment.

10. Financial institutions play a special role in the mediation of wealth creation. Banks bridge the gap between the needs of borrowers and lenders by transforming the size, maturity, and risk associated with surplus funds. For example, banks transfer safe, liquid assets (cash deposits) into risky, long-term illiquid assets (home mortgages), which yield higher expected returns that are then shared with banking clients and shareholders.

11. Financial institutions face a number of risks. These risk categories include *counterparty risk*: risks that each party of a contract will not live up to their obligation; *market risk*: risk that occurs with adverse movement in overall performance of the financial market; *credit risk*: risk that a borrower or counterparty will fail to meet its obligations; and *liquidity risk*: risk that a company or bank will be unable to meet short-term financial demands, among others. Financial institutions can mitigate these risks by diversifying their holdings through financial instruments, such as derivatives to insure against adverse price and market movements. As discussed by O'Halloran and Nowaczyk in chapter 13 of this volume, spreading risk across financial markets may change *firm-specific risk* exposure, but it does not change *systemic risk*, the aggregate level of risk in the system as a whole.

12. The TED-spread is calculated as: TED-spread = 3 Month LIBOR Rate / 3 Month Treasury Bill. If the default rate of U.S. government debt increases relative to the interbank rate of default, then the TED-spread ratio will fall below 1. When the credit risk of interbank lending increases, the ratio rises above 1, all else being equal.

13. The Federal Funds Rate is the interest rate depository institutions use to lend reserve balances to one another overnight without collateral.

14. In January 2008, Bank of America announced that it would buy the company for $4 billion, a fraction of what Countrywide was worth at its peak.

15. See Board of Governors of the Federal Reserve System (2007), Meeting of the Federal Open Market Committee, August 7, 2007.

16. See the Meeting of the Federal Open Market Committee on September 18, 2007.

17. Friedman and Schwartz (2008) argued that unleashed deflationary expectations and a tight monetary policy were the driving factors of the Great Depression.

18. For a history of Federal Funds Rate changes over time, see Amadeo (2019).
19. See Anderson (2016).
20. See figure 1.8 for more on foreclosure trends.
21. For a discussion of foreclosures by state, see James (2009).
22. After the Federal Reserve's traditional monetary policy of interest rates ran out of steam, it reverted to a number of unconventional monetary tools, directly intervened to stabilize financial markets and provided several rounds of quantitative easing through debt and asset purchases.
23. See data trends in McBride (2018).
24. See Bureau of Labor Statistics (2018).
25. See Moore and Mirzaei (2014) for a discussion of differential impacts of the crisis across industries.
26. Another distinctive feature of the recession was the length of time it took workers to find a new job. One of the scariest job charts ever (that is its title) plots the percent of job losses relative to the months of peak employment by the number of months after peak employment (McBride, 2019). The chart shows that by far the 2007–2009 recession had the highest percentage of job losses in post-World War II recessions for the most number of months.
27. Economic Report of the President, (2012, 40).
28. See De Haas and Van Horen (2012), Acharya et al. (2014), and Paltalidis et al. (2015) for a discussion of transmission channels of systemic risk and contagion.
29. Financial services firms are defined as all publicly traded firms; government sponsored enterprises (GSEs) are not included.
30. For our purposes here, shadow banks are all financial institutions that do not fit into other categories: banks, insurance companies, pension funds, public finance, and central banks.
31. For details of this analysis see the Independent Commission on Banking (2011, 11).
32. The full title of this rule is "Alternative Net Capital Requirements for Broker-Dealers That Are Part of Consolidated Supervised Entities," SEC Release No. 34–49830, RIN 3235-AI96. See "Rules and Regulations," *Federal Register* 69, no. 118 (June 21, 2004).
33. See Kalemli-Ozcan et al. (2012, 40).
34. See transcription of William Dudley's comments at http://www.newyorkfed.org/newsevents/speeches/2012/dud120508.html.
35. Notional value is the total value of options, forwards, futures, and foreign exchange currencies. The decline in gross market value reflects postcrisis regulations and ongoing structural changes in the OTC derivatives market.
36. BIS Statistical Release (June 2018).

References

Acharya, Viral, Robert Engle, and Diane Pierret. 2014. "Testing Macroprudential Stress Tests: The Risk of Regulatory Risk Weights." *Journal of Monetary Economics* 65 (July): 36–53. doi:10.1016/j.jmoneco.2014.04.014.

Amadeo, Kimberly. 2019. "Highest and Lowest Interest Rates and Why They Changed." *The Balance*. January 7. https://www.thebalance.com/fed-funds-rate-history-highs-lows-3306135.

Anderson, Dean. 2016. "Summing It Up: A Brief History of the Economy, Regulations, and Bank Data." Federal Reserve Bank of Atlanta. December 6. https://www.frbatlanta

.org/economy-matters/banking-and-finance/viewpoint/2016/12/06/history-of
-bank-regulation.

Bair, Sheila. *Bull by the Horns: Fighting to Save Main Street from Wall Street and Wall Street from Itself.* New York: Simon & Schuster, 2013.

Bank for International Settlements. 2018. "Statistical Release: OTC Derivatives Statistics at End June 2018." October 31. https://www.bis.org/publ/otc_hy1810.pdf.

Belvedere, Matthew J. 2018. "Warren Buffett: In the 10 Years Since Financial Panic, We've Learned We're 'all Dominoes.'" *CNBC.* September 10. https://www.cnbc.com/2018/09/10/warren-buffett-2008-financial-crisis-showed-we-are-all-dominoes.html.

Bianconi, Marcelo, Joe A. Yoshino, and Mariana O. Machado De Sousa. 2013. "BRIC and the U.S. Financial Crisis: An Empirical Investigation of Stock and Bond Markets." *Emerging Markets Review* 14: 76–109. doi:10.1016/j.ememar.2012.11.002.

Billio, Monica, Mila Getmansky, Andrew Lo, Loriana Pelizzon. 2012 "Econometric Measures of Connectedness and Systemic Risk in the Finance and Insurance Sectors." *Journal of Financial Economics*, vol. 104, no. 3: 535–59.

BNP Paribas. 2007. "BNP Paribas Investment Partners Temporarily Suspends the Calculation of the Net Asset Value of the Following Funds: Parvest Dynamic ABS, BNP Paribas ABS EURIBOR and BNP Paribas ABS EONIA." Press Release, August 9. https://group.bnpparibas/en/press-release/bnp-paribas-investment-partners-temporaly-suspends-calculation-net-asset-funds-parvest-dynamic-abs-bnp-paribas-abs-euribor-bnp-paribas-abs-eonia.

Board of Governors of the Federal Reserve System. 2007. "FOMC Statement." Press Release, August 7. https://www.federalreserve.gov/newsevents/pressreleases/monetary20070807a.htm.

——. 2008. Conference Call of the Federal Open Market Committee on March 10. https://www.federalreserve.gov/monetarypolicy/files/FOMC20080310confcall.pdf.

Buch, Claudia, and B. Gerard Dages. 2018. "Structural changes in banking after the crisis." Report prepared by a Working Group established by the Committee on the Global Financial System. CGFS Papers, No 60 (January).

Buffett, Warren. 2002. "Chairman's Letter to the Shareholders of Berkshire Hathaway Inc." February 28. http://www.berkshirehathaway.com/2001ar/2001letter.html.

Bureau of Labor Statistics. 2018. "News Release." November 6. https://www.bls.gov/news/.release/archives/jolts_11062018.pdf.

Cecchetti, Stephen G., and Kermit L. Schoenholtz. 2017. *Money, Banking, and Financial Markets*, 5th ed. New York: McGraw-Hill Education.

De Haas, Ralph, and Neeltje Van Horen. 2012. "International Shock Transmission After the Lehman Brothers Collapse: Evidence from Syndicated Lending." *American Economic Review* 102, no. 3 (May): 231–37. doi:10.1257/aer.102.3.231.

Dudley, William C. 2012. "What Does Interconnectedness Imply for Macroeconomic and Financial Cooperation?" Speech, Swiss National Bank-International Monetary Fund Conference, Switzerland, Zurich, May 8.

——. 2017. "Lessons from the Financial Crisis." Speech, The Economic Club of New York, New York City, November 6.

Executive Office of the President Council of Economic Advisers. 2009. *Economic Report of the President (2009)*. PR 44.9: U.S. Government Printing Office.

——. 2012. *Economic Report of the President (2012)*. PR 44.9: U.S. Government Printing Office.

Epstein, David, and Sharyn O'Halloran. 2008. "The Bear Stearns Takeover Game." Reflectivepundit. April 15. https://www.reflectivepundit.com/reflectivepundit/2008/04/the-bear-stearn.html.

Friedman, Milton, and Anna Jacobson. Schwartz. 2008. *A Monetary History of the United States 1867–1960*. Princeton, NJ: Princeton University Press.

Grima, Simon, and Luca Caruana. 2017. "The Effect of the Financial Crisis on Emerging Markets. A Comparative Analysis of the Stock Market Situation Before and After." ResearchGate. January. https://www.researchgate.net/publication/321155328_The_Effect_of_the_Financial_Crisis_on_Emerging_Markets_A_comparative_analysis_of_the_stock_market_situation_before_and_after.

Gros, Daniel, and Cinzia Alcidi. 2010. "The Impact of the Crisis on the Real Economy." SSRN. May 14. https://papers.ssrn.com/sol3/papers.cfm?abstract_id=1603944.

Haldane, Andrew, Simon Brennan and Vasileios Madouros. 2010. "What Is the Contribution of the Financial Sector: Miracle or Mirage?" in *The LSE Report on THE Future of Finance*. Edited by Adair Turner, London School of Economics and Political Science.

Independent Commission on Banking. 2011. *Final Report and Recommendations*. https://webarchive.nationalarchives.gov.uk/20120827143059/http://bankingcommission.independent.gov.uk/

Ivashina, Victoria, and David Scharfstein. 2010, "Bank Lending during the Financial Crisis of 2008." *Journal of Financial Economics*, vol. 97, no. 3: 319–38.

James, Frank. 2009. "Nearly One in Four U.S. Homes with Mortgages 'Underwater.'" NPR. November 24. https://www.npr.org/sections/thetwo-way/2009/11/one_in_four_us_homes_underwate.html.

Kalemli-Ozcan, Sebnem, Bent Sorensen, and Sevcan Yesiltas. 2012. "Leverage Across Firms, Banks, and Countries." *Journal of International Economics* 88, no. 2 (November): 284–98. doi:10.1016/j.jinteco.2012.03.002.

Kelly, Kate. 2009. "Inside the Fall of Bear Stearns." *Wall Street Journal*, May 9.

Lo, Andrew W. 2012. "Reading About the Financial Crisis: A Twenty-One-Book Review." *Journal of Economic Literature* 50, no. 1 (March): 151–78. doi:10.1257/jel.50.1.151.

McBride, Bill. 2018. "Housing Starts Decreased to 1.201 Million Annual Rate in September." *Calculated Risk* (blog), October 17. https://www.calculatedriskblog.com/2018/10/housing-starts-decreased-to-1201.html.

——. 2019. "Scariest Jobs Chart Ever." *Calculated Risk* (blog), January 13. https://www.calculatedriskblog.com/2019/01/update-scariest-jobs-chart-ever.html.

Moore, Tomoe, and Ali Mirzaei. 2014. "The Impact of the Global Financial Crisis on Industry Growth." *The Manchester School* 84 (2): 159–80. doi:10.1111/manc.12090.

Paltalidis, Nikos, Dimitrios Gounopoulos, Renatas Kizys, and Yiannis Koutelidakis. 2015. "Transmission Channels of Systemic Risk and Contagion in the European Financial Network." *Journal of Banking & Finance* 61 (December): S36–52. doi:10.1016/j.jbankfin.2015.03.021.

Reinhart, Carmen M., and Kenneth S. Rogoff. 2009. *This Time Is Different: Eight Centuries of Financial Folly*. Princeton, NJ: Princeton University Press.

Tarullo, Daniel K. "Regulating Systemic Risk: Remarks at the 2011 Credit Markets Symposium, Charlotte, N.C." *Joint Resolution Extending the Effective Period of the Emergency Price Control Act of 1942, as Amended, and the Stabilization Act of 1942, as Amended | FRASER | St. Louis Fed*, Federal Reserve Bank, Saint Louis Mo., 3 June 2011, fraser.stlouisfed.org/title/910/item/35358.

PART I

THE FINANCIAL CRISIS IN PERSPECTIVE

CHAPTER 2

IF "IT" HAPPENED AGAIN

A Road Map for Regulatory Reform

GLENN HUBBARD

The conventional assessment of the 2007–2009 financial and economic crisis places blame on a dearth of regulation. That assessment is simplistic at best and entirely inaccurate at worst. The truth is that the financial crisis was, in part, the result of a lack of *effective* regulation. And that challenge remains in today's climate of easier financial conditions.

Three themes emerge from the crisis. First, we certainly need more *effective* regulation. Although we needed new regulation in some previously under-regulated areas, the crisis has shown that the most precarious sectors of our financial system are those already subject to a great deal of regulation—regulation that just was not effective. Any call for further reform means that new or revised regulations should be based on solid *principles*, chief among them the reduction of *systemic risk* and *contagion*. Second, we must increase transparency in the financial system to promote investor protection. More information enables the market to price assets, risk, and other relevant inputs more accurately. Much of the present crisis can be attributed to a lack of critical information (and perhaps, in some cases, misinformation). Third, and critical for both ongoing U.S. and international regulatory discussions, we need to acknowledge and manage trade-offs between enhancing accountability for individual institutions and mitigating systemic risk from contagion.

The Crisis and the Regulatory Response

Severity of the Crisis

The 2007–2009 financial crisis was the most serious such event for the United States since the Great Depression. The crisis manifested itself in credit losses, write-downs, liquidity shocks, deflated property values, and a contraction of the real economy. The sharp contraction in U.S. gross domestic product in 2009 can be traced to the adverse effects of the crisis on household consumption and business investment. While originating in the United States, consequences of the crisis were felt globally, and U.S. monetary policy responses to the crisis generated global economic effects.

In the housing sector, banks took advantage of low interest rates and securitization opportunities to institute relaxed lending standards that drove the boom in mortgage lending from 2001 to 2006. Although the number of households in the United States increased only marginally between 1990 and 2008, the aggregate mortgage debt outstanding more than quadrupled during that same period. Increased borrowing by U.S. households was partially offset by climbing asset prices. The burst of the housing bubble virtually eliminated construction and sales activity for a while.

Globally, the financial crisis of 2007–2009 and its continuing aftermath have complex origins, but those origins share a four-letter word: *risk*. The mispricing of risk—with inflationary consequences for asset prices in the boom and a downward spiral of collapsing asset prices and economic activity in the bust, as well as contagion in the unwinding—must be central to economic analysis of and policy responses to the crisis. Underlying factors include (i) global saving and investment imbalances that contributed to low real interest rates and risk premia in international capital markets for many years, (ii) excessively expansionary U.S. monetary policy in the years 2003–2005, and (iii) significant gaps in regulation in theory and practice. For the purpose of this chapter, I will concentrate on some key weaknesses in regulation and on components of regulatory reform related to capital adequacy, resolution processes for insolvent institutions, and policies to manage contagion during a financial crisis.

Regulatory Goals and Principles

An obvious opening question in a debate over major regulatory reform is: *What problem are we trying to solve*? In the United States, considering the discussion leading up to and following the passage of the Dodd-Frank Wall

Street Reform and Consumer Protection Act of 2010, that question is tough to answer. For many economists and policymakers concerned about housing finance, the law was largely silent. The focus on lines of business in the so-called "Volcker Rule" appears somewhat disconnected from the painful problems actually experienced during the financial crisis (an issue under review by regulators now). And we must decide whether we are more interested in policies to address the likelihood of failure of individual institutions or the likelihood of contagion across assets, markets, and institutions (a tension dominating regulatory debate now).

Much of the early policy discussion in the aftermath of the Lehman failure and the AIG rescue concerned *interconnectedness* of assets and/or liabilities. While evidence on the significance of interconnectedness is mixed, the problem of *contagion*—particularly arising from reliance on short-term borrowings by both bank and nonbank institutions—was very important.

Going a step further, effective regulatory reform can occur only when policymakers take account of fundamental regulatory principles. *The most important of these principles is that regulation should reduce systemic risk.* Systemic risk is the risk of collapse of an entire system or entire market, exacerbated by links and interdependencies; with systemic risk, the failure of a single entity or cluster of entities can cause a cascading failure.

There are at least five externalities particular to financial markets that contribute to systemic risk. First, the spread of speculative information through the market can create the perception that economic difficulties affecting one financial institution will also affect similarly situated firms. Second, customers of failed institutions may subsequently find themselves in a less friendly market when looking to redirect their business. Third, interconnectedness exists among the financial institutions participating in modern financial markets, so that the failure of one firm can affect many others. Fourth, falling asset prices and resulting liquidity constrictions may create a negative spiral. Fifth, falling asset prices and liquidity crises may cause institutions to become reluctant to extend credit.

Regulation may be legitimately imposed for a variety of other reasons. Disclosure is important for investors' well-being, in view of the potential for an individual investor to undertake a less-than-adequate investigation before making an investment decision. Moreover, regulation can be used effectively to limit the influence of moral hazard that arises from state-provided safety nets and, in particular, to ensure that firms and capital suppliers are not permitted to take advantage of taxpayer support and engage in undue risk-taking.

A final principle of regulation applies to all the other principles as well: the cost-benefit rule. *That is, a regulation should be promulgated only when its benefits outweigh its costs.* Furthermore, if different kinds of regulation can achieve the same benefit, the regulation with the least cost should be adopted.

Reducing Systemic Risk

Again, the most compelling justification for financial regulation is the need to reduce externalities—particularly systemic risk. I now consider measures to reduce systemic risk in two areas: capital adequacy requirements and the resolution process for insolvent financial institutions.

Regulation of Capital

Historically, capital regulation has been the dominant regulatory mechanism for constraining risk-taking by banks. By providing a cushion against losses, capital is supposed to act as a first line of defense against bank failures and their secondary consequences for systemic risk. Yet the existing capital regime— effectively established by the Basel Capital Accords—failed to prevent several of the largest U.S. and European financial institutions from failing or becoming distressed to the point that they required government bailouts.

Institutional coverage. Until the crisis, it was well understood in the United States that firms that were not regulated as banks (or thrifts), and were not subject to capital regulation, were excluded from the Federal Reserve's safety net. The Fed's emergency measures during the crisis upended this understanding. These measures may have been justified by the exigencies of the crisis, but they have created structural moral hazards and impediments to a level playing field to the extent that institutions with access to the Fed's safety net are not subject to capital regulation. With the crisis behind us, we need to realign the institutional costs and benefits of capital regulation. Institutions with the ability to borrow from the central bank in its role as the lender of last resort should be subject to some form of capital regulation.

Calibration. Despite the critical role played by capital adequacy in the regulatory framework, existing capital requirements were set without an explicit link to a target standard of solvency for individual banks or for the system as a whole. Though an understandable reaction to the overleveraging of the system would be to raise capital requirements across the board, the lack of empirical research on capital calibration suggests that the costs and benefits of much higher capital requirements for banks remain uncertain.

Two categories of empirical research are useful for understanding arguments about raising bank capital levels. First, many studies have documented the relative costliness of external equity financing and of more junior as opposed to more senior debt claims. Second, evidence that credit supply responds to a loss of equity capital or to a higher required ratio of equity to risky assets necessarily demonstrates that equity financing is costly.

To the extent that bank equity financing is costly, a contraction in bank credit supply is socially costly when there is limited substitutability of bank credit and other funding to some or all borrowers. Both theoretical and empirical research has highlighted the imperfect substitutability of bank and nonbank sources of funds (for example, securities). Bank lending involves more information-intensive screening and contracting, and many borrowers face high information-related costs in nonbank lending.

The flip side of this point, of course, is that to the extent that there are non-bank sources of funds that are relatively close substitutes for bank credit, an increase in bank equity capital requirements will, all else equal, raise the volume of lending in those "close substitute" channels. I will return to this link between changes in capital requirements and shadow banking in a bit.

Before moving on, it is important to note that any argument that raising bank equity is costless is logically inconsistent with any policy argument for so-called macroprudential capital regulation. For such regulation to be effective, *it is necessarily the case* that (i) equity financing must be costly relative to other forms of financing, and (ii) changes in bank equity capital affect lending (that is, that capital requirements are binding and that bank and nonbank sources of funds are imperfect substitutes). But, of course, it is these very factors that relate to the *social cost* of higher capital requirements.

These arguments are not intended to suggest that banks should not hold more capital. They should—and now do. But ever-higher capital requirements are not a "free lunch" and require meaningful cost-benefit analysis.

Timing effects. Another feature of the current capital regulation framework is that minimum capital levels are fixed, while bank losses (or adverse earnings events) vary considerably over the economic cycle. The implication is that solvency standards are not constant during an economic cycle but are dependent on the "state of the world." The solvency level of a given capital requirement depends critically on the period over which it is calibrated and on assumptions of the state of the world going forward. In view of the cyclical nature of bank losses, the effect of a fixed capital requirement is to force banks to raise capital in the downturn as losses mount and capital levels are depleted. A key revision to the existing framework for the regulation of capital adequacy to be studied should be a shift to time-varying capital requirements. An alternative to letting capital requirements fall during a downturn would be to allow—or require—banks to hold some form of *contingent capital* that can be called upon as losses mount.

Countercyclical capital ratios can be achieved in two ways. The first would be to encourage dynamic provisioning. This encouragement could be done without conflicting with existing securities regulation or accounting standards by providing that additional reserves over "known" losses did not run through the income statement but rather constituted a special appropriation of retained earnings. The second way would be to require contingent capital.

One mechanism for reducing the cost of higher equity capital is to mandate the use of contingent capital that would increase a bank's equity when some prespecified action occurs. One manifestation, contingent convertibles, would convert into bank equity if regulatory capital (or in some forms, stock market value) declines below a prespecified value. An alternative manifestation is capital insurance, in which insurance provided by investors would pay off to a bank when a prespecified threshold event occurs.

Contingent capital offers important advantages in a reform to increase bank equity capital. The concept of shareholders' equity employed in the Basel Accord lags its true value (relying on accounting principles that combine book value, fair value, and market value constructs). As a consequence, regulators must keep pace with financial innovation in security design.

Well-designed contingent capital requirements can foster incentives for banks to maintain the right amount of capital (in the combination of equity plus contingent capital). Importantly, relative to costly equity financing, contingent capital offers a key benefit: issuing contingent capital need not reduce shareholder value, while mandated equity issues necessarily do so.

Systemically important institutions. In the United States, the crisis disproportionately affected the largest U.S. financial institutions. Very large banks may pose unique risks to the government because of their systemic consequences. As a result, unless policymakers comprehensively address the problem of too big to fail, one might argue that a large or important bank should be required to hold a larger capital buffer. The flip side of the point is also worth making: to the extent that we are willing to let very large banks fail, the high costs of extra capital are less necessary. And extra capital levels can be quite imperfect protection against contagion.

Having said that, certain types of financial institutions generally do not pose systemic risk to the financial system, including asset managers (mutual fund managers, as well as managers of private funds, like hedge funds and private equity funds) and traditional insurers, since their bankruptcy would not set off a chain reaction of financial institution failures. The government has rightly pulled back on this more expansive definition, though that shift has come about more from external commentary and judicial review than from internal analytical thinking.

From costly bank equity capital to "shadow banking." For very large banks lending to very large firms with access to nonbank sources of credit, higher bank cost of financing puts banks at a competitive disadvantage, leading to a search for ways to increase bank leverage. This search manifests itself in the quest for lending activity outside the regulated banking sector—"shadow banking." And arguments for macroprudential regulation of bank equity capital requirements must extend to more than just deposit-taking banks.

The experience of the 2007–2009 financial crisis offers lessons on the costs of "runs" and financial fragility in the shadow banking system. As many economists have emphasized, the collapse of the asset-backed securities market had in common with a textbook bank run the inability of purchasers of asset-backed securities to renew short-term financing.

Mechanically, the bank-run-like removal of short-term lending in shadow banking (the asset-backed securities market) can be understood in the context of "haircuts" in repurchase agreements used to finance conduits holding asset-backed securities in the shadow banking system. A haircut is akin to a down payment constraint, an amount to be posted when an investor borrows in the repo market. Prior to the financial crisis, haircuts on top-rated asset-backed securities were at most 2 percent. In the thick of the crisis, haircuts on both asset-backed securities linked to subprime mortgages and on consumer asset-backed securities increased substantially, in some cases to more than 50 percent. This change led to liquidations, further reducing asset prices.

Any change in bank equity capital requirements that does not incorporate the shadow banking system ignores important systemic risk; indeed, it is possible that a substantial increase in capital ratios could increase systemic risk by expanding the shadow banking system. To be effective, such regulation would need to extend to the shadow banking system through regulation of haircuts.

To be specific, consistent capital regulation reform in a macroprudential setting would require that a bank loan or the same holding within an asset-backed security be subject effectively to the same "capital requirement."

The alternative to this more expansive notion of bank capital regulation is to combat runs by extending the federal safety net, as, for example, in the financial crisis. But this policy extends the costly moral hazard built into the current banking safety net, requiring further thought about the pricing of such "insurance."

Back to goals and principles. The most basic arguments for government-mandated capital requirements (as opposed to levels determined by a purely market focus) reflect ex ante moral hazard concerns about the regulatory safety net. But there is a big point here: this ex ante reassurance is not costless. And, more important for reform in the aftermath of the financial crisis, capital requirements cannot be the complete answer in response to the ex post runs by short-term creditors whose investments are exposed to potential fire-sale losses.

Resolution Process for Failed Financial Institutions

The financial crisis and its aftermath revealed both the strengths and the weaknesses of insolvency regimes for complex financial institutions. Certain insolvencies have had a far greater systemic effect than others, in part because the law that governs the insolvency of a financial company depends on the company's form of organization. In the United States specifically, the insolvency of banks insured by the Federal Deposit Insurance Corporation (FDIC) is governed by the Federal Deposit Insurance Act (FDIA); the insolvency of registered broker-dealers is governed by the Securities Investor Protection Act; and the insolvency of most other financial companies is governed by the U.S. Bankruptcy Code.

The FDIA enables regulators to more effectively combat systemic risk. Notably, it creates a flexible insolvency regime that provides for preresolution action, receivership and conservatorship, and many methods of resolution, including liquidation, open bank assistance, purchase and assumption transactions, and the establishment of bridge banks. This regime has been very successful in promoting stability in the banking system by reducing uncertainty for depositors and counterparties while successfully mitigating losses for banks, counterparties, and the deposit insurance fund. However, the FDIA resolution regime is available only to resolve *banks*, excluding from coverage many systemically significant financial companies, including bank holding companies. One significant aspect of the FDIA, as compared to the Bankruptcy Code, is that it permits the transfer of certain derivatives and other qualified financial contracts to third parties, thus eliminating the downward spiral of prices that can result from a rush to liquidate collateral. A better alternative is to implement a comprehensive Financial Company Resolution Act, applicable to all financial institutions and based on the FDIA, that is applicable to all financial companies.

The path taken by the Dodd-Frank Act of 2010—the Orderly Liquidation Authority—still leaves some questions unanswered in this regard. Offering a general resolution antidote to too big to fail is particularly important, as the legislation's regulatory burdens advantage very large banks relative to smaller banks. And estimates of the value of the funding advantage via an implicit guarantee for very large institutions are in the tens of billions per year (and, in some estimates, hundreds of billions of dollars per year).

Back to goals and principles. Resolution mechanisms ranging from contingent capital and creditor bail-ins to good-bank/bad-bank structures to Dodd-Frank's Orderly Liquidation Authority focus on individual institutions. There is still an open question about the extent to which one should protect short-term creditors to reduce the likelihood of contagious runs. That is, while ex post resolution mechanisms are specifically designed to force losses on equity and debt holders of failing institutions, those mechanisms may do little to address contagion by exposing short-term creditors to greater risk. I will return to this point in a moment.

Back to the Problem of Contagion in a Financial Crisis

In some important ways, recent regulatory reforms have exacerbated problems of systemic risks through contagion. One way in which costly runs by short-term creditors can be reduced is through lender-of-last-resort support from the central bank. In the teeth of the financial crisis, the Federal Reserve expanded its provision of liquidity in new borrowing facilities. The Dodd-Frank Act, however, *reduced* the Fed's lending authority and raised collateral requirements for emergency lending. These limits, particularly given the additional power granted to the secretary of the Treasury, are unlikely to reassure short-term creditors, an essential problem given the fragile maturity transformation inherent in banking. While the law sought to reduce potential taxpayer losses from intervention, the trade-off in costs of contagion cannot be ignored.

A second regulatory intervention that makes contagion-fighting more difficult is restrictions on public capital injections. Bailouts were unpopular with much of the public and many policymakers because of ex post taxpayer expense and ex ante moral hazard. That bailouts of automobile companies occurred as well only enhanced public and policymaker concern that such interventions were politically motivated. And there are legitimate fears that such interventions allow politicians to prop up insolvent institutions for an extended period of time. Without guarantee or insurance systems for short-term creditors, however, public capital injections are a potentially valuable tool for addressing contagion and systemic risk during a financial crisis.

What, then, should governments do in the event of another significant financial crisis? Even if the government lacks standing authority to inject capital, it should be prepared to act early in the crisis in the context of a comprehensive plan of action. And the government should increase accountability for equity holders and management. Analyzing ways to resolve competing goals of institutional accountability and preventing contagion should rise in importance in both economic research and policy design—both for commercial banking and shadow banking.

Notes for a Path Forward

Five areas should guide a regulatory path forward for the Federal Reserve, the Trump administration, and Congress. The first step should be a thoroughgoing assessment of regulatory impact, including a rigorous quantitative analysis of the macroeconomic effects of regulation.

Second, bank regulators should review and potentially eliminate or recalibrate liquidity requirements, because liquidity requirements can *increase* stress during a crisis. As part of this analysis, bank regulators should revise "operational risk" capital requirements so that they are based on banks' *current* activities and risks.

Third, it is important that they ensure that rulemakings are adopted through a transparent and public process. I say this because the Federal Reserve's stress tests and the Federal Reserve and FDIC's living wills have been adopted in a secretive manner. The Federal Reserve and FDIC should adopt a more transparent process, in which outside review is possible.

Fourth, to address systemic risk, the Financial Stability Oversight Committee (FSOC) should replace nonbank systematically important financial institution (SIFI) designation with an activities-based regulatory framework to more effectively identify and reduce systemic risk. The FSOC should rescind its nonbank SIFI designations. And the FSOC should not apply rules for banks to nonbank financial institutions.

Fifth, the Federal Reserve's vital "lender of last resort" role should be grounded in a rule-of-law framework. The Federal Reserve should publish a detailed framework that outlines the procedures it would use to provide effective emergency liquidity to the U.S. financial system in a crisis. As with the conduct of monetary policy, I think of this approach as one of "maintain and explain" (maintain a clearly articulated framework and explain the rationale for departures from that framework). In so doing, the Fed should establish specific, observable criteria that will be used to determine whether emergency Fed lending becomes fiscal policy that should involve the Treasury. And as an ex post measure, Dodd-Frank's restrictions on Section 13 (3) lending should be reexamined.

* * *

The time for rethinking financial regulatory reform is now. But now is also the time for serious thinking and analysis. What is needed is a clear plan for reducing systemic risk, enhancing transparency, and modernizing regulatory institutions. The Trump administration's interest and that of new Federal Reserve leaders provides an opening.

That debate requires us to confront systemic risk and contagion. It also requires us to evaluate trade-offs between mitigating the failure of individual institutions and reducing systemic risk. Finance and the financial system are valuable for savers and borrowers and for the provision of risk-sharing, liquidity, and information services. Proper regulation can preserve and enhance this value. This reorientation is important both to improve macroeconomic outcomes and increase public and political support for the role of the financial sector in advancing economic well-being.

CHAPTER 3

TRENDS AND DELEGATION IN U.S. FINANCIAL MARKET REGULATION

THOMAS GROLL, SHARYN O'HALLORAN,
AND GERALDINE McALLISTER

The 2007–2009 financial crisis has been called a "perfect storm" of failures—Wall Street, hedge funds, banks, mortgage lenders, rating agencies, and the media all played their roles. Yet it is also important to ask whether regulators and the host of agencies that oversee financial markets had the necessary authority to carry out their mandates, or did they lack the tools to effectively supervise financial institutions and avert the financial crisis?

If the latter is true, then why did regulators fail to act at key points along the crisis time line? For instance, why did the Federal Reserve decline to provide liquidity in August 2007 when BNP Paribas halted redemption of mortgage securities as the secondary market experienced a drastic reduction in liquidity and price discovery proved impossible? Did members of Congress allocate insufficient regulatory authority to agencies to respond to changing market conditions and, instead, set policy on their own? Alternatively, did special interest groups pressure regulators and policymakers to enact softer regulations and limit agency discretion? Without understanding the sources of regulatory failure, it is difficult to understand what regulation will work in the future and under what conditions. Political and regulatory reforms mean little unless they are coupled with strong incentives for regulators to use the power delegated to them and resist being influenced by the industry they are supposed to oversee. Otherwise, giving bureaucrats more power will only hasten their capture and make regulatory outcomes even more inefficient, as we show in our analysis. This is an important discussion, for the different interpretations of history have different implications for the road ahead.

In this chapter, we provide a descriptive lens and an analytical characterization of changes in financial market regulation over time. We illustrate patterns in U.S. financial laws since 1950 and highlight recent lobbying activities aimed at the rules enacted in response to the financial crisis. Despite a growing financial sector in the United States, empirical trends document that regulatory discretion delegated to federal bank agencies has been on a downward trajectory for some time and only accelerated after the crisis. Our theoretical model highlights a partisan conflict between Congress and the presidency, which can explain a considerable amount of variance in these patterns. We also illustrate the empirical trends in lobbying and record when a financial crisis occurred, when a regulatory overhaul took place, the regulatory authority delegated to government agencies, and the lobbying efforts undertaken during both legislative enactment and agency rulemaking. The data show that lobbying of key financial agencies spiked when regulators were interpreting and drafting guidelines and procedures to implement the Volcker Rule, a rule that would have a significant impact on bank profitability.

In the second part of the chapter, we present our analytical frameworks, which expand the standard delegation models developed in Epstein and O'Halloran (1994, 1999). We employ a delegation framework of joint policymaking and analyze the constraints on administrative discretion when financial markets confront systemic risk or when lobbying pressure by special interests capture or limit regulators (Groll, O'Halloran, and McAllister, 2017). The evaluation recognizes that regulation must address (i) investment and systemic risk in financial markets as well as partisan influences and (ii) interest groups lobbying at the rulemaking stage to constrain or sway regulatory actions.

To understand the implications of lobbying activities in rulemaking, we extend the classical delegation setup and introduce interest groups lobbying regulators and legislators (e.g., note-and-comment period or legal action against "regulatory overreach"). Our model shows how a regulated industry may choose to undertake lobbying efforts at the administrative stage, when the regulated industry may exert costly lobbying pressure on the agency and influence its rulemaking. The agency, facing the burden of this lobbying pressure, may then choose to propose and implement a different policy that is within its delegated discretion.

The formal model highlights that the regulatory agency chooses a lower policy level in response to greater external policy shocks and lobbying pressure by the industry. Indeed, the mere threat of administrative lobbying by the industry may be sufficient to induce the agency to set policies closer to those preferred by the industry. Our analysis also shows that the policy conflict—the difference between the legislature's preferred policy and the agency's implemented policy—increases the agency's lobbying burden but also affects the interest group's lobbying effectiveness when the legislature prefers a higher policy level (more financial regulation). The implication of this finding is that administrative lobbying can either amplify or mitigate the impact of political conflict between the branches of government when setting policy. Our discussion further notes that the "ally principle" does not hold (Bertelli and Feldmann, 2006), and the legislature prefers an agency that is slightly more biased against the industry and can resist interest group pressure. Regarding regulatory design, we find that the legislature delegates greater discretion to the agency when there is more uncertainty around policy outcomes, when there is lower policy conflict between the legislature and the agency, and when administrative lobbying mitigates preference conflict.

The next two sections provide data trends to motivate our theoretical perspectives on delegation in financial markets and lobbying pressures on policymakers. Then we present our arguments and the theoretical results. The final section discusses the implications of our analysis for the recent push to roll back postcrisis regulatory reforms.

Trends in Financial Regulation Before the Financial Crisis

In a recently concluded study analyzing the legislation of U.S. financial regulation between 1950 and 2009, Groll, O'Halloran, and McAllister (2017) compiled a novel, comprehensive data set of all laws regulating the financial sector and constructed measures of agency discretion over time. The laws were first coded manually using observational data collection techniques developed in Epstein and O'Halloran (1999) but were also coded employing data science techniques, such as Natural Language Processing (NLP) and machine learning, to ensure the robustness of our measures (Groll et al., 2015). The legislation covers all the financial regulation laws, legislation that regulates the different parts of the financial markets, including banking, stock markets, financial intermediaries, state, and federal chartered banks, and so on. For this time period, we identified 121 major pieces of financial legislation and identified the various components of the laws subject to a given rubric, which is discussed in Groll et al. (2015) and Groll, O'Halloran, and McAllister (2017). The data provide information on regulatory design found in different types of legislation and how financial regulation has changed over time.

In particular, the data collected illustrate changes in authority delegated from Congress to regulatory agencies in financial regulation over time. To give some perspective, figure 3.1 illustrates the number of financial regulation laws enacted in each Congress: on average, about three and a half financial regulation laws are enacted in each congressional term. The figure also shows the distribution of laws enacted during the time period, including a spike in 2006

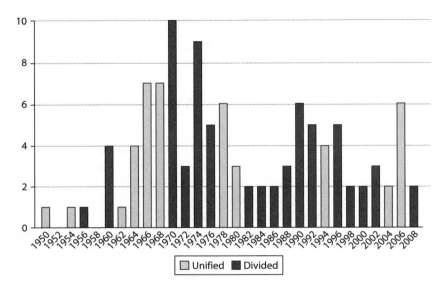

Figure 3.1 Financial bills passed per Congress, 1950–2009

as the financial crisis approached. The figure highlights when the executive and legislative branches were controlled by the same political party (unified government) and when this was not the case (divided government). The figure does not provide any evidence about the influence of partisan factors in passing financial laws; the average number of laws per Congress is almost identical during times of either type of control.

Parallel to the amount of enacted and changed legislation, the size of the financial sector, measured as a share of gross domestic product (GDP), increased substantially during this time period. As shown in figure 3.2, the importance of the financial sector in the national economy rose from 3 percent of GDP in 1950 to more than 8 percent in 2008, where it has largely remained. Despite financial sector growth, the amount of agency discretion—that is, the amount of authority delegated to the federal agencies to regulate the financial sector or individual key actors—declined over this period. A small number of exceptions led to increases in discretion, such as well-publicized financial crises and scandals, the Savings and Loan crisis, the Asian crisis, and the Enron scandal. Overall, however, Congress has given agencies less authority over time to regulate financial firms, even as the financial sector has increased in size and product innovations have become rapid and complex, making the need for regulatory oversight greater than ever.

Furthermore, within these trends we see two distinct developments. As illustrated in figure 3.3, the number of government agencies receiving authority and the amount of authority delegated rose significantly over time

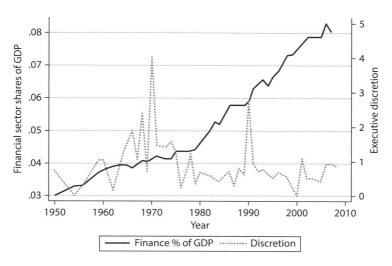

Figure 3.2 Financial sector size and regulation, 1950–2010

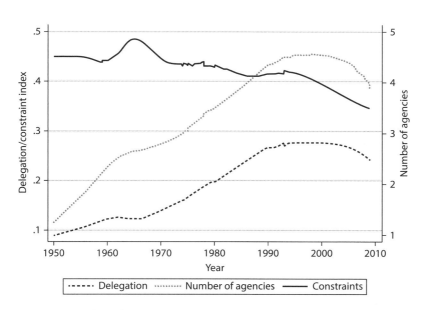

Figure 3.3 Financial regulation, 1950–2009: delegation, constraints, and agencies receiving authority

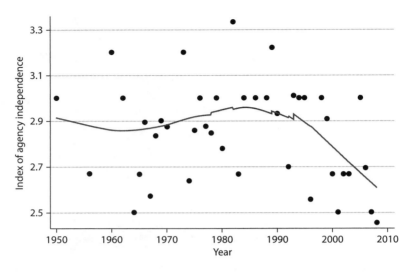

Figure 3.4 Agency independence

before declining from the 2000s onward, just before the financial crisis. However, the number of constraints remained relatively stable over a significant time span before decreasing from the 1990s onward.

Finally, the data illustrated in figure 3.4 show that the federal agencies receiving delegated authority are increasingly located within the political part of the executive apparatus, such as Cabinet-level agencies. This trend is in contrast to previous periods; authority is no longer delegated to independent agencies, such as the U.S. Securities and Exchange Commission (SEC) or Commodity Futures Trading Commission (CFTC). Rather, authority is delegated to agencies or departments that are politically controlled, that is, the Department of the Treasury and so forth.

Taken together, these general trends in financial regulation laws suggest that Congress has indeed continued to pass new laws regulating financial actors over this entire period. We further note that executive branch actors do possess an enormous amount of authority to regulate new products, but it is also true that this delegated authority has changed over time. Regulators are more constrained by administrative procedures, authority is more divided across political actors, there are more veto gates, and authority is invested in agencies more under the political control of the executive as opposed to independent regulatory commissions. In sum, our empirical findings fall between the two theories outlined at the beginning: Congress does indeed regulate the U.S. financial sector, but it has also systematically decreased the discretion of federal regulators, hampering their ability to oversee and regulate new developments and innovations in these growing markets.

Trends in Special Interest Group Activities Before and After the Financial Crisis

The prevalence of industry influence in financial regulation appears through the strategic interactions between legislators, agency rulemaking, and interest group lobbying. The Dodd-Frank Wall Street Reform and Consumer Protection Act of 2010 (Dodd-Frank) reforms demonstrate this dynamic. The massive legislation containing more than 2,300 pages directed regulators to issue more than four hundred rules and mandates. Parts of the law were vague and allocated significant discretionary rulemaking authority to regulatory agencies, as exemplified in the provisions that detailed the Volcker Rule. The opportunity for agencies to set policy guidelines in the overhaul of financial regulation in a significant and controversial area such as the Volcker Rule created a boom in lobbying activities. Immediately after enactment of Dodd-Frank and its Volcker Rule, industry representatives and interest groups lobbied to influence agency rulemaking and shape essential elements, including definitions, thresholds, and transparency. The financial industry sought to influence rulemaking by submitting comments during the rulemaking process as well as by providing analysis and testimony during public hearings.[1]

The passage of the Dodd-Frank Act highlights the political responsiveness of the design of financial regulation, which occurs at two sequential stages: the legislative stage (drafting and enacting bills) and the administrative stage (interpreting statutes and crafting rules). At the legislative stage, special interests provide campaign contributions or directly lobby members of Congress when they are drafting and voting on the legislation that will then be executed by regulators. At the administrative stage, industry participants directly lobby federal agencies that write the rules and enforce the laws by providing information, analysis, and impact statements to move policy in their favor.

Figure 3.5 shows the total amount spent on lobbying and the number of lobbyists at the legislative and administrative stages. The figure depicts a peak in lobbying activities around 2010 tracking passage of the Dodd-Frank Act.

Considering each stage separately, at the legislative stage a number of activities take place. First, as illustrated in figure 3.6, the insurance and security investment industries are among the largest spenders on lobbying in the financial sector.

These growing lobbying expenditures are not campaign contributions to legislators and challengers as in the normal electoral cycle. Rather, these outlays represent costs incurred by special interests to access and influence policymakers, legislators, and bureaucrats with information, analysis, and other resources. These expenditures are in addition to campaign contributions, which tend to receive much more public attention. However, campaign contributions by

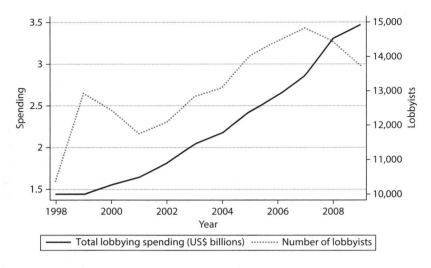

Figure 3.5 Dollars spent lobbying and number of lobbyists, 1998–2009

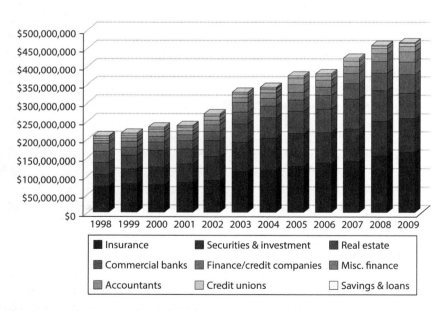

Figure 3.6 Lobbying spend (USD) on finance, insurance, and real estate, 1998–2009

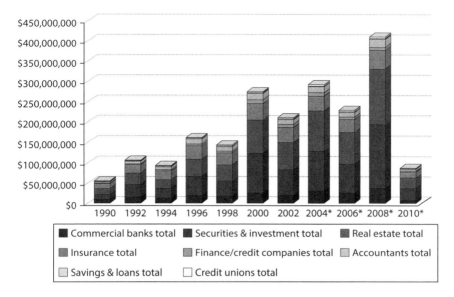

Figure 3.7 Finance, insurance, and real estate contributions (USD), 1990–2008

commercial banks, security investment firms, and credit unions, as illustrated in figure 3.7, are among the largest donations from the finance sector.

Second, looking at industry lobbying at the administrative stage, the number of times special interests directly contacted regulators peaked during the 2010–2011 period with the enactment of Dodd-Frank. Figure 3.8 further shows that the financial sector most frequently lobbied regulators at the CFTC and the SEC.

Figure 3.9 depicts the number of lobbyists' clients that are financial industry participants. As shown, once again the agencies lobbied most vigorously by the financial sector are the CFTC and the SEC. Lobbyists perceive these agencies to be most influential in rulemaking and to have the most regulatory discretion that could be swayed in favor of industry representatives—either by avoiding harsher regulation or by achieving even lower standards.

Furthermore, the amount of money spent on lobbying, as illustrated in figure 3.10, spiked around passage of Dodd-Frank, with the CFTC and the SEC again being the agencies most heavily lobbied.

To summarize, here, too, we find evidence that lobbying across federal agencies differs and that there is a strong political economy aspect. A significant spike in lobbying activity occurred around Dodd-Frank, both at the aggregate level and at the individual level, and there was a correlation between lobbying at the administrative stage and lobbying at the legislative stage. This correlation

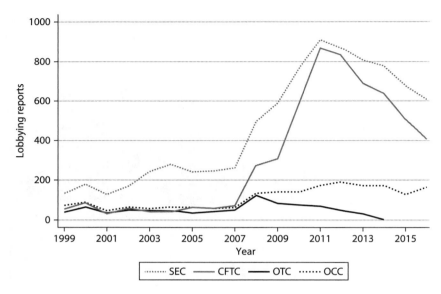

Figure 3.8 Number of annual lobbying reports by clients and agency

Source: https://www.opensecrets.org

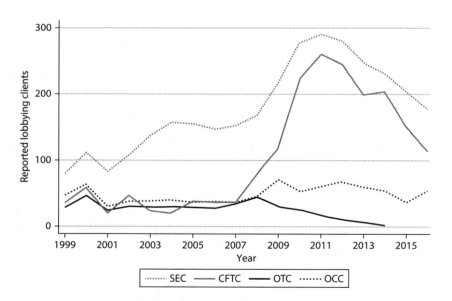

Figure 3.9 Number of reported lobbying clients by agency

Source: https://www.opensecrets.org

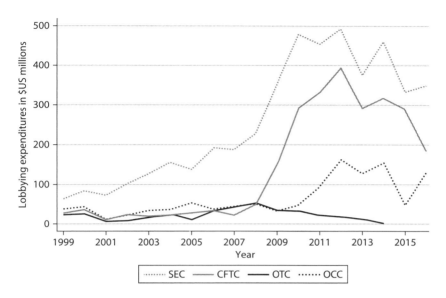

Figure 3.10 Amounts of reported lobbying expenditures by agency

Source: https://www.opensecrets.org

raises the question of whether legislative and administrative lobbying are substitutes for each other or complements.

Referring to the initial debate on regulatory design, when we think about the implications of the analysis of regulatory reform going forward, we can see that, in fact, agencies did have the authority to regulate the financial sector going into the financial crisis, but they were also hamstrung by political pressures to adopt less stringent policies than otherwise. A number of administrative procedures curtailed their delegated authority.

Delegation in Financial Regulation

A well-established theme in the political economy literature of regulatory design is that the structure of policymaking is shaped the political environment and the actors involved. Epstein and O'Halloran (1999) illustrate how lawmakers delegate regulatory authority to executive agencies when the policy preferences of the legislature and the executive are closely aligned, policy uncertainty is low, and the cost (political and otherwise) of the legislature setting policy itself is high.[2] A policy conflict between both branches may arise when there is a downstream moral hazard problem between the agency and the regulated firm, which creates uncertainty over policy outcomes.

In the following section, we illustrate recent work that addresses the sources of policy uncertainty and moral hazard problems arising from agency–firm interactions in financial regulation. We consider first the effects of the uncertainty of firm investments and the possibility of systemic risk arising from some financial investments. We then illustrate how lobbying pressure applied by potentially regulated firms to an executive agency that may or may not receive regulatory authority from the legislature increases or mitigates the policy conflict between the legislature and an executive agency that jointly determine financial regulation.

Regulating Systemic Risk

In the formal model of the policymaking process developed in Groll, O'Halloran, and McAllister (2017), Congress can delegate authority to the better-informed executive that can oversee both firm-level and systemic risk in financial markets. The model also incorporates a potential conflict between policymakers and regulators by considering differences in the salience of systemic failure and the potential cost of bailing out the finance and banking sector. The analysis highlights that Congress delegates more discretionary authority when (1) policy preferences between Congress and executive officials become more similar; (2) firms' risks become more uncertain; and (3) Congress's concerns about a bailout are greater. As a result, financial markets are more heavily regulated when firm-specific and systemic risks are uncertain and Congress's bailout salience and costs are greater. However, when interbranch preferences differ or perceived systemic risk is low, Congress may allow risky investments to be made that, ex post, it wished it had regulated.

To illustrate the tension between policy differences, the uncertainty over firm investments and systemic risks, the analysis focuses on the legislature's and the executive's policy preferences and possession of policy relevant information. The legislature favors, in general, less regulation than the executive because it puts less emphasis on the cost of a potential industry-wide bailout. The analysis denotes this as the preference conflict between lawmakers and the executive, which is part of the legislature's trade-off between the executive's information advantage and the preference conflict across both bodies.

Figure 3.11 illustrates the effects when the legislature would prefer to regulate itself and when it would rather hand over regulation to an executive government agency. The shaded triangle illustrates situations in which delegation to the executive arises; outside the shaded triangle the legislature regulates firms' investments itself. Firms may not consider a possible systemic failure when there is no regulation and could undertake investments

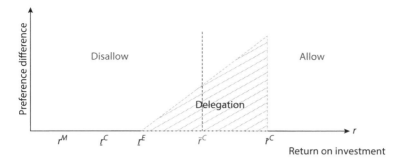

Figure 3.11 Effects when legislature regulates versus when regulation is delegated to an executive agency

deemed too risky from a social perspective. In the absence of regulatory interventions, however, firms may undertake any investment that yields them a nonnegative expected return—that is, any projects or investments at or above an unregulated individual return, which is labeled as r^M in figure 3.11. When the legislature implements a regulation without delegating the authority to an executive agency, it may not allow any investments that would yield a negative expected social return and actually include the cost of a possible bailout—that is, any investment returns below $\bar{r}^C$ in figure 3.11— but would allow any other investments above this threshold. However, when the legislature decides to delegate regulatory authority to the executive, the regulating agency sets a regulatory threshold similarly: disallowing investments with a negative expected social return that accounts for the cost of a possible bailout and the executive's salience but allowing all others. A better informed executive agency may know the likelihood of systemic risk that arises from correlated investments within the industry and can set a regulatory threshold for uncorrelated investments, $\bar{r}^E$, that are not causing systemic risk, and another one for correlated investments that are causing systemic risk and where the regulatory threshold follows from the legislature's preferred regulatory threshold of $\bar{r}^C$ when the executive agency received only limited discretion from the legislature.

A delegation from the legislature to an executive agency can then be described using these two regulatory investment thresholds. Looking at the level of regulatory thresholds, it can be said that all of them are increasing in (1) the absolute cost of a bailout, (2) the salience of a possible bailout, and (3) the probability of correlated investments and therefore the likelihood of systemic risk. However, regulatory thresholds are decreasing when the perceived probability of successful investments increases. Together this can explain the low regulatory thresholds in the 2000s when financial markets and new investment products were perceived to be stable and prosperous and investment and systemic risk well diversified.

Focusing on the preferences conflict between legislative lawmakers' and executive rulemakers' regulatory ideal points and the distribution of expertise, the government agency may put relatively more weight on the bailout cost than does the legislature. Therefore, the legislature may value the agency's expertise most when there is no difference in ideal points and delegate the greatest discretion to the agency then. However, when the government agency puts an increasing focus on the bailout cost, or the legislature has a decreasing focus, the preference conflict across both increases, and there will be less discretion delegated such that the executive cannot implement its preferred higher standards, which would simply be a movement along the vertical axis in figure 3.11. This implies that the delegation triangle shrinks as the conflict between lawmakers and executive rulemakers increases and the legislature prefers control over regulation. However, when a potential bailout may become more costly or when the legislature's uncertainty over correlated investments and systemic risk increases, the delegation triangle expands because the legislature could gain relatively more from the executive's expertise and more discretion would be delegated.

The policy conflict between the legislature and the executive also has implications for investments that are highly risky but high-returning when the legislature perceives a low likelihood of correlated investments and systemic risk. In such situations, the legislature regulates financial investments on its own—that is, Congress sets a return threshold of $\bar{r}^C$, which is most likely below the agency's preferred threshold for uncorrelated investments $\bar{r}^E$ in figure 3.11. The reason for this is that the agency's expertise in correlated investments is not sufficiently valued by the legislature, and the agency's regulatory threshold might be perceived to be too harsh due to different preferences over policies and the risk of a bailout.

Regulating Under Special Interest Group Pressure

In the following section, we present a formal model of rulemaking with delegation by Congress and lobbying pressure by special interests.[3] We use this model to address the question of how regulation is shaped from the legislative stage to the implementation stage when the regulated industry engages in lobbying efforts to influence the rulemaking shape. We apply our model to derive the predictions and discuss the implications with regard to the delegation of authority, the agency's implementation of regulation, as well as the industry's lobbying response. Our analysis highlights the various strategic considerations and interactions and provides policy recommendations to safeguard the law- and rulemaking process.

A Formalized Model

Our formal model examines the strategic interactions among the legislature, or simply Congress (C), the executive agency (A), and an interest group (I) representing a regulated industry. As in the standard delegation model, all actors have ideal points and quadratic preferences over outcomes in a unidimensional outcome space: $u_i(x) = -(x - x_i)^2$ for $x \in X = R_1$. Without loss of generality, we assume that $x_I = 0$ and $x_A > 0$. We further assume that $x_C > 0$, so if the value of x represents the strength of regulation, the industry prefers less regulation than either Congress or the agency.

Congress may delegate authority to make policy decisions to the agency, and final policy outcomes are a function of both the policy p chosen and an external shock ω according to the equation $x = p + \omega$. The external shock ω is uniformly distributed: $\omega \sim U \in [-R, R]$. When delegating, Congress can also place constraints on the agency's discretionary policy choices. Thus Congress sets a status quo policy p_0 and discretion limit d so that $|p - p_0| \leq d$.

Where we differ from the standard delegation model is in our assumption that the interest group can affect outcomes directly by lobbying the agency after the agency announces its proposed rule of p_A. In particular, we assume that $p = p_A - e$, where e is the amount of costly lobbying effort exerted by the interest group at the rulemaking stage. We envision this effort coming in the form of presenting analysis and testimony at the notice and comment stages of rulemaking, as well as broader lobbying efforts aimed at legislators, executive officials, and the public at large to weaken industry regulations. The group's cost of this effort is $c(e)$, with $c^e > 0$ and $c^{ee} > 0$.

For the sake of concreteness, we take $c(e) = \alpha e^2$, so that $\alpha > 0$ measures the relative cost of lobbying to the interest group, and low values of α indicate the ability to exert greater pressure on regulators. This lobbying also reduces the agency's utility by an amount $-\beta e$, where $\beta \geq 0$ is the cost to the agency of having its original proposals moved back toward the interest group's ideal point. It is possible to set $\beta = 0$, so that $\beta > 0$ indicates that the agency would prefer to implement a given policy outcome directly rather than propose a tougher regulation and have the industry lobby to weaken the agency's proposal.

Figure 3.12 Order of events in strategic interactions among Congress, an executive agency, and an interest group

Overall, then, $u_C = -(x - x_C)^2$, $u_I = -x^2 - \alpha e^2$, and $u_A = -(x - x_A)^2 - \beta e$, where $x = p_A - e + \omega$. The order of events is illustrated in figure 3.12. First, Congress sets the status quo and the discretion limit, (p_0, d). Then nature draws ω, which is observed by both the agency and the interest group. Third, the agency proposes its policy rule p_A. Fourth, the interest group observes p_A and chooses its lobbying effort level e. Finally, policy p is enacted and policy outcome x with corresponding utility levels is realized. We solve the game for its subgame perfect Bayesian-Nash equilibria in the appendix and discuss the results and intuition in the following section.

Administrative Lobbying, Rulemaking, and Policy Outcomes

Here we address our earlier question of how regulation is shaped from the legislative stage to the implementation stage when the regulated industry engages in lobbying efforts to influence the rulemaking. We apply our model to derive the predictions and discuss the implications with regard to the delegation of authority, the agency's implementation of regulation, as well as the industry's lobbying response. Our analysis highlights the various strategic considerations and interactions and provides first policy recommendations to safeguard the law- and rulemaking process.

Administrative Lobbying

Considering the policymaking process of the legislative and rulemaking stages, the industry's lobbying response is toward the agency's proposed policy and the realized policy shock. The agency's initially considered policy is obviously within its discretionary bounds, set by the legislature, but could now be influenced by the industry exercising pressure to affect the finalization of the rulemaking through comments and hearings. The regulated industry has, therefore, to ask if a lobbying response is valuable when it compares the marginal payoff from changing the agency's proposed policy to a different policy with the marginal cost of exercising costly lobbying activities. The industry's optimal lobbying activities are then an optimal response to the agency's initially proposed rule, the policy shock, and its lobbying effectiveness, which is the cost of lobbying (denoted by α) and the agency's resilience to lobbying pressure (denoted by β). As a result, if the interest group finds lobbying inexpensive or the agency's proposed policy too far away from its bliss point, it will respond with greater administrative lobbying to influence rulemaking.

Agency's Policy Choice

The agency will take into account the anticipated industry's lobbying response when proposing a policy rule. Hence, the agency considers the policy shock, its preferred policy, and the industry's response when it makes a proposal in the rulemaking process. Obviously, the agency proposes a lower policy level in response to greater external shocks or if the agency does not find a strong regulation desirable. Less obviously, the agency will respond to the lobbying pressure by proposing a lower policy level, and this policy level is increasing the industry's relative cost of lobbying α but decreasing the agency's lobbying burden β. These two elements, the relative cost of lobbying and the agency's lobbying burden, determine the *effective* administrative lobbying pressure, $\dfrac{\beta}{2\alpha}$, and the effect on the agency's proposed policy rule x_p as a deviation from the agency's preferred policy x_A. This effect of lobbying on rulemaking is illustrated in figure 3.13, as greater lobbying pressure moves the policy proposal x_p away from the agency's preferred policy, x_A, but toward the industry's preferred level of x_I.

Now the question is how far can administrative lobbying actually move the rulemaking? As usual, the answer is "it depends." If lobbying is relatively inexpensive, or the group is very efficient in undertaking lobbying (smaller α), then the interest group will increase its efforts and the agency will experience greater pressure, creating a greater lobbying burden on the agency and therefore a greater change in the proposed policy level. On the other hand, if the agency is easily burdened by lobbying pressure (greater β), possibly because of a lack of resources or little resistance to lobbying efforts, the interest group need not undertake much effort to burden the agency, and the agency's policy proposal can be easily captured. Consequently, if the burden to the agency of industry lobbying is high relative to the industry's lobbying cost, greater $\dfrac{\beta}{\alpha}$, the agency may propose a policy rule so that the industry gets its ideal point of no regulation, $x = x_I$, without the interest group having to actively lobby to obtain this outcome. This can serve as a convenient definition of agency capture: the mere threat of lobbying causes the agency to accommodate industry wishes, so that

Figure 3.13 Effect of lobbying pressure on agency policy rulemaking

in equilibrium the industry escapes effective government control without having to expend resources to do so.

If the ideal points are far apart or the effective administrative lobbying pressure is not sufficiently threatening, however, then the interest group undertakes a lobbying effort, as illustrated in the figure, that is (i) decreasing in the agency's lobbying burden, (ii) increasing in the agency's ideal point, and (iii) decreasing in the industry's lobbying cost if the agency's ideal point is greater than twice lobbying pressure, and vice versa. As a result, the agency's regulation is then (i) increasing in its ideal point, (ii) increasing in the interest group's lobbying cost, but (iii) decreasing in the agency's lobbying burden.

Legislature's Delegation Choice

The legislature, anticipating the agency's choices and the industry's lobbying efforts, has to decide which status quo policy it would like to set and how much discretion it would like to allocate to the better-informed agency to address policy shocks that are unobservable to the legislature. The traditional delegation trade-off arises: benefiting from the agency's expertise or moving policy outcomes closer to the agency's preferred levels. We refer to the differences in preferences as *preference conflict*, which is illustrated as the horizontal difference in ideal points in figure 3.13. The wider the gap between x_A and x_C the greater is the preference conflict. We know that the agency will be subject to lobbying pressure and may not announce its ideal point x_A as a policy proposal but at the regulation level x_P that has been shaped by administrative lobbying at the rulemaking stage. Lobbying pressure moves the policy outcome to the left, and we can see immediately that the "ally principle" fails to hold. The legislature prefers an agency, not with its own ideal point but one biased slightly against the industry, which serves as resistance against the industry's lobbying efforts.

Furthermore, lobbying has two effects on the preference conflict and the resulting *policy conflict* as the difference between the agency's announced regulation and the legislature's ideal point. If the agency is more biased against the industry than the legislature, as illustrated on the left side of figure 3.14, then administrative lobbying by the industry reduces the policy conflict between both branches. However, if the agency is more industry-friendly than the legislature, as illustrated on the right side of figure 3.14, then industry's lobbying pressure increases the policy conflict between the branches. Additionally, the policy conflict is driven by the effectiveness of administrative lobbying. If administrative lobbying is mitigating the policy conflict between the two branches, then the conflict is decreasing the agency's lobbying burden but increasing the industry's lobbying cost; if lobbying is increasing the policy conflict, then the opposite holds.

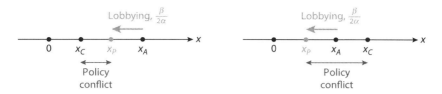

Figure 3.14 The effects of lobbying on the policy conflict between two branches of government

Balancing *status quo* and *discretion* are congressional considerations. Taking the preference conflict and the industry's lobbying pressure into account, Congress chooses its optimal status quo policy and delegated discretion to maximize its expected payoff from the industry that is regulated by the better-informed but differently biased agency.

The legislature's preferred status quo policy follows immediately from its ideal point. When the legislature's desire for greater regulation increases, the status quo policy increases as well. The optimal discretion follows from the legislature's policy uncertainty, the preference conflict between Congress and the agency, and the industry's lobbying pressure.

In more detail, the legislature delegates greater discretion when (i) there is more policy uncertainty for the legislature, (ii) its ideal point is closer to the agency's ideal point, and (iii) the lobbying pressure (agency's burden and lobby's cost) mitigates the preference conflict between the legislature and the agency. Regarding the policy conflict between both branches and combining the last two parts, we can state the following: If there is less policy conflict between the legislature and the pressured agency, the legislature delegates greater discretion. Hence, policy outcomes from the legislature's perspective improve with greater discretion whenever lobbying decreases the conflict between the legislature and the agency. Likewise, greater discretion would decrease policy outcomes if lobbying increases the conflict between both. Hence, we can summarize that regulatory outcomes are higher when (i) industry's lobbying costs are high, (ii) agency's lobbying burden is low, and (iii) agency's policy ideal point is higher.

Conclusion

The findings in this chapter advance our understanding of the interaction between governments and markets in the regulation of financial markets. The analysis highlights interest group pressure and interbranch politics as key factors that explain both the design of financial regulation and its implementation. Our analysis also points to a way out of what John C. Coffee Jr. refers to in chapter 19 as the "regulatory sine curve and statutory overcorrection," which is to develop models and simulations to understand the conditions under which a regulation interferes with the smooth operation of markets and the conditions under which a regulation is market-enhancing.

After the crisis, this question of regulatory design has taken on renewed urgency as the nation once again debates the architecture of the financial system. We are in the unthinkable situation of asking if the postcrash financial reforms overreached their intended mark. Did regulations go so far as to inadvertently create risk as a result of ill-conceived, overly aggressive policies that were inadequate for their purpose?

Indeed on October 31, 2018, the Federal Reserve and U.S. banking agencies proposed a "Tailored Regulatory Framework" that would divide financial institutions into four categories, determined by a combination of risk-based indicators, including size, cross-jurisdictional activity, nonbank assets, and off-balance sheet exposure.[4] The proposal signifies a move away from the one-size-fits-all regulatory framework based solely on asset size embodied in the Dodd-Frank Act. A move to tailor regulations, if taken to the extreme, can lead to the preposterous scenario that every bank is uniquely supervised, inevitably promoting regulatory arbitrage and ultimately no regulation at all.

Former Federal Reserve Chair Janet Yellen set out her reservations, noting that reductions in bank regulators' authority to address panics and pushes to deregulate leave "gigantic holes" in the financial regulatory fabric.[5] In addition, federal authorities can only regulate at the microprudential, individual bank level and not at the level of the system as a whole, limiting their ability to identify, measure, and mitigate systemic risk.[6] As a result, new financial instruments, such as leveraged loans that fund the massive corporate debt market, may trigger the next asset bubble that sparks a financial crisis.

Appendix: Formal Solution

Here we are solving our lobbying-delegation model and provide the mathematical solutions for our illustrative and intuitive discussions above.

Administrative Lobbying

Starting at the end of the game and working backward, for a given policy proposal p_A and shock ω, the industry will set its lobbying effort e to maximize $-(p_A - e + \omega)^2 - \alpha e^2$. This leads to lobbying in the amount of

$$e^*(p_A) = \frac{p_A + \omega}{1 + \alpha}. \tag{A.1}$$

Thus positive amounts of lobbying are exerted whenever $p_A + \omega > 0$, and it goes to zero when the agency accommodates the industry by making final policy outcomes equal to the interest group's ideal point. Note that $\partial e^*/\partial p_A > 0$, so that the interest group spends fewer resources lobbying an agency with preferences closer to their own. Further, the greater the shock, $\partial e^*/\partial \omega > 0$, the more lobbying effort the interest group undertakes.

Agency's Policy Choice

Knowing the interest group's best response to the announced policy rule, $e^*(p_A)$, the agency will propose policy rule p_A to maximize $-[p_A - e^*(p_A) + \omega - x_A]^2 - \beta e^*(p_A)$, yielding

$$p^*_A = \frac{(1+\alpha)(2x_A\alpha - \beta)}{2\alpha^2} - \omega \qquad (A.2)$$

iff $|p^*_A - p0| \leq d$ and constrained by (p_0, d), otherwise.

Combining equations (A.1) and (A.2), final policy outcomes will be:

$$x_P = p^*_A - e^*(p^*_A) + \omega = x_A - \frac{\beta}{2\alpha}. \qquad (A.3)$$

Notice that this point lies in the interval between the agency's and the interest group's ideal points as long as $x_A > \beta/2\alpha$. We refer to the term $\beta/2\alpha$ as the *effective* administrative lobbying pressure, which is a combination of the agency's lobbying burden and industry's lobbying cost. For values of β greater than or equal to $2\alpha x_A$, the agency sets p_A such that $x = 0$ and the industry does not lobby—the pure threat of lobbying results in industry-friendly outcomes. However, for greater ideal points of policy outcomes, $x_A > \beta/2\alpha$, the industry undertakes a lobbying effort and the effective administrative lobbying pressure is not sufficient to prevent regulation. Note that the agency's regulation is then (i) increasing in its ideal point, (ii) increasing in the interest group's lobbying cost, but (iii) decreasing in the agency's lobbying burden.

Congress' Policy Choice

Congress, on the other hand, would like the agency to set policy so that the outcome, net of industry lobbying, is Congress's ideal point: $p_A - e^*(p_A) + \omega = x_C$, which simplifies to $p^*_C = x_C \frac{(1+\alpha)}{\alpha} - \omega$. For any given value of ω, then, Congress's and the agency's ideal policies differ by an amount of

$$p^*_C - p^*_A = \left(\frac{1+\alpha}{\alpha}\right)\left(x_A - x_C - \frac{\beta}{2\alpha}\right). \qquad (A.4)$$

This expression goes to zero when $x_A = x_C + \dfrac{\beta}{2\alpha}$. Thus the "ally principle" fails to hold in our model: Congress prefers an agency not with its own ideal point but one biased slightly against the industry, because policy outcomes are a convex combination of the agency's ideal point and the industry's desire for no regulation and lobbying pressure. In other words, lobbying by the interest group mitigates the preference conflict between Congress and the agency if $x_C < x_A$, as illustrated on the left of figure 3.14, or increases the conflict if $x_C > x_A$, as illustrated on the right in figure 3.14, over policy outcomes x_P.

However, Congress is unable to observe the policy shock ω and can only determine the status quo policy and delegate discretion to the agency in order to affect policy outcomes to some extent.

Status Quo and Discretion

Congress anticipating the agency's policy rule proposal and the interest group's pressure—as well as a resulting policy conflict—can set its optimal status quo policy p_0 and discretion limit d. The policy outcomes given any status quo, discretion, and external shock are

$$
x^* = \begin{cases}
p_0 + d + \omega & \text{if } -R \le \omega < x_P - p_0 - d \\
x_P & \text{if } x_P - p_0 - d \le \omega \le x_P - p_0 + d \\
p_0 - d + \omega & \text{if } x_P - p_0 + d < \omega \le R.
\end{cases} \tag{A.5}
$$

Given these anticipated policy and outcome alternatives, Congress sets (p_0, d) to maximize its expected utility such that

$$
\begin{aligned}
EU_C(p_0, d) \;=\; & -\int_{-R}^{x_P - d - p_0} \frac{(p_0 + d + \omega - x_C)^2}{2R}\,d\omega - \int_{x_P - d - p_0}^{x_P + d - p_0} \frac{(x_P - x_C)^2}{2R}\,d\omega \\
& -\int_{x_P + d - p_0}^{R} \frac{(p_0 - d + \omega - x_C)^2}{2R}\,d\omega
\end{aligned} \tag{A.6}
$$

The optimal status quo policy follows from

$$
\frac{\partial EU_C}{\partial p_0} = \frac{2(d - R)(p_0 - x_C)}{R} = 0 \Rightarrow p_0^* = xc, \tag{A.7}
$$

In other words, Congress's optimal status quo policy is identical to its ideal point; and when Congress's desire for greater regulation increases, then the status quo policy increases. Further, the optimal discretion limit follows from

$$
\frac{\partial EU_C}{\partial d} = \frac{(d - R)^2 + (p_0 - x_P)(p_0 + x_P - 2x_C)}{R} = 0. \tag{A.8}
$$

which can be written as

$$d^* = R - \left| x_A - x_C - \frac{\beta}{2\alpha} \right| \qquad\qquad (A.9)$$

We can see immediately that a higher policy uncertainty, a greater R implying a wider range of possible policy shocks, yields a greater optimal discretion level. A greater preference conflict over policy outcomes, $x_P - x_C$, has a negative effect on discretion, which limits the interest group's influence and the agency's policy proposal.

The preference conflict, as the difference in Congress's ideal point and the agency's ideal point, $x_A - x_C$, has ambiguous effects on discretion. For example, if the agency is relatively more industry friendly than Congress, $x_A < x_C$, then a further increase in the preference difference, meaning the agency moving relatively closer to the industry, results in less discretion. However, if the agency is slightly more biased against the industry than Congress, $x_C < x_A < x_C + \frac{\beta}{2\alpha}$, then a further preference conflict increases actually discretion such that the interest group's pressure can offset the preference conflict. Finally, if the agency is too opposed against the industry and lobbying pressure cannot move the policy sufficiently close to Congress's ideal point, $x_A > x_C + \frac{\beta}{2\alpha}$, then here again, Congress places greater constraints on the agency.

The more responsive the agency is to the lobby's effective pressure, $\beta/2\alpha$, Congress increases or decreases discretion depending on the agency's preference relative to Congress's ideal point. For example, if the agency is industry friendly or slightly more opposed than Congress, $x_A < x_C + \frac{\beta}{2\alpha}$, then the more effective administrative lobbying is by the interest group, lower α or greater β, the smaller is discretion to prevent industry capture of the agency. However, if the agency is relatively more extremist against the industry than Congress, $x_A > x_C + \frac{\beta}{2\alpha}$, then more effective administrative lobbying can move the agency's policy rule closer to Congress's ideal point and Congress sets greater discretion.

Notes

1. The financial industry's efforts to sway agency rulemaking are well documented by Krawiec's (2013) case study on agency lobbying related to the Volcker Rule. Ban and You (2018) analyze the reported lobbying activities at the legislative stage and the SEC rulemaking stage around Dodd-Frank. Other studies have focused on the lobbying

and influence activities before the financial crisis (Mian, Sufi, and Trebbi, 2010, 2013; Agarwal et al., 2014; Lucca, Seru, and Trebbi, 2014).

2. For related influential work, see Melumad and Shibano (1991), Epstein and O'Halloran (1994), Volden (2002a, 2002b), Huber and Shipan (2002), Alonso and Matouschek (2008), Gailmard (2002, 2009), and Wiseman (2009).

3. There are several alternative frameworks to analyze lobbying. One modeling choice is the "menu-auction" approach introduced by Bernheim and Whinston (1986). Bennedsen and Feldmann (2006) applied Grossman and Helpman's (1994) menu-auction model to bureaucracies where special interests offer benefits to them in exchange for policy favors. Other lobbying models have focused on the provision of information (Crawford and Sobel, 1982), interactions between information provision and financial transfers (for a review see Groll and Ellis, 2014, 2017), or legislative subsidies as support for policymakers (Hall and Deardorff, 2006; Ellis and Groll, 2018). For a broader review see Grossman and Helpman (2001).

4. For a review of the proposed Tailored Regulatory Framework, see https://www.finregre form.com/wp-content/uploads/sites/32/2018/12/2018-12-10_Visual_Memorandum_A _New_Cut_Federal_Reserve_and_US_Banking_Agencies_Propose_Tailored _Regulatory_Framework.pdf. The proposal represents a move away from a one-size-fits-all regulatory framework based solely on asset size.

5. For a discussion with Paul Krugman on December 11, 2018, see https://finance.yahoo .com/news/yellen-warns-another-potential-financial-115500472.html.

6. See O'Halloran and Nowaczyk (chapter 14 in this volume) for a work-around to this limitation.

References

Agarwal, Sumit, David Lucca, Amit Seru, and Francesco Trebbi. 2014. "Inconsistent Regulators: Evidence from Banking." *Quarterly Journal of Economics* 129: 889–938.

Alonso, Ricardo, and Niko Matouschek. 2008. "Optimal Delegation." *Review of Economic Studies* 75: 259–93.

Ban, Pamela, and Hye Young You. 2018. "Presence and Influence in Lobbying: Evidence from Dodd-Frank, Business & Politics." (forthcoming)

Bernheim, B. Douglas, and Michael D. Whinston. 1986. "Menu Auctions, Resource Allocation, and Economic Influence." *Quarterly Journal of Economics* 101, no. 1: 1–31.

Bennedsen, Morten, and Sven E. Feldmann. 2006. "Lobbying Bureaucrats." *Scandinavian Journal of Economics* 108: 643–68.

Bertelli, A., and Sven E. Feldmann. 2006. "Strategic Appointments." *Journal of Public Administration Research and Theory* 17: 19–38.

Crawford, Vincent P., and Joel Sobel. 1982. "Strategic Information Transmission." *Econometrica* 50: 1431–51.

Ellis, Christopher J., and Thomas Groll. 2018. "Strategic Legislative Subsidies: Informational Lobbying and the Cost of Policy." (mimeo)

Epstein, David, and Sharyn O'Halloran, 1994. "Administrative Procedures, Information and Agency Discretion." *American Journal of Political Science* 38: 697–722.

——. 1999. *Delegating Powers: A Transaction Cost Politics Approach to Policy Making Under Separate Powers.* New York: Cambridge University Press.

Gailmard, Sean. 2002. "Expertise, Subversion, and Bureaucratic Discretion." *Journal of Law, Economics, and Organization* 18: 536–55.

——. 2009. "Discretion Rather Than Rules: Choice of Instruments to Control Bureaucratic Policy Making." *Political Analysis* 17: 25–44.

Groll, Thomas, and Christopher J. Ellis. 2014. "A Simple Model of the Commercial Lobbying Industry." *European Economic Review* 70: 299–316.

——. 2017. "Repeated Lobbying by Commercial Lobbyists and Special Interests." *Economic Inquiry* 55 (4): 1868–97.

Groll, Thomas, Sharyn O'Halloran, Sameer Maskey, Geraldine McAllister, and David Park. 2015. "Big Data and the Regulation of Banking and Financial Services." *Banking & Financial Services Policy Report* 34 (December).

Groll, Thomas, Sharyn O'Halloran, and Geraldine McAllister. 2017. "Delegation and the Regulation of U.S. Financial Markets." (mimeo)

Grossman, Gene, and Elhanan Helpman. 1994. "Protection for Sale." *American Economic Review* 84: 833–50.

——. 2001. *Special Interest Politics*. Cambridge, Mass.: MIT Press.

Hall, Richard L., and Alan V. Deardorff. 2006. "Lobbying as Legislative Subsidy." *American Political Science Review* 100: 69–84.

Huber, John D., and Charles R. Shipan. 2002. *Deliberate Discretion? The Institutional Foundations of Bureaucratic Autonomy*. New York: Cambridge University Press.

Krawiec, Kimberly D. 2013. "Agency Lobbying and Financial Reform: A Volcker Rule Case Study." *Banking & Financial Services Policy Report* 32: 15–22.

Lucca, David, Amit Seru, and Francesco Trebbi. 2014. "The Revolving Door and Worker Flows in Banking Regulation." *Journal of Monetary Economics* 65: 17–32.

Melumad, Nahum D., and Toshiyuki Shibano. 1991. "Communication in Settings with No Transfers." *RAND Journal of Economics* 22: 173–98.

Mian, Atif, Amir Sufi, and Francesco Trebbi. 2010. "The Political Economy of the US Mortgage Default Crisis." *American Economic Review* 100: 1449–96.

——. 2013. "The Political Economy of the Subprime Mortgage Credit Expansion." *Quarterly Journal of Political Science* 8: 373–408.

Volden, Craig. 2002a. "Delegating Power to Bureaucracies: Evidence from the States." *Journal of Law, Economics, and Organization* 18: 187–220.

——. 2002b. "A Formal Model of the Politics of Delegation in a Separation of Powers System." *American Journal of Political Science* 46: 111–33.

Wiseman, Alan E. 2009. "Delegation and Positive-Sum Bureaucracies." *Journal of Politics* 71: 998–1014.

CHAPTER 4

WE DID NOT REPEAT THE ERRORS OF THE PAST

Lessons Drawn from the Fed's Policy During the Great Depression

ANTOINE PARENT

U nlike 1929, the U.S. and European monetary authorities implemented expansionary monetary policies to prevent a recession
in 2008 and 2009. The purpose of this paper is to clarify the presumed lessons of the Great Depression for today. Indeed, since 2008, central
banks have acted as lenders of last resort to provide liquidity to banking systems to foster economic growth; in the 1930s they refrained from such action.
One question that comes to mind is, "Is this the right strategy to escape the
financial crisis?" A second question is, "Does it prove that we have a correct
understanding of the past?" The issue of the absolute validity of expansionary
monetary policy must be reconsidered to identify possible errors in the lessons
drawn from the past and in current monetary policy responses.

The literature contains many attempts at approaching the current crisis from
a historical perspective. Since 2008, the comparison between the two crises has
led to growing interest, and the related body of literature is considerable.

In section one, I review the current state of the literature that sets out to
compare "then with now." I identify a number of "chartist contributions,"
"the consensus view" (most notably developed by international institutions),
question Romer's "monetary lesson," and, ultimately, put this debate into perspective with the view expressed by Bordo and Rockoff (2013) that Friedman's
American Monetary History strongly influenced Fed policymaking during the
Great Recession. In section two, I review and compare the different readings of
the Fed's behavior during the Great Depression and discuss the conventional
wisdom among monetary historians about the Fed's policy conduct. In section

three, in light of new developments in cliometrics that apply Taylor rules in a nonlinear framework, I describe a revised monetary lesson from the past for application in current monetary policies. The Fed's behavior in 1929 was not necessarily the "monumental mistake" described at length in the literature, and doing the opposite of what was done in the 1930s is not necessarily the appropriate policy. On the contrary, that may well be another monumental mistake.

2007–2009 in Light of 1929: The Presumed Lessons of the Past

"Chartist" Contributions

Interest in a comparison between the Great Depression and the Great Recession was first evident at the very beginning of the latter crisis, but it should be noted that the focus gradually shifted after 2009 to finding an exit strategy and the appropriate monetary policy for central banks to end the crisis.

I shall limit myself here to the main features of this comparative literature, set out by Krugman (2009), Eichengreen and O'Rourke (2009), Helbling (2009), and Romer (2009). Krugman (2009) compared the fall in U.S. industrial production from its mid-1929 and late-2007 peaks, showing that the drop was milder during the latter crisis, which he described as only "half a great depression."

Eichengreen and O'Rourke (2009) felt that this was a misleading view because the Great Depression was a global phenomenon, and the comparison ought to be made for the world and not just for the United States. By comparing world industrial output, now and then, they painted a more disturbing picture than Krugman (2009), despite a similar decline in manufacturing production. Eichengreen and O'Rourke (2009) noted that stock markets fell faster during the Great Recession than during the Great Depression. International trade is another area where indicators at the beginning of the Great Recession were worse than during the Great Depression. This was seen as alarming in view of the prominence attached in the literature to trade destruction and protectionism as factors compounding the Great Depression. Obviously, these observations were made only one year into the current crisis, whereas the world economy continued to decline for more than three years after 1929. It is nevertheless true that, after one year, the world economy was doing worse during the Great Recession than during the Great Depression, whether in terms of industrial production, exports, or stock market performance.

What about monetary and fiscal policy responses then and now (immediately after the onset of the crises)? As an indicator, Eichengreen and O'Rourke (2009) calculated the weighted average gross domestic product (GDP) of central bank rates for seven countries. This indicator exemplified that monetary rates were lower in the Great Recession than in the 1930s and have been cut more rapidly, although with a similar five-month lag.[1] A clear-cut difference is apparent between the two episodes of crisis with regard to money supply: in 2008 the global money supply continued to grow rapidly, unlike in 1929 when it declined dramatically.

An analogous picture can be drawn for fiscal policy (for twenty-four countries) using as an indicator the fiscal surplus as a percentage of GDP. Fiscal deficits expanded only slightly after 1929, whereas they rose in 2008 to 2009, illustrating the will of governments to use countercyclical fiscal policies on a global scale. Thus, in contrast to Krugman (2009), Eichengreen and O'Rourke (2009) concluded that in 2009 the world experienced a shock similar to that of the Great Depression, but with opposite economic policy responses. They ultimately raised a crucial issue, wondering whether this economic policy response will work. This paper sets out to answer that question.

The Consensus View

In 2009, two years after the onset of the crisis, the European Commission delivered the report "Economic Crisis in Europe: Causes, Consequences and Responses," which devoted a full chapter to comparing the Great Recession with the Great Depression. Similarities and differences seem to be clearly identified in terms of geographic origin, causes, duration, transmission mechanisms, and policy responses. Obviously, this consensus should be considered with caution. The purpose of this paper is precisely to question its correctness.

First, this 2009 report states that the Great Recession was the deepest, most global, and synchronous since the Great Depression. In both cases, the roots of the crises are identified as financial: an insufficiently supervised financial sector and uncontrolled expansion of the shadow banking system led to massive bank failures and liquidity scarcity at the peak of the panic. Each episode was followed by a deep recession in the real economy. Major differences were nevertheless identified. First, we no longer live under the constraint of the gold standard—the attempt to restore this in the 1930s is thought to have had a contractionary impact on economic growth. The defense of the fixed rate to gold protected domestic gold bullion holdings but deepened the depression around the world. It was the tightening of monetary policies that turned the crisis into the Great Depression. According to the European Commission (2009) report, inadequate policy responses in the 1930s contrast with the appropriate monetary and fiscal policies that were implemented in our time. In the 1930s, the strong and persistent decrease in overall price levels that led to sharp deflation is identified as being due to the restrictive monetary policies pursued at that time. According to this report, mass unemployment, which reached an unprecedented level in the 1930s, was avoided during the Great Recession thanks to expansive monetary policy and automatic stabilizers. On the basis of these "well-understood lessons from the past," the European Commission forecasted a faster recovery than in the 1930s.

Despite greater use of financial leverage in the Great Recession, which reveals the persistence and depth of financial risks today, a consensus emerged among U.S. and European institutions that the monetary authorities were not repeating the errors of the past. This presumed consensus can be summarized as follows:[2]

- The macroeconomic policy response was the major factor contributing to the gravity and duration of the Great Depression;
- The lack of expansionary monetary measures by the Fed accentuated the Great Depression;
- Protectionism introduced by major countries during the 1930s amplified the phenomenon.

The European Commission (2009) identified five major lessons that showed proper exit strategies from the crisis were now being implemented based on a correct understanding of the past and learning from it:

- Lesson 1: maintain public confidence in the banking system and prevent a collapse in credit allocation;
- Lesson 2: maintain aggregate demand and avoid deflation, by means of expansionary monetary policies;
- Lesson 3: maintain international trade and avoid protectionism;
- Lesson 4: maintain international finance and avoid capital account restrictions;
- Lesson 5: foster closer international cooperation and avoid nationalism.

Thus, comparing the salient features of the Great Depression and Great Recession leads this mainstream literature to identify similar financial and economic vulnerabilities in both episodes and opposite policy responses to fight the crises.

This consensus view can be considered highly questionable for several reasons. Do these proposals rely on a correct reading of the past? A consensus is not necessarily right. It is also possible that this comparative analysis ignores parallels with the Great Depression. However, the essential point is that this reading, which emerged at the beginning of the crisis, was not challenged by the world's major monetary institutions (the Fed and the European Central Bank [ECB]). These expansionary monetary policies are still being implemented today in the United States and Europe. This shared "belief" among monetary authorities clearly demonstrates that the monetarist influence proved to be decisive in the monetary debate. Two important contributions prevailed in the economic policy debates and exerted a strong intellectual influence on the direction of monetary policy: Christina Romer's work and Friedman and Schwartz's *A Monetary History of the United States, 1867–1960* (1963; referred to as AMH).

Christina Romer's Influence: Breaking the Deflationary Spiral via Expansionary Monetary Policy

For the 2009 economic recovery, Romer (2009, referring to Romer, 1992) drew lessons from the Great Depression. She underlined that the fundamental causes of both downturns were the decline in asset prices and the failure of financial institutions. This, in turn, led to a collapse in the money supply (Friedman and Schwartz, 1963) and lending (Bernanke, 1983), with short-term interest rates close to zero. Regarding monetary policy response, Romer drew a key lesson from the 1930s: "monetary expansion can help to heal an economy even when interest rates are near zero" (2009, 4). This is a key issue because Romer clearly pinpoints a case of liquidity trap. If we refer to the historical context of the 1930s, after Roosevelt temporarily suspended convertibility to gold in April 1933, which caused a substantial depreciation of the dollar, the return to gold convertibility at a higher price led to massive gold inflows. Under the gold standard constraint, the U.S. Treasury was allowed to issue gold certificates in proportion to its gold holdings. Following the gold inflows, the Treasury issued more notes. Friedman and Schwartz (1963) calculated that the money supply grew 17 percent a year over the period 1933–1936. These figures illustrate that expansionary monetary policy was not completely absent after the Great Depression but began after the devaluation of the U.S. dollar. Could it impact interest rates?

"This monetary expansion could not lower nominal interest rates because they were already near zero . . . what it could do was break expectations of deflation" (Romer, 2009, 5). Romer argued that because there were expectations of continued deflation, although the nominal rate was near zero, this rate was still considered exceedingly high by agents. Increasing money supply would facilitate a reversal in expectations and "break the deflationary spiral" (5). Replacing expectations of deflation with expectations of price stability should bring a reduction in real interest rates and enhance consumption and investment. Romer noted that "the first thing that turned around was interest-sensitive spending. Car sales surged in the summer of 1933. One sign that lower real interest rates were crucial is that real fixed investment and consumer spending on durables both rose dramatically between 1933 and 1934" (5–6).

Thus, the experience of the 1930s suggests to me that even in a situation of liquidity trap[3] expansionary monetary policy can continue to play an important role even when interest rates are low by affecting expectations and, in particular, by preventing expectations of deflation. Romer's proposition, according to which expansionary monetary policy (EMP) is still efficient in a context of liquidity trap constituted the major argument in favor of EMP as the unique relevant exit strategy today.

The Legacy of AMH and the Triumph of Friedman's Ideas About the Great Depression

Bordo and Rockoff identified three core reasons *A Monetary History of the United States, 1867–1960* (Friedman and Swartz, 1963) has endured and become "a classic whose reputation has grown with time:" (2013, 64): "it was designed to provide long-run historical evidence (with the underlying statistics presented in Monetary Statistics)" (62); "it was designed to provide evidence for the modern quantity theory" (64); and ultimately "its narrative approach (and not an explicit model) captures the imaginations of new generations of economists" (64). Bordo and Rockoff underline the "continuing influence of AMH on the monetary policy debate" (64). They contend that clearly "the GR did not become the GD because the Fed and other central banks learned the lessons of AMH and flooded financial markets with liquidity" (64; see also Bordo and Landon-Lane, 2010). The authors recall an episode of

> the Bernanke Fed, taking a page from AMH's discussion of the expansionary gold and silver purchase programs of the U.S. Treasury in 1933–34, where FS argued that the Fed itself should have conducted expansionary open market purchases, engaged in massive open market purchases of long-term government bonds and mortgage backed securities in December 2009 (Bordo and Rockoff, 2013, 64).

Friedman and Schwartz (1963, chap. 7) contend that the heart of the explanation of the Great Depression can be found in the strong declines in output that were preceded by strong declines in money supply: the Great Depression of 1929–1933 is viewed as a consequence of the major collapse in the stock of money that the Fed could (or should) have prevented. In the Great Recession versus Great Depression debate, it is clear that Friedman and Schwartz continue to play a key role and that the motto repeated at length by the world's monetary authorities—We did not repeat the errors of the past—is a tribute to Friedman and Schwartz in the sense that the monetary authorities contend that if they are avoiding deflation and a contraction of GDP at the present time, it is because they correctly learned the lessons from Friedman and Schwartz and implemented appropriate expansionary monetary policy to fight against the financial crisis.

In section two, I survey the cliometrics literature on the Fed's policy with regard to the Great Depression and discuss the influence and limits of this dominant view.

The 'Inept' Policy of the Fed During the Great Depression as the Cornerstone of Conventional Wisdom

Hsieh and Romer (2006, 140) described the Fed's failure to respond to the banking panics during the Great Depression as "one of the great mysteries of the 1930s." This issue has received considerable attention in the literature, with two main explanations for the Fed's behavior during the depression.

The first, most notably supported by Friedman and Schwartz (1963), stressed that Fed officials exhibited an erroneous understanding of monetary conditions and used an erroneous implicit model of the economy. Using domestic monetary aggregates rather than interest rates, Friedman and Schwartz argued that the Great Depression was caused by domestic monetary contraction and that the Fed could have prevented and even reversed it with an appropriately expansionary monetary policy. They contended that the Fed's refusal to combat monetary contraction was a monumental policy mistake, and this judgment became the dominant view thereafter. Bordo, Choudhri, and Schwartz (2002) supported this monetarist conviction by conducting a counterfactual analysis of expansionary monetary policy in the United States during the 1930s. They found that the United States, the largest economy in the world, with massive gold reserves, was not constrained from using expansionary policy to offset banking panics, deflation, and declining economic activity. Expansionary open market operations by the Fed at two critical junctures—from October 1930 to February 1931 and from September 1931 to January 1932—would have been successful in averting the banking panics that occurred. Had expansionary open market purchases been conducted in the 1930s, the contraction would not have led to the international crises that followed.

The second principle explanation blames the crisis on international causes and highlights the desire on the part of Fed officials to defend the gold standard. U.S. adherence to the gold standard acted as the fundamental constraint on monetary policy that prevented the Fed from taking action. Chandler (1958, 199) argued that both domestic and international goals were important in 1924 and 1927, and Wheelock (1991, chap. 2) found empirical support for this view. Eichengreen (1992), Temin (1976), and Bernanke (1983) suggested that the Fed did not implement expansionary monetary policy in the aftermath of the crisis because such expansion would have led to devaluation under the constraint of the gold standard. In this view, the Great Depression was not the result of domestic policy mistakes but the outcome of the Fed's commitment to the gold standard.

Hsieh and Romer (2006) questioned this view by testing whether expectations of devaluation forbade the Fed from continuing the 1932 open market purchase program. To that end, they used two indicators to measure devaluation expectations: the three-month forward premium exchange rates of the dollar against a panel of currencies and interest rate differentials. Their conclusion was that no expectations of devaluation could be found in 1932 regardless of the indicator. They held the view that their analysis of the 1932 open market purchase program supported the view that the American Great Depression was largely the result of inept policy, not adherence to the gold standard. "We are inclined to agree with Friedman and Schwartz that the Fed's failure to act was a policy mistake of monumental proportions, not the inevitable result of the US adherence to the gold standard" (175). This refutation of the idea that international causes affected the conduct of the Fed's policy and a focus on domestic causal factors of the crisis seem dominant today in the literature.

Why did Fed officials supposedly fail to respond appropriately to the crisis? Wheelock (1992) surveyed the existing approaches and alternative views about the incidence of monetary policy on the development of the crisis. He identified some core questions that still shape the debate today: Were domestic monetary conditions easy or tight? What was the impact of Strong's death? How consistent was the Fed's strategy? Was there a shift in monetary policy driven by a change in policy tools after the onset of the crisis?

"Most Fed officials felt that money and credit were plentiful. Short-term market interest fell sharply after the stock market crash of 1929 and remained at very low levels throughout the 1930s. Exceptionally low yields on short-term securities have suggested to many observers an abundance of liquidity" (Wheelock, 1992, 9). Proponents of the Austrian theory of the business cycle, such as Hayek (1932) and Adolph Miller and George Norris among the Fed's officials, argued that conditions were "easy," that excessively easy monetary policy in the 1920s had fostered the depression, and believed that "artificial" increases in the money supply in response to the depression, as in 1932, were mistakes. Other indicators of monetary conditions, however, suggest the opposite: the money stock fell by one third from 1929 to 1933. Irving Fisher (1932) argued that the Fed should prevent deflation by increasing the money supply. Friedman and Schwartz (1963, 375) contended that "it seems paradoxical to describe as "monetary ease" a policy which permitted the stock of money to decline [. . .] by a percentage exceeded only four times in the preceding fifty-four years and then only during extremely severe business-cycle contractions." Keynesians tend to support the idea that monetary ease prevailed during the depression. Temin (1976, 169) asserted: "There is no evidence of any effective deflationary pressure from the banking system between the stock market crash in October 1929 and the British abandonment of the gold standard in September 1931. [. . .] There was no rise in short-term interest rates in this two-year period. [. . .] The relevant record for the purpose of identifying a monetary restriction is the record of short-term interest rates." At the same time, however, I denounced the inability of the Fed to combat bank failures, which counterbalances the view that monetary conditions were patently easy. More recently, Field (1984) and Hamilton (1987) emphasized that the real interest rate increased sharply during the Great Depression in contrast with the apparent signal of nominal interest rates, which suggests that monetary conditions were far from easy.[4]

The impact of the death of the Fed's chairman Benjamin Strong also divides the community of scholars. Friedman and Schwartz (1963) considered Strong's death in 1928 to have been a decisive event that provoked a dramatic change in policy orientation that was harmful to the country due to ignorance of the underlying model of the economy and the abandonment of an aggressive policy. Wicker (1966), Brunner and Meltzer (1968), and Temin (1989) contended that Strong's death was a minor event that changed nothing; there was simply a continuation of erroneous policies. Chandler (1958) and Friedman and Schwartz (1963) took the view that under Strong's leadership the Fed stimulated economic activity during recessions by promoting monetary ease. In contrast, therefore, Strong's death would lead to a systematic contractionary bias in monetary policy during the depression. Wheelock (1992, 27), however, called this assertion into question. Underlying the ambiguity of several of Strong's quotations, Wheelock stressed "the difficulty of inferring what policies he would have pursued in the 1930s" (14). Wheelock's thesis was that there was no fundamental change in regime after the death of Benjamin Strong and that "Fed errors seem largely attributable to the continued use of flawed policies" (27).

Was the Fed's policy simply inept, or consistent with clear objectives? Chandler (1958, 199) argued that by 1924, "Federal Reserve officials had developed three major objectives or considerations that were to shape their policies for about a decade. These were 1) promotion of high and stable levels of business activity and employment and stability of price levels; 2) curbing excessive use of credit for stock market speculation, and 3) assistance to monetary reconstruction and stability abroad." Wicker (1966) and Brunner and Meltzer (1968) argued that there was no inconsistency in Fed policy. They contended that the Fed used the volume of discount loans and nominal interest rates as policy guides, and because these variables fell sharply from 1930–1931, Fed officials inferred that money was easy and that open market purchases were unnecessary. According to Wicker (1966, 172–184) and Chandler (1971, 198–204), the Fed measured the effects of its purchases by the excess reserve position of New York banks, and by mid-1932 they had begun to set explicit targets for excess reserve. Thus, the Fed's strategy for evaluating credit conditions seems to have evolved slightly from focusing on the discount loan volume to focusing on "free reserves," that is, excess reserves less borrowed reserves.

Consequently, Wheelock suggested focusing on Federal Reserve Credit (FRC). The FRC was the sum of holdings of federal government securities, bankers' acceptances, and discount loans to member banks. "Open market operations, gold flows, changes in the public's currency holdings and other causes of reserve flows affected the extent to which banks turned to the Fed for credit, either in the form of discount loans or through acceptance sales to the Reserve banks" (1989, 466). Wheelock described the Fed's policymaking as follows: "The Fed had three policy tools: open market operations in government securities, the discount rate and the buying acceptance rate. In general, the three tools were used consistently with another, i.e. open market purchases (sales) were made in conjunction with discount acceptance buying rate reductions (increases)" (454).

In the literature, there is a debate about how these instruments were coordinated. Trescott (1982) and Epstein and Ferguson (1984) treat the Fed's operations in government securities and its operations in bankers' acceptances as pure substitutes. Friedman and Schwartz (1963) and Wicker (1966) note that some Fed officials did not view operations in government securities and bankers' acceptances as perfect substitutes. Although probably not perfect substitutes, Wheelock (1989) acknowledged that operations in government securities and acceptances could be seen as "somewhat interchangeable" (459). Very interestingly, he suggests that "most often, the Fed's directives did not specify specific targets for interest rates or loans. At most, the Fed used these variables as 'indicators' of credit conditions, rather than 'targets'" (459). In his analysis, the most relevant indicator to capture the driving forces of Fed officials' decisions remains the stock of non-borrowed reserves: The change in unborrowed reserves accurately measures the Fed policy intent if open market operations were to be used to offset undesired changes in the gold and currency stocks and in acceptance sales to the Fed" (464). He states that "it may be that open market operations did not reflect the Fed's policy intent as well as the flow of unborrowed reserves" (464) and concluded that in the 1930s the Fed "continued to rely on bank reserve positions and market interest rates as policy guides (473).

Wheelock's work (1989) must be acknowledged as pioneering in that it proposed the first econometric regression of the Fed's policy reaction function to be based on the *volume* of federal government security holdings, bankers' acceptance holdings, and discount loans to member banks. Nevertheless, some reservations apply. Notably, Toma (1989) challenges this view. He contests the use of the total volume of outstanding FRC as a guideline for monetary policy. Open market operations produced opposite changes in the volume of discount loans. His analysis indicated that changes in discount loan volume offset open market operations dollar for dollar. Toma's study implies that the Fed's response to its policy goals could not be reflected in the evolution of FRC. Because they were offset by the other forms of outstanding FRC, open market operations did not produce systematic changes in bank reserves or the supply of money. Therefore, the FRC did not reflect the Fed's response to its policy goal. Moreover, as reported by Wheelock (1992, 9), data on excess reserves before 1929 are not available.

Consequently, with regard to the study of this period, volume-based indicators might be misleading. The lack of data on volume over a long period prohibits us from performing econometric tests on quantities. As a result, nominal interest rates could be more relevant for evaluating the consistency of the Fed's policy over the period (see section three).

New Insights from the McCallum and Taylor Rules in a Nonlinear Historical Perspective

The use of McCallum and Taylor rules in a historical perspective provides new insights into the presumed inept policy followed by Fed officials during the Great Depression. In this section, I survey two articles that illustrate this point. In "Did the Fed Follow an Implicit McCallum Rule During the Great Depression?", Damette and Parent (2016) address the issue of the consistency of the Fed's action during the interwar period using McCallum's rule. By developing backward-looking models, forward-looking models, and performing counterfactual historical simulation, they found that the McCallum rule provides some interesting historical lessons, enabling us to identify some possible driving forces behind the Fed's policy setting. They provided evidence that the Fed followed an imperfect and partial McCallum rule over the period 1921–1933, moving the money base instrument according to an output target but not correcting for any deviation from this target. This suggests that the Fed was probably more active than reported in the literature.

Economists should not refrain from using retrospective econometrics to test the robustness of presumed relationships. Testing an implicit monetary rule helps to highlight the motives underlying the Fed's behavior during the Great Depression. Obviously, new and valuable historical lessons can be drawn from this kind of exercise. In this way, Damette and Parent (2016) have reassessed the continuity and consistency of the Fed's action during this period. In themselves, the limits encountered in this exercise reveal the imperfections and hesitations in the decisions taken by Fed officials. For instance, they recognize that they have only been able to reproduce the dynamics of the monetary base according to a McCallum rule to some extent: with their estimated McCallum function (which links the actual money base to the estimated target), the target is always significant, not the output gap. The interpretation is meaningful: throughout the period, Fed officials monitored the output target, whereas they did not correct for any deviation from it. This finding has been corroborated with forward-looking models. As a result, Damette and Parent conclude that the Fed followed a partial or imperfect McCallum rule during the interwar period.

Does the absence of any correction for deviation from the target in the estimated McCallum rule necessarily reveal policy mistakes and prove that the Fed implemented erroneous and inappropriate policy during the period? Damette and Parent (2016) pointed out that such a conclusion would be overly hasty because it would imply that the Fed could not combine the two instruments of the monetary base and the interest rate. In this paper, I simply explore all the possibilities from a McCallum rule in terms of money base policy. Damette and Parent also conduct a counterfactual historical simulation by comparing the actual base money policy with a calibrated standard McCallum model (imposing a coefficient of 0.5 for the output gap), which also is very informative with regard to whether the Fed's monetary policy was too restrictive, too lax, or about right (still subject to ongoing debate in the literature, as mentioned in the previous section). They found that, in general, before 1929 the Fed did not seem to deviate much from an optimal calibrated McCallum rule. Indeed, the difference between actual and calibrated monetary base variations was near zero and relatively stable until the crisis of 1929. Between 1929 and 1933, they found the dynamics of the gap to be less stable but, interestingly, these dynamics reveal that the Fed adopted accommodative policies, increasing the monetary base more rapidly than the optimal (calibrated) amount. This finding contrasts strongly with Friedman and Schwartz's (1963) analysis because it provides evidence that the Fed used the monetary base to compensate for the collapse of the economy after 1929.

In "Did the Fed Respond to Liquidity Shortage Episodes during the Great Depression?", Damette and Parent (2018) set out to test whether the Fed had recognized the impending liquidity crisis of 1929 and whether its long-term policy took account of this danger. They wondered whether the Fed was well aware of liquidity risks and attempted to prevent them from occurring. Here, too, they performed retrospective econometric analysis to assess the significance of the Fed officials' decisions during the interwar period. For this purpose, they used an Ireland–Taylor type rule in a nonlinear framework.

The theoretical grounds for the use of a nonlinear framework to study the Fed's policy conduct during the interwar period have been described in Cukierman and Muscatelli (2008). They referred to objective functions that display features in which abnormal circumstances may cause central bankers to implement asymmetric objectives that lead to the implementation of nonlinear reaction functions. They documented how the dominant type of asymmetry in monetary policy (recession avoidance versus inflation avoidance) changes with the economic environment. Damette and Parent (2018) transposed this rationale to the study of the Fed's preferences during the interwar period.

To parametrize the nonlinearities during the interwar period, they applied smooth-transition models (STRs), the modeling strategy proposed by Granger and Teräsvirta (1993) and Teräsvirta (1994, 1998). This specification is based on the theory that it is unlikely that interest rate responses in the reaction function will remain constant over a long period characterized by dramatic changes in the economy. This method allows the coefficients of the variables that might play a nonlinear role in the model to depend on a transition variable that governs smooth transition. Damette and Parent (2018) used an indicator of liquidity tensions on the market as a transition variable to test whether, during these troubled times, the Fed monitored liquidity tensions. They highlighted three distinct periods in the conduct of the policy, all of them driven by the Fed's perception of liquidity risks (identified by a proxy that expressed "liquidity shortage"). After a regular period prior to 1927, they found that the Fed lost control of monetary policy between 1927 and 1929 and, then, reestablished the drivers of monetary policy conduct as early as the early 1930s.

Damette and Parent (2018) suggested that, due to the Fed's insensitivity to signs of tensions in liquidity in the 1920s and a total loss of control over monetary policy from 1927–1929, the Fed adopted a radical position in its subsequent decisions. From creation of the Open Market Policy Conference (OMPC) in 1930, the Fed's decisions seem to have been driven by the fear of a repetition of the previous episodes of dramatic liquidity shortage. Thus, Damette and Parent (2018) provided a new reading of the Fed's behavior during the 1930s. They highlighted that, in contrast to the twenties, the 1930s were marked by what amounted to "liquidity shortage avoidance" preferences on the part of the Fed. It should be noted that it would have been impossible to arrive at these results with a linear form of the monetary rule. Linear econometric tools are unable to characterize the shock of the Great Depression and the behavior of the Fed during the interwar period. It is clear that implementing nonlinearity made it possible to demonstrate the Fed's asymmetric preferences during the interwar period.

Conclusion: Can We Learn from the Past Without Making Use of History?

By warning against making use of history for economic policy purpose, I have dealt with some implicit broad issues: Can we rely on cliometrics to draw clear-cut lessons from history? Is there a systematic bias in the cliometric attempt to understand the present through the past? Is the cliometric project legitimate by its very nature or doomed to fail? I conclude that the attempt to infer policy recommendations from the study of the systematic relationship between variables in the past has proved to be misleading in the case of the presumed monetary lessons drawn from the Fed's policy conducts during the Great Depression. I have highlighted three pitfalls: Cliometrics can relate current issues to the past but cannot predict the future. Trying to draw a single definite lesson from the past for the future would be illusory. Cliometrics should never consist of using a framework that is not appropriate for the topic.

I have provided an important example of the misuse of history that had important side-effects because it served as a pretext for economic policy recommendations. In particular, I have shown that lessons from retrospective econometric analysis do not make sense when the analysis is not combined with rigorous economic modeling and econometric analysis. As illustrated here, it is striking how the consensus view came to be one of unconditional support for unconventional monetary policies, presumably in light of the correct understanding of the Fed's policy mistakes during the interwar period. I presented evidence that caution and accountability for economic policy recommendations is required when assessing previous episodes of crisis. The American and European monetary authorities implemented expansionary monetary policies to prevent the recession in 2008 and 2009, unlike in 1929.

In this paper, I have clarified the presumed lessons from the Great Depression for today. The motto of the consensus view and conventional wisdom—we did not repeat the errors of the past (and we were right not to)—was based on three major errors or shortcomings:

1. The idea that a single lesson can be drawn from monetary history.
2. The absence of appropriate methodology. Notably, the need for nonlinear studies of monetary policy rules in the presence of brutal transitions or sudden jumps such as occurred in the Great Depression and the Great Recession.
3. The failure to question a single reading of events and blindness to the fact that an invalid or erroneous interpretation of history can lead to a policy mistake today.

I believe that the Fed's behavior in 1929 was not necessarily the monumental mistake described at length in the literature. However, doing the exact opposite of what was done in the 1930s is not necessarily the appropriate policy and may well have been another monumental mistake.

Notes

1. It would have been better to distinguish between the Fed rate and the European Central Bank rate, as using a weighted central bank rate introduces bias. Indeed, this may explain why the interest rate levels found by these authors are, surprisingly, lower now than then. The absence of central bank cooperation during the interwar period and the Gold Standard constraint may explain the propensity of each central bank to increase its domestic discount rate in order to capture gold resources. The weighted indicator captures this effect, whereas if we use single domestic discount rates, and notably the Fed rate, the level of central bank interest rates then and now is not very different (see, for instance, Romer, 2009).

2. See the section titled "Policy Response Then and Now," in the European Commission report (2009).
3. Romer (2009, 5) characterized this situation as follows: "Consumers and businesses wanted to sit on any cash they had because they expected its real purchasing power to increase as prices fell." She thus assimilated the period 1929–1933 to a context of liquidity trap.
4. Another set of explanations (namely, interest group pressure explanations of the Fed's behavior) departs from the others, maintaining that the Fed's contractionary policy was deliberate and that its officials were well aware that tight monetary conditions prevailed during the depression. "Epstein and Ferguson (1984) and Anderson, Shughart, and Tollison (1988) contend that Fed officials acted only to promote the interests of commercial banks rather than economic recovery, notably in aiding its member banks. They argue that monetary policy was designed to cause the failure of non-member banks" (as cited by Wheelock, 1992, 4).

References

Anderson, G. M., W. F. Shughart, and R. D. Tollison. 1988. "A Public Choice Theory of the Great Contraction." *Public Choice* (October): 3–23.
Bernanke, B. 1983. "Nonmonetary Effects of the Financial Crisis in the Propagation of the Great Depression." *American Economic Review* 73 (3): 257–76.
Bordo, M., and H. Rockoff. 2013. "Not Just the Great Contraction: Friedman and Schwartz's *A Monetary History of the United States 1867 to 1960.*" *American Economic Review: Papers & Proceedings* 103 (3): 61–65.
Bordo, M., and J. Landon-Lane. 2010. "The Banking Panics in the United States in the 1930s: Some Lessons for Today." *Oxford Review of Economic Policy* 26 (3): 486–509.
Bordo M., E. Choudhri, and A. Schwartz. 2002. "Was Expansionary Monetary Policy Feasible During the Great Contraction? An Examination of the Gold Standard Constraint." *Explorations in Economic History* 39 (1): 1–28.
Brunner, K., and A. H. Meltzer. 1968. "What Did We Learn from the Monetary Experience of the United States in the Great Depression?" *Canadian Journal of Economics* 1 (2): 334–48.
Chandler, L. V. 1958. *Benjamin Strong, Central Banker.* Washington, D.C.: Brookings Institution.
——. 1971. *American Monetary Policy 1928–1941.* New York: Harper & Row.
Cukierman, A., and A. Muscatelli. 2008. "Nonlinear Taylor Rules and Asymmetric Preferences in Central Banking: Evidence from the United Kingdom and the United States." *The B. E. Journal of Macroeconomics* 8 (1): art. 7.
Damette O., and A. Parent. 2016. "Did the Fed Follow an Implicit McCallum Rule During the Great Depression?" *Economic Modelling* 52 (January): 226–32.
——. 2018. "Did the Fed Respond to Liquidity Shortage Episodes During the Great Depression." *Macroeconomic Dynamics* 22 (October): 1727–49. doi: 10.1017/S1365100516001073.
Eichengreen, B. 1992. *Golden Fetters: The Gold Standard and the Great Depression, 1919–1939.* Oxford: Oxford University Press.
Eichengreen, B., and K. O'Rourke. 2009. "A Tale of Two Depressions." *VoxEU.org* 1 (September).
Epstein, G., and T. Ferguson. 1984. "Monetary Policy, Loan Liquidation, and Industrial Conflict: The Federal Reserve and the Open-Market Operations of 1932." *Journal of Economic History* 44 (4): 957–83.

European Commission. 2009. "Economic Crisis in Europe: Causes, Consequences and Responses." *European Economy* 7: 1–90.

Field, A. J. 1984. "A New Interpretation of the Onset of the Great Depression." *Journal of Economic History* 64 (1): 489–98.

Fisher, I. 1932. *Booms and Depressions, Some First Principles.* New York: Adelphi.

Friedman, M., and A. Schwartz. 1963. *A Monetary History of the United States, 1867–1960,* Princeton, N.J.: Princeton University Press.

Granger, C. W. J. and T. Teräsvirta (1993) *Modelling Non-Linear Economic Relationships.* Oxford: Oxford University Press.

Hamilton, J. D. 1987. "Monetary Factors in the Great Depression." *Journal of Monetary Economics* 19: 145–69.

Hayek, F. A. von. (1932) 1984. "The Fate of the Gold Standard." In *Money, Capital and Fluctuations: Early Essays of F. A. von Hayek,* ed. Roy McCloughry, 118–35. London: Routledge and Kegan Paul.

Helbling T. 2009. "How Similar Is the Current Crisis to the Great Depression?", *VoxEU.org,* April 29.

Hsieh, C. T., and C. Romer. 2006. "Was the Fed Constrained by the Gold Standard During the Great Depression? Evidence from the 1932 Open Market Purchase Program." *Journal of Economic History* 66 (1): 140–76.

Krugman P. 2009. "The Great Recession Versus the Great Depression." *New York Times,* March 20.

Romer, C. 1992. "What Ended the Great Depression?", *Journal of Economic History* 52: 757–84.

——. 2009. "Lessons from the Great Depression for Economic Recovery in 2009." Presentation at Brookings Institution, Washington, D.C., March 9.

Temin, P. 1976. *Did Monetary Forces Cause the Great Depression?,* New York: Norton.

——. 1989. *Lessons from the Great Depression.* Cambridge: MIT Press.

Teräsvirta, T. 1994. "Specification, Estimation and Evaluation of Smooth Transition Autoregressive Models." *Journal of the American Statistical Association* 89: 208–10.

——. 1998. "Modelling Relationships with Smooth Transition Regressions." In *Handbook of Applied Economic Statistics,* ed. A. Ullah and D. E. Giles, 507–52. New York: Dekker.

Toma, M. 1989. "The Policy Effectiveness of Open Market Operations in the 1920s." *Explorations in Economic History* 26: 99–116.

Trescott, P. B. 1982. "Federal Reserve Policy in the Great Depression: A Counterfactual Assessment." *Explorations in Economic History,* 19: 211–20.

Wheelock, D. C. 1989. "The Strategy, Effectiveness and Consistency of Federal Reserve Monetary Policy 1924–1933." *Explorations in Economic History* 26 (4): 453–76.

——. 1991. *The Strategy and Consistency of Federal Reserve Monetary Policy, 1924 to 1933.* Cambridge: Cambridge University Press.

——. 1992. "Monetary Policy in the Great Depression: What the Fed Did and Why." *Federal Reserve Bank of Saint Louis Review* 74 (March/April): 3–28.

Wicker, E. 1966. *Federal Reserve Monetary Policy 1917–1933.* New York: Random House.

CHAPTER 5

REGULATION AND COMPETITION IN THE EU FINANCIAL SECTOR

PIERRE-CHARLES PRADIER

I n his inauguration speech, Michel Barnier, then European Union commissioner for internal market and services, noted that "financial integration and stability go hand in hand" (Barnier, 2010). The impact on financial stability of the 42 directives and regulations he passed has been dissected and assessed by every possible stakeholder, but integration is often overlooked. Perhaps Barnier's appointment as liquidator of the Anglo-European Union obfuscated his contribution to integration. However, the creation of a banking union, of a capital markets union, of European supervisory agencies, and the complete overhaul of the regulatory framework to *level the playing field* should have had definite consequences on integration. The European Central Bank (ECB) provides some statistics, and Dirk Schoenmaker, professor of banking and finance at the Rotterdam School of Management, Erasmus University Rotterdam, has made a remarkable series of contributions on financial sector integration, but no one appears to care. Nevertheless, financial integration is likely to increase the provision of cross-border services between member states and the number of cross-border mergers, and, thus, it will have an impact on competition through increased concentration. Once again, no one appears to care. Even without the global financial crisis and without the European sovereign debt crisis, competition in the financial sector should have been a hot topic in Europe because interstate competition may raise distribution issues between member states, and intrastate competition may denote capture of the regulator by the financial sector. No one cares, but perhaps the crisis made the topic so hot that it became urgent to not talk about it.

By comparison with the current EU situation, a brief glance at the recent financial history of the United States has shown that leveling the playing field and promoting financial integration may have a definite impact on the structure of the banking sector; the Riegle-Neal Interstate Banking and Branching Efficiency Act of 1994, for instance, triggered a host of mergers that eventually drove the market share of the five largest players from 20 to almost 50 percent in just fifteen years. Apparently the EU banking sector already enjoys the same level of integration (European Central Bank [ECB], 2017). Did the Barnier legacy change this competitive structure?

It seems rather unlikely that such a huge regulatory change could be completely neutral, but the available data seem to confirm that it is; however, discussions with industry professionals provides diverging points of view: professional services providers saw no difference until Brexit became probable, but insurers appear to think that Solvency II favors concentration, and bankers are concerned. Is it possible, then, to clarify these mixed feelings? I first look at facts and data to assess the state of the question (section one). This will lead to distinguishing sectors whose competitive structure over the past decade was not affected from sectors where the potential impact could be significant (section two), such as the banking sector (section three) and the insurance sector (section four), where apparent stability may mask different latent changes. I analyze the impact of regulation and the possible evolution in the coming years. This method does not rely on a model fitted to a dataset, but on the a priori analysis of distinctive characters of the regulation, which match a number of observed facts. The reader should not look for proofs, therefore, but rather for insights that raise awareness of potentially troublesome issues, namely, the concentration process in the insurance industry and the dismemberment of the business model of European banks. Both of these trends are invisible from the existing statistics.

Regulatory Overhaul and EU Financial Integration

The ECB provides many potentially interesting statistics, such as a class of financial integration indicators (1) and a yearly report on financial structures (2). Unfortunately, they contain little information relevant to competition in the financial sector.

Financial Integration Indicators

Each year since 2005, the ECB has published a report on the financial integration of European member states. The current methodology relies on thirty-nine statistical series aggregated into three main indicators measuring (1) price convergence

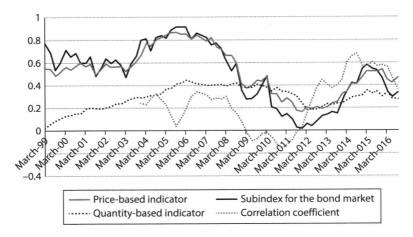

Figure 5.1 ECB financial integration indicators

Source: Author, based on ECB data.

on financial markets (money market, bond market, equity market, and banking market), (2) quantitative aspects such as cross-border holding of assets, and (3) other aspects of integration such as risk-sharing, that is, the correlation of each member state's consumption to EU gross domestic product (GDP). These methodologies, as shown in Figure 5.1, produce an assessment of EU financial integration, which essentially shows a regressive trend since the mid-2000s, with a low in 2013 and a slight rebound subsequently by the first two composite indicators (the third is much flatter but exhibits overall the same pattern over the past ten years).

At first sight, the common "V" pattern appears to fit the crisis-and-regulatory-overhaul story: early signs of the financial crisis triggered rising risk premia and flight to quality led to a retreat on domestic assets, hence, a fall in price- and quantity-based indicators, which would later recover as Barnier's reforms were introduced. Figure 5.1 also displays a fourth line: the subindex for the sovereign bond market. Although its weight in the price index is less than 30 percent, it explains 85 percent of variance in the price-based indicator and also traces the pattern of other indicators. The data also can be explained in a second manner: the interest rate convergence-divergence-convergence may result from the European sovereign crisis, which resulted in rising spreads and diminishing cross-border holding of assets. ECB financial integration indicators tell us little about the integration of a financial sector providing services to consumers and businesses. These indicators may have relevance in macro matters, such as the timing of the business or credit cycle, but they tell us little about issues of competition. Shall we then look at the *report on financial structures* for data on concentration?

Concentration Indicators

The ECB's "Report on Financial Structures" (2017) provides sectorwide concentration ratios, which we show in Figure 5.2 .

The data presented in Figure 5.2 are somewhat surprising. The European insurance sector appears much more concentrated than the banking sector, which is not at all obvious. From an international comparison perspective, the European banking sector appears to be as concentrated as the U.S. banking sector (where, in 2015, the market share of the five largest banks was 46.5 percent according to Federal Reserve Economic Data [FRED]). However, figures provided by the yearly NAIC Competition database for U.S. industry show less concentration there: the market share of the four largest U.S. firms was just 25.1 percent in 2014 (whereas in the EU this exceeds 50 percent in non–life insurance and 70 percent in life insurance). It should be noted, however, that the insurance industry data indicate a "simple average" of member states' statistics. Repeating this exercise with state-level NAIC data would give a figure of 32.0 percent rather than 25.1 percent, although still far below the EU figures. In fact, averaging concentration statistics is rather pointless (see Appendix 1). Rather than using a poor indicator of concentration in the United States, we should correctly measure EU concentrations.

Unfortunately, neither the ECB nor the European Insurance and Occupational Pensions Authority (EIOPA) provide public data for use in calculating an

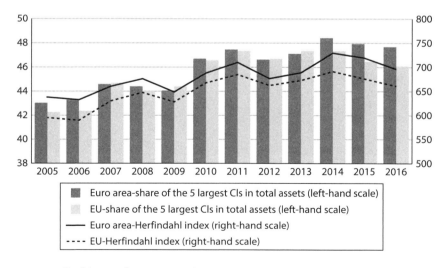

Figure 5.2 Banking market concentration

Source: ECB, "Report on Financial Structure," (2017), 31, 48.

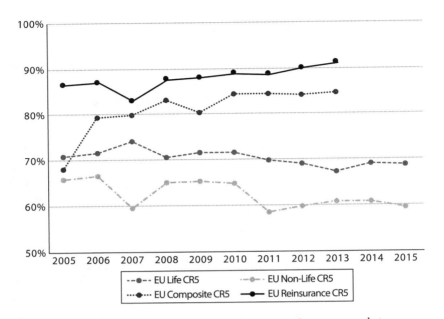

Figure 5.3 Average of CR5 concentration ratios in euro-area insurance markets

Note: Simple average over euro area countries, for which data are available and relevant, are based on gross written premiums of the five largest companies as a percentage of total gross written premiums in the domestic sector of each country.

Sources: Author, based on EIOPA data.

EU-wide concentration index. Schoenmaker (2015) and Schoenmaker and Sass (2014) provide data (Figure 5.3) that can be used to calculate concentration ratios for eurozone banking and insurance in the European Economic Area (EEA) and Switzerland. These data are based on country-by-country reporting for banks, with a careful matching of three different insurance data sources (see Schoenmaker and Sass, 2014). The final data (see Appendix 2) show the EU financial industry to be much less integrated than its U.S. counterpart. We can, therefore, infer that ECB banking data rely on the same averaging of member state concentrations and are, therefore, misleading as this is not indicated, unlike the insurance data.

It seems clear, therefore, that we lack the relevant data to produce the ultimate study on financial sector concentration. Nevertheless, Schoenmakers us understand that the classic view of the EU—that banks were large at the level of the member state—is no longer the case, as demonstrated in Table 5.1 (see, for example, Bertay et al., 2013). Unfortunately, the absence of time series data prevents us from understanding the trends, and we must rely on hypotheses to disentangle the complexity of recent history.

If we want to portray what is happening in the markets, we are left to rely on partial data. I would hazard a guess that a number of financial industry

TABLE 5.1 Financial Subsectors Concentration Ratios in 2012

	U.S.	EU ECB/EIOPA	EU Schoenmaker and Sass
Banking sector	46.8% (U.S.)	47.9% (EU)	18.0% (eurozone)
Insurance sector	26.3% (U.S.)	>55.0% (EU)	20.6% (EEA+ Switzerland)

Sources: U.S. banks, FRED, Insurance, NAIC Competition database, EU banks and insurance, ECB (2017b), Schoenmaker (2015), Schoenmaker and Sass (2014).

sectors are so specialized that changes in the regulatory environment have not fundamentally altered the supply side structure. The following section provides a number of intuitive examples. The case of banking is complex to analyze due to the aggregation of different activities, and it is likely that changes in market structure go unnoticed. Literature on the insurance sector emphasizes the possibility of increasing returns induced by new regulations, and I explain why such a concentration is not visible concentration.

Sectors Largely Untouched by Regulatory Change

What justifies the statement that little has changed in certain subsectors and little is likely to change in the coming years? When the distribution of activities across member states is highly asymmetric and did not change, there are reasons to believe that the competitive advantage enjoyed by the leaders will continue ("indefinitely, except insofar as we have specific reasons to expect a change," as Keynes wrote in chapter 12 of the *General Theory*). Consider, for instance, the investment fund sector. Although this sector has been significantly reregulated, with at least three new EU directives,[1] the distribution of net assets under management across members states has barely changed postcrisis. Figure 5.4 shows the ratio of the share of assets under management in the EU to the share of EU GDP for the largest member states; the only countries with a share of assets larger than their share of GDP are Luxembourg and Ireland. The Czech Republic and Greece experienced capital flight on the order of 10 percent of GDP, and Malta attracted significant inward investment. Asset management firms, therefore, appear to be *niche* specialists, providing services for the entire EU (although many member states have an industry serving their domestic clients). I describe *specialized services* as those services that are offered to the entire EU from specific locations through EU passporting rights contained in the relevant directives.

Unfortunately, we lack data as striking as assets under management to characterize each segment of the EU financial sector and to identify those member states that provide specialized services, so we cannot test whether events of the past decade have had an impact on their activities. What we can guess is that most sub-sectors exhibiting the same specialization have, more or less, experienced the same stability. Considering the insurance industry, for example, specialized services are provided from London, captive insurance is provided from Luxembourg and Ireland, and life insurance is provided from Lichtenstein—bordering the EU and an EEA member (see Figure 5.4) More generally, the City of London is well known for aggregating a number of specialized services, including clearing, corporate and investment banking, legal counsel, and other professional services sometimes excluded from financial sector data, such as finance-related IT services.

My thesis is simply that past regulatory overhauls seem not to have significantly affected the competitive advantage of the providers of these specialized services. Whether they adapted a posteriori or lobbied a priori, both are efficient. Brexit, of course, casts a veil of uncertainty over the future.

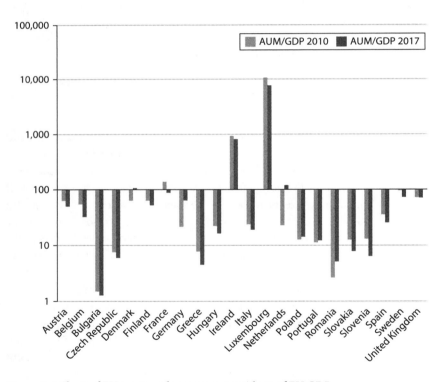

Figure 5.4 Share of EU assets under management/share of EU GDP

Source: Author, based on European Fund and Asset Management Association data; Quarterly Statistical Report Q3 2017, https://www.efama.org/Publications/Statistics/Quarterly/Quarterly%20Statistical%20Reports /171211_Quarterly%20Statistical%20Release%20Q3%202017.pdf; and Quarterly Statistical Report Q3 2011, https://www.efama.org/Publications/Statistics/Quarterly/Quarterly%20Statistical%20Reports/Quarterly%20 Statistical%20Report%20Q3%202011.pdf#search=Quarterly%20Statistical%20Report%20Q3%202010.

Banking

In this section, I introduce key regulatory changes before introducing the current enigma of delayed consolidation and two scenarios for the future.

Europe Banking Reform 101

The EU not only implemented a Basel III package (under CRD IV and CRR), with some minor degrees of freedom,[2] but has, since 2013, created a banking union through a series of regulations[3] with a Single Supervision Mechanism (SSM) and an intergovernmental agreement establishing a Single Resolution Mechanism (SRM). Deposit insurance, intended to be the third pillar of the banking union, continues to function at the level of the member states and without a common guarantee fund. Crisis management is a work in progress because the European Resolution Fund will not be fully funded before 2025. Some consider the banking union incomplete given the absence of an EU deposit guarantee fund, but the current arrangement resolves the problem developed in Schoenmaker (2011), which showed that, in a region where the financial sector is significantly integrated, the absence of a common supervisor may pose a severe threat in case of systemic risk because no single country will bear the cost of avoiding a systemic failure. This instance of the classic free rider problem is resolved with the combination of a common supervisor and common resolution mechanism, whereas deposit guarantee may be left to the discretion of member states to avoid moral hazard.

The EU has a complex topology of intertwined subsets. Each country follows the single rulebook (i.e., Basel III + Bank resolution, and recovery rules + local deposit guarantee schemes), but only nineteen are eurozone members. The number of SSM and SRM participants falls between the number of EU member states and the number of eurozone states; eurozone members are required to participate, and EU member states with "close cooperation agreements" are not required to join the eurozone in order to be part of the banking union. Currently, twenty-six of the twenty-eight EU members (all but the United Kingdom and Sweden) have signed the intergovernmental agreement establishing the SSM, but only twenty-one have actually ratified the treaty.

Those members of the banking union are now part of a legally integrated market, where mergers, and particularly cross-border mergers, should be expected given that state markets are already highly concentrated. However, after a wave of postcrisis restructuring, especially in Belgium and Spain, there has been little merger activity in the EU since 2012. This should be explained.

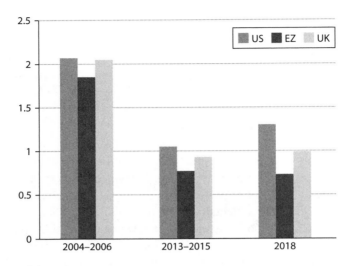

Figure 5.5 Bank average price-to-book ratios by area

Source: Author, based on Bloomberg data,

Where Are the Expected Mergers?

The lack of merger activity is especially puzzling because the price-to-book ratio of European banks has remained low postcrisis while increasing in the United Kingdom and United States (albeit with a significant variance in the latter case), as shown in Figure 5.5

Another way to consider the low European bank market valuation is to compare the MSCI indices for stocks. As shown in Figure 5.6, although the

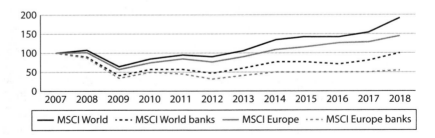

Figure 5.6 MSCI indices of stocks

Source: Author, based on MSCI data (MSCI world banks index, MSCI Europe banks index), https://www.msci.com/documents/10199/5aba8305-c399-4057-8159-3c96eb30c3ef ; https://www.msci.com/documents/10199/e72ea9be-ae79-4bb5-8ce0-054d4f371549.

world index recovered from the crisis in 2011 and is now at twice the 2007 level, the European index is lagging, and the situation for banks is even worse. Global banks have only recently recovered, with their stock returning to 2007 valuations, and banks stocks in Europe are still at a 50 percent discount ten years after the financial crisis.

Banks stocks are discounted; hence, the least efficient banks should be bought and restructured, as happened in Spain. Two issues explain the current state of delayed consolidation: latent risks seem not to be compensated by expectations of profits.

Let's look at risks first. Mergers would be uncertain because of underwriting and political risks. *Underwriting risk* is a euphemism alluding to asset quality: Banca Monte dei Paschi di Siena is famous for having acquired Banca Antonveneta from Santander with a large number of nonperforming loans on its balance sheet. It is well known that Europe is struggling with nonperforming loans and has failed to date to reduce their amount (Figure 5.7), thus delaying economic recovery. Politics may be the issue here because states protect their home market (see, for example, how Italy insisted on dealing with Banca Monte dei Paschi di Siena, sidelining the European Single Resolution Mechanism). In this political risk category, rising populism will make takeovers of foreign banks difficult because we cannot exclude the possibilities that further local or EU regulation would alter the business model and profit perspective.

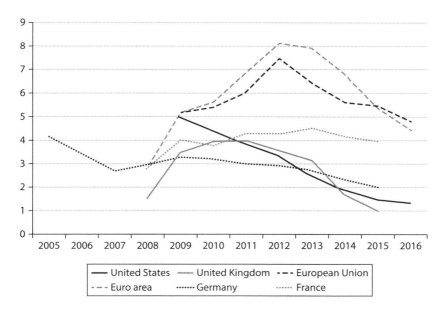

Figure 5.7 Nonperforming loans (percent)

Source: Author, based on BoE, ECB, and FRED data.

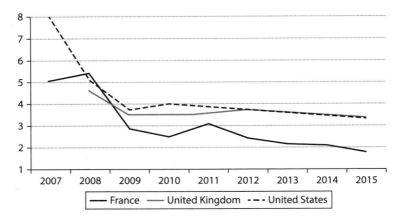

Figure 5.8 SME lending rates

Leaving aside politics and other risks, the problem is probably less non-performing loans (which cannot, however, be ignored, especially in Southern Europe) than it is very low interest rates. A simple comparison shows, for instance, that financing for small- and medium-sized enterprises in the United Kingdom costs 150 basis points more there than in the eurozone, and U.S. financial markets can provide firms with cheap money. However, mortgage rates in continental Europe are less than 2 percent, 150 basis points, cheaper than in the United States. In a recent paper, Claessens et al. (2017), show that falling interest rates lead to a margin crunch for banks.

The authors also show that this margin crunch is stronger when the interest rate is already low and that it grows stronger still over time (hysteresis). This analysis (Figure 5.8) has been conducted on pre-2015 data; but there are good reasons to believe this phenomenon endures, and the margin for banks is extremely low. It seems quite convincing, then, that the *perspective* of stagnating low interest rates results in very low bank valuation.

The very low interest rates in Figure 5.9 provide a consistent account for the underdevelopment of shadow lending and, in particular, crowd- and peer-to-peer lending, as Foata (2017) argues. Butler et al. (2014) have shown unambiguously that peer-to-peer lenders and banks compete on interest rate. In the United Kingdom, alternative finance can provide clear advantages to risky borrowers, but the banking sector does appear cheaper on the continent. The same might be true for securitization techniques, which can hardly be profitable in an environment as low-yield as the current eurozone.

The question then is, "How could competition evolve given this legal and economic environment?" We see at least two reference scenarios.

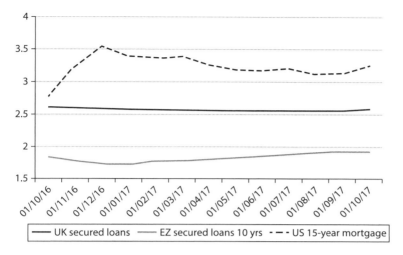

Figure 5.9 Bank lending rates to households

Source: Author, based on BoE, ECB, and FRED data.

Two and a Half Possible Scenarios

One credible scenario would be that the cycle picks up earlier in northern Europe because balance sheets are healthier. As restructuring is completed in France, the Netherlands, and the Nordic countries (see Oliver Wyman, 2017), and large investments are made in digitalization, those banks will likely enjoy a competitive edge. They would benefit from an interest rate rise to boost their interest rate margin, restore their profitability and market to book value, and could then buy their southern and eastern European counterparts, providing those institutions with sounder processes. They also would benefit from diversification, cycle decorrelation, and more regulatory capital. This scenario is compatible with the constraints explained by Schoenmaker (2015): megamergers are unlikely for reasons of financial stability, and intrastate fusion in smaller member states is equally unlikely as banking there is already concentrated; so the most likely EU bank mergers are cross-border mergers between small banks of smaller states or takeovers of these small banks by larger banks.

Obstacles to this *continental consolidation* scenario should not be ignored. The political problems have been mentioned, but a number of business model uncertainties remain. The imposition of credit floors will likely require additional capital for large universal banks and further delay consolidation. Even precrisis, the business of retail banking was not highly profitable (see Petracco-Giudici et al., 2013), and additional competition may render it unpalatable. Eventually, the alternative scenario would make it impracticable.

Scenario two could be called *profit skimming by shadow banking*. The idea is simply that clever competitors target the more profitable lines of business, separating them from banking conglomerates. Two examples will help highlight the nature of the implied risks. Consider, for instance, boutique FinTech firms such as Kantox, a foreign exchange broker and payment solution provider. Founded in London in 2011, in a matter of months it conquered a volume of activity comparable to a large universal bank because it is not required to provide regulatory capital and enjoys simplified compliance procedures. Lower-cost competitors thus drain profit margins. Others can capture future market opportunities, thereby lowering prospects and valuation—see, for example, Malta's three recent acts[4] creating a special regulatory regime for technical arrangements (Tendon, 2018) that considers computer protocols such as block chains, DAOs, and other DLT applications as legal persons. Of course, such legal persons do not have reporting or compliance obligations at present, but banks cannot rely on these kinds of maneuvers to outsource or diminish their regulatory costs. These examples show how banks may suffer from *negative complementarity* once certain business lines become less costly to operate outside of banks. This creates a significant threat to the current banking model.

Scenarios one and two can be partially combined in a *zombie consolidation with profit skimming* scenario, possibly the worst outcome. FinTech boutiques located in complacent jurisdictions would drain profitable business lines, leaving larger banks with unprofitable networks of physical branches and other legacy activities. Under this scenario, the banking industry could become more concentrated if measured by assets under management (boutique firms do not hold significant assets) or by the number of firms (as the ECB does in its 2017 "Report on Financial Structures"). This would create the impression that increasing returns will eventually bring larger banks to their break-even point, but becoming larger would only add costly additional systemic requirements. This scenario is reminiscent of the steel industry in the 1960s and 1970s when a headlong rush toward concentration was supposed to bring salvation, which never came.

The bifurcation toward one scenario or the other depends on complementarity between lines of business and the possibility of regulation based on activity, not entities. The real problem with the large regulatory package enabled after 2010 is that no one has a precise idea about the possibility of restoring the profitability of banking conglomerates to precrisis levels. Some professionals (see, for instance, Lencquesaing, 2018) plead for national competent authorities to fine-tune regulation and business models. The current top-down ECB approach does not seem adequate if its intent is to outsmart agile firms operating from agile financial centers, with relaxed regulators trying to skim the cream of the profit.

By contrast, the perspectives for insurance appear a bit clearer.

Insurance

Schoenmaker and Sass (2014) have shown the insurance sector to be more integrated than the banking sector; that is, the share of cross-border premiums written by insurers is larger than the share of cross-border assets held by bankers. According to Schoenmaker (2011, 2016), this should mandate a drive toward an insurance union. Comparisons with banking may be dangerous because, for example, contracts vary enormously across the EU. They do not include the same guarantees, and although continental Europe has essentially automatic renewal, the U.K. customer must sign a new contract annually (and so use price comparison websites more intensively). Close attention must be paid to the peculiarities of the sector when introducing the regulatory framework before looking at the actual consequences for concentration and related problems.

Does Solvency Incentivize Consolidation?

In the insurance sector, Solvency II (Directive 2009/138), first scheduled for entry into force in 2010, was delayed to January 1, 2016, with a transition period lasting until 2019. In the decade since the financial crisis, insurance firms have been readying themselves for implementation of this still-delayed directive. The regulation was designed to prevent regulatory arbitrage with banking, which Allen and Gale (2007) consider to be a major source of risk. Solvency II mimics Basel II and features the same three pillars. Pillar 1 establishes quantitative, that is, capital requirements; Pillar 2 relates to governance and supervision; and Pillar 3 is concerned with public disclosure and market transparency. The proposed regulation has been supported by larger insurers and criticized by smaller ones because many have found incentives to concentration between the lines of the project:

1. Stoyanova and Gründl (2014, 417) have introduced to the academic literature the idea of a "trend towards consolidation in the insurance sector due to recognition of geographic diversification effects in Solvency II's standard formula." To be more explicit, the "standard formula" for computing Solvency Capital Requirements (i.e., Pillar 1) sums up different capital requirements for different "risk modules," each of them being defined as a 99.5 percent

value-at-risk. Geographical diversification may lower those values-at-risk and thus the overall SCR, although the authors insisted that this capital-saving feature should be balanced with merger costs.

2. Pillar 1 feature another incentive toward consolidation: the capital requirements under Solvency II are usually higher than under the previous regulatory regime unless an "internal model" is researched by the company, as demonstrated by the fifth Quantitative Impact Study (EIOPA, 2011). Many companies choose not to build an internal model because of the implied cost, which can be amortized only by larger firms: capital requirements then turn internal models into a fixed cost, commanding increasing returns to scale.

3. Pillar 2 and Pillar 3 add up to the "fixed costs-increasing returns" in the insurance sector, and Chneiweiss and Pradier (2017) have shown that reporting costs were vastly increased for the smaller insurance companies.

These interpretations of Solvency II are speculative, and there a number of reasons to believe that it will lead to consolidation and increased concentration in the sector. Point 1, above, suggests the possibility of cross-country consolidation. Let us now look at whether the facts and figures confirm or refute our hypotheses.

Considering the Data

As I have shown, concentration statistics provided by EIOPA cannot be used to assess actual industry concentration. We are, therefore, left to consider the number of firms, however imprecise this measure may be is:

1. As reported by Insurance Europe, the number of firms exhibits signs of concentration, which must, nevertheless, be interpreted carefully. To the table, we added the *rate of reduction* in the number of insurance firms, where a positive rate indicates that the number of firms is falling and a negative rate indicates a rising number of firms. Perimeter is crucial to the understanding of concentration in Europe. In the EU28, the number of firms is most often rising, with an exception between 1998 and 2003. The EU12 appears to be less dynamic, with between 0.5 percent and 1 percent greater concentration per year, probably because the market is more mature. Only the United Kingdom has a rising number of firms. Excluding the United Kingdom, the EU12 market is experiencing accelerating concentration, with more than 3 percent of insurance firms disappearing annually between 2008 and 2013. I include a line showing the EU28 minus the United Kingdom for symmetry. It should be pointed out that without the United Kingdom the entire EU insurance sector has been undergoing consolidation since the beginning of the century, which has been accelerating in the old EU12 countries since 2008.

TABLE **5.2** Concentration Rates in the EU Insurance Industry

	1993	1998	2003	2008	2013
EU28 yearly concentration rate	5,083	5,173	4,756	4,914	4,968
		−0.35%	−1.70%	−0.65%	−0.22%
EU28-UK yearly concentration rate	4,255	4,341	3,984	3,942	3,739
		−0.40%	1.73%	0.21%	1.06%
EU12 yearly concentration rate	4,284	4,212	3,804	3,741	3,611
		0.34%	2.06%	0.33%	0.71%
EU12-UK yearly concentration rate	3,456	3,380	3,032	2,769	2,382
		0.45%	2.20%	1.83%	3.06%

Source: European Insurance in Figures 2015 data, https://www.insuranceeurope.eu/european-insurance-figures
-2015-data. The author based on BoE/ECB/FRED data.

2. Including EIOPA data would not change the overall picture, but it is worth noting that, according to EIOPA data, the number of firms falls in only certain countries, including Denmark, France, and Germany.

Eventually, since the number of firms is falling and the concentration ratios are not increasing, we can infer that *small* firms are disappearing and the consolidation is occurring between smaller firms. The correct instrument to study ongoing concentration would then be an EU28-wide data (to test Stoyanova and Gründl's hypothesis) and preferably the Herfindahl-Hirschman Index (i.e., sum of squares of market shares). With more than 3,500 insurance firms in existence today, extracting this data from EIOPA Financial Stability Reports would not be an inexpensive exercise.

Delayed Consolidation in Insurance Too?

Although the number of insurance firms has fallen during the past ten years, the speed of the consolidation process probably does not reflect the increasing returns embedded into Solvency II. The reason here is probably not the same as with the banking sector (i.e., low profitability and high risks).I shall cite rather:

1. Of the European insurance market, 32.4 percent is held by mutual insurers (AMICE, 2017). This market share exceeds 50 percent in Austria and the Netherlands and is only slightly below 50 percent in France, Germany, and Sweden. Consolidation among mutual insurers is difficult as there is

no mechanism for profitable firms to take over unprofitable firms. France passed a law in 2001 to enable the creation of hybrid Mutual Insurance Group Holdings (sociétés de groupe d'assurance mutuelle), but this was an offensive rather than a defensive strategy. Consequently, there are only a handful of such mutual insurance group holdings in existence (see, for example, AG2R and COVEA) and still no clear consolidation mechanism.

2. According to conversations with insurers, it seems that a number of small mutual insurers now rely on external solutions providers for the new actuarial, reporting, and capital requirements under Solvency II, while distributing insurance products from these solutions providers to complement their business lines. Hence, a number of smaller insurers are now serving as fronts for larger groups, although it is difficult to measure this phenomenon.

3. Low interest rates limit the additional capital charges and their significance for the smallest business. Rising interest rates, however, may trigger a wave of consolidation.

Eventually, there are reasons to think that the new regulatory framework should lead to sectoral consolidation, but the relevant data has not been examined at present. Even if consolidation took place, many non-capitalistic actors cannot be targets for consolidation. This may become a concern as the EU approaches full employment, which is not the case in every member state.

Conclusion

Although there does not appear to be any significant trend toward concentration across the financial industry, the regulatory package implemented under Commissioner Barnier may have had—and may continue to have—contrasting impacts on financial subsectors. Existing data do not provide a clear view of what is happening, and the only indicator of consolidation is the number of firms. It might be enough to say that the dominance of specialized services providers in their niche markets is unchanged overall but that banking and insurance may have been deeply affected. In the insurance sector, it is likely that increasing returns remain latent and that concentration is hampered by the low interest rate environment and the unsuitability of mutual insurers for consolidation. Workarounds are being found, and there are few concerns as delayed consolidation means relative stability of employment. The situation of the banking sector is more difficult to analyze, and it cannot be said whether complementarity between business lines will lead to cross-border mergers (mainly large Western European banks taking over smaller eastern European banks) or whether negative complementarity will result in the skimming of the most profitable activities by shadow banking boutiques. In this area, the regulator has a role to play, not only to secure bank stability but also to help banks move toward sustainable business models by enabling activity-based regulation. This is an important concern for the coming years, and Brexit changes relatively little as other countries, such as Malta, can offer a relatively relaxed regulatory environment, especially to shadow banking firms.

The focus of European data on the macroeconomic aspects of financial integration may appear to be a lack of concern, and without complete information it is difficult to make efficient choices. I have shown, however, a number of ways in which data can be dangerous. This is not a plea for ignorance but rather for further inquiry into this topic.

Appendix 1

Fallacies of Composition in Concentration Measures

Hardy, Littlewood, and Polya have shown that concentration ratios for the whole are always less than or equal to the weighted average of concentration ratios for the parts. Table 5.A1 shows why. Consider two countries (1 and 2) with five insurance firms operating in their market of equal size; thus, a 34 percent market share in one country is equal to 17 percent of the whole.

The concentration ratios in member states are almost 50 percent higher than the actual concentration ratio for the EU.

The concentration ratio of the whole is always less than the simple average of the concentration ratios of the parts, but there is no definite relative position of the true concentration ratio for the whole and the simple average of concentration ratios for the parts, as Table 5.A2 shows.

Here, the true concentration ratio takes into account the relative size of the domestic insurance markets, with the market in Country 2 being 9 times larger than the market in Country 1. The simple average thus vastly overestimates the concentration. If the proportions of countries 1 and 2 were swapped, the simple average would underestimate the true ratio.

TABLE 5.A1

Insurance Firm	Country 1	Country 2	Countries 1+2
A	34	0	17
B	33	0	16,5
C	33	33	33
D	0	33	16,5
E	0	34	17
Concentration ratio (3 first)	99	99	67

TABLE **5.A2**

Insurance Firm	Country 1	Country 2	Countries 1 & 2 Simple Average	Countries 1 & 2 Weighted Average with Weights = 0,1/0,9
A	40	30		
B	30	20		
C	20	10		
D	1	5		
Others	9	35		
Concentration ratio (3 first)	90	60	75	63

Combining those two effects, it is clear that we can deduce nothing from studying concentration ratio averages. Let us consider the following example, where firms A and B are leaders in their respective home countries and hold a competitive position in one-half of the other member states of the EU. Firm A and Firm B want to merge, but their national competition authority believes this would give them too much market power on the local market; hence, Firm A takes over Firm B's foreign subsidiaries and branches, and the local branches of Firm B are taken over by foreign competitors. The result is a decreasing concentration on the local market; hence, the average concentration ratio drops while the overall market experiences real consolidation (Table 5.A3a and Table 5.A3b).

TABLE **5.A3a** Before the Merger

Firm	Country 1	Countries 2–15	Countries 16–28
A	30	20	0
B	30	0	20
C	15	0	0
D	1	30	0
E	1	0	30
Others	23	50	50
Concentration ratio (3 first)	75	50+	50+

TABLE **5.A3b** After the Merger

Firm	Country 1	Countries 2–15	Countries 16–28
A	30	20	20
B	–	–	–
C	15	0	0
D	16	30	0
E	16	0	30
Others	23	50	50
Concentration ratio (3 first)	62	Unchanged	Unchanged

Hence an EU-wide concentration ratio must be calculated to understand the real impact on competition.

Appendix 2

Calculation of Concentration Ratios for the EU Insurance Sector

Schoenmaker and Sass (2014) provided data for the space distribution of gross written premiums of the thirty largest European insurers, that is columns 1–5 in Table 5.A4.

TABLE **5.A4**

Name	GWP (World) €m	Home	Europe	Rest of World	GWP (Europe) €m	Market Share
Generali	69,61	29%	65%	6%	65,44	5.9%
AxA	84,59	23%	50%	27%	61,75	5.6%
Allianz	72,09	25%	44%	31%	49,74	4.5%
Lloyds	31,39	82%	5%	13%	27,30	2.5%
CNP Assurances	26,44	81%	8%	11%	23,53	2.1%
Aviva	27,99	50%	34%	16%	23,51	2.1%

TABLE **5.A4** (*continued*)

Credit Agricole Assurances	22,91	66%	30%	4%	22,00	2.0%
Achmea	20,46	94%	6%	0%	20,46	1.9%
Zurich	38,84	11%	40%	49%	19,81	1.8%
Talanx	26,66	35%	32%	33%	17,86	1.6%
Ergo	17,09	77%	18%	5%	16,24	1.5%
BNP Paribas Cardif	19,81	32%	45%	23%	15,26	1.4%
Covéa	14,82	89%	10%	1%	14,67	1.3%
ING	20,28	36%	23%	41%	11,96	1.1%
Unipol	11,93	100%		0%	11,93	1.1%
Groupama	10,76	80%	20%	0%	10,76	1.0%
Aegon	19,53	19%	35%	46%	10,54	1.0%
Vienna	9,69	43%	57%	0%	9,69	0.9%
Ageas	9,95	64%	33%	3%	9,65	0.9%
Swiss Life	9,98	49%	47%	4%	9,58	0.9%
Mapfre	21,58	37%	7%	56%	9,49	0.9%
Prudential	36,81	23%	0%	77%	8,47	0.8%
RSA Insurance	11,57	36%	30%	34%	7,63	0.7%
SCOR	9,51	22%	20%	58%	4,00	0.4%
ACE	21,59	18%	0%	82%	3,89	0.4%

I used the data in the table to compute columns 6 and 7:

- (6) is (2) × [(3) + (4)]
- (7) is (6) divided by the total gross written premium, as they appear in the Insurance Europe database.

Concentration ratios can then be computed for 2012:

- CR3 (market share of the three largest insurers) = 16 percent
- CR5 = 20.6 percent
- CR10 = 30 percent
- CR20 = 40.9 percent

Notes

I would like to thank Fabrice Borel-Mathurin, Arnaud Chneiweiss, Matthieu Lacaze, Jean-Paul Laurent, Jean-François Lepetit, and Christophe Moussu for their advice and comments on earlier versions of the papers. Any errors are mine.

1. Namely, the Alternative Investment Fund Managers Directive (2011/61/EU) plus the Undertakings for Collective Investment in Transferable Securities IV (Directive 2009/65) and V (Directive 2014/91).
2. The Basel Committee deemed the EU "materially noncompliant" on Basel III on the definition of bank capital and provisions around the use of internal models (FSB, 2017).
3. Regulation (EU) No. 1024/2013 of October 15, 2013, conferring specific tasks on the European Central Bank concerning policies relating to the prudential supervision of credit institutions; Regulation (EU) No. 1022/2013 of the European Parliament and of the Council of October 22, 2013, amending Regulation (EU) No. 1093/2010 establishing a European Supervisory Authority (European Banking Authority).
4. Namely, an Innovative Technology Arrangements and Services Bill 2018, a Virtual Financial Assets Act 2018, and a Digital Innovation Authority Bill 2018.

References

Allen, F., and D. Gale. 2007. "Systemic Risk and Regulation." In *The Risks of Financial Institutions*, ed. M. Carey and R. M. Stultz. Chicago: University of Chicago Press.

AMICE. 2017. European Market InSights 2015. https://www.amice-eu.org/publications/studies_reports.aspx

Barnier, M. 2010. Speech at the Financial Integration and Stability: The Legacy of the Crisis conference, Brussels, April 12. http://europa.eu/rapid/press-release_IP-10-417_en.htm.

Bertay, Ata Can, Asli Demirgüç-Kunt, and Harry Huizinga. 2013. "Do We Need Big Banks? Evidence on Performance, Strategy and Market Discipline," *Journal of Financial Intermediation* 22 (4): 532–58.

Butler, A. W., J. Cornaggia, and U. G. Gurun. 2014. "Do Local Capital Market Conditions Affect Consumers' Borrowing Decisions?" Mimeo.

Chneiweis A., and P.-C. Pradier. 2017. "The Evolution of Insurance Regulation in the EU Since 2005." In *Financial Regulation in the EU: From Resilience to Growth*, ed. R. Douady, C. Goulet, et al. London: Palgrave MacMillan.

Claessens, Stijn, Nicholas Coleman, and Michael Donnelly. 2017. "'Low-For-Long' Interest Rates and Banks' Interest Margins and Profitability: Cross-Country Evidence." International Finance Discussion Papers, No. 1197.

EBA. 2017. Risk Assessment of the European Banking System, November. https://eba.europa.eu/risk-analysis-and-data/risk-assessment-reports.

ECB. 2017a. Financial Integration in Europe, May. https://www.ecb.europa.eu/pub/pdf/other/ecb.financialintegrationineurope201705.en.pdf.

ECB. 2017b. Report on Financial Structures, October. https://www.ecb.europa.eu/pub/pdf/other/reportonfinancialstructures201710.en.pdf.

EIOPA. 2011. "Report on the Fifth Quantitative Impact Study (QIS5) for Solvency II." EIOPA-TFQIS5-11/001. March 14.

Foata J. D. 2017. What Holds Back the French Crowdlending Market? *AltFi News*, July 20. http://www.altfi.com/article/3235_what_holds_back_the_french_crowdlending_market.

FSB. 2017. "Implementation and Effects of the G20 Financial Regulatory Reforms: Third Annual Report." http://www.fsb.org/2017/07/implementation-and-effects-of-the-g20 -financial-regulatory-reforms-third-annual-report/.

Lencquesaing, E. F. 2018. "Brexit: l'arbre qui cache la forêt." *Agefi.* http://communautes.agefi .fr/status/15002.

Oliver Wyman. 2017. *Beyond Restructuring: The New Agenda.* https://www.oliverwyman .com/content/dam/oliver-wyman/v2/publications/2017/oct/European-Banking-Report _2017.pdf.

Petracco-Giudici M., M. Marchesi, A. Rossi, N. Ndacyayisenga, and J. Cariboni. 2013. "Analysis of Possible Incentives Towards Trading Activities Implied by the Structure of Banks's Minimum Capital Requirements." In *Impact Assessment Accompanying the Document Proposal for a Regulation of the European Parliament and of the Council on Structural Measures Improving the Resilience of EU Credit Institutions . . .*, https://eur-lex .europa.eu/legal-content/EN/ALL/?uri=CELEX:52014SC0030.

Schoenmaker, Dirk. 2011. "The Financial Trilemma." *Economics Letters* 111 (February 10): 57–59.

——. 2015. "The New Banking Union Landscape in Europe: Consolidation Ahead?" *Journal of Financial Perspectives* 3: 2.

——. 2016. "European Insurance Union and How to Get There." Policy Brief . http://bruegel. org/2016/12/european-insurance-union-and-how-to-get-there/

Schoenmaker D., and J. Sass. 2014. "Cross-Border Insurance in Europe." DSF Policy Paper, No. 45, November.

Stoyanova, R., and H. Gründl. 2014. "Solvency II: A Driver for Merger and Acquisitions?" *The Geneva Papers on Risk and Insurance-Issues and Practice* 39: 417–39.

Tendon S. 2018. *Malta Blockchain Regulation Proposal: Legal Personality for DAOs and Smart Contracts*, https://chainstrategies.com/2018/03/11/malta-blockchain-regulation-proposal -legal-personality-for-daos-and-smart-contracts/amp/.

CHAPTER 6

TRENDS IN FINANCIAL MARKET REGULATION

NOLAN MCCARTY

A s a political scientist, I would like to follow up on what Sharyn O'Halloran did earlier, which was to reintroduce the political dimension to questions of policy, regulatory design, and performance.

It is exciting to participate in this discussion because five years after the onset of the crisis I wrote a book with Keith Poole and Howard Rosenthal in which we assessed the performance of the regulatory reforms undertaken. Ten years later, I am very interested to see whether some of the things we said then held forth in this assessment of reforms. Unfortunately, *Political Bubbles: Financial Crises and the Failure of American Democracy* (Princeton University Press, 2013) faced a number of problems after publication. It was the 258th book pertaining to the financial crisis to be published, so nobody got around to reading it. Moreover, the phrase "political bubbles" has now become the terminology of choice for epistemic closure that creates the effectiveness of fake news. The result is that the book was not widely read by the public and our title was co-opted.

Our principal argument, which I think resonates well with the work of O'Halloran et al., Antoine Parent, and Pierre-Charles Pradier, was that the politics of financial reform creates a procyclical regulatory behavior. Therefore, exactly when regulators should be stepping in to manage systemic risks, to destimulate the economy, or to do any of the things that we might imagine they would do to prevent financial crisis, they begin to deregulate and overstimulate the economy.

We rooted this behavior in several features of U.S. politics. We highlighted the evolution of beliefs, both the beliefs that market actors have about the true value of assets and when there is a bubble and the ideological beliefs about the proper role of markets and government in the U.S. economy. We also rooted it in the institutional incentives and constraints of various actors, whether it be Congress, the president, courts, states, or financial regulators. We argued that if you consider in depth the political economy of policymaking decisions, it is very unlikely that elected politicians will ask that the punch bowl be taken away at the appropriate time. If those incentives are not bad enough, we noted the role of interest group politics and lobbying as being an additional incentive not to intervene at appropriate times.

We developed a complementary approach to thinking about the political economics of finance that is similar to the one that Groll et al. developed in "Delegation and the Regulation of U.S. Financial Markets" (see Groll et al. 2017 in the reference list to chapter 3). Perhaps more relevant today as we consider the response to the crisis, we also examined the history of financial crises in the United States and noted four findings—features that hold across financial crises from the nineteenth century through to 2007–2008.

First, and relevant for this discussion, we noted that legislative responses to financial crises and economic downturns have typically been limited and delayed. The political incentives that prevent political institutions and actors from intervening effectively and efficiently have been borne out over time. Ideological concerns about excessive regulation have always placed some limits on responses. Thus, delays are often caused by the ideological rigidity of our parties. Second, our two political parties have very different beliefs about the relative roles of the economy and the state. Oftentimes, a transition in power is required before policies change. We noted that the silver lining of the 2007–2008 crisis was the fact of a presidential election right when the crisis was taking root—unlike 1929 when we awaited a new presidential election three and a half years into the crisis. Third, and clearly relevant for this discussion, the legislative process has often been undone by changes in power. Some rollbacks in regulations have taken place over the past year, and some regulations have been undone by executive orders or by canceling rules that were made at the end of the Obama administration. Other rollbacks used the less transparent means of nonenforcement or nonimplementation by agencies, which are now controlled by Republicans. We argued that short-term election concerns have been important in how politicians structure responses. Once those short-term election issues disappear, there is less pressure to reform. That is my background on this topic.

Let me now try to apply this to the papers by O'Halloran et al., Parent, and Pradier. These papers complement the framework I outlined and incorporate the role of beliefs and ideological preferences in institutions into regulatory decisions. However, their primary focus is on congressional decisions to delegate new authority and constrain regulatory agencies. Within that framework, it is presidents and regulators who seek to do most of the regulating. Because of their national electoral incentives, presidents pay a larger cost for political bailouts and, therefore, care much more about systemic risk. Less controversially, presidents have much better information than legislators do about that systematic risk. Thus, their framework suggests that the dynamics of regulation depend on the extent to which Congress is willing to delegate to a much more regulatory-sympathetic executive or to one that has more information.

A number of other factors should be taken seriously. It is worth considering the role of beliefs and the dynamics: how beliefs about systemic risk change over time and how those beliefs are politically inflected. Within the U.S. regulatory system, it is also worth considering the extent to which regulators and presidents really do care about controlling systemic risk and bailout costs. Clearly, they care about a constituency of an entire country, but presidents also have other roles. As leaders of their party, they are responsible for fund raising for their party. When asked why he robbed banks, Willie Sutton responded, "That's where the money is." Presidents, as party leaders, will be engaged and supportive of the financial sector.

O'Halloran et al. touch on the capture of regulators. That is a very important political dynamic. By "capture" I do not simply mean out-and-out bribery. There are many ways in which regulators see the world in a very similar way to that of the regulated industries, either as the revolving door, the dependence of regulators on industry-expertise, or even simply the cognitive capture caused by social ties. This is, however, simply a way of setting out, once more, my basic agreement with them that thinking about these decisions and how regulations have evolved over time are both an important political matter and an important economic matter.

The papers by Parent and Pradier are less explicitly political. However, there are ways in which a better engagement with the political economy of economic and financial policymaking strengthens their arguments. In "We Did Not Repeat the Errors of the Past," Parent takes on the view that restrictive monetary policies prolonged the Great Depression and that expansionary monetary policy is the right response to financial crises. As he argues, based on nonlinear versions of the McCallum and Taylor rules, it does not appear that the monetary response to the Great Depression was a policy error. There is a tantalizing suggestion that today's expansive monetary policy is a policy error, and it would be interesting to see more evidence on this.

I would like to address what I see as the underlying political dimension. The folk theory of central banks is that they are independent and insulated from political pressure. In comparison with other regulatory agencies, that is probably true, but it is probably not true in an absolute sense. Taking a central bank's independence as a starting point, it is a question of finding the right kind of rules to produce sound policy responses. I would push back on that folk theorem by suggesting that central banks are political actors—in other words, they are not perfectly insulated. Therefore, when we think about rules of behavior for central banks in times of a financial and economic crisis, we want them to be politically incentive-compatible. It is worth considering the extent to which responses are politically incentive-compatible by evaluating the history of the response in the 1930s and comparing it to the response in 2008–2009. When one thinks about the current expansionary monetary approach, I would argue that the approach is very politically implementable. Such an approach would be a very aggressive thing to do in a crisis, especially in a world in which these kinds of targeted interventions have been ruled out. In the United States, through Dodd-Frank, expansionary monetary policies are very compatible with the incentives of the Fed as well as all the political actors. On the flipside, we also want to think about whether the exit from these policies is politically incentive-compatible and whether or not there might be increased pressure on central banks to continue these policies for too long. The political aspect of that might be the catalyst that causes the policy error, as well as the misunderstanding of the underlying economics.

Considering Pradier's paper on regulation and competition in the EU, one of the critiques that we received about our book was that we were extremely critical of the U.S. response to the financial crisis, whereas most people would conclude that the U.S. response was much better than that of Europe. Pushing back on this critique, we argued that each European member state had political dysfunctions similar to those in the United States, as well as those associated with having to regulate at the EU-level. In that context, this paper nicely illustrates the political dynamics of making these decisions at the EU-level. As Pradier points out, the goals of financial regulation in the EU postcrisis were twofold: financial stability and leveling the playing field on an EU-wide basis. Once that second criterion is introduced, these policies naturally become excessively political. They become political for the firms involved in getting leveled-down and leveled-up, but they become political also as member states, whose politicians care about local employment and manipulate economic outcomes at a local level for electoral and other political reasons. It would be interesting to see the paper expand on the political dimensions of the choices that were made. Perhaps those dimensions played a larger part in the explanation of why the regulatory changes in the EU had less effect on competition and integration than the designers of those regulations had envisaged.

PART II

CREATING THE RIGHT (DIS)INCENTIVES

CHAPTER 7

PROGRESS AND CHALLENGES AFTER THE FINANCIAL CRISIS

JACOB J. LEW

Ten years after the worst financial crisis since the Great Depression, the U.S. financial system is safer and more resilient than it was before the crisis. After thirty-seven quarters, our economy continues the longest period of uninterrupted growth since World War II, with the longest period of uninterrupted jobs growth since 1939. From March 2010 to today, private employers have added more than 20 million jobs, and the unemployment rate has fallen from 10 percent to 4 percent. At the same time, the stock market has reached new highs, with the Dow breaking 26,000 from a low of 6,443.27 on March 6, 2009.

Coming out of the financial crisis, household balance sheets were in terrible shape, and many families were underwater. We have seen a tremendous amount of rebuilding of household balance sheets since then, and if you look at where households are today versus at the end of the financial crisis, a lot of repair has occurred. Some of it is because bad mortgages and bad loans have been written off; some of it is because savings have come back.

There should be much to celebrate in terms of both successful policy and the grit and determination of the American people to bounce back with a vigor that is so characteristic of the United States. But to the contrary, policymakers now act as if that were anything but the case. We hear a steady drumbeat about the state of the economy and the need to deregulate the financial sector. Ten years ago, when a struggling economy needed even more of a boost, members of Congress were reluctant to increase the deficit, but in 2017 they rushed to pass a tax cut that will greatly expand our debt as we reach full employment.

This poorly timed fiscal stimulus has already raised concerns about inflationary pressures, as monetary policy moves in the direction of tightening. Ironically, after a populist revolt driven in part by anger at public policies during the financial crisis that saved major financial institutions to prevent the recession from becoming a depression, this same tax bill confers massive economic benefits on the financial services industry while offering little to working men and women.

As we consider how things have changed ten years after the financial crisis, we need to unpack these contradictory observations and remember clearly how the last crisis developed, what tools might have made it possible to either prevent it or respond earlier, and what safeguards we need for the future.

It is impossible to predict when the next financial shock will occur, but history tells us that it is not a question of whether there will be a future crisis but whether we will see it coming in time to act effectively. I begin by looking back on the policy steps that produced this sustained recovery and long period of stable growth. I also compare our experience to the response of other countries, and I conclude with some cautionary thoughts about the dangers of significantly rolling back protections that safeguard our financial system today.

Any discussion of how we reenergized the U.S. economy has to begin by recognizing the resilience of the American people, whose determination to look ahead to better days, as always, was the engine driving our consumer economy and confidence in the future. But policy was also critical.

At the peak of the crisis, policymakers used all of the levers available to them. Fiscal stimulus provided a critical boost to a struggling economy, regulators pressed financial institutions to recognize losses and replenish their capital, and the Federal Reserve used low interest rates and both conventional and unconventional monetary tools to provide conditions for restoring economic growth. Along with fiscal and monetary policy, we also addressed structural problems that had allowed the crisis to develop and took decisive steps to repair a broken financial system. We replaced an outmoded regulatory structure that missed the signs of approaching crisis with a new approach to financial regulation. Financial reform shifted from a reactive and backward-looking focus to one that is forward-looking and aimed at identifying and addressing emerging risks.

The last comprehensive overhaul of the financial regulatory system in 1929 was a response to the crash that led to the Great Depression. Congress passed landmark laws such as the Securities Act of 1933, which required securities to be registered with the U.S. Securities and Exchange Commission (SEC), and the Glass-Steagall Act, which established the Federal Deposit Insurance Corporation (FDIC) and separated commercial and investment banking.

By 2008, the financial system was dramatically different. New products such as collateralized debt obligations, credit default swaps, asset-backed commercial paper, options, and derivatives had become routine. Much financial activity had moved from banks and securities issuers and brokers to less highly regulated firms—mortgage finance companies, hedge funds, and money market funds. New practices, such as algorithmic trading, altered the dynamics of familiar market behavior, and new points of concentrated risk created questions about our ability to see all the points where the failure of a single firm or activity might present a systemic risk. Complex overnight funding operations, such as tri-party repo, which are critical to the liquidity of traditional and non-traditional businesses, presented a new form of risk with potential global consequences in an increasingly interconnected financial world.

Globalization and technology have produced many benefits in terms of efficiency and financial access, but the interconnectedness of the global financial system also means that financial contagion can spread quickly. The financial world went through a dramatic transformation in the seventy years after the Great Depression, but the financial regulatory framework fell behind. Deregulation opened the door to more complex firms and created largely unregulated space for nontraditional financial institutions. After each intervening small crisis, improvements focused heavily on fixing specific glaring deficiencies related to the most recent problems but failed to address broad systemic change. In short, on the eve of the financial crisis, we lacked sufficient visibility to see the crisis coming. No agency had the authority and the responsibility to review the entire system and ensure its stability. Many have argued that these deficiencies directly contributed to the global financial crisis.

Faced with the collapse of Wall Street giants, immediate stabilization methods were needed to halt financial panic. Leaders in Congress worked with President Obama to fix the structural weaknesses of the regulatory system, and they enacted a new generation of comprehensive financial reforms in the Dodd-Frank Wall Street Reform and Consumer Protection Act. Unlike other laws enacted since the Great Depression, Wall Street Reform built a forward-looking system to identify and address emerging risks, no matter where the activities are conducted or by whom.

These reforms started by addressing many of the specific causes of the crisis: too little capital, risky investment strategies, lack of planning for resolution in the event of distress, opaque derivatives markets, abusive consumer practices, and poor mortgage underwriting standards. As a result, banks today have roughly twice as much capital as before the crisis. With the Volcker Rule, banks no longer have proprietary trading businesses and are required to focus solely on serving their clients rather than trading for their own benefit. The majority of derivatives are now cleared, traded transparently, and reported to regulators. Every year the Federal Reserve conducts stress tests on those banks that exceed a certain capital threshold, initially set at $50 billion, to make sure they can withstand a severe recession before they are allowed to pay dividends or reduce their capital, and these stress test results are made public to ensure greater transparency. There was a strong case to increase the minimum threshold to US$100 billion, but recent revisions to Dodd-Frank will eventually raise the limit to US$250 billion, leaving fewer than fifteen institutions subject to the stress test, and limiting visibility into other very large and interconnected banks.

A key driver of the financial crisis was the lack of planning for resolution in the event of distress for large interconnected financial companies. Financial reform requires banks to undertake continual resolution planning and work with regulators to simplify legal structures so there is a roadmap to resolve a troubled firm. Dodd-Frank created a new Orderly Liquidation Authority to help safely unwind large financial firms such as Lehman Brothers. And, in a positive step, the Trump administration opposed congressional proposals to repeal this critical authority, which is fully funded by the financial services industry. Should we face a crisis again, it is one of the few tangible tools available to stop contagion from spreading. Repealing an industry-funded tool to manage a crisis, such as Orderly Liquidation Authority, must not be mischaracterized as ending too big to fail.

Wall Street Reform also tackled abusive consumer practices that threatened financial stability. In 2008, ambiguous or nonexistent underwriting standards led to the widespread origination of risky mortgages. Fraud and abuse in the mortgage market hurt consumers and investors and contributed to a financial stability crisis. Today regulators can see and stop mortgage practices like this. With the creation of the Consumer Financial Protection Bureau (CFPB), we now have a regulator whose charge is to protect consumers and our economy from predatory practices that might cause a similar crisis in the future. Though still new, the CFPB has already made a difference. Disclosure requirements benefit more than 49 million households, and over US$12.4 billion has been returned to roughly 31 million consumers. In 2016, the CFPB revealed that Wells Fargo employees opened two million accounts without consumer permission, and the company was fined US$100 million. After receiving more than 50,700 complaints about private and federal student loan practices, the CFPB acted to return more than US$750 million to student loan borrowers. The CFPB also responded to complaints about credit card practices, payday lending abuses, and discriminatory lending.

Opponents of the CFPB tell a very different story. Actions that even many stakeholders privately describe as careful and well founded are attacked as massive government overreach. Unfortunately, this perspective has gained traction among the CFPB's current leadership. As a result, the CFPB has begun limiting and rolling back vital rules enacted during the Obama administration, including payday lending regulations designed to protect the most vulnerable from predatory practices. Despite the failure of legal challenges to the Bureau's structure, the future of this important body is far from clear, as the Trump administration projects a dim view of the Bureau's mission.

Internationally, the United States has worked with other G20 countries and with the Financial Stability Board (FSB) to promote financial standards and to reduce the risks of financial contagion spreading. Global markets are safer and more transparent thanks to increased global bank capital and a toughening of liquidity, leverage, and disclosure standards. The United States should continue to lead by example in these international efforts that help protect our own economy from external risks. But critics of financial reform often describe the FSB, incorrectly, as usurping the sovereign independence of U.S. policymakers, conjuring up conspiratorial images to undermine a project that has helped to spread high U.S. standards around the world. Importantly, higher global standards level the playing field and leave the United States more competitive than it would be if our competitors were held to lower and more dangerous standards. Still, the erosion of relations with key allies undermines our ability to spread higher standards and threatens our capacity to coordinate an international response to a future shock.

Dodd-Frank not only tried to prevent a recurrence of past crises, but also it established processes to help detect and protect against new and different threats in the future. The focus has been to identify risks, not only from particular firms but also from products, categories of activities, and markets as a whole, regardless of where activities are conducted and who is conducting them. For example, mortgage regulation applies regardless of the originating entity, whether it is a national bank, a credit union, or a mortgage finance company. New rules from the SEC or from the U.S. Commodities Futures Trading Commission (CFTC) in the derivatives market apply regardless of whether the institution involved is a commercial bank or an independent investment bank.

Wall Street Reform also tackled a glaring gap in the precrisis regulatory landscape that left no agency with authority to look broadly across the whole financial system to identify emerging signs of systemic risk. The law created the Financial Stability Oversight Council (FSOC) and charged it with precisely that mission. Chaired by the secretary of the Treasury, FSOC also includes the chairs of the Board of Governors of the Federal Reserve system, the SEC, the FDIC, and the CFTC, the directors of the CFPB and the Federal Housing Finance Administration, the head of the Office of Financial Research (OFR), and experts on insurance regulation and state practices in that area. The objective was to break down barriers between agencies and to better monitor the financial system as a whole to identify and track risks and, when necessary, take action.

A key tool given to FSOC is the power to designate nonbank financial companies for enhanced prudential standards and supervision by the Federal Reserve. This prevents firms with varying business structures from slipping through the regulatory cracks even though they are large enough to affect the entire system. An early example was General Electric (GE), one of four nonbank financial companies designated for Federal Reserve supervision. Historically a manufacturing company, GE had grown to include a large banking arm, which by 2008 accounted for more than 50 percent of its overall business. But the nonbank financial company designation is subject to annual review, and after GE made a business decision to exit the financial services business, it was dedesignated.

A great deal of energy has been invested by opponents of FSOC to characterize its actions as far-reaching and even overreaching. The image that the critics conjure up is that dozens or maybe hundreds of nonbanks were designated and that many more were likely to follow. This is simply false. The decisions were all fact-based, analytically driven, and highly circumscribed, which is why you can count on one hand the number of nonbanks designated for heightened scrutiny. After the Trump administration dedesignated Prudential Insurance, it withdrew the government's appeal in a court battle over the designation of the insurer MetLife, and there are currently no designated nonbank financial companies. Those who call for limiting the designation authority going forward increase the chance that in the future we will go back to a system in which we lack the radar to see a problem coming.

FSOC has also reviewed the different risks that may be associated with the growing role of asset managers and hedge funds. From 2008 to 2016, assets under management of the twenty largest asset managers in the United States rose from US$20 trillion to over US$34 trillion. And in the subsequent year, the total increased to some US$40 trillion. FSOC decided to take a closer look at the use of leverage by hedge funds through a newly created interagency hedge fund working group. No single regulator currently has the ability to assess the risk hedge funds pose to financial stability, and FSOC is uniquely positioned to bring together regulators to share information and review a cohesive strategy. This working group is consistent with the essential mission laid out in Dodd-Frank, and it is crucial to the goal of looking ahead, not in the rearview mirror, to identify future risks. The standard of effectiveness is not simply how much action is taken but whether regulators are asking the right questions to understand when they might need to act.

In the years after the financial crisis, the United States recovered more quickly than other developed economies. Underlying the recovery in the United States was a clear sense that the U.S. financial system is much safer than it was before the crisis. In Europe, the United Kingdom also moved swiftly on multiple fronts, particularly in the area of financial reform and restoring the soundness of the financial system, but the European Union was slower to act. And with the political winds blowing against more mutualized action, the work of fully reforming deposit insurance and other steps to protect the European financial system remains incomplete. In Japan, the policy of Abenomics calls for the use of three arrows—fiscal, monetary, and structural reforms—but coordinating these tools to be effective has proved challenging, and the benefits of mutually reinforcing policy moves has not been fully realized. In both Europe and Japan, stable and organic growth did eventually emerge, but the lost years can be measured in reduced economic benefits to their citizens, and economic headwinds are growing.

Policymakers are often tempted during times of stability to roll back regulations, weaken reforms, and reduce oversight. Facts matter, and ten years after the financial crisis proposals to disempower the CFPB, repeal the Orderly Liquidation Authority, weaken the FSB, roll back the authority of FSOC, or to curtail the activities of the OFR must be seen for what they are: a return to the far riskier world we lived in before the financial crisis. We need to be extremely skeptical about proposals that would take down the radar to detect a future crisis or eliminate tools we may need to address such a crisis. It would leave our economy on weaker footing to return to the world as it existed in 2007 when a financial crisis came very close to causing a depression. The long growth that we have enjoyed since the recovery began in 2009 is built on the foundation of a safer and sounder financial system.

In the decade since the financial crisis, we have all become more focused on exposures to cyberattacks or accidents, and it is important that this focus remain. Cybersecurity went from being an issue for technical teams to requiring attention from senior executives—it belongs with the Secretary and the CEO. Even though I am not a technical expert on cybersecurity, I made it clear within the Treasury Department that it was my responsibility to make sure we set appropriate standards inside Treasury and across the financial sector. One of the first things I did when I became secretary was to make sure we could share classified information to cleared private sector actors, so if we had information about a threat, we could pass it along. I also made it a priority to set an expectation that targeted firms would overcome their fear of reputational damage to come forward, say "we've been attacked," and share information. It is important there not be any shame associated with saying you have been attacked. Every individual and institution, public and private, is exposed to cyber risks, and this risk is not going away.

I conclude with one further observation about the upside-down nature of politics in the United States today. Notwithstanding the fact that taxpayers were fully repaid for the direct costs of using tax dollars to recapitalize failing banks, anger that elites and financial institutions were bailed out from a financial crisis that they created helped to stoke populism in both major political parties. This populism shaped a presidential election that weakened traditional candidates and led to a rejection of elites that makes it fair game in political discourse to challenge experts and to deny facts. Part of what makes people angry is that the indirect cost of the Great Recession left lasting scars and a sense that many who made the decisions that led to the crisis are now doing well, whereas working people feel stuck in jobs with stagnant wages and uncertain futures. This only underscores the bitter irony that the winners from the recent tax bill are the very elites who are so resented.

The White House and Congress moved heaven and earth to pass a tax bill before the American people could fully see that the legislation provides tremendous benefits for those very elites who were the object of public scorn in the last election. The tax cut spends money we do not have and will run up the debt perhaps by US$2 trillion over the next ten years, and it does little or nothing for most working men and women. Instead, the benefits have accrued to the very wealthy and corporations, and tax savings are more often leading to stock buybacks rather than investments in capital projects or workers.

The challenges we face in the economy of the future are different from the aftermath of the financial crisis, and the question of how we maintain stable middle-class incomes is a separate question from addressing the aftermath of the financial crisis. This tax bill, for example, could have been a moment to take steps to help middle-class families rebuild their financial foundations, addressing the concerns of those worried about job stability, how to pay for child care so that both parents can work, and the threat that categories of jobs (like driving trucks) they now rely on may not exist in five, ten, or fifteen years. It was a lost opportunity that leaves the coffers bare for future efforts to address middle-class anxiety. When the time comes to pay the bill, as it always does, programs like Social Security, Medicare, and Medicaid, which are critical to the security of the middle class, will not be safe from proposed cuts.

The case for the tax bill rested on denying mainstream fact-based analysis and leaving no time for serious review or debate. That approach must not be allowed to shape how we handle proposed changes to the financial system. The progress we have made must be understood, and facts must be the foundation for any change. Weakening financial stability and hurting our economy is not reform. Working men and women count on a sound economy that produces reliable paychecks to make ends meet every month, and financial reform has helped create sustained economic growth. We need to be vigilant as proposals to roll back reforms suggest that we roll back the clock.

CHAPTER 8

BANKS AND TAX HAVENS

First Evidence Based on Country-by-Country Reporting

VINCENT BOUVATIER, GUNTHER CAPELLE-BLANCARD,
AND ANNE-LAURE DELATTE

Increased transparency regarding the activities of institutions, and in particular regarding profits made, taxes paid and subsidies received, is essential for regaining the trust of citizens of the Union in the financial sector. Mandatory reporting in that area can therefore be seen as an important element of the corporate responsibility of institutions towards stakeholders and society.

—Recital (52) to CRD IV

I n the aftermath of the "great financial crisis," several scandals have shed light on the presence of banks in tax havens[1] (UBS, 2008; Offshore leaks, 2013; Luxleaks, 2014; Swissleaks, 2015; Panama Papers, 2016; Paradise Papers, 2017). The leaks documented the intermediation role of global banks in setting up shell companies, foundations, and trusts to ease tax avoidance for their clients. Although the topic made headlines, there is little academic evidence regarding banks in tax havens. The main objective of this study is to gauge the role played by banks in facilitating tax and transparency avoidance. At stake is whether a more stringent regulation of bank activity in tax havens can reduce tax evasion and money laundering.

The academic research on tax havens accounts for less than 0.4 percent of the academic literature on taxation,[2] which is probably related to the scarcity of data on tax havens. A first part of the literature is based on macroeconomic (aggregated) data and examines the characteristics of the countries or jurisdictions considered as tax havens (Hampton and Christensen, 2002; Hines, 2005, 2010; Dharmapala and Hines, 2009). A number of works on offshore financial centers (OFCs) address, somewhat independently, similar issues (Masciandaro, 2006; Rose and Spiegel, 2007). A second stream of papers relies on aggregated data with a focus on cross-border deposits and capital flows (Grilli, 1989; Alworth and Andresen,1992; Huizinga and Nicod`eme, 2004; Lane and Milesi-Ferretti, 2011). Third, a number of papers specifically examine the banking sector (Demirgc-Kunt and Huizinga, 2001; Zucman, 2013; Johannesen and Zucman, 2014). Overall, cross-country studies on tax havens use incomplete data sets and no papers focus on the financial or banking sector at the microeconomic level, using individual data. Our study attempts to address this gap.

Since January 1, 2015, all European banks regarded as global systemically important institutions are required to publicly disclose country-by-country data, as stipulated by the Capital Requirements Directive (CRD) IV of the EU. This paper precisely exploits newly published data to assess the role of tax havens in international banking. These new data are individual, regulatory, and comprehensive. The CRD IV requires all the largest banks to report activity in every jurisdiction where they have a commercial presence. In other words, for the first time, we work on a data set covering the location choices of banks at the individual level without missing data.

Our data include the reported information, on a country-by-country level, for the largest EU banks: turnover, number of employees, profit or loss before tax, tax on profit or loss, and public subsidies received. We focus on activity through the information on turnover. The data set is cross-sectional and concerns 2015, the first year for which the reports were available. Bank headquarters are located in ten EU countries; their foreign affiliates have activity in 138 countries in total, including approximately thirty tax havens jurisdictions. Tax havens represent 0.8 percent of our sample in terms of population, 2 percent in terms of gross domestic product (GDP), but EU banks record 18 percent of their foreign turnover and 29 percent of their foreign profit in these countries.

The main new findings are: (1) tax havens generate an extra 200 percent presence of foreign banks; (2) the favorite destinations of tax evasion intermediated by European banks are Luxembourg and Monaco; (3) British and German banks display the most aggressive strategies in tax havens; (4) new transparency requirements imposed in 2015 have not changed European banks' commercial presence in tax havens; and (5) banks intermediate €550 billion in offshore assets, which is 5 percent of their home countries' GDP.

Section two describes our database and provides some stylized facts. Section three presents the main results. Section four offers conclusions.

New Data on International Banking Activity

As the basis of the usual recommendations to preclude aggressive tax planning and profit shifting, country-by-country reporting (CbCR) requires the largest firms to provide detailed information regarding the allocation of their income, profit, and taxes. From 2015, according to CRD IV of the EU (Article 89), all European banking groups with a consolidated turnover above €750 million are required to publicly disclose the activity of all their affiliates (subsidiaries and branches). More precisely, the public CbCR requires banks to disclose information on a country-by-country basis together with their financial statements on the following items: turnover (net banking income), number of employees (on a full-time equivalent basis), profit or loss before tax, tax on profit or loss, and public subsidies received.

Our sample is composed of the thirty-seven largest EU banks in terms of assets, located in ten EU countries in 2015. All these banks are large, with a leverage ratio exposure measure above €200 billion and, therefore, are considered as either Global- or Local-Systemically Important Institutions (SIIs) by the European Banking Authority.

The banks in our sample employ 1.2 million people in 138 partner countries and record a total turnover of €278 billion abroad. They have foreign affiliates in one to seventy-nine countries and are located in twenty-six tax havens (out of forty or so usually considered). Table 8.1 displays country summary statistics.

We extend the number of destination countries to 228 to account for the absence of activity. The small tax havens correspond to countries of fewer than two million people. The small tax havens represent 0.1 percent of our sample in terms of population and 0.3 percent in terms of GDP; big tax havens represent 0.7 percent of the population sample and 1.7 percent of the GDP. Tax havens experienced high level of income per capita (more than twice that of the rest of the world). Unsurprisingly, the implicit tax rate is much lower in tax havens, 5 percent versus 17 percent, and the financial infrastructures are more developed.

Table 8.2 displays the turnover, number of employees, profits, and tax on profits of foreign affiliates reported by the EU banks included in our sample. The activity is broken down into nontax havens, small tax havens, and big tax havens. EU banks in our sample employ about 1.2 million people abroad and a little more than 100,000 people in tax havens. Although tax havens represent only 9 percent of the workforce abroad, they account for 18 percent of the turnover and 29 percent of the profits recorded abroad. More specifically, small tax havens represent 5 percent of the turnover recorded abroad, only 2 percent of the employment, 10 percent of the profits, and 5 percent of the taxes.

TABLE **8.1** Countries Summary Statistics

		Nonhavens	Small Havens	Big Havens
Number of countries		185	35	8
GDP (PPP, EUR bn)	Total	112,000	308	1,880
	Av.	605	9	235
	%	98.1%	0.3%	1.6%
Population (thousand)	Total	7,260,000	6,942	48,500
	Av.	39,300	198	6,064
	%	99.2%	0.1%	0.7%
GDP/capita (EUR)	Total	15,427	44,369	38,763
	Av.	17,786	36,643	38,763
Implicit tax rate		17%	5%	5%
Financial infrastructures		54	67	68

Source: Authors. Effective tax rate is taken from the Bureau of Economic Analysis. Financial infrastructure development is measured with the GFSI Index from Z/Yen Group.

TABLE **8.2** Bank Activities in Foreign Countries

	Nonhavens (112)	Small Havens (19)	Big Havens (7)	Tax Havens (26)	Total Foreign (138)
Turnover	229,959	13,585	34,959	48,544	278,503
In % of foreign	83%	5%	13%	17%	100%
Employees	1,116,115	22,649	81,553	104,202	1,220,317
In % of foreign	91%	2%	7%	9%	100%
Profits	54,126	7,599	14,492	22,090	76,216
In % of foreign	71%	10%	19%	29%	100%
Tax on profits	15,016	827	1,695	2,521	17,538
In % of foreign	86%	5%	10%	14%	100%
Turnover/GDP	0.2%	4.9%	1.9%	2.2%	0.3%
Turnover/employees	21%	61%	43%	47%	23%
Profit/turnover	24%	55%	41%	45%	27%
Profit/employees	5%	34%	18%	21%	6%
Tax/profit	28%	11%	12%	11%	23%

Source: CbCR (2015).

Note: The thirty-seven largest European banks are represented. The sample includes only countries in which European banks declare affiliates.

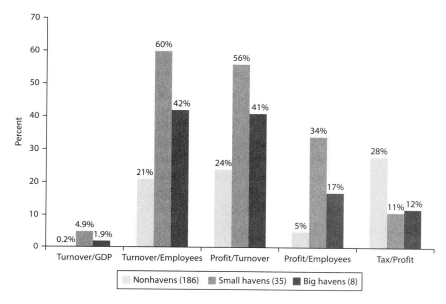

Figure 8.1 Business ratios across jurisdictions

Source: Authors, based on CbCR (2015). See Bouvatier et al. (2018)

Figure 8.1 compares business ratios across jurisdictions. Turnover as a ratio of GDP is 9.5 times higher in big tax havens and 24.5 times higher in small tax havens. Productivity calculated as the turnover per employee is twice as high in big tax havens as in nontax havens and three times higher in small tax havens. The profit rate is 1.7 higher in big tax havens and 2.5 higher in small tax havens (profit/turnover). Lastly, the implicit tax rate in tax havens is 2.5 times lower than in nontax havens (tax/profit). In total, raw statistics indicate that banks record significantly higher activity and profit per employee in tax havens than in nonhaven countries.

Some Unpleasant Geography

In Bouvatier et al. (2018), we depart from a standard gravity specification of banks' foreign presence by including tax havens, determinants, and we rely on a Poisson pseudo-maximum likelihood estimator to account for zeros in the dependent variable (see paper for details). Beyond the traditional gravity factors (the size of the country and the geographical and cultural distance), the effect of a tax haven dummy is significant: tax havens attract a greater commercial presence than nontax havens once we control for standard factors. More precisely, the average effect of being a tax haven is an additional presence of 200 percent, that is, a multiplication by 3 of the activity compared to nonhavens.[3] This first estimate informs us about the average magnitude of tax havens' effect, but there is a large heterogeneity among countries.

Which countries attract the greatest unexplained banking activity? The majority of tax havens display a low abnormal banking activity and serve only few banks (rarely more than 2 percent); a few tax havens (the Channel Islands, Hong Kong) are more aggressive and entertain specific bilateral relationships for historical reasons. In turn, Luxembourg benefits from a widespread presence of foreign banks, which record a substantial abnormal activity.

Which banks are the most active in intermediating tax evasion? Our model uncovers null or negative abnormal activity in tax havens for the Austrian and Spanish banks in our sample. In turn, we observe a group of countries in the middle horizontal band where abnormal activity represents less than 3 percent of their global activity (Denmark, Sweden, Italy, the Netherlands, and France). It is worth observing that the French banks, which have a strong foreign commercial presence in general, report a widespread presence in tax havens, yet with a quasi-null abnormal activity (0.9 percent of their global activity). In comparison, data reveal that two British banks and two German banks are particularly aggressive: Standard Chartered and HSBC have abnormal activity in havens equal to 21 percent and 17 percent of their global activity, respectively; and DZBank's and Deutsche Bank's abnormal activity in havens represents 15 percent and 8 percent of their global activity, respectively.

What is the bank contribution to tax evasion intermediation? Banks are part of a chain of financial intermediaries between tax evaders and tax havens, including also mutual funds, funds of funds, insurance companies, et cetera. To assess the relative role banks play in intermediating wealthy individuals' offshore wealth, we can get an approximate idea of corresponding offshore assets from turnover (income) amounts using banks' business ratios (cost to income and cost to assets). More precisely, we sum up the abnormal turnover for all country j listed as a tax haven, which yields the euro amount of unexplained banking activity in tax havens of all banks in our sample. We apply the income to deposit ratio collected from the World Bank GFD database to this euro amount to get the corresponding amount of offshore assets. In total, we estimate that the banks in our sample contribute to intermediating a total of €549.2 billion in offshore assets, that is 4.2 percent of the contributing countries GDP (see Bouvatier et al., 2018).

Finally, in Bouvatier et al. (2018) (using a difference-in-difference approach), we do not observe any impact of the CbCR in 2016 on the commercial presence of banks in tax havens.

Conclusion

The main contribution of this paper is to explore the geography of banking: this is the first paper to take advantage of the CbCR data set, which offers a comprehensive and reliable coverage of firm location choices. By providing a number of new stylized facts on the drivers of the activities of banks in tax havens, we underline the value of such data. As expected by its proponents, the CbCR is an effective tool to enhance transparency.

This new data set raises subsequent research avenues. First, the CbCR under CRD IV also applies to investment firms, that is, mainly broker-dealers and asset management entities. A natural continuation is to focus on these much less-documented entities. Second, only 2015 data are so far available. There is no requirement to report prior years' comparative figures, but in the future we shall be able to examine changes in banking locations by exploiting exogenous changes of the environment. Finally, the CbCR has first been applied to financial institutions, but there are currently strong pressures in Europe and the United States to impose the CbCR on all large multinational enterprises. Such an extension would constitute a highly valuable source in corporate finance research.

It is also possible to improve the collection of information, at no significant cost. For now, the data need to be manually and separately collected for each bank. The data are usually provided within the financial reports, not readily available, and with notable differences across banks. Several recommendations of the International Open Data Charter could be applied.[4] First, the data need to be provided in open, multiple, and standardized formats, so data can more easily be processed and used by a wide range of parties (scholars, journalists, NGOs). Second, additional information reporting could be required without additional costs: the number of subsidiaries and some aggregate items of the balance sheet to better reflect affiliates' underlying activities, such as total assets. Third, the data need to be published on a central portal managed, for example, by the European Central Bank or the European Banking Authority.

Notes

The authors thank Jezabel Couppey-Soubeyran, Mathieu Crozet, Dhammika Dharmapala, Thierry Mayer, Tom Neubig, Franz Reiter, Bert Scholtens, Shyam Sunder, Farid Toubal, Michael Troege, Gabriel Zucman, and the participants of the 2017 National Tax Association Conference, Princeton University EU seminar, Columbia University (SIPA) seminar, CEPII, EU Policy Network, Groningen University, and University of Buenos Aires for helpful discussions. They thank Manon Aubry and Thomas Dauphin from Oxfam for sharing their database. They also gratefully acknowledge Mona Barake and Pranav Garg for excellent research assistance. This research has benefited from the support of Research fellowships 2016–2017 with reference 2016 ECFIN 013/B. The usual disclaimer applies. This synopsis is a short version, prepared for the Conference at Columbia University. See Bouvatier et al. (2018) for the details.

1. Dharmapala and Hines (2009, 1058) propose the following definition for tax havens: "locations with very low tax rates and other tax attributes designed to appeal to foreign investors." The Organization for Economic Cooperation and Development (OECD) adds the lack of transparency and of exchange of information as a common feature of these countries/jurisdictions.
2. Comprehensive and stimulating academic surveys on international tax competition, profit shifting by multinational enterprises (MNEs), and tax havens are provided by Devereux (2007), Hines (2007, 2010), Dharmapala (2008, 2014), and Zucman (2015).
3. The result is confirmed with various alternative specifications.
4. In July 2013, G8 leaders signed the G8 Open Data Charter, which outlined a set of core open data principles. See http://opendatacharter.net/.

References

Alworth, J., and S. Andresen. 1992. "The Determinants of Cross-Border Non-bank Deposits and the Competitiveness of Financial Market Centres." *Money Affairs* 5 (2): 105–33.

Bouvatier, V., G. Capelle-Blancard, and A.-L. Delatte. 2018. "Banks Defy Gravity." Working Paper 2017-16, CEPII research center.

Demirgc-Kunt, A., and H. Huizinga. 2001. "The Taxation of Domestic and Foreign Banking." *Journal of Public Economics* 79: 429–53.

Devereux, M. 2007. "The Impact of Taxation on the Location of Capital, Firms and Profit: A Survey of Empirical Evidence." Oxford University Centre for Business Taxation. Working Paper 07/02.

Dharmapala, D. 2008. "What Problems and Opportunities Are Created by Tax Havens?" *Oxford Review of Economic Policy* 24: 661–79.

——. 2014. "What Do We Know About Base Erosion and Profit Shifting? A Review of the Empirical Literature." *Fiscal Studies* 35 (4): 421–48.

Dharmapala, D., and J. R. Hines Jr. 2009. "Which Countries Become Tax Havens?" *Journal of Public Economics* 93: 1058–68.

Grilli, V. 1989. "Europe 1992: Issues and Prospects for the Financial Markets." *Economic Policy* (October), 4 (9): 387–421.

Hampton, M. P., and J. Christensen. 2002. "Offshore Pariahs? Small Island Economies, Tax Havens, and the Reconfiguration of Global Finance." *World Development* 30 (9): 1657–73.

Hines, J., Jr. 2005. Do Tax Havens Flourish?" In *Tax Policy and the Economy*, ed. J. Poterba, 65–99. Cambridge: MIT Press.

——. 2007. "Corporate Taxation and International Competition." In *Taxing Corporate Income in the 21st Century*, ed. A. Auerbach, J. Hines, J. Slemrod, and J. Poterba, 65–99. Cambridge, UK: Cambridge University Press.

——. (2010). "Treasure Islands." *Journal of Economic Perspectives*, 24 (4):103–25.

Hines, J., Jr., and E. Rice. 1994. "Fiscal Paradise: Foreign Tax Havens and American Business." *Quarterly Journal of Economics* 109: 149–82.

Huizinga, H., and G. Nicod`eme. 2004. "Are International Deposits Tax-Driven." *Journal of Public Economics* 88 (6): 1093–1118.

Johannesen, N., and G. Zucman. 2014. "The End of Bank Secrecy? An Evaluation of the G20 Tax Haven Crackdown." *American Economic Journal: Economic Policy* 6 (1): 65–91.

Lane, P., and G. Milesi-Ferretti. 2011. "Cross-Border Investment in Small International Financial Centres." *International Finance* 14 (2): 301–30.

Masciandaro, D. 2006. "Offshore Financial Centres: Explaining the Regulation." Paolo Baffi Centre Bocconi University, Working Paper 170.

Rose, A. K., and M. M. Spiegel. 2007. "Offshore Financial Centres: Parasites or Symbionts?" *Economic Journal* 117 (523): 1310–35.

Zucman, G. 2013. "The Missing Wealth of Nations: Are Europe and the US Net Debtors or Net Creditors?" *Quarterly Journal of Economics* 128 (3): 1321–64.

——. 2015. *The Hidden Wealth of Nations: The Scourge of Tax Havens.* Chicago: University of Chicago Press.

CHAPTER 9

"DYNAMIC PRECAUTION" IN MAINTAINING FINANCIAL STABILITY

The Importance of FSOC

JEFFREY N. GORDON

T his chapter addresses the problem of maintaining financial stability once the immediate shock of the financial crisis of 2007–2009 has subsided. Financial stability is the ultimate public good; in particular, it's "nonexcludable," meaning that every institution, financial and nonfinancial, and every person benefits from financial stability. Yet maintaining financial stability is costly. Institutions face seemingly onerous constraints on their plans and activities, and we have set up a complicated administrative and supervisory apparatus in the name of maintaining financial stability.

I encounter this problem—the problem of memory and belief—with every fall's teaching in a course called "Financial Crises and Regulatory Responses" (cotaught with economist Patrick Bolton, for law and business students). The course focuses on the recurrent nature of financial crises rather than their singularity; nevertheless, we devote particular energy to the financial crisis that began to unfold in 2007. Unlike the savings and loan crisis of the 1980s, the crisis of 2007–2009 upended the entire U.S. financial sector and spread globally. The economic impact is measured in trillions of dollars, a massive regulatory project is still under way, and the political consequences continue to ramify in the United States and its global partners. And this is in the aftermath of a "good" crisis outcome.

One ambition of the course is to give students a sense of the existential dread of living through the crisis while cognizant of the fear and uncertainty. In fall 2008 I was coteaching a course in comparative corporate governance. This was overtaken by the cascading failures of Lehman Brothers, AIG, and the Reserve Primary Fund, then followed by the fitful efforts of congressional rescue. Stock markets and debt markets continued to deteriorate. On the way to class on many a day, I wondered whether I should draw extra money from the ATM because, who knew, maybe the ATM will be closed down later. Sophisticated people scrambled to divide their assets among insured deposit accounts at multiple banks. The day Congress voted down the initial rescue legislation—the Troubled Assets Relief Program (TARP)—was a moment of dysfunction piled on dystopia, a day *New York Times* columnist Tom Friedman described as one of the three days in his lifetime when he feared for the future of the United States. The other two were the assassination of John F. Kennedy and the 9/11 attacks. Even after the TARP infusions—alongside the guarantees of money market fund issuances, bank deposits and loans, and the massive liquidity injections, even after all of those extraordinary measures—the financial sector continued to unravel, and the economy went into a tailspin. These effects were not limited to the United States. The globalizing pattern of finance, reflected both in global financial firms and global financial flows, spread the disorder worldwide, particularly to western Europe.

Most alarming was the risk of a financial collapse that would rip apart the post–World War II economic order. For all its imperfections, that economic order had transferred nationalistic impulses away from the military realm to the economic realm and produced interlinked systems of trade and production that would reinforce cooperative rather than competitive impulses at times of stress. We in the United States had been living in a sweet spot in world history, and it all seemed very much at risk. What would Great Depression II look like? And what twist in U.S. and world history would follow?

The worst was avoided, as we now know. The emergency measures were necessary but not sufficient, however. What definitively turned confidence around was the first stress tests undertaken in the early spring of 2009, which demonstrated that the likely loan losses of major U.S. financial institutions would not render them insolvent. This demonstration was made credible by the assurance that TARP funds would be available to backstop the institutions that would otherwise fail the stress test. The stress test, the fiscal stimulus enacted in the early months of the Obama presidency, the fall 2008 financial sector emergency measures, and the rescue of the automobile industry—all of it, in proportions we can never know, made the difference.

Even though the worst had been avoided, the costs were still enormous. These costs were not just the lost trillions of dollars in gross domestic product (GDP), the millions unemployed, and the lives disrupted, but also the terrible political costs. The actions that were necessary to save the financial system from collapse (and to avoid an even worse economic and human outcome) produced a pattern of winners and losers that could not be defended on any principle of desert. The consequence of "bailouts" for Wall Street alongside defaults for Main Street and foreclosures and job loss for ordinary citizens produced intense and long-lasting resentments. The disparate outcomes fed the belief that the system was "rigged" and that the experts who failed to foretell the danger and then insisted on the remedies were in on the rigging. This, in turn, makes all of the problems of a complex global economy more difficult to resolve and compromises more difficult to accept. To repeat, this political turn followed a crisis resolution that, at least in the United States, was on the high side of reasonable expectations.

The lesson of the financial crisis of 2007–2009 is that the maintenance of financial stability must be the apex goal of the financial regulatory system. As noted above, financial stability is costly to maintain. For example, under the present regulatory structure, the largest banks must limit payouts to shareholders and maintain a prescribed ratio of assets to shareholders' equity, using two different measures: one adjusted for the purported riskiness of bank assets, the other without such adjustments. These banks face asset composition and funding rules that will limit the amount of liquidity and maturity transformation they can undertake. Efforts to offload liabilities through securitization are constrained by risk-retention requirements. Proprietary trading is off limits, and the banks must monitor the boundaries between "market-making," which is permitted, and proprietary trading, which is not. This description hardly exhausts the list of regulatory constraints nor weighs the compliance costs of staying within the rules.

Part of the reason Bolton and I teach our course is to put successive generations of students—each further distant from a lived experience—into that existential moment, so they may have a glimmer of the urgency that justifies those costs. For example, when reading the staff memo that accompanied the financial deregulatory proposal that emerged from the House Financial Services Committee in summer 2016, the so-called CHOICE Act (short for **C**reating **H**ope and **O**pportunity for **I**nvestors, **C**onsumers, and **E**ntrepreneurs),[1] those who lived through the crisis will probably think it was written by a smart twenty-seven-year-old staffer who was a sophomore in college as the world teetered on the edge of Great Depression II.

One very important lesson of the financial crisis is that the maintenance of financial stability is an ongoing project that requires an approach of what I will call "dynamic precaution." The threat comes along four different avenues: (1) the effort by institutions within the financial stability regime to find loopholes and other sorts of regulatory arbitrage to avoid the regime's costs; (2) the effort by institutions outside of the regime to produce financial intermediation services that are the functional equivalent of within-the-regime firms; (3) "innovation," which includes the unexpected consequence of existing rules in new application; and (4) macroeconomic forces that magnify the threat of financial instability. These elements, separately and in combination, can reshape the financial system; these elements can move a formerly stable system into one that is systemically susceptible to either an internal or external shock.

Dynamic precaution calls for a governmental institution whose principal function is to monitor the financial system as it evolves, call attention to emerging risks to financial stability, and then catalyze the necessary regulatory intervention. This institution should sit outside the existing regulatory agencies. This distance will cost some deep knowledge about particular institutions and financial system segments, but it also avoids the blinders associated with the inevitable desire of a functional regulator to advance the interests of its regulatory clients. The institution must also be obliged to disclose what it observes to the public and to the legislative branches. Such required disclosure provides some measure of independence from actors who may have political and economic investments in existing arrangements and also puts other responsible actors on public notice. This general scheme is embodied in the Financial Stability Oversight Council (FSOC), created by the Dodd-Frank Act, and its companion, the Office of Financial Research.

Financial systems are a bundle of financial activities and financial institutions (entities). Although the way certain financial activities are carried out can create financial fragility and add to systemic risk, ultimately it is institutions that carry on the business of financial intermediation. It was the failure and near-failure of financial institutions that produced the sudden stop in the world economy in the fall of 2008. These points appear to have been confused in current efforts by the U.S. Treasury to cut back the FSOC's power to designate additional financial institutions as systemically important and thus subject to a regime of "enhanced prudential supervision" established by the Federal Reserve Board.

In developing a case for dynamic precaution, I first explain why financial institutions need to remain the focus of the FSOC regime even while observation and regulation aimed at activities is also important. Second, I describe how FSOC can serve dynamic precaution by using its designation authority to negotiate "off-ramps" for firms whose instability or failure would otherwise have systemic implications. And third, I discuss the reason cost-benefit analysis can play only a limited role in financial regulation if the maintenance of financial stability is the apex goal.

Activities and Institutions

Why Activities Matter

There is no doubt that the structure and volume of financial activities can measurably affect the level of systemic risk generally and the fragility of particular institutions. The case of derivatives (or "swaps") provides a good demonstration of activity-based concerns that are transinstitutional, as illustrated by these three examples. First, derivatives trading was initially undertaken among a small group of financial firms, especially investment banks, and the trades were documented via casual record keeping even as the volume of derivatives trading vastly increased. This was perceived as laying the groundwork for a systemic "back office" crisis similar to securities trading in the late 1960s. Prodded by the New York Fed, an industry task force undertook a concerted effort to resolve this activity-based risk, which, as one participant put it, was "one dog that didn't bark" during the financial crisis.

Second, prior to the financial crisis, most derivatives were entered into on a bilateral basis, meaning that all the players were exposed to counterparty risk. The failure of Lehman Brothers meant that millions of open positions needed to be closed (under applicable netting rules). The uncertainty about the incidence of financial losses in this process on firms that were highly leveraged was certainly a factor in the financial freeze in the fall of 2008.

Third, because of the Lehman Brothers experience and because of the unexpected (and catastrophic) warehousing of credit default swap risk by AIG, one of the major Dodd-Frank Act reforms now shifts most derivative trading activity to Central Clearing Parties (CCP). This means that each side of a "swap" is protected by the clearinghouse, backed by its capitalization and additional callable commitments of clearinghouse members. The CCP also gets additional protection as a "Financial Market Utility" as described in the Dodd-Frank Act.

The Dodd-Frank Act also contains many other instances of activity-based regulation. For example, it establishes a regime of "safe securitization," which tries to control the moral hazard in origination by requiring a securitizer to retain a certain portion of risk that otherwise would be transferred. The Volcker rule's separation of "market-making" (permitted for a large bank holding company) and "proprietary trading" (forbidden) is an effort to place certain risky activities outside of systemically important financial firms. Financial fragility can be created by the activities that facilitate short-term finance. This funding strategy comes with greater susceptibility to runs, the consequent sudden need to shrink balance sheets, which in turn yields fire sale pricing and the resultant threats to bank solvency. The activities in question include securities lending and the short-term secured lending known as "repo." Regulation can target the activity directly, for example, by focusing on the value stability of the underlying collateral or by devising settlement protocols that reduce the daylight risk of the banks that intermediate the tri-party repo market. But sometimes activity risks are best addressed at the institutional level, by limiting reliance on short-term wholesale finance by large financial firms, as exemplified in the so-called "Net Stable Funding Ratio" in the Basel III rules.

Institutions (Entities) Are Nevertheless the Critical Regulatory Focus

Financial institutions bundle various financial activities. Thus, notwithstanding the independent importance of activities in systemic oversight, institutions must be the critical regulatory focus. All activities are channeled through institutions. Institutions are, in effect, bundles of activities. The fragility of the institution is commonly a function of the elements of that bundle, including the weighting. The risks associated with short-term wholesale finance, for example, depend upon its importance to the institution's balance sheet, both as a proportion of its liabilities and its liquid assets.

Institutions are nodes in the financial system. They bring together customers, markets, fund flows, relationships, and provide multiple sorts of interconnection. The failure of a large financial firm tears a hole in that network. Switching and recontracting costs can disrupt the real economy. The financial crisis provided strong evidence that the failure of even a single important financial firm could ramify in escalating ways. This is why the Dodd-Frank Act took up systemically important financial firms so extensively, in three particular respects: first, in empowering the Federal Reserve to devise a system of "enhanced prudential standards" to minimize failure risk for a category of firms that Congress deemed to be systemically important both because of their direct linkage to the banking system and their asset size; second, in devising a general strategy for "orderly liquidation" of a failed or failing institution deemed to be systemically important to minimize the knock-on effects of its failure; and third, in giving FSOC the power to designate "nonbank" financial institutions as systemically important and thus subject to enhanced prudential standards as devised by the Fed.

FSOC Designation Authority and Dynamic Precaution

FSOC designation authority, which has been used sparingly, has nevertheless become a source of great controversy. In appreciating the critical role of this designation authority, it is important to recall the financial crisis itself. The crisis was, in historical terms, a "banking crisis." Such a crisis generally arises from a credit-fueled asset bubble in which much of the banking sector faces insolvency when the bubble collapses and loans go unpaid. Insolvent banks will default on obligations to depositors and other creditors and, of course, can no longer funnel credit to businesses or consumers. Bank insolvencies also can disrupt the payments system, meaning that consumers and businesses lose the channels for making or receiving payments for goods and services. Before deposit insurance, the risk of bank insolvency could readily become self-fulfilling because a run by self-protecting depositors could force the rapid sale of a bank's assets at "fire sale" prices, producing insolvency even for relatively well-capitalized banks. Banking crises are commonly associated with real estate, in the belief that the supply inelasticity of real estate assets means that prices will invariably increase, but, as exemplified by the stock market crash of 1929, banking crises can be associated with any asset that investors mistakenly believe will always appreciate.

An essential fact about the financial crisis of 2007–2009 is that a banking crisis emerged outside of the traditional commercial banking sector. The investment bank Bear Stearns failed when short-term credit suppliers grew suspicious of the value of the mortgage-backed securities on its balance sheet. Lehman Brothers, another investment bank, failed because of similar suspicions about its commercial real estate assets. AIG, an insurance company, failed because it was unable to make good on its guarantees of mortgage-related derivatives. Reserve Primary Fund "failed" because the write-down of its credit extension to Lehman meant that it was unable to cover redemption requests by its own short-term claimants. Bear and AIG were, of course, rescued; Lehman was not. The crisis demonstrated that a significant portion of the U.S. "banking" system had migrated outside of the official commercial banking sector to institutions that operated through securities markets. Investment banks and money market funds performed all three "transformations" that characterize banking: credit, maturity, and liquidity; that is, the conversion of risk-laden, illiquid, long-term assets into short-term risk-free liabilities. The counterparty relationships sundered by the Lehman failure also revealed the existence of a private payments system that tied together financial firms.

Thus, one of the most important lessons of the financial crisis was that systemic risk could arise outside of the official banking system. A further lesson was that reforms designed to protect the banking sector may prompt the migration of such systemic risk. For example, the Glass-Steagall Act was designed to protect the banking sector by separating commercial banks from securities market activities. In achieving this separation, Glass-Steagall also energized freestanding investment banks to use securities markets to create functional substitutes for credit provided by commercial banks. A substitute "shadow banking" system emerged—but without the oversight, deposit insurance, and public lender-of-last-resort backstop that we have come to think necessary to assure the stability of the banking sector. More generally, measures that strengthen the official commercial banking sector almost invariably produce financial innovation outside the official sector, with the goal of providing equivalent credit intermediation while not bearing the financial stability costs.

The core regulatory problem is this: maintenance of financial stability requires the adjustment of the regulatory perimeter to cover new financial intermediaries as they become systemically important. This is true for three reasons. First, the failure of such a large intermediary could eliminate an important credit channel for a significant group of borrowers. Second, its failure may well have knock-on effects for the official banking sector through balance sheet linkages or correlated asset holdings that will damage banks' financial position. Banks may have extended credit to the new financial intermediary, either through a direct loan, purchase of a debt security, or purchase of an asset backed by the intermediary's guarantee. Banks may have entered into contingent credit (or guarantee) arrangements with the intermediary. Banks may hold similar assets as the new intermediary, which are subject to abrupt devaluation as the troubled intermediary disposes of assets to meet claims of counterparties and the official sector hoards liquidity. Thus, directly and indirectly, the failure of such an institution will damage the real economy through an abrupt contraction in credit availability.

And third, the success of new intermediaries will presumably come at the expense of institutions in the official banking sector and will be attributable at least in part to a lighter, less costly regulatory burden. This competitive success will put pressure on the overseers of the official sector to relax regulatory constraints so that official banking institutions can compete, even though these costs were necessary to maintain financial stability. Thus, financial stability free-riding by extra-perimeter systemically important financial intermediaries undercuts the capacity of regulators to maintain financial stability over the long term.

One of the most valuable, if imperfectly realized, achievements of the Dodd-Frank Act is the recognition of evolving and migrating systemic risks and the design of a regulatory apparatus to address this, FSOC. FSOC is a council of U.S. regulators charged with identifying "potential emerging threats to the financial stability of the United States." FSOC was given a research arm, the Office of Financial Research, and also various tools to engage with these threats. One of the most important tools is the power to designate a nonbank financial institution as systemically important and subject it both to "prudential standards" devised by the Board of Governors (of the Fed) and to the Fed's general supervision. To designate the nonbank firm for such treatment, the council must "determine that material financial distress [at this firm], or the nature, scope, scale, concentration, interconnectedness, or mix of activities of [this firm] could pose a threat to the financial stability of the United States." Let's call this the designation of the firm as a "systemically important financial institution" (SIFI). To guide the FSOC in this determination, the act specifies that FSOC "shall consider" ten wide-ranging "considerations" "and any other risk-related factors that the Council deems appropriate." The council's designation decision is reviewable, but the applicable standard of review is the deferential test of "arbitrary and capricious."

This SIFI designation authority has been controversial. Its opponents bring out the heavy artillery: the broad grant of discretion is said to be inconsistent with the rule of law because, by regulatory determination, a large financial firm can be made subject to a potentially stringent prudential regime of a regulator, the Fed, with whom it may have had no prior engagement. One of the few designated firms, MetLife, challenged FSOC in court and achieved success.[2]

A major reason for pushback is that most of the initial targets of FSOC designation have been insurers who, despite their $1 trillion-plus balance sheets, claim they could not be a source of systemic risk because their liabilities (insurance policies of various types) are not readily runnable. This claim is asserted despite the business fact that insurers have used this balance sheet stability as a selling point for nontraditional insurance financial activities (AIG was only an extreme example). Before the financial crisis, it was common to hear that all financial institutions were, like happy families, alike in their core function of risk management and allocation. Postcrisis, the insurers strenuously assert that they are unalike. The United States has historically relegated the regulation of insurers to the states, and a suspicious mind might think that insurers prefer a predictably laxer regulatory diffusion to concerted oversight by a single federal regulator. It is also true that the Fed has no experience with insurance regulation and reflexively inclines to banklike regulation—capital bolstering and balance sheet strengthening—rather than a tailored consideration of insurance company specific risks.

Thus, a major reason for the controversy over SIFI designation is that no one knows exactly what it entails. The Fed becomes a regulator of the designated firm, responsible for setting prudential standards and engaging in supervision, but it has significant flexibility in fulfilling these tasks.[3] The council has a mandate to offer "recommendations" to the Fed,[4] including recommendations tailored to the designated firm's business.[5] The Fed is invited to "consult" with the council about alternatives to risk-based capital and leverage that achieve "similarly stringent" risk control.[6] The Fed is required to "consult" with the primary "functional" regulator of the subject firm (if any).[7] Nevertheless, the Fed has the last word on the substance of the standards and the nature of the supervision. The only statutory structural requirement is that the designated firm must prepare a "living will" for its resolution in bankruptcy, just like the large bank holding companies that were designated as systemically important under the Dodd-Frank Act.[8] The concern that the Fed will apply banklike capital and liquidity standards to every designated SIFI, no matter its business model, has created much of the resistance to FSOC's designation power, whether or not such fears are justified. The discretion granted to the Fed for "tailored application,"[9] necessary in the circumstances, is an incomplete solution.

This analysis of the FSOC designation authority misunderstands how the FSOC scheme should function. The key point is this: the optimal number of new SIFIs is zero. The FSOC designation process and the subsequent annual review for each designated SIFI is designed to provide an off-ramp for firms whose size, business strategy, interconnectedness, and other characteristics would raise questions about their systemic import. In other words, the FSOC's designation authority becomes the mechanism for *avoiding* the creation (or continuation) of firms that are "too big to fail." The designation process is a way to identify systemic concerns and to give firms the opportunity to mitigate them. It is not a mechanism by which new classes of financial firms are ported over to the Fed for regulation and supervision.

Moreover, FSOC's designation authority often spurs other regulators to expand their perimeters and set stability-promoting standards. One example is the recent program of the Comptroller of the Currency to offer special national banking charters to FinTech firms, which could bring some prudential oversight to this rapidly expanding sector.[10] The recent initiative of the U.S. Securities and Exchange Commission (SEC) to require mutual funds to plan for adequate liquidity buffers came in response to FSOC's investigation of systemic concerns in asset management.[11] Liquidity buffers reduce the risk of runs and fire sale dispositions that could have knock-on effects to other financial institutions holding similar assets. FSOC's possible designation of particular asset managers prompted the SEC's action, which aims to reduce systemic risk by other means.

Understanding how FSOC's designation authority can best discourage the creation or maintenance of a SIFI requires looking at both the statutory mandate and a "Three Stage Process" described in FSOC's interpretive guidance.[12] In Stage 1, FSOC will use quantitative thresholds to identify a set of nonbank financial firms "that merit further evaluation," in particular a consolidated asset threshold ($50 billion) plus one other quantitative measure in specific categories pertaining to the firm's size or risk appetite (such as leverage or short-term funding). In Stage 2, each firm identified in Stage 1 will be subject to analysis of its potential threat to U.S. financial stability using existing public and regulatory resources. For firms that present a prima facie case for designation after Stage 2, FSOC will collect information directly from the particular firm, including, presumably, proprietary information; this is Stage 3. Based on its assessment, FSOC may move to a "Proposed Determination" that the firm presents a risk to financial stability that requires oversight by the Fed. Before the determination becomes final, FSOC must provide notice to the candidate firm, "including an explanation of the basis of the proposed determination." The firm is entitled to respond with written submissions and, at the council's invitation, oral testimony and argument.

Consider the factors that FSOC says it will consider in Stage 3, in addition to the quantifiable ones, that "could mitigate or aggravate" the firm's potential threat to financial stability: "the opacity of the [firm's] operations, its complexity, and the extent to which it is subject to existing regulatory scrutiny and the nature of such scrutiny." The analysis will include "an evaluation of the [firm's] resolvability . . . [that] entails an assessment of the complexity of the [firm's] legal, funding, and operational structure, and any obstacles to the rapid and orderly resolution of the [firm]." Resolvability factors include "legal entity and cross-border operations issues;" "the ability to separate functions and spin off services or business lines; the likelihood of preserving franchise value in a recovery or resolution scenario, and of maintaining critical services within the existing or in a new legal entity or structure; the degree of the [firm's] intra-group dependency for liquidity and funding, payment operation, and risk management needs; and the size and nature of the [firm's] intra-group transactions."[13]

Each of these elements is an invitation to the targeted firm to try to eliminate its threat to financial stability and avoid a designation. The firm can restructure to reduce its systemic profile; subject itself to regulatory oversight as a substitute for the Fed (e.g., OCC for FinTech firms); and, in particular, subject itself to a "living wills" process designed to facilitate the resolution of a significant financial firm. In other words, the FSOC review process is designed to *avoid* designation by giving a firm the opportunity to address the issues that trouble FSOC. The targeted firm and FSOC can negotiate a solution that mitigates the systemic risk that would otherwise call for the Fed's oversight. One analogy is Justice Department review of a significant merger: the parties and the department negotiate to look for acceptable accommodation to antitrust concerns before the department brings an enforcement action. There is no serious criticism that this practice, which is common to competition regimes worldwide, is inconsistent with the rule of law. The interaction between FSOC, the targeted firm, and the Fed is quite similar.

Even after designation, the nonbank financial firm is entitled to annual review of its designation.[14] This, too, is an invitation for the designated firm to address FSOC's financial stability concern. The goal of the FSOC designation process is to avoid the creation or maintenance of systemically important firms. Subjecting nonbank financial firms to the Fed's oversight is a backup where accommodation cannot be found. In short, the FSOC process is set up to provide off-ramps from designation.

Evidence for this dynamic is in FSOC's designation of GE Capital in July 2013[15] and its rescission of that determination in June 2016.[16] The basis for the initial determination was straightforward: GE Capital, a wholly owned subsidiary of General Electric Corp., was "one of the largest financial services companies in the United States, ranked by assets," $539 billion as of yearend 2012, and was "a significant source of credit to the U.S. economy," extending credit to 243,000 commercial customers, 201,000 small businesses, and 57 million consumers. Through many different channels, "material financial distress at the company, if it were to occur, could pose a threat to U.S. financial stability."

Yet over the subsequent three years, "GE Capital has fundamentally changed its business model. Through a series of divestitures, a transformation of its funding model, and a corporate reorganization, the company has become a much less significant participant in financial markets and the economy. GE Capital has decreased its total assets by over 50 percent, shifted away from short-term funding, and reduced its interconnectedness with large financial institutions. Further, the company no longer owns any U.S. depository institutions and does not provide financing to consumers or small business customers in the United States."[17] The 2016 rescission decision described how company officials met with council staff regarding how it might undertake strategic actions that would reduce its systemic risk. In short, in response to guidance by the FSOC, the company steered away from those activities and mechanisms that would render its failure a systemic threat. The head of GE Capital said the decision reflected the transformation of GE Capital into a "smaller, safer financial services company."[18] It was once a SIFI but no longer,[19] and the U.S. economy is now more stable because of the change.

Moreover, the Fed played a role in this process of negotiated dedesignation. It both issued enhanced prudential standards for GE Capital and substantially suspended them while the company was in the process of restructuring.[20]

In sum, GE Capital's travels through the FSOC designation process underscore that the ultimate goal is to reduce the number of systemically important financial institutions, not to increase the Fed's regulatory reach and regulatory burden. Presumably this is an objective that all sides of the debate can embrace. Those who think that SIFI designation means the firm will be regarded as "too big to fail" and thus a bailout candidate should welcome a process aimed at reducing the number of firms that are "systemic." Those who think that FSOC needs to expand the regulatory perimeter to protect financial stability should appreciate that ex ante reduction of systemic risk is better than greater ex post regulation. The key legislative fact is this: FSOC's designation authority is essential to this dynamic. The credible possibility of designation is what disciplines managerial decisions about the size, scope, leverage, and interconnectedness of a financial firm's activities.

FSOC's designation authority thus can play a major role in maintaining financial stability over the long term. FSOC intervention (or its threat) can help keep some firms below the systemic threshold, induce some firms to back off if they have crossed it, and lead other regulators to constrain some of the systemically risky behavior of firms that they oversee. In short, there will be fewer SIFIs with FSOC designation authority than without. And for firms that are unavoidably systemic, FSOC designation (and Fed oversight) will be very important.

Cost Benefit Analysis vs. Dynamic Precaution in Financial Regulation

Cost-benefit analysis (CBA) has become a familiar prescription in financial regulation. Courts have taken great license with existing statutes to require a quantified tally of costs and benefits, even in one remarkable case insisting that this methodology was required under the "arbitrary and capricious" judicial review standard of the Administrative Procedure Act,[21] which is quite remarkable in light of the recency of CBA in judicial review of administrative action and the 1946 origins of the APA. The fundamental flaw with CBA in the financial regulatory area is the poor fit with the dynamic nature of the financial system itself. Even if it were possible to tally the costs and benefits of a particular financial regulatory rule at a given moment in a nonarbitrary,[22] nontrivial[23] way, the point is that, for any important rule, the relevant effect will be prospective. The rule will play a role in reshaping the financial sector, meaning that the prior assessment of costs and benefits will be obsolete. As I have elsewhere argued,

> The financial system is not a natural system. It is constituted by regulation, a constructed system. . . . [T]he system itself is not stable: parties will adapt in light of the regulation, the system of finance will change, and with it the benefits and costs of the regulation in question.[24]

Where CBA has been commonly used, in health and safety and environmental areas, the primitives of the system—the laws of physics, chemistry, and biology, for example—are invariant to the rules that are founded on their operation. There are no comparable primitives in finance. The rules constitute the financial system, and changing major rules will change the system, often in quite unpredictable ways.

To reject CBA analysis in its quantified form is not the same as rejecting pragmatic efforts to assess the likely impact of regulation, which includes the thoughtful use of the available empirical evidence and sophisticated modeling of financial system dynamics. Instrumental rationality has value in financial regulation. In context, CBA is an irrational facsimile. Precisely because of the humility a regulator should bring to the exercise, the most appropriate stance of a systemic regulator is dynamic precaution. The point is to observe the financial system as it evolves, to monitor the build up of stresses and potential sources of financial instability, and to propose intervention as necessary. This consists of monitoring on at least two dimensions: First is the tracking of financial stress on its time-series dimensions, reflected, for example, in the rapid expansion of credit or an unusual escalation of asset prices.[25] Second is the tracking of cross-sectional institutional development, such as the growth of a new class of financial intermediaries or a rapid move to a new form of financial intermediation or new financial activity.[26]

Cost-benefit analysis encourages a "one and done approach," which is exactly the wrong attitude necessary for the maintenance of financial stability. Modern financial systems are always a work in progress, dynamic not static. The energy comes from multiple sources: First are the efforts by institutions within the official perimeter to innovate to evade regulatory constraints, for example, the Special Investment Vehicles that banks devised precrisis to move assets off the balance sheet and thus avoid the need to augment regulatory capital. Second are the institutions outside the official perimeter that attempt to provide functional equivalent financial intermediation as "banks" without paying the financial stability tax. Precrisis, credit intermediation shifted in significant measure to institutions outside of the official banking system, such as securitization vehicles, money market funds, and investment banks.[27] Innovations in contractual arrangements (securitization) and in finance ("repo") appeared to offer a lower cost strategy for housing finance than plain vanilla mortgages run through the banking system. Third, technology itself can be transformative. Neither sophisticated securitization (nor other forms of structured finance) nor derivatives would have been possible without high-powered computers. Dynamic precaution inclines the regulator to be forward-looking, not backward or presentist.

The case for dynamic precaution is well illustrated by the many financial regulatory rules that produced outcomes far outside the assessment of the costs and benefits contemplated by the rule's enactors, outcomes that were an integral part of the financial crisis. One example, of course, is the case of money market funds (MMFs), which the SEC introduced in the late 1970s as a vehicle for retail investors to benefit from high short-term money market fund rates at a time when bank deposit rates were constrained by regulation.[28] Throughout the 1990s, MMFs increasingly became a short-term wholesale investment vehicle for institutions looking for liquidity, safety, and cash management. This produced a set of very large financial intermediaries in a $3.5 trillion industry (as of 2008) outside the official banking system—without capital or a lender of last resort. The run on MMFs after the failure of the Reserve Primary Fund was an accident waiting to happen.

The second example, a 2005 Bankruptcy Act change,[29] justified via a thinly reasoned cost-benefit analysis as reducing systemic risk, turned out almost immediately to be the vector of systemic risk throughout the financial system. The Bankruptcy Abuse Prevention and Consumer Protection Act of 2005 (BAPCPA) made what might seem to be a limited, technical change (described hereafter) to the operation of a bankruptcy "safe harbor" for financial contacts, and made this in the name of *reducing* systemic risk. Yet the change made it easier to finance extensions of credit to residential real estate, which both inflated an already overheated subprime mortgage market and heightened susceptibility to bank runs throughout the financial system. The lens of quantified cost-benefit analysis, which assessed the stability of the financial system as it then was, brought exactly the wrong regulatory attitude. Instead, the question needs to be, how is the financial system changed through these new rules? Will that require intervention?

To understand this requires some unpacking.[30]

Financial intermediaries commonly finance assets on their balance sheets with short-term collateralized loans called "repo." "Dealer banks" can earn a "spread" on the difference between higher long-term rates and lower short-term rates. Similarly, financial intermediaries commonly collateralize transactions with one another (especially derivatives) via repo. A leading text on financial regulation describes repo this way:

> Repo [is] a collateralized loan structured as a sale and repurchase transaction in which the "seller" (borrower) sells a security to the "purchaser" (lender) with the understanding that it will repurchase the security [at a higher price that reflects the interest charge]. Commonly the market value of the security exceeds the loan, and the difference is the so-called "haircut" (or "margin") and reflects the extent to which the loan is over-collateralized. If the borrower defaults on its repurchase obligation (repayment of the loan), the lender can . . . sell [the security] and apply the proceeds to the loan. *Laws of most jurisdictions protect the lender (purchaser) from insolvency laws that might otherwise stay a secured party's foreclosing on the borrower's collateral, a bankruptcy safe harbor.* By protecting the value of the lender's "deposit," repo provides a kind of private deposit insurance.[31] [emphasis added]

The key to the counterparty's security in this short-term lending arrangement is the capacity to foreclose on collateral that is at least equal to the loaned amount and then immediately to realize on this value. This means that such creditor self-help must be excluded from the "automatic stay" that is generally triggered by a bankruptcy filing, designed to preserve the going concern value of the debtor. This "safe harbor" for repo in financial contracts was initially added to the Bankruptcy Act in 1984, with the proviso that the collateral eligible for such treatment was limited to U.S. Treasury securities, agency securities, and certain bank issuances thought to be protected through the social safety net. The increasing volume of derivatives transactions in the 1990s led to a push to expand the range of collateral that would be eligible for repo safe harbor treatment.[32] After an eight-year effort, such a provision was added as a title to bankruptcy legislation (in 2005) otherwise aimed at a purported increase in fraud and abuse in consumer bankruptcy.

The general argument for the bankruptcy safe harbor in financial contracts is that it reduces systemic risk. Financial firms at the center of the financial system have a huge book of trades with one another, secured through repo, and are thinly capitalized relative to the notional value of their trading books, on the view that (1) their trading book is roughly balanced and (2) their counterparty credit risk is eliminated through collateral arrangements like repo. If firm A could not immediately realize on the value of its outstanding credit extensions to Firm B, then Firm A could not meet its obligations to Firm C—a falling dominoes theory of systemic risk. Moreover, without the assurance of immediate realization, A would refuse to roll over existing credit extensions to B, triggering a liquidity crisis for B that could easily lead to B's failure and the potential systemic runoff from that. The justification invoked for expanding the collateral eligible for bankruptcy safe harbor treatment, in particular to add mortgage-backed securities, was that financial firms were in fact using such securities in their repo transactions.[33] So systemic stability would be served by including this sort of collateral in the safe harbor.[34]

The assumption that this expansion of the safe harbor provision would add to systemic stability underpinned an explicit assessment of costs performed by the Congressional Budget Office in connection with a 2000 version of the legislation.[35] The benefits of greater systemic stability were assumed; the quantified assessment of costs focused on record keeping. In no respect did the CBO consider the impact of the collateral eligibility provisions on the financial system overall or any other vector of systemic risk. In light of the complicated politics relating to other elements of the bankruptcy legislation, the financial contracting provisions were enacted into law after significant delay, in 2005, as part of a consumer-focused bankruptcy package. An examination of the eight-year odyssey of the provision, reflected in legislative proposals and committee hearings and reports in the 1998–2005 period, produces ample evidence of a single-minded focus on one-way systemic risk implications, with the quantification of costs limited to the most banal.

Yet this seeming technical change to a piece of financial system architecture was a significant accelerant to the financial distress that broke out in fall 2008.[36] How so? First, the legislative change produced an immediate increase in mortgage-backed securitization. Now that mortgage-backed securities could for sure serve as collateral for repo, they could be cheaply financed through short-term credit provided by money market funds and other wholesale short-term creditors. A recent paper by Srinivasan demonstrates this by showing the growth of repo and securitization immediately after the passage of BAPCPA.[37] He shows, first, a consistent linear relationship between the growth of repo and growth in structured finance; second, a growth in repo after BAPCPA's passage in 2005; third, concentration of such growth in structured finance among the banks that regularly traded in repo and thus would find it easiest to ramp up; and fourth, an increase among those banks in their securitization activity immediately after BAPCPA took effect.

Second, these mortgage-backed securities were structured in a way to produce the financial alchemy of transforming pools of subprime mortgages into a large fraction of securities rated AAA. These highly rated securities were then used to collateralize the repo loans. How did this matter for the crisis? As mortgage foreclosures accelerated in 2007–2008 and the methodology behind mortgage-backed securitization became suspect, the value of the AAA securities used as collateral became suspect. The lenders demanded increasingly large haircuts or simply withdrew from the repo market. This rapid reduction of short-term credit provision amounted to a "run," and correspondingly required financial firms to rapidly sell off assets; the two sides of the balance sheet must match, after all. The accelerating asset sales were at prices that imposed huge losses, not only on the selling institutions but also at other firms holding similar assets, required by mark-to-market accounting. This negative spiral threatened systemic insolvency.

Thus an important engine of the financial crisis was a bank run originating in the shadow banking system and then spreading, principally through fire sale externalities, to the financial sector more generally.[38] The "Run on Repo" is a critical element in the financial contagion story,[39] and the way that BAPCPA brought fragile collateral into the repo system dramatically exacerbated the risk of runs.

In short, one consequence of BAPCPA was to increase the demand for securitized products (because they could be financed more cheaply) and thus to bring additional funds into already overheated real estate markets and add additional volume to the bubble. And, because no one seemed to appreciate that the stability of the financial system depended upon the repo collateral holding its value within a predetermined range (the "haircut") no matter what, BAPCPA produced a channel through which financial distress spread virally throughout the financial system. The parties did not consider the risk that the new collateral would produce a new form of systemic risk. The cost-benefit analyses, formal and informal, were predicated upon the existing state of the world, not the world that resulted from adoption of the new rule. Congress, of course, was not required to perform a cost-benefit analysis, but they seemed to think they had, and that they changes they implemented would produce the benefit of greater systemic stability rather than mere redistribution.

The point is this: a cost-benefit analysis of the change in the bankruptcy safe harbor, a kind of technical-seeming rule change that the financial regulatory agencies commonly make, would not have picked up the way the change would significantly change the financial system itself. The challenge of financial stability is not to assess cost and benefits of the system as it presently exists but to observe the system as it evolves, and to observe the effects of new rules on the system as a whole. This is the stance of dynamic precaution.

Conclusion

This chapter concludes where it started. The financial crisis was an extraordinarily costly set of events, even though it resolved somewhere in the top half of potential outcomes. That is a sobering thought. The maintenance of financial stability must therefore be an apex goal of the financial regulatory system. Because the financial system is a continuous work in progress, the right regulatory approach is dynamic precaution. This calls for institutions such as FSOC to play a vigorous monitoring role over the financial system as it evolves. It calls for regulators (and, more so, courts) to avoid overclaiming what can be obtained through quantification of costs and benefits.

Notes

Many thanks to Adrienne Ho, LLM '17, for assiduous research on complicated legislative history questions.

1. House Committee on Financial Services, "Explanatory Statement Accompany the Financial CHOICE Act," June 23, 2016.
2. MetLife, Inc. v. Fin. Stability Oversight Council, 177 F. Supp. 219 (D.D.C 2016), appeal dismissed, 2018 WL 1052618 (Jan. 23, 2018).
3. See, generally, DFA § 165.
4. DFA §§ 115, 165 (a)(1).
5. DFA §§ 115(a)(3), 165 (a)(2)(A).
6. DFA § 165(b)(1)(A).
7. DFA § 165(b)(4).
8. DFA § 165(b)(1).
9. DFA § 165(a)(2) (caption of section).
10. "OCC Begins Accepting National Bank Charter Applications from Financial Technology Companies," Office of the Comptroller of the Currency Press Release, July 31, 2018; "Comptroller's Licensing Manual Draft Supplement, Considering Charter Applications from Financial Technology Companies," July 2018.
11. See "Investment Company Liquidity Risk Management Programs," SEC Rel. No. 33–10233; IC-32315, October 13, 2016 (adding Rule 22e-4 under the Investment Company Act of 1940); FSOC, "Notice Seeks Comment on Asset Management Products and Activities," 2014; Office of Financial Research, "Asset Management and Financial Stability," 2013.
12. See 12 CFR § 1310 and Appendix thereto, and discussion at 77 Fed. Reg. 21637–21662.
13. See 77 Fed. Reg. at 21662 (April 11, 2012).
14. DFA § 113(d).
15. See U.S. Treasury, "Basis of the Financial Stability Oversight Council's Final Determination Regarding General Electric Capital Corporation, Inc.," July 8, 2013, https://www.treasury.gov/initiatives/fsoc/designations/Pages/default.aspx.
16. See U.S. Department of the Treasury, "Basis of the Financial Stability Oversight Council's Rescission of Its Determination Regarding General Electric Capital Global

Holdings, LLC," June 28, 2016, https://www.treasury.gov/initiatives/fsoc/designations /Pages/default.aspx.

17. U.S. Department of the Treasury, "Basis of the Financial Stability Oversight Council's Rescission," 2.

18. Ted Mann and Tracy Ryan, "GE Capital Sheds 'Systemically Important' Label," *Wall Street Journal*, June 29, 2016 (quoting Keith Sherin).

19. A similar process of down-sizing and restructuring is under way in the case of MetLife, which is separating its U.S. individual life insurance business from its remaining insurance and financial services businesses. This is described in Form 10-K, Brighthouse Life Insurance Co, FY 2016, March 28, 2017, available through the SEC's EDGAR site. For current developments, see Leslie Scism, "MetLife Closer to Spinning Off U.S. Life Insurance Business," *Wall Street Journal*, June 28, 2017.

20. Federal Reserve System, "Application of Enhanced Prudential Standards and Reporting Requirements to General Electric Corporation," 80 Fed. Reg. 44111, July 24, 2015.

21. See MetLife, Inc. v. Fin. Stability Oversight Council, 177 F. Supp. 219 (D.D.C. 2016), appeal dismissed, 2018 WL 1052618 (January 23, 2018); Business Roundtable v. SEC, 647 F.3d 1144 (D.C. Cir. 2011).

22. John Coates, "Cost-Benefit Analysis of Financial Regulation: Case Studies and Implications," *Yale Law Journal* 124, no. 4 (2014): 882–1345 (identifying arbitrary choices in cost/benefit choices).

23. Such as by assessing the attorney time (and costs) in regulatory filings regarding rules that shape an industry.

24. Jeffrey N. Gordon, "The Empty Call for Benefit-Cost Analysis in Financial Regulation," *Journal of Legal Studies* 43, no. 2 (June 2014): S351, S366–67.

25. The Office of Financial Research has devised the "Financial Stress Index," which provides "a daily snapshot of stress in global financial markets," and the "Financial System Vulnerabilities Monitor," "designed to provide early warning signals of potential U.S. financial system vulnerabilities." See www.financialresearch.gov.

26. These two approaches to macroprudential regulation are more fully developed in John Armour, Dan Awrey, Paul Davies, Luca Enriques, Jeffrey Gordon, Colin Mayer, and Jennifer Payne, *Principles of Financial Regulation* (Oxford: Oxford University Press, 2016), 409–30.

27. For a more detailed discussion, see Armour et al., *Principles of Financial Regulation*, 439–44, 481–87.

28. This is drawn from Gordon, "Empty Call," supra note 24; Jeffrey N. Gordon and Christopher M. Gandia, "Money Market Fund risk: Will Floating Net Asset Value Fix the Problem?" *Columbia Business Law Review* (2014): 313–32.

29. Bankruptcy Abuse Prevention and Consumer Protection Act of 2005, Pub. L. No. 109–8, § 907, 119 Stat. 23, 171–72 (codified as amended at 11 U.S.C. § 101(47) (2012)) ["BAPCPA"].

30. For more extensive accounts, see Edward R. Morrison, Mark J. Roe, and Christopher S. Sontchi, "Rolling Back the Repo Safe Harbors," *Business Lawyer* 69, no. 4 (August 2014): 1015–47; Edward R. Morrison and Joerg Riegel, "Financial Contracts and the New Bankruptcy Code: Insulating Markets from Bankrupt Debtors and Bankruptcy Judges," *American Bankruptcy Institute Law Review* 13 (2005): 641–64.

31. Armour et al., *Principles of Financial Regulation*, supra note 26, 440–41.

32. See "Financial Contract Netting Improvement Act of 2000," Report from Comm. on Banking and Financial Services, 106th Congress 19–20, September 7, 2000; "Safety and Soundness Issues Related to Bank Derivatives Activities—Part 3: Hearings Before the

Comm. on Banking, Finance, and Urban Affairs, H.R. (Part 3—Minority Report)," 103d Cong 4, October 28, 1993.

33. "The Business Bankruptcy Reform Act: Business Bankruptcy Issues in Review: Hearings on S. 1914," before the Subcomm. on Administrative Oversight and the Courts of the S. Comm. on the Judiciary, 105th Cong. 56, 1998 (Bond Market Ass'n statement).

34. The Business Bankruptcy Reform Act, at 38–39 (U.S. Treasury position).

35. See "Financial Contract Netting Improvement Act of 2000," Report from the Comm. on Banking and Financial Services, 106th Cong. 22, September 7, 2000.

36. See, generally, Mark J. Roe, "The Derivative Market's Payment Priorities as Financial Crisis Accelerator," *Stanford Law Review* 63, no. 3 (2011): 539–90.

37. See Kandarp Srinivasan, "The Securitization Flash Flood," August 2017, https://ssrn.com/abstract=2814717.

38. For a useful literature survey on the triggers for the crisis, see Gary Gorton and Andrew Metrick, "Getting Up to Speed on the Financial Crisis: A One Weekend Guide," *Journal of Economic Literature* 50, no. 1 (2012): 128–50.

39. See Gary Gorton and Andrew Metrick, "Securitized Banking and the Run on Repo," *Journal of Financial Economics* 104, no. 3 (2012): 425–51.

PART III

USE AND (AB)USE OF MODELS IN PREDICTING FINANCIAL OUTCOMES

CHAPTER 10

REFLECTIONS ON THE GLOBAL FINANCIAL CRISIS TEN YEARS ON

JOSEPH E. STIGLITZ

It has been ten years since the financial crisis dealt the biggest blow to the world economy since the Great Depression. Although growth has returned and the job market has now tightened—especially in the United States where the crisis originated—reverberations from the crisis continue to affect us in ways both large and small, both obvious and obscure and subtle.

The devastating damage to our economy calls for profound reflection and change, in economics, politics, the financial sector, among policymakers, and in our behavior. Now that the United States has staved off total disaster with emergency measures, it is time for the country to root out the causes of the crisis and make deep adjustments to protect against another such painful and utterly wasteful episode.

Although the lessons learned have not been totally ignored, a sober accounting of what has actually been done to respond to the crisis shows that only a relatively small number of these lessons have been acted upon. The glass is probably three-quarters empty and one-quarter full: We have identified the problems that gave rise to the financial crisis, but our solutions to those problems have been highly incomplete—and are yet at risk of being undone.[1]

The experience of the crisis should have led us to change our economic models, our economic priorities, and our regulations for the financial sector. In this chapter, I trace how mistakes in each of these areas made the financial crisis all but inevitable. I then take stock of which of the necessary reforms have been undertaken since the crisis, and which have not. Finally, I offer some perspective on how the U.S. response to the crisis has influenced our political system and what this bodes for our future.

Bad Models Facilitated the Crisis

It can be easy to forget, a decade later, just how blindsided many economists and bankers were by the financial crisis. In light of what has become common knowledge about the financial sector's excesses and mismanagement, in retrospect it seems obvious that the sector and the economy were headed for serious problems. A few of us did warn—with increasing alarm in the middle of the century's first decade—that something was terribly wrong. For others, however, the crisis was truly unexpected. The reason for this widespread surprise was fairly straightforward: Economists were relying on models that not only didn't predict the crisis but almost said that it couldn't happen. And this was true not just of academic economists, but those immersed in policy, in the "real world," at central banks and the IMF.

Not long before the crisis, people like Ben Bernanke were talking about how well the economy was doing. Even after the housing bubble broke, Bernanke would say not to worry—that the problems had been contained. He could get away with saying something so absurd because the models he was relying on indicated that the problems *were* (or should have been) contained. Those models were based on the notion that risk was diversified and that the subprime mortgage market was a small fraction of the wealth of the global economy. If risk were well-diversified and there was a perturbation in a small part of the world's wealth, the economy could well absorb it. As the crisis made obvious, these models were totally inadequate to deal with what happened. In fact, they made the crisis more likely.

On the basis of these standard models, the IMF and the U.S. Treasury promoted diversification, claiming that it would spread the risk widely and that that would make the system more stable. What happened in this crisis was not that risk was distributed and spread but that risk was propagated and amplified. There was not a diminution of risk through diversification but rather an amplification, through contagion.[2] Diversification simply turned what could have been contained cases of financial failure into a global pandemic.

Using a public health analogy highlights just how misguided this emphasis on diversification was. Say that a hundred people arrive in New York City with Ebola. If one followed the precrisis IMF recommendation, one would try to soften the risk to public health by sending the Ebola victims to every state— voila, the risk is diversified! The correct way to deal with such a situation is, of course, quarantine.

The mathematics one uses to analyze contagion are totally different from those used in models in which diversification helped manage risk. With economists and policymakers clinging to the flawed models, the crisis we experienced was almost inevitable. Policymakers encouraged more diversification, and this greater diversification itself led to greater instability. What remains mysterious is why these models were never questioned. There was a cognitive dissonance: at times (before the crisis) discussions focused on the benefits of linkages (diversification); at others (after the crisis) on the costs (contagion). Yet no one in these institutions thought to formulate (or even look for) a model integrating both kinds of effects, within which one could ascertain, perhaps, an optimal degree of diversification.

Even more remarkable, the flaws in the models and their implications were known well before the crisis. Bruce Greenwald and I devoted a chapter to the subject in our 2003 book *Towards a New Paradigm in Monetary Economics* (written and given as lectures years earlier);[3] Franklin Allen and David Gale in Pennsylvania wrote about the consequences of financial interlinkages in 2000.[4] But the IMF and the Federal Reserve were not interested and ignored the findings. The willful ignorance was, fortunately, not universal. At least one central bank was interested, the Bank of England, under its research director Andy Haldane; and it was actually engaged in serious work before the crisis. For others, perhaps, these insights were simply too inconvenient to acknowledge in the years before the bubble burst; it might have meant that the regulators would have had to think harder about regulation.

There were many other ways in which the standard models being used by economists and by central banks, such as dynamic stochastic general equilibrium models or DSGE models, were very badly flawed. For one, they assumed that the source of the shock was an exogenous shock. The models could not conceive of a shock from within—a credit bubble created by the market itself—which was exactly what happened. They could not conceive of markets lending beyond people's ability to repay, which was also exactly what happened. Underlying these misconceptions were standard beliefs about how our economy worked—beliefs in rationality, rational expectations, and incentive alignment between social and private returns. The standard models and their backers argued that we had developed sound incentive structures for the participants in our marketplace.

After the crisis, defenders of these models claimed that they were never meant to work 100 percent of the time. The models had failed because we were hit by a once-in-a-century flood, they said, and a model that was meant for normal times is not going to work in a once-in-a-century flood. To the contrary, I believe that, in fact, reliance on the flawed models contributed to the crisis. The Fed was not an innocent victim of some outside force—a war or a plague. The Fed bears the responsibility for what happened, both in what it did and what it did not do. It chose to be influenced by certain models and ways of thinking, even when it had access to information and research showing that the models they were using were deeply flawed; and it ignored other models and analyses that provided clear warning signs.

An especially odd aspect of the economic models used by central banks was that there were no banks; it was peculiar, because without banks there would not have been central banks. Because these models completely ignored banks and ascribed no function to them, no one raised questions about the consequences of their interdependencies. No one seemed fully aware of the consequences of letting Lehman Brothers go down. They knew that there would be some consequences, of course, but they thought they would be limited. But when the firm collapsed, it sent shockwaves throughout the entire financial system for simple reasons: other people had money that they were not able to access. The problems echoed throughout the financial system.

Deepening the mystery about why so many people clung to these broken models is that, as we know from data that came out after the crisis, it was clear in 2007 and 2008 that the financial system was freezing up. People knew there was a problem. Yet their mind-set was so shaped by their flawed models that they did not ask whether Lehman's collapse would lead to the demise of other financial institutions, or a cascade of bankruptcies.

Even today, ten years later, blind fidelity to flawed models continues to contribute to disagreements about the causes of the crisis, the appropriate remedies, and what could or should be done to prevent another crisis.

Deregulation and Secularization

Of the many bad policy decisions for which the flawed models paved the way, one of the most consequential was deregulation of the financial sector. This deregulation, which had begun more than twenty-five years earlier, allowed the other problems brewing in the financial sector to become supercharged. Among these was the housing bubble—a bubble that was allowed to inflate to massive proportions because it created the illusion of widespread wealth and wealth creation, at least for a short time.

Growth of gross domestic product (GDP) was chugging along in the middle of the decade, thanks in part to low interest rates that facilitated high levels of lending. Anybody looking closely at banks' balance sheets, however, should have been horrified by what was going on. Americans were not just borrowing; the mortgages they were borrowing were exceptionally dangerous. They were short-term mortgages—with variable interest rates, some with negative amortization, others with balloon payments— requiring the mortgage to be totally refinanced every few years. There were all kinds of mortgages that seemed to shift risk to the borrowers—though if the borrower defaulted, of course, the risk shifted back to the owners of the mortgages. But the borrowers were often poor, and not in an economic position to assess or bear that risk. If interest rates increased or the bubble broke, they would not be able to roll over the loans, and there would be a crisis.

To the attentive observer, it was evident (a) that there was a bubble and (b) that when the bubble broke, there would be problems. Rob Schiller and I, and others, spoke about the very high probability that we were in a housing bubble. One can never be completely sure that a bubble exists until it breaks, but in this case, the possibility that we were not in a housing bubble was remote. Given the nature of the mortgage markets, with the growth of "risky mortgages," it was very clear that, when that bubble broke, the mortgage market would be put into extreme distress.

Proper regulations should have prevented such borrowing from being possible. Instead, for years the brakes had steadily come off, giving dangerous and deceptive lending practices free rein. Policymakers were in thrall to the mania for free markets; in their view, bad practices might emerge but would not survive because they would be unprofitable. Credit would dry up for unsustainable ideas (such as poorly designed mortgages) before they grew large enough to cause widespread problems.

As I have argued for decades, the logic behind such free market fundamentalism is seriously defective and is based on numerous false assumptions. The models largely ignored information imperfections and asymmetries, yet these are at the heart of financial markets. The models assumed that private and social returns were well aligned, and yet it should have been obvious that that was not the case with the prevailing incentive structures in the financial sector; and it was not the case for the too-big-too-fail (or too-interconnected or too-correlated-to-fail) financial institutions: they reaped the rewards from excess risk taking while society picked up the costs. There were massive externalities, long recognized: a failure of the financial system has large macroeconomic consequences—the reason that bailouts occur so frequently. Yet our regulators, including the heads of the Federal Reserve who were steeped in market fundamentalism, paid no heed: they simply assumed that the banks knew how to manage risk better than the regulators.

Banks came up with "innovations"—new, high-risk mortgages that could be stuffed into large securitizations and then "structured" so that the top tranches could be sold off as AAA securities, making such lending appear less dangerous than it was. Securitization was supposed to insure against catastrophe, by diversifying risk, pooling the risks together and spreading them around, so that each investor would in fact bear little risk. Instead, securitization, as designed and practiced, ended up being just one more amplifier of the crisis.

It is true that by sharing risks sometimes they become less "dangerous"—that was the argument for diversification noted earlier. But one can share risk through the ownership structure of banks. If one wants to have a diversified portfolio of mortgages, a diversified portfolio of bank ownership can help achieve this. We know how to create bank mutual funds, and they indeed can accomplish diversification. Whether there were any significant further benefits from securitization was ambiguous, even before the crisis; but there was surely a cost associated with the perverse incentives to which it gave rise.

Securitization was done in such a way that the incentives of mortgage originators were not aligned with the people who were going to buy the mortgages. The originator of the mortgage got his fees upfront, and he sold it on. He wanted to originate as many mortgages as he could, and he would pass them on up the chain to the investment bank, who would sell them to someone else. There was seemingly no pecuniary reason for the mortgage originator to care whether the borrower would ever be able to repay the loan. Securitization separated out origination from accountability, misaligning incentives and creating a classic moral hazard problem.

A closer examination of the details of mortgage contracts, though, shows that some thought went into their design. They included provisions to mitigate this incentive problem. Many included so-called put-back provisions, which were supposed to ensure that, if the mortgage was not as described by the originator, it would be considered a faulty, flawed mortgage, and it could be put back to the originator. The contracts even had provisions saying that banks would pay legal costs in the event of a legal dispute. In effect, the originators provided to the investment banks, and the investment banks to the mortgage insurers, a money-back guarantee on the quality of their mortgages. (The mortgage insurers were the so-called monoline companies that helped with "credit enhancement" so the top tier of the structured financial products could achieve a AAA rating.) However, there were two factors that nobody had fully anticipated: the massive fraud that characterized the mortgage originators and the investment banks, and the massive breaches of contract that occurred in enforcement and compliance.[5]

A financial system that was rife with such fraud and deception was almost bound to fail. A framework that says economic activity is entirely based on rational expectations with no deceptive and fraudulent practices was bound to miss the huge amount of irrational activity and the irregularities in the financial markets in the years before the crisis. It was willful neglect that the Federal Reserve and other regulators did not keep a closer eye on what was going on in the years before the crisis—a neglect partially based on a misguided ideology and flawed models that ignored these possibilities. There had been cognitive capture of the regulators, who took seriously the financial sectors' claim that they knew best how to manage risk, totally ignoring the flawed incentive structures, the massive externalities, and the rampant moral turpitude (to which I will come shortly).

Inequality

Rampant predatory and reckless lending papered over a growing underlying fact about the U.S. economy: inequality was on the rise, and this was creating a shortfall in aggregate demand. The scale of the problem only became fully obvious after the crisis, but it was there beforehand, too, both in the United States and in many other countries. Inequality leads to economic weakness because those at the top save a lot more than those at the bottom. At the top, savings rates are generally somewhere between 20 and 35 percent. The average household savings rate of the bottom 80 percent of Americans was some negative 10 percent. When you move money from the bottom of the economic pyramid to the top, aggregate savings goes up, and aggregate consumption goes down.

Thus high inequality causes aggregate demand to be weaker than would otherwise be the case, unless the weakness is made up for in some other way. There are intelligent ways to do so—say, through increased government spending on badly needed infrastructure improvements. But before the crisis, U.S. policymakers chose one of the worst possible ways to make up for weaker aggregate demand—making it easier and cheaper to lend to people who might not be able to pay it back. This gave a short-term boost to aggregate demand, but it also made the economy frail—as noted above, most Americans had exceedingly low, even negative, savings rates. That was not sustainable. A financial system based on that level of overextension of credit is headed toward crisis.

This lending was made possible not only because of deregulation but also because the Fed had lowered interest rates. The doctrine at the time in those simplistic models held that lower interest rates would stimulate the economy, without addressing inequality. And they did, but at great cost, opening the door to a different set of problems. The crisis occurred during a period of financial deregulation; lowering interest rates in that deregulated environment made it easy to create a bubble.

A Culture of Bad Financial Behavior

The poor performance of the mortgage market, the securitization process, credit rating agencies, and the system of risk sharing among banks, including through credit default swaps, were exposed as time went on. But it was not only that these systems were broken. Another large factor that contributed to the crisis was the bad behavior of banks, which was so rampant that it can accurately be called a culture. This bad behavior extended into every corner of finance.

The extent of the bad behavior was only exposed after the crisis. The Wells Fargo scandal encapsulates this kind of bad behavior: opening up accounts without people's knowledge, charging them huge amounts, and forcing them to buy auto insurance. Throughout the financial system, there were tax and money laundering havens, where secrecy's main function was to hide a wide variety of nefarious activities, the kinds of abuses revealed in the Panama Papers and the Paradise Papers. Some people point to these phenomena and accuse banks of participating in a criminal enterprise. That may be an exaggeration, but it is clear that banks and others in the financial sector were very much engaged in tax avoidance—and, in many cases, tax evasion—and other actions that facilitated corruption. They aided and abetted money laundering.

Over the decade since the crisis, we have become aware of countless such examples where bankers moved to the edge of legality, and many went over that edge, where even if there had been no laws proscribing what they did, the bankers should have known that what they were doing was wrong. Market manipulation in the foreign exchange market was one example of banks proving themselves untrustworthy. Wells Fargo and predatory lending showed the extent of the moral depravity on the part of our financial institutions. Many of these examples were not directly responsible for the crisis, but others—such as the pervasive fraud in the mortgage origination process—clearly were.

Banks thrive on secrecy, but that secrecy has far-reaching costs. My work was on the economics of information, problems of asymmetries of information, and the problems of trying to expose and reduce asymmetric information, guided by the basic belief that efficient markets require good information. Bank secrecy erodes this foundation of well-functioning markets. In fact, the secrecy went so far that it contributed to the erosion of trust in the financial sector, even between banks. (Goldman Sachs's creation of securities that were designed to fail has become the poster child for this erosion of trust.) Because each bank's practices were opaque, banks stopped lending to each other in times of need: each possible lender assumed that the inner workings of the other banks were just as rotten as their own. This contributed in a very big way to the freezing up of the financial markets, and the freezing up of the financial markets was at the core of the financial crisis.

I do not think we have really changed the culture since the financial crisis. There is still a lack of transparency.

What Has Changed—And More, What Has Not

Despite the scale of the financial crisis, there has never been a full reckoning within the economics profession of just how inadequate the models were—too many prominent economists have simply held that the problems were with the implementation of the models, and not with the models themselves. There are Ptolemaic efforts to make the models better, little tweaks here and there. But to my great disappointment, the fundamental flaws continue—the rational expectations equilibrium framework (the DSGE models) remains dominant, though the critiques have gradually become more accepted by younger economists, who have less of a vested interest in the old models.[6]

New Efforts in Economics Provide a Ray of Hope

There are, however, several important new strands of work breaking out of the models that helped shape the crisis. This new work rejects rational expectations, tries to explore financial interlinkages, and acknowledges the presence of pervasive macroeconomic externalities—that, for instance, when one large group in the economy borrows more abroad, it affects exchange rates, which has effects on others.

These ideas are very important. The most important theorem in economics has been Adam Smith's invisible hand—the idea that the pursuit of self-interest leads as if by an invisible hand to the well-being of society. It took 150 years of work to prove exactly the conditions under which that is true. Years ago, Bruce Greenwald and I subsequently showed a very general result that whenever there are imperfect risk markets (which is always), whenever there is imperfect information, and particularly asymmetric information (which is always), then Adam Smith's "hand" is not just invisible but is, in fact, absent. That is to say, in general, the market is not constrained Pareto efficient (taking into account the costs of obtaining information and creating new markets).

Ours was a very general theorem. But now a whole group of economists—from Harvard, Columbia, Johns Hopkins, and UC Berkeley, to name a few universities in which this research is moving forward—have developed macroeconomic representations of these market failures. They have showed that there are systematic failures *at the macroeconomic level*. There could be too many interlinkages among banks (which was the problem with the credit default swap markets) or, as we noted earlier, too much foreign-denominated borrowing.

Another strand of research that had begun well before the crisis but which the crisis brought to the fore focuses on corporate governance. Eighty years ago, Berle and Means pointed out that there is a separation of ownership and control in modern capitalism, and they argued that this had important consequences. My research and that of others in the 1970s and 1980s laid information theoretic foundations for this delegation of decision making (in what came to be called the principal agent problem) and explored the consequences, including for the design of incentive contracts to align managerial interests with those of the owners. Regrettably, the macroeconomic models popular before the crisis left the issue out. Even Alan Greenspan, when he testified to Congress, acknowledged that this oversight was a flaw in his model: he and others believed that banks would be able to self-regulate. Self-regulation is an oxymoron, but remarkably, he and other regulators argued not only that the banks were in the best position to assess risk but also that they had the incentives to manage it well. What Greenspan forgot was that the bankers' interests were not well aligned with the banks' interests, and the banks' interests were not perfectly aligned with the rest of society's. Look at the design of the incentive systems at banks and it should be obvious, even to someone not trained in economics, that they encouraged taking on too much risk. In fact, given those incentive structures, if the bankers had *not* engaged in excessive risk, it would have proven our economic theories were wrong.

Academics have convincingly shown the importance of these problems of incentives and corporate governance, but it has not been fixed in practice. There have been some attempts to do so, but unsurprisingly, there has been pushback, as there has been in almost every other aspect of the regulatory environment.

Another big advance is in models exploring effects of financial market integration. One of the most important questions now before us is what a good financial structure should look like—a structure that absorbs risk, that does not explode when there is a big shock.

This is a research agenda that is just opening up, and one that I became interested in during the East Asia crisis. When I was chief economist at the World Bank, I had seen how the collapse of one bank led to the collapse of another bank, the failure of one firm led to the failure of another firm, to the point where 70 percent of Indonesian firms were bankrupt. This made it obvious that interdependence was important, so one had to start thinking about financial interlinkages. I have been working with several people, including Agostino Capponi at Columbia and Stefano Battiston at the University of Zurich, on questions such as whether it is best to have dense networks (financial systems with many linkages) or sparse networks. Dense networks are good in that they do a better job of sharing risk, but because they share risk, one can have a systemic crisis when there is a big correlated shock. Unless the government engages in a very costly bailout, the macroeconomic consequences of the resulting financial crisis are large. But either way, the costs to government and society are large.

An interesting idea that the IMF and a number of European countries have tried or talked about or advocated for themselves or the IMF (Germany has been particularly vocal) is a bail-in. But can you get the banks to voluntarily contribute? The United States tried that in 1998 in the Long-Term Capital Management crisis, where one hedge fund went bankrupt and, with one-and-a-half trillion dollars of debt, its disorderly collapse would have threatened general financial stability. LTCM needed large amounts of money to satisfy its creditors—the kind of money that the Central Bank would have naturally provided if LTCM had been a bank. But LTCM was not a bank, though many banks had lent LTCM money, and many bankers had too. That incident showed how interrelated and frail our financial system was. The New York Fed took the lead and got all the firms involved save two to cooperate in a bail-in. (There were some disquieting aspects of the bail-in: to get the cooperation of the managers of LTCM, its partners were given a 10 percent equity stake in the "resolved" enterprise, even though under normal bankruptcy, they could have gotten nothing; the heads of the banks used capital from the banks that they headed to save a hedge fund in which they had a personal stake—an obvious conflict of interest.) The degree to which the contributions of those who joined in the bail-in were "voluntary" is still debated. There were implicit threats: one never wants to cross one's regulator. The two that did—the two that didn't go along with the New York Fed's orchestrated "private" bailout of LTCM—were Bear Stearns and Lehman Brothers, and both were effectively allowed to go into bankruptcy in 2008, with shareholders being wiped out. (Some have suggested that this was their deserved payback for their earlier lack of cooperation.) But the question then becomes: can you have a credible bail-in if the regulator doesn't resort to such implicit or explicit threats of retribution? To have a credible bail-in "on its own merits," it has to be credible to each of the banks asked to contribute that the government will not bail out the financial system without its own cooperation. That is to say, for a bail-in to be credible, if the entities who are supposed to participate know that the government is going to bail them out anyway, why would they contribute to the bail-in?

Our recent research on networks relates to this. It turns out that with sparser networks and less interdependence, there are lower probabilities of bankruptcy cascades (where one bankruptcy leads to another, the specter that seemed to follow from Lehman's collapse), and bail-ins are more credible. Because the cascades will not occur, it is less credible that the government will perform a bailout. Taking account of the resulting lower expected bailout costs to the government, sparser networks work out to be the more efficient financial structure. These conclusions reverse what had been the common wisdom on the design of good financial structures.

The next step in this vein of research is to look at endogenous network formation: how it is affected by the rules, how a variety of risks can be controlled within any given network, and how this links to preventing systemic risk.

In all these ways, the crisis has brought about some good. It has spurred some interesting research that had previously been proceeding at a very slow pace.

Policy Has Not Adapted

Although there are benefits from the crisis arising from the academic response to the crisis, policy has lagged far, far behind, in almost every area. Banks do have larger buffers now, which is good. And there is more discussion of better macroeconomic regulation. But the changes in mortgage regulation have been far from adequate—for instance, the U.S. government is still the ultimate holder of a large percentage of U.S. mortgages. The government is absorbing the risk just like it was before the crisis. For all of Americans' pride in being a private market economy, the financial market for housing is run by the state. And, at that, it is done in the worst kind of private-public partnership, in which the private sector walks off with the profits and the public bears the risk.

But when proposals were made that the banks should bear at least 10 percent of the risk, the banks told the government that it would be impossible to function as a lender if they had to bear such risk. This is, of course, illogical: if you separate out loan origination—or "skin in the game," as it's called—from holding loans, moral hazard will be rampant.

The fact of the matter is that we have not been able to fix the mortgage market, and it does not seem likely that we will be able to due to the unwillingness of banks to bear responsibility for the mortgages they originate. The real estate industry wants to continue doing real estate, and the financial sector does not want to bear the risk associated with mortgage origination, and no one wants to square that circle. So the current system of ersatz capitalism with the government bearing the risk persists.

There are other areas where the policy reaction since the crisis has been very disappointing. Capital requirements have been raised for banks, but the banks complain about the high costs this has imposed on them—costs they say they have to pass on to borrowers (in spite of their record profits). The banks seem not to understand one of the basic ideas in modern finance, which is the Modigliani-Miller Theorem. That theorem says that, when one gets more debt, it simply pushes risk onto the resulting smaller amount of equity; what one saves on one account, one loses on the other. An increase in leverage does not magically reduce the true cost of capital. Banks have probably ignored this simple lesson because they want to push the risk onto the American taxpayer: they want to increase the bailout premium that they get.

That banks continue to fight these logical regulations is worrisome, and the banks have already scored some victories, turning back the clock toward the precrisis world. Outside the sphere of bankers, there is a broad consensus that the U.S. government should not bear the risk of derivatives and credit default swap. In response, the United States passed the so-called Lincoln Amendment to Dodd-Frank (the 2010 bill regulating the financial sector) to prevent government-insured institutions like banks from writing these derivatives. But the banks countered with their own amendment—which has come to be known as the Citibank Amendment because it was written by Citibank—and it effectively repealed the Lincoln Amendment. Thus today taxpayers still bear the residual risk of these risky financial products.

There are many ways of dealing with this risk consistent with the tenets of capitalism. Those who participate in derivatives markets could be made to be jointly liable so that they monitor what is going on. But banks clearly want the government to continue to pick up the risk.

Another important part of Dodd-Frank was an effort to monitor risk by establishing a research agency for that purpose. But the Trump administration has said it wants to take away spending for that important effort.

Further, nothing has really been done to counter the risk posed by too-big-to-fail banks. In fact, the problem with too-big-to-fail is worse because of mergers that occurred during the crisis—and which the government encouraged. And it is not just too-big-to-fail that imposes systemic risk. There are problems of too-intertwined-to-fail (or too-connected-to-fail) and too-correlated-to-fail. None of these problems have been fixed. Some of the too-correlated-to-fail issues would have been addressed if the United States had reenacted Glass-Steagall, but that opportunity was missed.

One morsel of good news at the policy level is that, in the aftermath of the crisis, the IMF changed its mind about a topic that has been a very big point of contention: cross-border regulation of short-term capital flows. Instability in these capital flows has, around the world, been a major source of financial and economic instability. The regulation of such flows was one of the most contentious aspects of my 2002 book, *Globalization and Its Discontents*. The IMF now says (in agreement with what I said there) that there ought to be special regulations of these cross-border capital flows because they do represent a special kind of risk.

Deeper Issues with Our Political System

The gap between the academic response to the crisis and what has happened in policy is not just about finance. This says a lot about how our political system works.

First, there has been no accountability for the bankers who undermined the trust in our system. The accountability that occurred after the Savings and Loan crisis, which was minute compared to the 2008 crisis, was orders of magnitude greater. The robo-signing scandal, in which people lost their homes sometimes even when they did not owe any money, showed that our country did not really adhere to the rule of law. Few of the people who engaged in practices like these that led to the crisis were held to account—even though there was much that could have been done. One example is that the government could have removed the board of directors at Wells Fargo for their actions; that could have happened at other banks as well.

There were many such measures that could have been taken, which were far short of putting people in prison but which would have sent a clearer signal that running a bank in certain ways will not be tolerated.

There are some other aspects of the financial system that may not have contributed to the crisis but have contributed to the lack of confidence in our economic system. One is the fact that, as people were losing their jobs and losing their homes, so many bankers walked off with bonuses—often euphemistically called "retention bonuses" to paper over the fact that people were being rewarded for failure. These types of things sent a message to the public that there was no justice or integrity in finance or in the parts of government that were charged with regulating it.

The fundamental reason that the big banks have so thoroughly avoided painful consequences for the problems they caused is their excessive market power, their abuse of that power, and their conversion of their economic power into political power. One of the big fights in Dodd-Frank was getting through the Durbin Amendment, which was to curtail the abuse of monopoly power associated with debit cards. In other countries, such as Australia, this power has been curtailed, proving that it is possible to get rid of this monopoly power. These countries have outlawed the use of certain contract provisions that amplify and maintain banks' market power in debit and credit cards, and monopoly profits have come way down as a result. The United States was only willing to impose some regulations on the abuse of market power for debit cards, not for credit cards. The government then made the mistake of delegating the issue of regulating the fees that the debit cards could charge merchants to the Federal Reserve, which is partially captured by the financial sector. The Fed's technical experts recommended a rate that I thought was 2 to 4 times the rate that it should have been, but then the Federal Reserve itself doubled that rate.

Such clear abuses of market power contribute to Americans' sense that the political system and the institutions it controls are rigged. Captured institutions undermine faith in the political system, and a disregard for the rule of law does as well. There was a proliferation of fraud in the credit rating agencies and investment banks before the crisis. Banks even refused to comply with contracts in which they had provided "money back guarantees" to investors and others who bore the risks of the mortgages that the mortgages were as described—that, for instance, they were for owner-occupied housing rather than rental properties (the default on the former is typically much lower than on the latter). And yet these contract provisions were seemingly well-designed to contain moral hazard. But if a legal system is broken, contracts are not worth the paper on which they are written. This type of trust is foundational to the functioning of our society.

And then there is a much broader issue. Almost all of the regulatory efforts have been directed at trying to *prevent* the banks and the financial sector from imposing harms on the rest of us: imposing harms from excessive risk taking, abusive credit card practices, market manipulation, predatory lending. Banks should be prevented from doing bad things, but they also need to be encouraged to do things that are beneficial to our society and our economy. There should have been far more discussion about what kind of a regulatory system would have created a financial system that actually worked. Better mortgages could be designed to help individuals manage the financial risk of home ownership—rather than the mortgages our private financial sector provided, which were designed to maximize the fees extracted from the financially unsophisticated. We have examples to inspire us: a Danish mortgage system that has worked for a long time and systems with income-indexed mortgages. There is a lot of financial innovation—not of the kind that gave us the crisis but of the kind that would make the U.S. economy stronger in the long term and less susceptible to crises. However, our industry does not seem to be interested in such innovations. It is up to the regulators to do more, and so far they have not. And if the private financial sector cannot do what it should, the government should step in with a *public option*, providing mortgages to reliable taxpayers at an interest rate just above that at which government itself can obtain funds.

We are already getting familiar with the fallout of our policy and political failures in response to the crisis. It is no abstraction; the lack of trust in our economic system and our financial system, and the well-deserved belief that we have a rigged system, have provided the context for the rise of a demagogue.

Notes

1. This chapter is adapted from remarks delivered at the conference "Ten Years After the Financial Crisis," Columbia University, December 7–8, 2017. After this speech was delivered, Congress took a major step toward undoing key provisions of Dodd-Frank.

2. The mathematics of this has been set forth in a series of papers with Stefano Battiston and other coauthors. See Tarik Roukny, Stefano Battiston, and Joseph E. Stiglitz, "Interconnectedness as a Source of Uncertainty in Systemic Risk," *Journal of Financial Stability* 35 (2018): 93–106; Stefano Battiston, Guido Caldarelli, Robert M. May, Tarik Roukny, and Joseph E. Stiglitz, "The Price of Complexity in Financial Networks," *Proceedings of the National Academy of Sciences of the United States of America* 113, no. 36 (2016): 10031–36; and Stefano Battiston, Domenico Delli Gatti, Mauro Gallegati, Bruce Greenwald, and Joseph E. Stiglitz, "Liaisons Dangereuses: Increasing Connectivity, Risk Sharing, and Systemic Risk," *Journal of Economic Dynamics and Control* 36 (2012): 1121–41. Anyone who has taken an elementary course in mathematics knows what matters is the convexity of the relevant functions. The models used by the Federal Reserve and by the IMF always assumed diminishing returns, with no nonconvexities, and so they always concluded that diversification was good. But bankruptcy costs or learning or large fixed costs of production change this.

3. Joseph E. Stiglitz and Bruce Greewald, *Towards a New Paradigm in Monetary Economics* (Cambridge: Cambridge University Press, 2003).

4. Franklin Allen and David Gale, "Financial Contagion," *Journal of Political Economy* 108, no. 1 (2000): 1–33.

5. The federal government won a multibillion dollar suit, and there have been some very large settlements, but more than a decade after the crisis, multiple big banks are refusing to honor their contracts and are fighting billion-dollar suits over breach of contract and fraud. Closer inspection of the mortgage files showed that large proportions were "defective" (i.e., significantly different from what they were represented to be), often seemingly fraudulently so. It seemed that the banks were simply hoping that *somehow* something might happen that would enable them not to pay their due, either some judge ruling that the statute of limitations (limiting how long after a bad act is committed it can be sued) had passed or that some corporate-friendly judge would somehow forgive them for what they had done. (I have served as an expert witness in several of these suits.)

6. See, in particular, the special symposium on the subject in the *Oxford Review of Economic Policy* in 2017, including my paper, Joseph E. Stiglitz, "Where Modern Macroeconomics Went Wrong," *Oxford Review of Economic Policy* 34 no. 1–2 (2017): 70–106. For a more establishment defense of the old models, see the 2018 symposium in the *Journal of Economic Perspectives*.

CHAPTER 11

THE RIGHT WAY TO USE MODELS

EMANUEL DERMAN

Metaphors

Sleep is the interest we have to pay on the capital which is called in at death; and the higher the rate of interest and the more regularly it is paid, the further the date of redemption is postponed.

So wrote Arthur Schopenhauer, comparing life to finance in a universe that must keep its books balanced. At birth you receive a loan—consciousness and light borrowed from the void, leaving an absence in the emptiness. Nightly, by yielding temporarily to the darkness of sleep, you restore some of the emptiness and keep the absence from growing limitlessly. Finally you must pay back the principal, make the void complete again, and return the life originally lent you.

By focusing on the common periodic nature of both sleep and interest payments, Schopenhauer extends the metaphor of a loan to life itself. The principal is life and consciousness, and death is the final repayment. Along the way, sleep is the periodic little death that keeps the borrower solvent.

Good metaphors are expansive; they compare something we don't understand (sleep), to something we think we do (finance). They let you see in a new light both the object of interest and the substrate you rest it on, and enlighten upward and downward.

The common basis of Schopenhauer's metaphoric extension is periodicity. Taking an analogy based on matching regularities and then extending it into distant regions is a time-honored trick of mathematicians. You can

see it at work in the extension of the definition of the factorial function
$n! = n \times (n-1) \times (n-2)...1$.

Using the exclamation point is traditional but clumsy. Because $n!$ is a function of $n!$, it's more elegant to express it via the function $F(n)$ defined by $F(n) = (n-1)!$, which satisfies the recursive property $F(n+1) = nF(n)$. You can regard this property as almost a definition of the factorial function. If you define $F(1) = 1$, then $F(n)$ for all integers greater than 1 can be found from the recursive definition.

The definition $n! = n \times (n-1) \times (n-2)...1$ works only for positive integers n. The definition $F(n+1) = nF(n)$ seems more malleable. Why shouldn't there be a function $F(x)$ that satisfies the relation $F(x+1) = xF(x)$ where x is not necessarily a positive integer? Why shouldn't the factorial function exist both for $x = 3$ and, say, $x = 3.2731$?

The Swiss mathematician Leonhard Euler discovered (invented?) the gamma function $\Gamma(x)$ that does indeed satisfy $\Gamma(x+1) = x\Gamma(x)$ for all x. For integer values of x, it agrees with the traditional factorial function. For noninteger or even complex values of x, $G(x)$ serves as a smooth extrapolation or interpolation of the factorial from integer to noninteger arguments. It's smooth because it coincides with the factorial function for positive integer arguments but maintains the crucial recursive property for nonintegers. Mathematicians call this kind of extension *analytic continuation*.

The gamma function is a metaphorical extension of the factorial, in which one property, its recursion, becomes its most important feature and serves as the basis for extending it. It's a bit like calling an automobile a horseless carriage, preserving the essence of carrying and removing the unnecessary horsefulness, or like calling a railroad *ferrovia* in Italian or *Eisenbahn* in German, focusing on the fact that it's still a road, but one made instead of iron. Analytic continuation is a method of modeling a function. But whereas most models are restrictive—a model train is less than a real train—in mathematics, a new model can be something greater rather than diminished. That's because mathematics deals entirely with its own world, and everything you do extends it rather than confines it.

Most of the words we use to describe our feelings are metaphors or models. To say you are elated is to say you feel *as though* you have been lifted to a high place. But why is there something good about height? In the gravitational field of the earth, all nonfloating animals recognize the physical struggle necessary to rise and experience wonder when they see the world spread out beneath them. Being elated is feeling as if you'd overcome gravity. People dream of flying.

Conversely, we speak of feeling depressed *as though* we'd been pushed down to a low place. Things are looking up, we say, looking brighter, or less dark. These are metaphors too, derived from our physical senses. Metaphors nest, recursively. When we say the economy is depressed, we are comparing the economy's spirits (another metaphor) to the spirits of a person who feels as though he or she were pulled down by gravity.

Language is a tower of metaphors, each "higher" one resting on older ones "below." Not every word can be a metaphor or language would be meaningless. At the base of the tower are words such as *push* and *down*, two of the nonmetaphorical word-concepts on which the tower rests. *Push* and *down* are understood by us viscerally because we are "wetware," collections of chemicals rather than silicon or computer code, that experience the world through the sensations of which chemicals are capable. You cannot have lived without knowing what it is to have struggled against gravity and responded to light and warmth and, hence, to know that *down* and *dark* are bad and *up* and *light* are good.

Had life arisen in outer space, free of gravity and light, there would be no perceptible down or up and, hence, no possibility of depression or elation. You could be disheartened perhaps, but not depressed. You could feel full or empty, but not light or heavy, bright or dark. And you couldn't take a dim view of your surroundings.

Models

We use the word *model* in many contexts. A model airplane is a scaled-down version of an actual plane, similar in some respects, but not all. The four-year-old's plastic plane, the twelve-year-old's radio-controlled glider, and the aeronautical engineer's wind-tunnel airplane are all model airplanes, though they differ from each other. The similarities to the real thing are important, but different users require different similarities.

What do we mean when we call some construct a model?

The *Model T* is a version of a Ford, one of a class of things belonging to the Ford category. Model T is an instance, less general, not everything a Ford might be.

A *fashion model* can be an actual person used to display clothing or cosmetics. It's not everything a person might be. When you're a model, only parts of you are important. A person is complete, the real thing.

An *artist's model* is a proxy for the real thing. A mannequin is a proxy for a proxy. (The work of art that uses the proxy becomes a real thing again.)

A *computer model of the weather* tries to predict the weather in the future from the weather today. "Weather" is an abstraction for a collection of an indefinite number of qualities and quantities and the way they vary over the short term, among them temperature, pressure, humidity, wind speed. A weather model's equations focus on a limited number of features of a limitlessly complex system. Even with the right equation, there is always the danger that one has omitted something ostensibly negligible but whose tail effects over long times are crucially important.

An *economic model* aims to do for the economy what the weather model does for the weather. It, too, embodies a set of equations that attempts to represent the behavior of the people and institutions interacting in an economy. But just as the notion of weather is more abstract than the notion of an airplane, so the concept of an economy is even more diffuse. Money, supply, demand, and utility, just a few of the many variables in an economic model, are much harder to define (let alone quantify) than temperature and pressure. A "market" and an "economy" are even more clearly a construct of the mind. When you model the economy, you are modeling abstractions.

Hayek[1] pointed out that in the physical sciences the macroscopic concepts (gases, pressure, etc.) are concrete and the microscopic one (atoms and molecules) are abstractions. But in economics, he argues, individuals are concrete and the "economy" is the abstraction.

The *Black-Scholes model* tells you how to estimate the value of an option in terms of its underlying risk. It's a recipe, an engineering model, a Sol LeWitt painting that contains instructions for how to create a work of art. Just as a weather model makes assumptions about how fluids flow and how heat undergoes convection, just as a soufflé recipe makes assumptions about what happens when you whip egg whites, so the Black-Scholes model makes assumptions about how stock prices fluctuate up and down. But our assumptions about the behavior of stock markets are much less believable than our assumptions about how egg whites turn fluffy. Fluids and egg protein don't care what people think about them; markets and stock prices do. Like a weather model (but even more so), Black-Scholes is a limited, ingeniously clever mental model of a complex system, a small box that tries to imitate the actual world outside.

The *standard model*, for which Sheldon Glashow, Abdus Salam, and Steven Weinberg received the 1979 Nobel Prize in Physics, is a unified description of the smallest elementary particles (quarks and leptons) and the forces between them. The description incorporates into one coherent framework Maxwell's nineteenth-century theory of electromagnetism, the 1928 Dirac theory of the electron, and Fermi's 1934 theory of beta decay, in which all of these apparently disparate forces are only superficially different aspects of a single more general force. The standard model is not really a "model" at all but rather a description and, hence, a theory.

A theory, as I argue below, attempts to provide an accurate description of the nature of things, unifying the outward with the inward, not just saving the appearances but identifying their essence. A model arises out of conscious analogy. A theory arises out of a deep intuitive identification of the inner and the outer.

Why Is a Model a Model?

A model airplane, however complex, is simple when compared to the real thing.

There is a gap between the model and the object of its focus. The model is not the object, though we may wish it were.

A model is a metaphor of limited applicability, not the thing itself. Calling a computer an electronic brain once cast light on the function of computers. Nevertheless, a computer is not an electronic brain. Calling the brain a computer is a model too. In tackling the mysterious world via models, we do our best to explain the thus-far incomprehensible by describing it in terms of the things we already partially comprehend. Models, like metaphors, take the properties of something rich and project them onto something strange.

A model focuses on parts rather than the whole. It is a caricature that overemphasizes some features at the expense of others.

A model is a fetish in which the importance of one key part of the object of interest is obsessively exaggerated until it comes to represent the object's quintessence, a shoe or corset standing in for a woman. (Is that perhaps why most modelers are male?) But the shoe or corset isn't the woman, just the most important part of the woman for this model user.

The most valuable knowledge is unconscious. Until you can do something without thinking, you can't move farther up the hierarchy of metaphors of description in language or science. In *Zen in the Art of Archery*, Eugen Herrigel recounts the struggle to make mental knowledge visceral. Thinking for yourself is hard work. Models provide ways of letting other people do the thinking for you. With Feynman diagrams, almost anyone can calculate elementary particle cross-sections mechanically.

In physics or finance, the first major struggle is to gain some intuition about how to proceed; the second struggle is to transform that intuition into something more formulaic, a set of rules anyone can follow, rules that no longer require the original insight itself. One person's breakthrough becomes everybody's possession.

The world is multidimensional. Models allow us to project the object into a smaller space and then extrapolate or interpolate within it. At some point, the extrapolation will break down. What's amazing is how well it sometimes works, especially in the physical sciences.

But extrapolation based on limited information is dangerous; extrapolation depends on a model, not a fact. Estrogen supplements cause their own problems, and margarine only seemed better than butter.

When unconsciously used, models result in paradoxes or conflicts, and it becomes necessary to expose and then examine unconscious assumptions.

This is what Einstein did with the concept of simultaneity, what Lee and Yang did with parity invariance.

Why Is a Theory a Theory?

Models are analogies, and always describe something *relative* to something else. Theories, in contrast, are *the real thing*. They don't compare; they describe the essence, without reference. Every fact, as Goethe wrote, is a theory.

In that sense, a theory is the ultimate nonmetaphor.

Moses, tending the flock of his father-in-law Jethro near the mountain of Horeb, saw a burning bush whose flame would not consume it. God, from within the bush, declared himself to Moses and commanded him to deliver the Israelites from Pharaoh.

Whom shall I tell them sent me? asks Moses.

Tell them: I am that which I am, said the voice.

God is riffing on his true name: the Hebrew word for *I will be* is *EHYH*. Its root is *HVH*, the last three letters of God's name. *HVH* means *being*, and is also the name of the *present tense* in Hebrew grammar. YHVH (Yahweh or Jehovah) is the irreducible substance, the ultimate nonmetaphor, too, the bottom-level primitive out of which everything else is constructed. Hence, no graven images, no models, are possible. You can't ask "*Why?*" about YHVH; you can ask only "*How?*"

Theories tell you what something *is*. Models tell you only what something is *more or less* like. Unless you constantly remember that, therein lies their danger.

My favorite theory is Dirac's 1928 theory of the electron, still correct today. He sought an equation that satisfied both quantum mechanics and special relativity. The one he found had four solutions. Two of them described the electron that physicists already knew about, a particle with negative charge and two spin states. But Dirac's equation had two additional solutions, similar to the ones he'd already found, but with incomprehensibly negative energy. The positive-energy solutions described the electron so well that Dirac felt obliged to make sense of the negative-energy ones too.

Dirac postulated that the void—the medium that we call empty space, what physicists call the vacuum—is in fact filled to its rim with negative-energy electrons, and they constitute an infinite sea. This metaphorical *Dirac sea* is the vacuum we inhabit, and, accustomed to it, we don't notice the infinite number of negative charges surrounding us. (We smell only pollutants, not air itself.) If this is true, argued Dirac, then when you shoot light into the vacuum and eject a negative energy electron, a hole is left behind. This absence of an electron and its negative charge behaves exactly like an electron with a positive charge. Anderson discovered this so-called positron in 1932 and astounded all the physicists uncomfortable with what had been a metaphorical stretch. Just as life is a temporary hole in the darkness, so here, too, absence becomes a presence.

Dirac's equation transcended its metaphor and became a theory of reality. A brain may be *like* a computer, an atom may be *like* a miniature solar system, but an electron *is* the Dirac equation. Dirac's theory of the electron stands on its own two feet, beyond metaphor, the thing itself. Like God in the burning bush identifying himself to Moses, the theory of the electron pronounces, "I am that which I am."

Theories are deep and inexplicable, difficult to find; they require verification; they are right when they are right. Models are shallow and somewhat easier to invent; they require explanation. We need models as well as theories.

Spinoza's Theory of the Affects

Spinoza approached what he called the *affects*, human emotions, in the same way that Euclid approached triangles and squares, aiming to understand their interrelations by means of principles, logic, and deduction. Spinoza's avowed aim was to find a method to escape the violent sway emotions inflict on human beings caught in their grip.

The Primitives

Spinoza's primitives are *pain*, *pleasure*, and *desire*. Every adult with a human body knows by direct experience what these feelings are, although Spinoza, following Euclid's definitions of points and lines, makes an attempt to define them.

Desire, he writes, *is appetite conscious of itself.*

Its cohorts are two more primitives: *pleasure* and *pain*.

Though he defines them, as is the case with Euclid's points and lines, we can recognize neither pain nor pleasure from their verbal definitions; we need to have experienced them directly and had them named. They lie beneath all the other affects and can conveniently be thought of as closer to organic conditions than psychic ones.

Spinoza distinguishes finely between local and global sensations. "*Pleasure* and *pain*," he writes, "Are ascribed to a man when one part of him is affected more than the rest, whereas *cheerfulness* and *melancholy* are ascribed to him when all are equally affected." *Suffering*, therefore, is localized *pain*, whereas *melancholy* is globalized *pain*.

His definitions of good and bad are utilitarian at the individual level. "By good I here mean every kind of pleasure, and all that conduces thereto, especially that which satisfies our longings, whatsoever they may be. By evil, I mean every kind of pain, especially that which frustrates our longings." *Good* is that which brings *pleasure*, and *bad* is that which brings *pain*.

The Derivatives

The primitives are the most fundamental affects, and the more complex emotions bear a more indirect link to the three just named. Just as financial stock options are derivatives that depend on the underlying stock price, so more complex human emotions derive their force from their relation to the three underlying sensations of pain, pleasure, and desire. Spinoza elaborates:

> *Love* is *pleasure* associated with an external object.
> *Hate* is *pain* associated with an external object.
> *Hope* is the expectation of future *pleasure* when the outcome is uncertain and doubtful.
> *Joy* is the *pleasure* we experience when that doubtful expectation is fulfilled.
> *Disappointment* is the *pain* of unfulfilled pleasure.
> *Pity* is *pain* accompanied by the idea of evil which has befallen someone else whom we conceive to be like ourselves.

More complex emotions, like exotic financial derivatives, depend on two underlying primitives. *Envy* is *pain* at another's *pleasure*, like a convertible bond whose value depends on stock prices and interest rates. Conversely, though Spinoza doesn't name it, *Schadenfreude* is *pleasure* at another's *pain*.

Cruelty involves all three primitives: Spinoza defines it as the *desire* to inflict *pain* on someone we *love* or *pity*. Financially speaking, *cruelty* is a convertible bond whose value depends on the stock price of the underlying stock, riskless interest rates, and credit spreads.

Spinoza adds to his system three additional primitives that are meta-emotions. The first is *Vacillation*, the state of oscillation between two emotions. Thus *Jealousy*, he explains, is the *vacillation* between *hate* and *envy* toward an object of *love* in the presence of a rival for it. *Jealousy* is a derivative of *envy*, and *envy* is a derivative of *pleasure* and *pain*. If we follow the links far enough, we end up always at *pain*, *pleasure*, and *desire*.

The second addition is *Wonder*. *Wonder* is what we experience when confronted by something that fills the mind to the exclusion of all else, something unrelated to anything else. *Wonder* is what we experience in the presence of Yahweh in the burning bush, who is what he is, and bears no relation to anything else.

Spinoza's final primitive is *Contempt*, the feeling we have when we contemplate something that most forcibly reminds us of all the qualities it lacks. An absence becomes a nameable presence.

I call what Spinoza created a theory rather than a model. He doesn't make analogies; he doesn't attempt to explain how humans behave by comparing them to some other system we already understand. He begins with observations about human beings, obtained through experience, introspection, and intuition. He produced a theory accessible to everyone because it analyzes everyday human experiences.

Figure 11.1 illustrates the dependency of all the emotions on *desire, pleasure,* and *pain.*

Intuition

It takes intuition to discover theories. Intuition may sound casual, but it results from intimate knowledge acquired by careful observation and painstaking effort. John Maynard Keynes wrote a speech for the Newton tercentenary in which he commented on Newton's qualities:

> Newton came to be thought of as the first and greatest of the modern age of scientists, a rationalist, one who taught us to think on the lines of cold and untinctured reason. I do not see him in this light. Newton was not the first of the age of reason. He was the last of the magicians, the last of the Babylonians and Sumerians, the last great mind which looked out on the visible and intellectual world with the same eyes as those who began to build our intellectual inheritance rather less than 10,000 years ago. . . .
>
> I believe that the clue to his mind is to be found in his unusual powers of continuous concentrated introspection. . . . His peculiar gift was the power of holding continuously in his mind a purely mental problem until he had seen straight through it. I fancy his pre-eminence is due to his muscles of intuition being the strongest and most enduring with which a man has ever been gifted. Anyone who has ever attempted pure scientific or philosophical thought knows how one can hold a problem momentarily in one's mind and apply all one's powers of concentration to piercing through it, and how it will dissolve and escape and you find that what you are surveying is a blank. I believe that Newton could hold a problem in his mind for hours and days and weeks until it surrendered to him its secret. Then being a supreme mathematical technician he could dress it up, how you will, for purposes of exposition, but it was his intuition which was pre-eminently extraordinary—"so happy in his conjectures," said De Morgan, "as to seem to know more than he could possibly have any means of proving."[2]

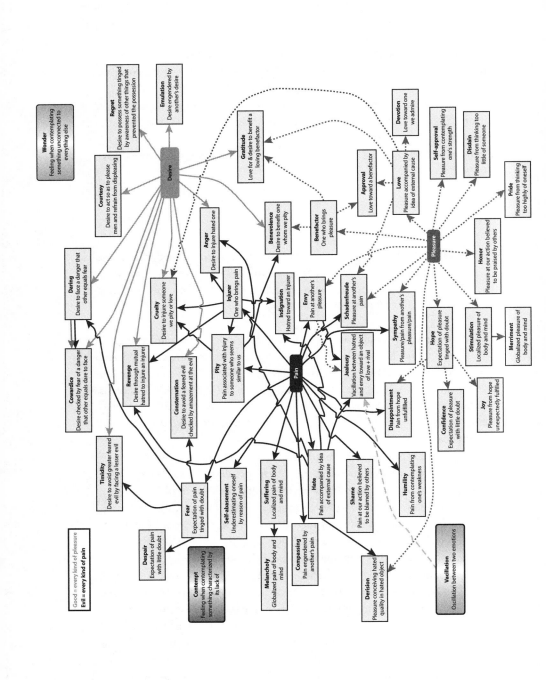

Wonder
Feeling when contemplating something unconnected to everything else

Regret
Desire to possess something tinged by awareness of other things that prevented the possession

Emulation
Desire engendered by another's desire

Courtesy
Desire to act so as to please men and refrain from displeasing

Gratitude
Love for & desire to benefit a loving benefactor

Devotion
Love toward one we admire

Self-approval
Pleasure from contemplating one's strength

Disdain
Pleasure from thinking too little of someone

Daring
Desire to face a danger that other equals fear

Cruelty
Desire to injure someone we pity or love

Anger
Desire to injure hated one

Benevolence
Desire to benefit one whom we pity

Approval
Love toward a benefactor

Love
Pleasure accompanied by idea of external cause

Benefactor
One who brings pleasure

Honor
Pleasure at our action believed to be praised by others

Pride
Pleasure from thinking too highly of oneself

Desire

Pleasure

Cowardice
Desire checked by fear of a danger that other equals dare to face

Revenge
Desire through mutual hatred to injure an injurer

Injurer
One who brings pain

Indignation
Hatred toward an injurer

Envy
Pain at another's pleasure

Schadenfreude
Pleasure at another's pain

Sympathy
Pleasure/pain from another's pleasure/pain

Stimulation
Localized pleasure of body and mind

Merriment
Globalized pleasure of body and mind

Timidity
Desire to avoid greater feared evil by facing a lesser evil

Pity
Pain associated with injury to someone who seems similar to us

Consternation
Desire to avoid a feared evil checked by amazement at the evil

Jealousy
Vacillation between hatred and envy toward an object of love + rival

Hope
Expectation of pleasure tinged with doubt

Joy
Pleasure from hope unexpectedly fulfilled

Fear
Expectation of pain tinged with doubt

Pain

Disappointment
Pain from hope unfulfilled

Confidence
Expectation of pleasure with little doubt

Despair
Expectation of pain with little doubt

Self-abasement
Underestimating oneself by reason of pain

Suffering
Localized pain of body and mind

Hate
Pain accompanied by idea of external cause

Shame
Pain at our action believed to be blamed by others

Humility
Pain from contemplating one's weakness

Contempt
Feeling when contemplating something characterized by its lack of

Good = every kind of pleasure
Evil = every kind of pain

Melancholy
Globalized pain of body and mind

Compassing
Pain engendered by another's pain

Derision
Pleasure conceiving hated quality in hated object

Vacillation
Oscillation between two emotions

This perception—that his insight arose independent of his proof—was also James Clerk Maxwell's opinion about André-Marie Ampère, who, in 1820, discovered the connection between electricity and magnetism. Referring to Ampère as the "Newton of electricity," Maxwell, who extended Ampère's discoveries into Maxwell's equations and found that they described light, wrote:

> We can scarcely believe that Ampere really discovered the law of action by means of the experiments which he describes. We are led to suspect, what, indeed, he tells us himself, that he discovered the law by some process which he has not shown us, and that when he had afterwards built up a perfect demonstration, he removed all traces of the scaffolding by which he had built it.[3]

When you struggle with a field of inquiry for a long, long time, and you eventually master and incorporate not only its formalism but its content, you can make use of it to build things one level higher.

Intuition is a merging of the understander with the understood. It is the deepest kind of knowledge.

Models in Finance

There are no genuine theories in finance. Financial models are always models of comparison, of relative value. They are metaphors. The efficient market model assumes stock prices behave *like* smoke diffusing through a room. These are comparisons that have some reasonableness, but they're not even remotely fact. Newton's laws and Maxwell's equations are. There is almost no gap between the object and their description. You can say that stock prices behave *like* smoke. You cannot say that light behaves like Maxwell's equations. Light *is* Maxwell's equations.

Therefore, the advanced mathematics in a financial model is to some extent deceptive. The syntax is similar to that of accurate physical theories, but the semantics is not. One should not mistake the similarity of style for similarity of truthfulness.

All concepts, perhaps all things, are mental. But there are no genuine theories in finance because finance is concerned with value, an even more subjective concept than heat or pressure. Furthermore, it is very difficult to find the scientific laws or even the regularities governing the behavior of economies: there are very few isolated economic machines, so one cannot carry out the repeated experiments that science requires. History is important in economics. Credit markets tomorrow won't behave like credit markets last year because we have learned what happened last year and cannot get back to the initial conditions of a year ago. Human beings and societies learn; physical systems by and large don't.

For an experiment to be approximately repeatable, history has to be unimportant. That requires that the system couple very weakly to the rest of the universe. A coin flip can be repeated ad infinitum under almost the same conditions because external conditions affect its outcome hardly at all. That's not the case in finance.

What Is the Point of a Model in Finance?

It takes only a little experience to see that it's not the same as the point of a model in physics or chemistry. Mostly, the point of a model is not prediction or divination. Here's a simple but prototypical financial model that has most of the characteristics of more sophisticated models.

How do you estimate the price of a seven-room apartment on Park Ave. if someone tells you the market price of a typical two-room apartment in Battery Park City? Most likely, you figure out the price per square foot of the two-room apartment. Then you multiply by the square footage of the Park Ave. apartment. Finally you make some rule-of-thumb higher-order corrections for location, park views, light, facilities and so on. You might develop a model for those too.

The model's critical parameter is the implied price per square foot. You *calibrate* the model to Battery Park City. Then you use it to interpolate or extrapolate to Park Ave. The price per square foot is *implied* from the market price of the Battery Park City apartments; it's not the *realized* construction price per square foot because there are other variables—exposure, quality of construction, neighborhood—that are subsumed into that one implied number.

Calibration is dangerous; it's always fitting a wrong model to the only world we know, and then using it to extrapolate or interpolate. The closer your model to the behavior of the world, the less dangerous your extrapolation.

The Aim of Financial Models

The way property markets use implied price per square foot illustrates the functions of financial models more generally.

Models Are Used to Rank Securities by Value

Apartments have manifold features. Implied price per square foot can be used to rank and compare many similar but not identical apartments. It provides a simple one-dimensional scale on which to *begin* ranking apartments by value. The single number given by implied price per square foot doesn't truly reflect the value of the apartment; it provides a starting point after which more qualitative factors must be taken into account.

Models Are Used to Interpolate from Liquid Prices to Illiquid Ones

In finance, models are used less for divination than in order to interpolate or extrapolate from the known prices of liquid securities to the values of illiquid securities at the current time—in the example above, from the Battery Park City price to the Park Ave. value. The Black-Scholes model proceeds from a known stock price and a riskless bond price to the unknown price of a hybrid, an option, similar to the way one estimates the value of fruit salad from its constituent fruits.

No model is correct—a model is not a theory—but models can provide immensely helpful ways to make initial estimates of value.

Models Transform Intuitive Linear Quantities Into Nonlinear Dollar Values

In finance a model is also a means of translating acquired *intuition* into dollar values. The apartment value model transforms price per square foot into the value of the apartment. It's easier to begin with an estimate of price per square foot because that quantity captures so much of the variability of apartment prices. Similarly, it's easier to convert one's intuition about future volatility into current options prices than it is to guess at the appropriate prices themselves.

The One Law of Finance

Research papers in quantitative finance look superficially like those in natural science, but the similarity is deceptive. There are no deep laws or theories in finance that can be expressed in mathematics.

The one law you can rely on in finance is the law of one price, which, roughly put, dictates: "If you want to know the value of a financial security, use the known price of another security that's *as similar to it* as possible."

The wonderful thing about this law—it's valuation by analogy—when compared with almost everything else in economics, is that it dispenses with utility functions, the unobservable hidden variable whose ghostly presence permeates most of faux-quantitative economic theory.

The law of one price is not a law of nature. It's a general reflection on the practices of human beings, who, when they have enough time and enough information, will grab a bargain when they see one. The law usually holds in the long run, in well-oiled markets with enough savvy participants, but there are always short- or even longer-term exceptions that persist.

How do you use the law of one price to determine value? If you want to estimate the unknown value of a target security, you must find some other replicating portfolio, a collection of more liquid securities that, collectively, is similar to, i.e., has the same future payoffs as the target, *no matter how the future turns out*. The target's value is then simply that value of the replicating portfolio.

Where do models enter? It takes a model to demonstrate similarity, to show that the target and the replicating portfolio have identical future payoffs *under all circumstances*. To demonstrate the identity of future payoffs, you must (1) specify what you mean by "all circumstances" for each security, and (2) you must find a strategy for creating a replicating portfolio that, in each future scenario or eventuality, will have payoffs identical to those of the target. That's what the Black-Scholes options model does—it tells you precisely how to replicate an option out of stocks and bonds, under certain assumptions. It's like a recipe that tells you how to make fruit salad—an option—out of fruit: the stocks and bonds. And, ingeniously used, it tells you how to do the inverse—to figure out the value of one type of fruit given the price of other fruits and fruit salad.

Most of the mathematical complexity in finance involves the description of the range of future behavior of each security's price. Trying to specify all circumstances reminds me of the 1967 movie *Bedazzled*, starring Peter Cook and Dudley Moore. In this retelling of the German legend of Faust, Dudley Moore plays a short-order cook at a Wimpy's chain restaurant in London who sells his soul to the devil in exchange for seven chances to specify the circumstances under which he can achieve his romantic aims with the Wimpy's waitress he desires. Each time the devil asks him to specify the romantic scenarios under which he believes he will succeed, he cannot get them quite specific enough. He says he wants to be alone with the waitress in a beautiful place where they are both in love with each other. He gets what he wants—with a snap of the devil's fingers, he and his beloved are instantly transported to a country estate where he is a guest of the owner, her husband, whom her principles will not allow her to betray. In the final episode, he wishes for them to be alone together and in love with each other in a quiet place where no one will bother them. He gets his wish: The devil makes them both nuns in a convent where everyone has taken a vow of silence. This difficulty is the same difficulty we have when specifying future scenarios in financial models—like the devil, markets always eventually outwit us. Even if markets are not strictly random, their vagaries are too rich to capture in a few sentences or equations.

So die the dreams of financial theories. Only imperfect models remain.

The Right Way to Use Models

Given that finance's best tools are shaky models, the best strategy is to use models as little as possible, and to replicate making as few assumptions as you can. Here are some other rules I've found to be useful as a practitioner.

Avoid Too Much Axiomatization

Axiomatization is for mathematics. Finance is about the real world. Every financial axiom is pretty much wrong; the practical question is: *how* wrong, and can you still make use of it?

Good Models Are Vulgar in a Sophisticated Way

In physics it pays to drop down deep, several levels below what you can observe (think of Newton, Maxwell, Dirac), formulate an elegant principle, and then rise back to the surface to work out the observable consequences. In financial valuation, which lacks deep scientific principles, it's better to stay shallow and use models that have as direct as possible a path between observation of similarity and its consequences.

Markets are by definition vulgar, and correspondingly the most useful models are wisely vulgar, too, using variables that the crowd uses, like price per square foot, to describe the phenomena they observe. Build vulgar models in a sophisticated way.

Of course, over time crowds and markets get smarter and the definition of vulgarity changes to encompass increasingly sophisticated concepts.

Sweep Dirt Under the Rug, but Let Users Know About It

One should be very humble in applying mathematics to markets, and be extremely wary of ambitious theories, which are, when you face facts, trying to model human behavior.

Whenever we make a model of something involving human beings, we are trying to force the ugly stepsister's foot into Cinderella's pretty glass slipper. It doesn't fit without cutting off some essential parts. Models inevitably mask as well as expose risk. You must start with models and then overlay them with common sense and experience.

The world of markets doesn't exactly match the ideal circumstances a model assumes, but a robust model allows a savvy user to qualitatively adjust for those mismatches. A user should know what has been assumed when he uses the model, and he should know exactly what has been swept out of view.

Think of Models as Gedanken Experiments

It's impossible to make a correct financial model. Therefore, I like to think of financial models as *gedanken* experiments, like those Einstein carried out when he pictured himself surfing a light wave or Schrodinger when he pictured a macroscopic cat subject to quantum effects.

I believe that's the right way to use mathematical models in finance, and the way experienced practitioners do use them. Models are only models, not the thing in itself. So, we can't expect them to be truly right. Models are better regarded as a collection of parallel thought universes you can explore. Each universe should be consistent, but the actual financial and human world, unlike the world of matter, is going to be infinitely more complex than any model you make of it. You are always trying to shoehorn the real world into one of the models to see how useful an approximation that is.

Beware of Idolatry

The greatest conceptual danger is idolatry, imagining that someone can write down a theory that encapsulates human behavior and relieves you of the difficulty of constant thinking. A model may be entrancing, but no matter how hard you try, you will not be able to breath true life into it. To confuse the model with a theory is to embrace a future disaster driven by the belief that humans obey mathematical rules.

Financial modelers must therefore compromise, must firmly decide what small part of the financial world is of greatest current interest, decide on its key features, and make a mockup of only those. A model cannot include everything. If you are interested in everything, you are interested in too much. A successful financial model must have limited scope; you must work with simple analogies; in the end, you are trying to rank complex objects by projecting them onto a low-dimensional scale.

In physics, there may one day be a Theory of Everything; in finance and the social sciences, you have to work hard to have a usable Model of Anything.

A Manifesto

Because of the inherent unreliability of models in the social sciences, in 2009 Paul Wilmott and I wrote The Financial Modelers Manifesto, outlining the right way to think about financial models.[4] We concluded with the Modelers' Hippocratic Oath.

The Modelers' Hippocratic Oath

- I will remember that I didn't make the world, and it doesn't satisfy my equations.

- Though I will use models boldly to estimate value, I will not be overly impressed by mathematics.
- I will never sacrifice reality for elegance without explaining why I have done so.
- Nor will I give the people who use my model false comfort about its accuracy. Instead, I will make explicit its assumptions and oversights.
- I understand that my work may have enormous effects on society and the economy, many of them beyond my comprehension.

More Principles, Fewer Regulations

Though there are wise ways of using them, the foolish use of models is only a part of the story of the financial crisis and the subsequently inadequate poultices applied to it. Listed below are a few more suggestions for avoiding catastrophes.

- Nature runs on principles rather than regulations.
- Everyone is a grownup, and no one is more grownup than anyone else.
- Your words are as valuable as money.
- If you want the benefits of taking risk, you must also suffer the disadvantages.
- Corporations are neither governments nor people.
- Don't treat only some people's insolvency as illiquidity.
- Optimization in human affairs is an illusion. You always need more capital than you think.
- Provide golden parachutes for no one; provide tin parachutes for everyone.
- "If you believe that capitalism is a system in which money matters more than freedom, you are doomed when people who don't believe in freedom attack using money."[5]

Notes

1. Friedrich Hayek, *The Counter-Revolution of Science*, 2nd ed. (Indianapolis, IN: Liberty Fund, 1979).
2. This speech appears in chapter 35 of *The Collected Writings of John Maynard Keynes*, ed. Elizabeth Johnson and Donald Moggridge (London: Royal Economic Society, 1978).
3. James Clerk Maxwell, *Treatise on Electricity and Magnetism* (1873), https://en.wikisource.org/wiki/A_Treatise_on_Electricity_and_Magnetism/Part_IV/Chapter_III.
4. Paul Wilmott and Emanuel Derman, "The Financial Modelers Manifesto," https://en.wikipedia.org/wiki/Financial_Modelers%27_Manifesto.
5. Edward Lucas *The New Cold War: Putin's Russia and the Threat to the West* (New York: Palgrave Macmillan, 2008), 100.

CHAPTER 12

THE FUNDAMENTAL VOLATILITY OF THE DIGITAL ECONOMY AS A CONTRIBUTOR TO FINANCIAL INSTABILITY

ELI NOAM

Dot-Com Bust and Financial Meltdown

In 2008, financial markets plummeted and took much of the global economy down with them. This was not, however, the only significant drop in the early twenty-first century. The decade began with the boom and bust of the dot-com bubble, or, more generally, of the InfoTech sector. Viewing the 2008 financial crisis through a wider lens that includes the preceding InfoTech boom-bust, one can draw conclusions about the nature of economic volatility in the information economy and about the tools of government to deal with such volatility.

There are several similarities in the two crises. These include deregulatory laws—the Gramm-Leach-Bliley Act of 1999 in the financial sector and the Telecommunications Act of 1996 in the information sector—which helped unleash tremendous activity, much of it financed by debt. Although debt levels were lower in the information and communication technology (ICT) industry than in the real estate industry, their growth had been extraordinary. Telecom alone saw an investment boom of US$1.3 trillion, much of it debt-funded. Between 1999 and 2001, U.S. telecom companies borrowed more than US$320 billion. In Europe, the seven major telecom companies, formerly government organizations with almost no financial liabilities, collectively took on debt greater than the entire gross domestic product (GDP) of Belgium.

However, after a few years of exuberance, things turned sour. Figure 12.1 shows the default rate in the telecom industry relative to the default rate of other industries. Clearly, the failure rate in telecom was much higher, and faster

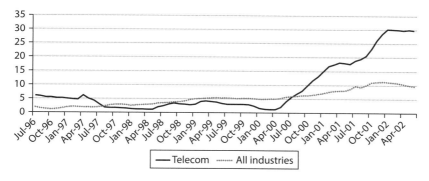

Figure 12.1 Twelve-month rolling average default rates in the telecommunications sector versus all industries

growing. This resulted in an enormous drop in sectoral employment beyond that due to technological progress. Similarly, telecom hardware manufacturing, research, and development experienced major downsizing.

Factors for Volatility

Why did this happen and what lessons can one learn? There are a number of possible explanations for the dot-com bust. There was no demand shortage, so a classic Keynesian-type downturn did not occur. Nor does a monetarist and interest rate–oriented explanation hold. To a limited extent, a credit cycle theory explanation holds (debt secured by collateral led to credit constraints, and shocks were then amplified and spilled over to other sectors). Nevertheless, this only partially describes what had happened.

There are two major possible explanations for severe recessions. The first category can be described as the *perfect storm* scenario. Cycles are caused by random shocks and a rare confluence of events. In both crises, a combination of a slowing economy, bumbling regulators, fraudulent and overwhelmed managers, greedy financial institutions, starry-eyed academics, hyperventilating consultants, gullible journalists, and irrationally exuberant investors came together and combusted. Such a confluence of factors was not likely to repeat itself for a long time. For many, the conclusion is that the shocks are rare as well as random, and therefore there is no governmental solution.

An alternative scenario is that there is a *fundamental instability* in a sector, industry, or an economy. It goes beyond individual fraud, bumbling regulators, or fraudulent management. The fundamental factors are not random but systematic and inherent to the sector. It is a variation of the "Austrian" perspective, which focused on overcapacity, with a pattern of boom, price wars, bust, shake-out, and new investments. These fundamental factors are apparent in both the InfoTech and financial sectors. And, since both are key parts of the information economy, this instability affects the emerging economic system.

The characteristics of information products include high fixed costs and extremely low marginal costs. Whether it is content, software, networks, semi-conductors, data, games, platforms, or devices—they are all expensive to create (produce) and cheap to reproduce, which means high economies of scale. A second characteristic is network effects. The more people consume or use a product or a service, the more benefits they gain from having it. This means that there are incentives both on the scaling, which is on the supply side, and on the network effects, which is on the demand side. There are benefits to being large, having a large market share, being there early, and to expand or possibly overexpand. This leads to the third related characteristic, which is an excess supply. Production increases exponentially while consumption increases lin-early and slowly. Intense competition for "mindshare" and "attention" follows with consequences on product style and on marketing. A similar excess supply exists in networks. From 1996 to 2001, capital expenditures in the United States increased at an annual rate of 29 percent, and the incremental cost of band-width fell by approximately 54 percent annually. Some carriers had over 90 per-cent of their fiber "dark." Stock market analysts judged firms by fiber capacity or cell sites, which led telecom firms to overinvest in such physical elements.

Figure 12.2 illustrates the overcapacity in Transatlantic fiber. The line ris-ing to the right shows the capacity of Transatlantic fiber to move information. In just a few years, 1998 to 2002, capacity increased enormously as new fiber cables came online. The descending line represents prices, which fell rapidly. The third line, hugging the bottom of the graph, shows actual capacity utilized. Everything between the utilization line and the capacity line is excess capacity, which is fiber that went dark.

It has been observed by electronic futurist Stewart Brand that "informa-tion wants to be free," uncensored and gratis, which means without a direct price. For many decades, information has become cheaper to the point that it is becoming difficult to charge anything for it. Music, video, online publishers, and newspapers are all struggling to charge relatively small prices.

The entire competitive part of the information sector—from music to tele-coms to consumer electronics and anything in between—has become subject to a gigantic price deflation in slow motion. The price for everything has fallen enormously. This chronic price deflation shows no sign of abating. It is a great deal for consumers but spells disaster for providers, as prices drop toward mar-ginal cost, which is close to zero, and typically do not cover the full cost. The more efficient the information market becomes due to technology, the faster this process advances. Arbitrage reduces or removes the ability to maintain higher or differentiated prices.

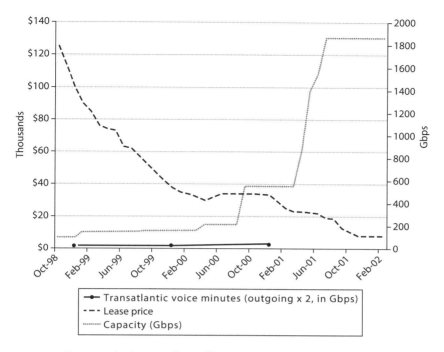

Figure 12.2 Overcapacity in transatlantic fiber

Other factors were also at play, including lags in regulation, technology shocks, and credit cycles based on equity prices. The more a firm built out, the more credit it would receive, and the more the stock market would value the expansion and finance further expansion. But the network effects that seemed such a positive thing on the way up also have a tendency to exacerbate things on the way down. Together these factors lead to expansion and contraction cycles, more general instability, a winner-takes-all type of industry organization, inequality in the benefits from the industry, and a tendency toward oligopoly. Observing the worldwide experience, we can conclude that market equilibrium for InfoTech is not infrastructure competition but oligopoly. One can see this in the emergence of dominance by Google, Facebook, et cetera.

The Impact of the Financial Crisis on the InfoTech Sector

Having examined in brief the instability of 2000 to 2001, let us now turn to the impact of the 2008 financial crisis on the InfoTech sector. As the cost of capital rose and consumer spending dropped, the most immediate impact of the credit crunch and financial crisis was a lack of readily available credit and higher commercial interest rates. The cuts in central bank interest rates in some countries were not reflected in rates for commercial lending, as banks sought to revive their balance sheets. Meanwhile, banks' risk profiles veered to ultra-caution, with banks imposing stringent lending requirements on borrowers. The difficulties in the credit market saw refinancing costs rise sharply, with telecom debt issuances interest rates higher by 3 to 4 percent compared to the precrisis situation. As the entire market dropped, stocks in the telecom, IT, and consumer electronics (CE) industries collapsed, even though there was nothing fundamentally wrong in the industries themselves. This effect was also reflected by the decline in IPOs. There were twenty-eight IPOs in 2007, but once the crisis hit, IPOs almost vanished, with only two in 2008 and four in 2009. Venture Capital deals dropped by 40 percent. Leading tech companies Microsoft and IBM reduced their workforce by approximately 16,000 people, and Motorola by 4,000 people. Intel's revenues decreased by 20 percent in one quarter. Thus the ICT industry was heavily affected.

Governmental Tools and Their Effectiveness

How did the U.S. government respond to these crises? This gives us an indication of governmental responses to new generation economic volatility. There are several strategies for recovery in an economic downturn: stimulation of demand, stimulation of competition, or stimulation of subsidies. The conceptual problem for InfoTech, both in the dot-com bust and the financial crisis, was that there were no real problems with demand. The second potential approach, the encouragement of competition, was potentially reducing investments by large ICT firms, so the focus was on inequality, particularly in rural areas and poor communities. However, the main government response involved a system of *subsidies* in the form of the American Recovery and Reinvestment Act of 2009. Although not industry-specific, this legislation earmarked US$7.2 billion in stimulus funding for broadband internet access and projects. These funds were channeled through two programs, with more general type projects in a Broadband Technology Opportunities Program (BTOP), implemented through the Department of Commerce, and programs for rural areas implemented through the Department of Agriculture's Broadband Initiative Program (BIP). In addition, Congress mandated a national broadband plan, an international benchmarking, and a national broadband map that described the broadband capacities around the country. BTOP awarded grants to new and established service providers and offered grant terms and regulations more attractive to new carriers, with the goal of deepening competition in broadband infrastructure. More than 250 awards were made across all fifty states through BTOP sponsorship of basic infrastructure construction, community computing centers, and community interventions. BIP focused on grant and loan combinations to established service providers. However, public investment represents only a small fraction of the total investments needed, so its net impact was small. It was further diluted by being sprinkled across the entire country, and much of it went to incumbents who would often have made the investments anyway. Federal monies did not necessarily reach areas of high need. New York, for example, despite its large rural and mountainous areas, economically stagnant upstate, and large low-income population, hugely underperformed in receiving broadband upgrade grants. At that time, New York was the third largest state by population, but it ranked twenty-first in terms of grant funding received. It had 6.1 percent of the nation's population but received only 2.2 percent of grant money. In terms of actual dollars, New York received less funding than the tiny state of Vermont. Program administration was weak, and the result analysis was virtually nonexistent. This plan benefited some, but it did not seem to have had a significant effect on national infrastructure or the health of the InfoTech industry. Thus neither the subsidy model nor demand-stimulation nor pro-competition policies had a significant impact on the Info-Tech sector.

The Future of Macroeconomic Policy Tools

And what about macroeconomic policies through the banking system? Information and money go hand in hand. From the days of the telegraph, and even before, InfoTech has been integral to the financial sector. Any change in the technology of information distribution affects money, and any change in financial instruments affects the ability of governments to manage the financial economy.

Today the emergence of encrypted and decentralized e-money will affect the ability of governments to conduct monetary policy. Monetary policy is conducted through central bank control of short-term interest rates, the money supply, the relending by banks (the reserve requirements), and reporting requirements. With electronic money rising, these tools all carry question marks.

The central bank system is based on the ability to control interest rates. E-money reduces the demand for liabilities—that is, of public debt—issued by the central bank and, therefore, its ability to control liquidity through open market operations.

Mobile payment accounts will not simply be debit accounts but also credit accounts. In other words, they will create credit, especially microcredits, which will expand the supply of money. Demand deposits are affected by individuals depositing money in their mobile accounts or depositing it instantly in other jurisdictions. By moving money to nonbanks, e-finance reduces the type of deposits that are subject to reserve requirements, leaving less and less for central banks to control.

There is also a deterritorializing of money. Already, for the U.S. dollar, three-quarters of new cash is moving abroad. The privatization of money adds another dimension, the degovernmentalization of money. We return to an emergence of private monies outside of governmental fiat issuance. Current examples of this are cryptocurrencies, such as those based on blockchain arrangements, which exist outside of government controls. We will see new types of money and money creators. We will also see technical progress in that standardized and staid commodity—money—the emergence of smart money, money that can do things. Cash that pays interest. Cash that can deposit itself. Cash that can time its own spending. Some of this may be foreign, and some may be domestic.

Governments are losing control over money creation. The volume of cash is altered by stored value in mobile terminals. With widespread m-finance terminals in every pocket, pocketbook, and automobile, the volume of stored value dwarfs the actual currency in circulation. In addition, e-money is created endogenously by economic activity and is, therefore, procyclical, rather than anticyclical, exacerbating instability.

Furthermore, the velocity of financial flows is enormously accelerated. Once individuals have money stored on or controlled by their phone, they may program it to seek the bank that pays the highest rate of interest. If Bank 1 in Country B raises its interest rate slightly, billions of cell phones around the world might shift money to that particular bank and to that particular country, and, as that happens, major instabilities will emerge.

Offshore tax havens and shadowy cyberbanks will emerge and become much more accessible. Reduction of the cash economy will reduce tax cheating, but the abilities to shift money, to hide money, and to anonymize money will grow exponentially. There will also be issues with reserve requirements, such as deposit insurance.

When money is deterritorialized from an actual economy, much of it beyond regulation, and with money being able to move instantly to other countries, the ability of governments and central banks to control the money supply and the macroeconomy is reduced.

The Need for New Thinking

What we witnessed in 2001 was that the new economy—dot-coms, InfoTech companies, app sites, telecom entrants, new media companies, e-commerce sites, et cetera—became an old-style bust. Collectively, in the United States alone, investors lost approximately US$3 trillion. The Enron scandal was, in comparison, peanuts.

It was also the collapse of an intellectual atmosphere in which mindless hype was left unchallenged: how digital bits play by different economic rules than physical atoms, how the silicon economy is different from the carbon one, and how a price-earnings ratio need not have any E that stands for earnings. Yet these analysts of the ICT sector were not alone in donning rose-colored glasses. A few years later, other subdisciplines of economics also failed in anticipating deep problems in their areas, whether in real estate, banking, or macroeconomics.

Where was adult supervision in all this—the journalists, the academics, the rating agencies? When it comes to the dot-com crisis, the economics and policy research community performed terribly in interpreting or anticipating almost anything dealing with the internet and its business. We might consider why that has been so. The internet had many of its origins in the university community, and its early critical mass rose among researchers and students. The academic community viewed it, rightly, with some parental pride, and, like most parents, suspended some critical judgment. There was also a generational gap at work. The younger generation saw it as a means to leapfrog its seniors; experience seemed to matter little in an environment where the rules were all new. The elder generation feared being seen as obsolete and pulled their punches. Other academics became bogged down in the relatively small issues of domain names and flat rate pricing, laudable but narrow. If there was one societal-oriented criticism of the internet from academia, it was that there was not enough of it—the digital divide. This was something that leftist reformers and rightist business tycoons could agree on.

In conclusion, the great advances in technology and entrepreneurship led to a collective enthusiasm that was reflected by exuberant stock market valuations. Our view of the future of society and economy in the information age was shaped by various purveyors of hype in industry, academia, the press, and government. They painted a vision of a world in which all mankind would be linked and well informed, in which information would conquer illness, ignorance, and poverty, and in which economic prosperity, technological innovation, and political democratization would thrive. How wonderfully inspiring—and how naïve. No wonder danger signals were missed and policymakers were left unprepared.

There is more trouble ahead. The various subindustries of the information sector affect each other more and faster than before. Therefore, as countries become information-activity-based societies, they also become more volatile economies. The information industries will go through boom-bust cycles, of which we have merely experienced the first. There will be greater instability and fewer effective tools to deal with it.

Academic researchers failed in the dot-com and InfoTech bubble and in the real estate and financial bubble. We suspended our critical faculties and lost our detached skepticism. Having absorbed these lessons, it is time for the academic community to become less like cheerleaders and more like thought leaders, to understand the fundamental factors at work, and to establish new analytical theories and policy tools for the information economy.

CHAPTER 13

THE IMPACT OF REGULATION ON SYSTEMIC RISK

SHARYN O'HALLORAN AND NIKOLAI NOWACZYK

Models in Crisis

Since the turmoil following the collapse of Lehman Brothers led to lively debate over how to regulate the financial system to avoid another crisis. In particular, after the 2007–2009 financial crisis, governments enacted numerous laws to reduce systemic risk—risk that arises when the actions of individual firms trigger instability in an industry or even an entire economy. U.S. legislators introduced regulations, for example, to clear derivative trades through centralized counter-parties and collateral payments to reduce losses in case of default. Nonetheless, the soundness of these policies, or if they reduce systemic risk at all, remains uncertain, leaving open a number of questions: 1) Have recent regulations improved stability in the financial system? 2) How can we predict and evaluate the impact of a regulation before it is implemented? 3) What configuration of regulations reduces the probability of systemic failure under various scenarios?

These questions are not simply academic. Ten years after the financial crisis and the most comprehensive reworking of financial regulation since the Great Depression, Congress is once again rolling back key parts of the regulatory fabric put in place to prevent similar crises from taking place. It is usual that legislation over-shoots after a crisis, and when the crisis subsides, regulation also retreats. However, it is important to know which regulations are necessary to ensure the safety and soundness of the financial system and which add undue burdens to markets.

In this paper, we develop a model and analytic tool that enable prospective evaluation of alternative regulations under various conditions. Building on advances in data science methods, these analytic tools that enable scenario testing derived from real case data and thereby provide a unique opportunity for regulators to make informed decisions about the impact of public policy before the next crisis strikes.

Transparency and Open Source

The 2007 to 2009 financial crisis was the perfect storm of failures: Wall Street, regulators, hedge funds, all played a part. Governments responded by introducing a number of new regulations to improve the safety and soundness of the banking system as well as to mitigate systemic risk. These include capital buffers, leverage requirements, and restrictions on derivatives at both domestic and global levels.

The question is, given all these regulations, are we better off now than before? In particular, is the financial system more transparent and accountable than before the crisis? After all it was the oblique, complex derivatives that exasperated the mortgage crisis that brought down the international system in the first place.

The financial industry's response to these regulations has been to build black box risk models developed, for the most part, in institutional silos. The implication is that financial firms currently conduct risk exposure analysis absent shared standard models to use as benchmarks and validate results. Yet, the regulations require transparency and flexibility, and these requirements cannot be met by traditional silo-ed approaches. In response, collaborative efforts between academia, industry, and government have formed. Even the banks have come together in a previously unheard of data consortium, AcadiaSoft.

This reorganization has been accompanied by a paradigm shift from proprietary, homegrown software to open source. Even in financial risk management, open source solutions such as ORE, see (see opensourcerisk.org), have emerged. This trend has facilitated the use of new technologies in the solution space, including machine learning, natural language processing, artificial intelligence, and neural networks. These methods provide powerful tools to augment risk analysis. In addition, these technologies provide new ways of developing models.

Open Source Risk Engine (ORE)

ORE computes the risks in a derivative portfolio from the perspective of a single bank. Schematically, it works as follows, see also figure 13.1: It consumes trade data, market data and some configuration files as inputs, identifies all risk factors of the trade portfolio, and performs a Monte Carlo simulation. This allows the computation of risk analytics at portfolio, asset class, and counterparty levels.

These analytics provide a benchmark that can be shared among regulators and industry participants to calibrate models around risk tolerance. As the

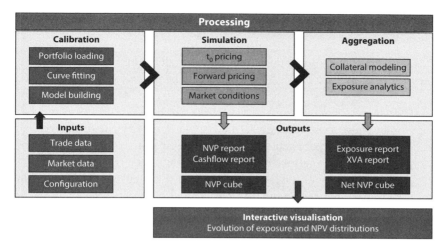

Figure 13.1 Open Source Risk Engine (taken from [ORE User Guide, Fig. 1])

assumptions of ORE are commonly known, it enables conversations around why and how various models deviate from the standard benchmarks.

A Systemic Risk Engine

One can aggregate firm specific risk metrics produced by the ORE into a systemic risk engine to assess the impact that regulations have on the financial system as a whole. This requires that the analysis takes into account not only the impact that financial transactions have on a financial institution but also the impact that each institution has on the system. Netting these input and output effects provide a more realistic picture of the impact of a regulation on the risks in the financial system. Moreover, adopting graph modeling enables visualization, calculation, and testing of the robustness of various hypotheses under alternative parameter assumptions. More technical details on the technology stack used in the simulation can be found in O'Halloran, Nowaczyk, and Gallagher (2017).

Columbia Data Science Institute FinTech Lab

The Columbia FinTech Lab housed in the Data Science Institute provides an easily accessible demonstration of how these tools can produce risk analytic measures. The Fintech Lab website provides a graphic display and interface that demonstrates how this analysis can be conducted.

Pivot: Systemic Risk

ORE has been built to computes the risks in a derivatives portfolio from the perspective of a single bank and can serve as a bank's risk management system or can validate such a system. Its applications have an interesting pivot, however. Because the computations of those risks from the perspective of one bank requires the above mentioned inputs, market data, trade data, netting agreements, and other simulation parameters, ORE can compute systemic risk by running the computation from the perspective of all banks in a system.

The aggregate are all risks of all banks in a financial system. As the same models are used for each bank, the resulting risk metrics are consistent and comparable across all banks. Those metrics then can be computed under different regulatory regimes, allowing for a consistent evaluation of the impact of financial regulation on systemic risk.

In practice, performing such a computation is difficult as one crucial input, the trade data of all the banks in the system, is proprietary and thus inaccessible. However, if the purpose of such a computation is to evaluate the impact of a financial regulation in general or to guide regulatory decision making bodies, it is, in fact, undesirable for the outcome to depend overly on current trade data. Trading activity in the global financial system is significant. Millions of transactions change the trade portfolios of the market participants every day, even every second. Changes in financial regulation, however, happen over a period of decades. The regulations around Initial Margin, for instance, a direct reaction to the financial crisis in 2007 to 2009, are still not fully implemented and will not be implemented fully before the early 2020s. Given the different time scales for changes in trade portfolios and changes in financial regulation, it would be an undesirable feature of financial regulation if its impact strongly depended on current trade data as this would signal overfitting of regulation to the current market.

Ideally, financial regulation should have the desired impact and that impact should be largely invariant of trading activity. Consequently, the evaluation of a regulation should similarly be largely independent of changes in trade data. The precise trade data of the current financial system, therefore, should not be needed to evaluate the impact of a regulation. What is needed to study the impact of a regulation on a financial system is simply trade data, preferably as realistic as possible, but not necessarily the live deals of the current dealer banks. Our approach is to use a simulation technology. We randomly generate entire financial systems, including trade data, and calibrate those random generators to realistic distributions. The result is a representative sample of possible financial systems, which is transparent and completely accessible at all levels, from a single trade to the entire system.

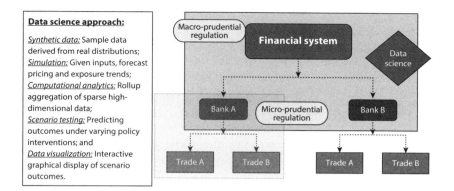

Figure 13.2 Using Data Science to Close the Gap between Micro- and Macro-Prudential Regulation

Risk Metrics

The simulation approach adopted here has the advantage of bridging the gap that traditionally separates micro- and macro-prudential regulation, see figure 13.2. The micro-prudential side considers a single bank in all its complexity and is primarily interested in the risks this bank is exposed to as a result of the trades in its portfolio. The metrics that measure those risks are standardized and their use is enforced globally by regulators. Examples include Value-at-Risk (VaR) to measure market risk, Effectivized Expected Positive Exposure (EEPE) for credit risk, Liquidity Coverage Ratio (LCR) for liquidity risk, or a Basel-II traffic light test for model risk. Even though the concrete value of a metric like EEPE can differ between two banks that use internal models, the regulatory framework around internal models is designed to minimize those differences and the method, at least, is consistent. The only drawback of the micro-prudential view is that it considers only one bank in isolation, making it difficult to study systemic risk.

In contrast, macro-prudential regulation considers an entire financial system with all its banks, but considers each and every bank from a high level perspective only. From a macro-prudential view, the amount of risk a bank is exposed to is of less interest than the amount of risk a bank induces into the financial system. In particular, the question of whether or not a bank default could result in the default of the system is of particular importance ("too big to fail"). In sharp contrast to the micro-prudential risk metrics, there is not even a clear definition on what *systemic risk* precisely means or how it should be measured. In Bisias et al. (2012) the U.S. *Office for Financial Research* discusses thirty-one different metrics of systemic risk. A closer look reveals that these are not simply different metrics measuring the same quantity, but that they are different underlying notions of systemic risk. Most of these metrics focus on the analysis of market data such as housing prices or government bonds and their correlations. For instance, Billio et al. (2010) use Principal Components Analysis (PCA) and Granger Causality to study the correlations between the returns of banks, asset managers, and insurance. Unfortunately, most of those macro-prudential metrics are unsuited to guiding decision making bodies or regulatory interventions precisely because their micro-prudential nature remains unclear (with CoVaR, which relies on a quantile of correlated asset losses, being a notable exception, see Adrian and Brunnermeier 2016).

Weighted Degree Metrics

This twofold divergence in metrics—the gap between micro- and macro- prudential regulation and the different notions of systemic risk—is unfortunate from a methodological point of view. The various notions of systemic risk are a consequence of the fact that this is a relatively new field and that the financial system and hence systemic risks are very complex and have many different facets. The gap between micro- and macro-prudential regulation has historic origins: The obvious approach of studying the macro-prudential impact of a regulation on an entire financial system as an aggregation of all its micro-prudential impacts has failed in the past due to the complexities of both levels. In recent years there have been tremendous technological advances in handling big and highly complex data sets. Therefore, our approach is to use the standardized micro-prudential risk metrics and aggregate them in a graph model of systemic risk.

Graph Model of Systemic Risk

The trade data in a financial system is naturally organized in an undirected *trade relation graph* $G = (B, T)$: The nodes B represent the banks and the links T represent the trade relations. The graph is undirected because a trade relation is symmetric: a deal is only a done deal if both sides sign it. An example of a trade relation graph is shown in figure 13.3, where six banks (labeled A-F here) are trading bilaterally with each other in five trade relations. The nodes represent the banks, the links represent the trade relations, and the labels on the links represent the trade or portfolio identifiers. Any additional data on the trade portfolios can be attached to the links, for instance as a list of trade identifiers. The details of the trades are then stored in a database. This model serves both as a representation of a financial system and as a data format for the random generation of financial system (c.f. Section V-A). Optionally, one can also attach more information on the nodes in that graph, for instance a bank's core capital ratio.

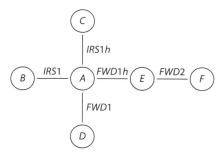

Figure 13.3 Trade Relations

Each trade in a trade relation imposes various types of risks (as well as rewards) on potentially both banks, and these risks can be computed in various metrics by means of mathematical finance. By computing a fixed set of risk metrics for all trade relations in a trade relation graph, we obtain a *risk graph* that captures the risks between all the various banks in the system, see figure 13.4 for the example. Formally, the risk graph $RG = (B, A, w)$ is computed out of the trade relation graph as follows: The risk graph has the exact same nodes B as the trade relation graph, but each undirected trade relation $t \in T$ is replaced by two directed arrows $a_1, a_2 \in A$ representing the risks the bank at the tail induces onto the bank on the head and vice versa as a consequence of their trade relation. Finally, we attach a (possibly multivariate) weight function $w(a)$ onto the arrows $a \in A$ that quantify the risks. An example we will use later is EEPE to measure credit risk. Another example could be the PFE (Potential Future Exposure) over a certain time horizon at a fixed quantile (analogous to U.S. stress testing). Notice that the amount of risk that is induced by a bank b_1 onto a bank b_2 may or may not be the same as the amount of risk induced from b_2 onto b_1 even though both are in the same trade relation. For example, the loss

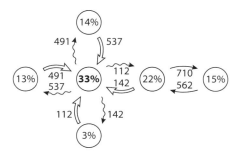

Figure 13.4 Exposures

an issuer of an FX option might suffer as a result of the buyer defaulting is at most zero, whereas the buyer can in theory suffer a unlimited losses.

The weight functions, that is, the risk metrics, can be computed using ORE. The resulting data produces a weight $w(a)$ for each arrow $a \in A$ in a risk graph. This provides a complete picture of risk in the financial system modeled by the trade relation graph in established micro-prudential risk metrics. We then aggregate this data by a purely graph theoretic construction from the arrows of the risk graph to the nodes and then further to a systemic level as follows: For each bank $b \in B$, we compute the *weighted in/out-degree*

$$w^-(b) := \sum_{\substack{a \in A \\ a \text{ ends at } b}} w(a), \quad w^+(b) := \sum_{\substack{a \in A \\ a \text{ starts at } b}} w(a). \tag{1}$$

The in-degree $w^-(b)$ represents the total amount of risk the bank b is exposed to from the system and thus corresponds to the micro-prudential view of b. The out-degree $w^+(b)$ represents the total amount of risk the bank b induces into the system and thus corresponds to the macro-prudential view of b. Therefore, this graph theoretic construction bridges the gap between the micro- and the macro-prudential by providing a coherent metric of both in the same model. In the example shown in figure 13.4, the in-degree of the big bank A in the middle is $w^-(A) = 537 + 142 + 112 + 491 = 1282$ and the relevant arrows going into A are highlighted as $\Rightarrow$. The out-degree is $w^+(A) = 491 + 112 + 142 + 537 = 1282$ and the outgoing arrows are highlighted as $\rightsquigarrow$.

In a second step, we aggregate the risk metrics to a systemwide level by computing $w(G) := \sum_{a \in A} w(a)$ the total weight in the system. It is instructive to express the weighted in- and out-degree as a percentage of that total, i.e., to compute

$$\rho^-(b) := \frac{w^-(b)}{w(G)}, \quad \rho^+(b) := \frac{w^+(b)}{w(G)}, \tag{2}$$

a relative version of the weighted in/out-degree. In the example shown in figure 13.4, the total amount of risk in the system in $w(G) = 3836$ and, e.g., counterparty A has $\rho^+(A) = w^+(A) / w(G) = 1282 / 3836 = 33\%$. Any of the quantities

$$w(G), \quad \max_{b \in B} w^+(b), \quad \max_{b \in B} \rho^+(b) \tag{3}$$

are (possibly $\mathbb{R}^k$ valued) metrics that capture the total amount of weight in the graph and its concentration. These metrics serve as weighted degree metrics of systemic risk.

Collateralization

The financial crisis vividly exposed the credit risk component in derivative contracts. Any two banks that enter into a derivative contract fix the terms and conditions of the contract at inception, and both commit to payments according to the contract until it matures. Although the rules on how to compute the payment amounts are fixed at inceptions, the payment amounts themselves are not as they depend on future market conditions. In particular, in the interest rate derivatives market that has an estimated total aggregated notional in the hundreds of trillions, the maturities of these contracts can be several decades. This exposes the two trading counterparties to each other's credit risk: A payment in ten years would simply not happen if one of the counterparties defaults in nine years. As a derivative contract with a defaulted counterparty is worth zero, a default induces a significant shock to the value of a derivatives book of a bank.

A standard financial regulation to mitigate those credit risk exposures is collateralization. That means that the two counterparties exchange collateral (typically in cash or liquid bonds) with each other during the lifetime of the trade. In a first step, counterparties exchange *variation margin* (*VM*) to cover the current exposure to daily changes in the value of a derivatives portfolio, sometimes subject to thresholds and minimum transfer amounts. This regulation is already fully phased in. In a second step, they can post *initial margin* (*IM*) to each other to cover for the potential exposure to close out risk after a default would occur. A more detailed description of these regulations can be found in [9, Sect. IV].

These collateralization regulations lead to four different regulatory regimes:

1. All derivative trades are uncollateralized.
2. All derivative trades are VM collateralized, but some may only be partially collateralized due to thresholds and minimum transfer amounts.
3. All derivative trades are fully VM collateralized.
4. All derivative trades are fully VM collateralized and also fully IM collateralized.

For reasons of clarity, we exclude regime (2) from the present discussion. It is obvious that collateralization mitigates the exposure to credit risk on a micro-prudential level from the perspective of each counterparty.[1] We now test the hypothesis that collateralization also reduces systemic risk using the graph model from Section IV and simulated financial systems.

Simulation Technology

The first step in our simulation is to generate financial systems like figure 13.3, and calibrate the distributions of our random generator to realistic data. A statistical

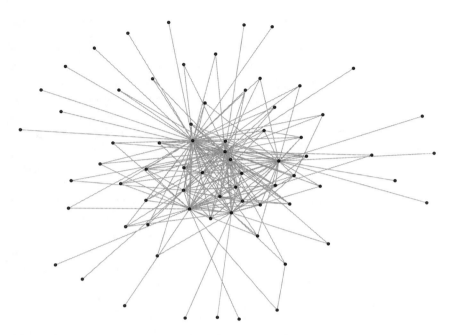

Figure 13.5 A Randomly Generated Trade Relation Graph

analysis of the macro exposures in the Brazilian banking system carried out in Cont, Moussa, and Santos (2013) has shown that the degrees of the nodes in the trade relation graph, i.e., the number of links attached to each node, follow approximately a Pareto distribution. Therefore, we randomly generate Pareto distributed sequences and then compute a graph, which realizes that sequence. Although the first step is straightforward, the second is a hard problem in discrete mathematics, which is still under active research. For the purposes of this paper, we use the so called *erased configuration model* as implemented in the Python library networkx and described in Newman (2003). Further details can also be found in Britton, Deijfen, and Martin-Löf (2006), and Bayati and Saberi (2010). The resulting graphs look like figure 13.5. We can see that the Pareto distributed node degree yields to graphs that have a few nodes with many links representing a few big banks, and many nodes with only one or a few links representing a large number of smaller firms in the system.

To test our collateralization hypothesis, we run a simulation with the following parameters:

- Risk Type: Counterparty Credit Risk
- Risk Metric (choice of weight function w): EEPE (Effectivized Expected Positive Exposure)

- Asset classes: IR/FX Derivatives
- Number of financial systems: 10
- Number of banks in each system: ≤ 50
- Number of trades: 2360
- Number of netting sets: 1378
- Number of Monte Carlo paths: 500

Results

In figure 13.6 we see a highly aggregated overview of the results of the simulation. We can see that measured in average total levels of credit risk (i.e. $w(G)$) measured in $w = $ EEPE collateralization reduces this risk. The relative reduction between regime (1), that is the uncollateralized business, and regime (3), that is the fully VM collateralized business, is 74 percent; and the relative reduction between regime (1) and regime (4), that is the fully VM and IM collateralized business is even 95 percent. Notice that this level of aggregation is even higher than in macro-prudential regulation as we aggregate across multiple financial systems representing possible future states of the world.

As all data are created during the simulation and completely accessible, we can now drill down to the macro-prudential view and study the impact of those

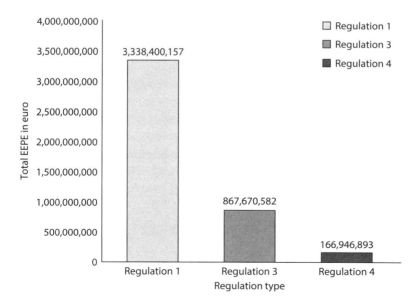

Figure 13.6 Total Reduction of EEPE

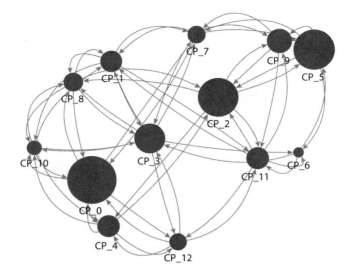

Figure 13.7 Example of a Financial System (Uncollateralized)

regulations on an example system. In figures 13.7 to 13.9, we see the risk graph of a financial system under the three regulatory regimes. The size of the node indicates the amount of risk the bank at that node induces into the system, that is, the $w^-(b)$. We see that collateralization significantly reduces risk in the entire system.

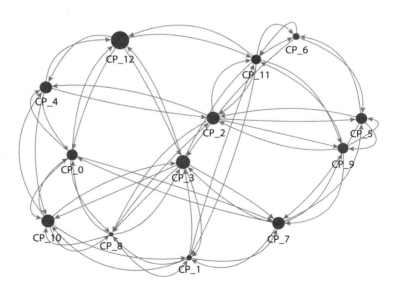

Figure 13.8 Example of a Financial System (VM Collateralized)

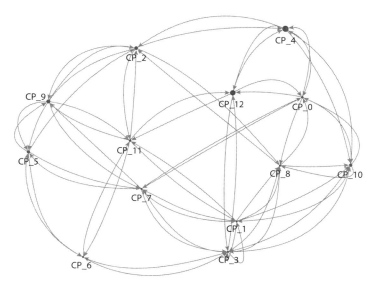

Figure 13.9 Example of a Financial System (VM & IM Collateralized)

This optical impression can be confirmed by drilling down further to the micro-prudential view. In figure 13.10, we plot the EEPE + (b) for every bank b in the system. We can confirm that the impact of collateralization on every bank is qualitatively the same as on the average, that is it reduces individual risk, but the amount of reduction can vary among the banks. It is interesting to

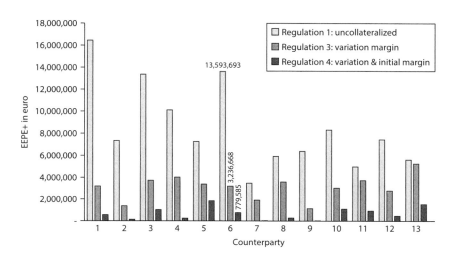

Figure 13.10 Impact of Collateralization on Individual Banks (EEPE +)

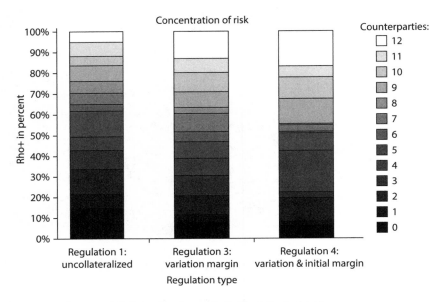

Figure 13.11 Impact of Collateralization on Individual Banks ($\rho +$)

note that the concentration of those risks, see figure 13.11, i.e., the $\rho^+(b)$ stays mostly the same across the regulations, and for banks where it does change, it is not necessarily smaller. We conclude that collateralization has the desired effect of reducing total levels of risk of each counterparty but is inadequate to address concentration risks.

We can now drill down even further than the mirco-prudential level. As a byproduct of the simulation, we obtain exposure data of 1,378 netting sets, which we can mine to gain insight into all the micro impacts of the various regulations. In figure 13.12, we see the distribution of relative reductions in EEPE of the various netting sets when comparing REG_1 (uncollateralized) with REG_3 (VM collateralized). Although most of the netting sets show a significant relative reduction in exposure, some of them also show a significant relative increase in exposure. The explanation for this is as follows: Assume bank A has trades in a netting set with bank B. These trades are deeply out of the money for bank A, meaning the markets have moved into bank B's favor. Then the uncollateralized exposure for bank A is very low.[2] Under VM collateralization, however, as the trades are deeply in the money for bank B, bank B will call bank A for variation margin. Bank A will then pay the variation margin to bank B, where it is exposed to the default risk of B, because B might rehypothecate[3] this variation margin. In some situations, this results in higher exposure under VM collateralization than under no collateralization. We see that on a

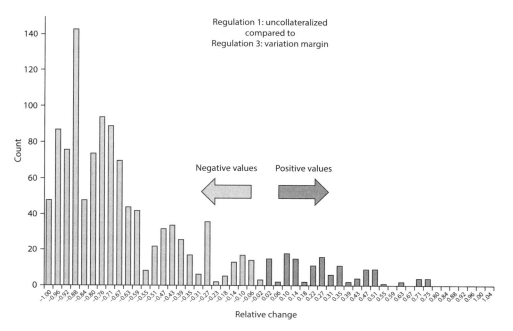

Figure 13.12 Histogram of Relative Reduction in EEPE over All Netting Sets. (197 out of 1,378 have more than 150 percent increase and are not shown, 29 of those have zero uncollateralized EEPE). Mean: −57.42 percent, SD: 38.33 percent

micro level, VM collateralization can have an adverse effect in rare cases of netting sets, which are deeply out of the money.

Initial Margin cannot be rehypothecated and, therefore, posted Initial Margin is not treated as being at risk.[4] In figure 13.13, we see the relative reductions in EEPE of the various netting sets when comparing REG_3 (VM collateralization) vs. REG_4 (VM & IM collateralization). Here we can see that the effect of the additional IM overcollateralization unambiguously reduces the exposure further.

When comparing REG_1 (uncollateralized) vs. REG_4 (VM & IM collateralization) directly, we can see in figure 13.14 that the reduction in exposure is larger and distributed more narrowly compared with just the VM collateralization, see figure 13.12. There are still some netting sets left, which show an increase due to posted variation margin. However, this increase is smaller than under REG_3, as it is partially mitigated by the additional IM collateral.

It should be noted that although the increases in exposure we see in figures 13.12 and 13.14 are large in relative terms, they are actually quite small in absolute terms. In figure 13.15, we compute the total increases and decreases in EEPE of all the netting sets separately.

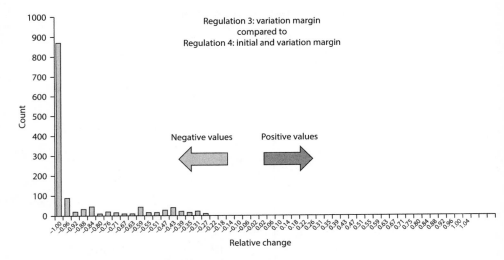

Figure 13.13 Histogram of Relative Reduction in EEPE over All Netting Sets. (0 out of 1,378 have more than 150% increase and are not shown, 0 of those have zero VM collateralized EEPE). Mean: −85.78 percent, SD: 20.76 percent

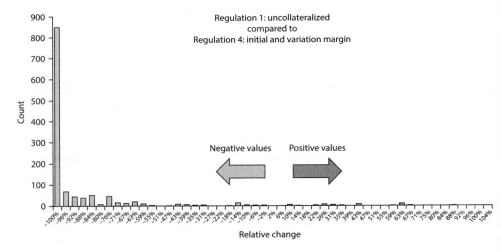

Figure 13.14 Histogram of Relative Reduction in EEPE over All Netting Sets. (69 out of 1,378 have more than 150 percent increase and are not shown, 29 of those have zero uncollateralized EEPE). Mean: −83.83 percent, SD: 34.44 percent

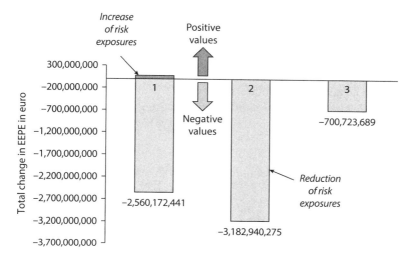

Figure 13.15 Total Increases and Decreases in EEPE of All Netting Sets between the Various Regimes

Synopsis

The directed weighted graph metrics provide a useful comparative statistics to evaluate the impact of various regulatory regimes on systemic risk. Applied to our hypothesis testing we arrive at the following conclusions:

- Collateralization reduces systemic credit risk significantly (measured in EEPE, i.e., the cost of resolving a failed system).
- Collateralization does not materially change the concentration of credit risk in a financial system.
- In corner cases (deeply out of the money portfolios), VM collateralization can increase credit risk.

Notice that these results are an interplay of the aggregated macro-exposures and a systematic analysis of all micro-exposures, which would not be possible outside of the present framework.

Outlook

The financial crisis highlighted the dangers of relying too heavily on proprietary models developed in silos. The open source paradigm provides a means to benchmark models and to have common standards across the industry.

We plan to expand the research at hand into various directions:

Large scale simulation The simulation performed to obtain the results in Section V-B ran on a standard desktop computer. We plan to deploy the systemic risk engine in a cloud environment and run a large scale simulation to achieve an even higher statistical robustness.

Dependence on distributions of the trades During the random generation of the trade relations, various distributional choices have to be made. It is interesting to study the dependence of the results on those choices. We expect them to be fairly stable under distributions.

Agent-based creation of trade relation graphs The current model assumes a Pareto distribution of the trade relations. It would be interesting to enhance the nodes representing the banks in the graph model with dynamic agent-based rules of trading and study under what conditions the resulting trade relations are Pareto distributed.

Joint modeling of all major risk classes In the present article we study the impact of collateralization on credit risk. However, regulation can affect all types of risk and the metrics used to measure it. We plan to conduct a joint analysis of market risk, credit risk, liquidity risk, operational risk and model risk.

Initial margin and funding costs We believe that the key to understanding the interplay between credit risk and liquidity risk, in particular when studying the impact of collateralization, is its effect on funding costs and other value adjustments of derivative trades, the so called *XVAs*. These quantify the price of the reduction in risk.

Derivatives market vs. money market It is to be expected that collateralization will impact not only the derivatives market but also the money market. As initial margin cannot be rehypothecated, its impact could be large. It is therefore interesting to study the interplay between those markets, both in case studies and simulations.

Central clearing The current analysis focuses on the study of the impact of collateralization on systemic risk as this was one of the major regulatory responses to the crisis. Another response was the incentivization of central clearing, which can be studied in a similar fashion. Notice that the graph model presented in Section IV is already able to capture the effect of this regulation: Any bilateral trade relation of a bank A with a bank B has to be replaced by two trade relations: one of bank A with the clearing house and another one for bank B with the clearing house. We expect to obtain results quantifying how much safer a clearing house needs to be in order to reduce systemic risk compared to bilateral trading.

Notes

Acknowledgments We would like to thank Donal Gallagher (CEO of Quaternion Risk Management), for helpful comments and support of our research.

1. In the language of Section IV, this means that collateralization reduces the $w^-(b)$, i.e., the amount of risk bank is exposed to, where w is a credit risk metric (EEPE in our case).
2. Due to the finite number of MonteCarlo paths, it is sometimes even numerically zero in the simulation.
3. That is, posting margin received from one counterparty to another.
4. It should be highlighted that in our simulation we model the bilateral trading between various banks, where Initial Margin is posted into segregated accounts. Derivatives that are cleared through a central counterparty (CCP) or exchange traded derivatives (ETDs) are not in scope of this simulation.

References

Adrian, T., and M. K. Brunnermeier. "CoVaR." 2016. *The American Economic Review* 106 (7): 1705–41.

Bayati, M., J.-H. Kim, and A. Saberi. 2010. "A Sequential Algorithm for Generating Random Graphs." *Algorithmica* 58, no. 4 (December): 860–910.

Britton, T., M. Deijfen, and A. Martin-Löf. 2006. "Generating Simple Random Graphs with Prescribed Degree Distribution." *Journal of Statistical Physics* 124, no. 6 (September): 1377–97.

Billio, M., M. Getmansky, A. W. Lo, and L. Pelizzon. 2010. "Econometric Measures of Systemic Risk in the Finance and Insurance Sectors." NBER Working Paper 16223.

Bisias, Dimitrios, Mark Flood, Andrew W. Lo, and Stavros Valavanis. 2012. "A Survey of Systemic Risk Analytics." *Office of Financial Research*, Working Paper #0001, January 5, 2012.

Cont, R., A. Moussa, and E. Santos. 2013. "Network Structure and Systemic Risk in Banking Systems." In *Handbook on Systemic Risk*, ed. J. Fouque and J. Langsam, 327–68. Cambridge: Cambridge University Press. doi:10.1017/CBO9781139151184.018.

Columbis Fintech Lab, http://fintech.datascience.columbia.edu/.

M. E. J. Newman. 2003. "The Structure and Function of Complex Networks." *Siam Review* 45 (2): 167–256.

O'Halloran, S., N. Nowaczyk, and D. Gallagher. 2017. "Big Data and Graph Theoretic Models: Simulating the Impact of Collateralization on a Financial System." Proceedings of the 2017 IEEE/ACM International Conference on Advances in Social Networks Analysis and Mining. *ASONAM '17*: 1056–64. doi:10.1145/3110025.3120989.

O'Halloran, S., N. Nowaczyk, and D. Gallagher. 2017. *A Data Science Approach to Predict the Impact of Collateralization on Systemic Risk*. December. SSRN: https://ssrn.com/abstract=3090617.

"Open Source Risk Engine." www.opensourcerisk.org. First release October 2016.

"ORE User Guide." https://github.com/OpenSourceRisk/Engine/blob/master/userguide.pdf.

CHAPTER 14

BIG DATA, PROCESS SCALABILITY, AND FINANCIAL STABILITY

MARK D. FLOOD

I briefly present a big-data perspective for understanding what happened in financial markets, both in the run-up to the crisis of 2008 as well as in the ten years after it occurred. Big-data scalability challenges are certainly not the only important force underlying the crisis, and they may not be the most important. But the pervasiveness of these challenges in the financial system makes the big-data perspective a useful lens for interpreting some of the research papers presented at the conference "Ten Years After the Financial Crisis," and included in this volume.

In particular, the big-data perspective helps in understanding three seemingly disparate papers in this volume. Emanuel Derman (chapter 12; 2011) engages in a philosophical discursion on the meaning of models and theories in finance; Eli Noam (chapter 13; 2006) highlights how some basic forces of information economics have driven industrial organization in the telecommunications and financial sectors; and Sharyn O'Halloran and Nikolai Nowaczyk (chapter 14) present the Open Source Risk Engine (ORE) and apply it to simulation experiments on the impact of collateral on systemic risk in a financial network. The big-data perspective helps synthesize these particular papers, but it also highlights issues that are more fundamental and more general.

As a touchstone, begin with the following classic equation, which encapsulates the efficient markets hypothesis (Fama, 1976):

$$E_m\left(p_{j,t} \mid \varphi_{t-1}^m\right) = E\left(p_{j,t} \mid \varphi_{t-1}\right) \tag{1}$$

The left side of the equation represents the expectation at time t, as implied by the market (m), of the price, p_j, of the jth asset, conditional on the information set, φ^m, available to the market at time $t-1$. On the right, the m sub- and super-scripts are missing, indicating a more omniscient expectation. The equation states that, when it comes to assessing the expected economic value of an asset or portfolio, wearing the blinders of the market—however we define "market"—is as good as wearing no blinders at all.

There are good reasons to question whether this assertion was ever fully true; see, for example, Sanford Grossman and Joseph Stiglitz (1980), Andrew Lo and Craig MacKinlay (2002), or Lasse Pedersen (2015). I once worked in a foreign exchange trading room in which our chief trader was able to fund his bonus by catching pure arbitrage opportunities—simultaneous and nonoverlapping bid-ask quotes from competing dealers—in the largest financial market in the world, namely, spot foreign exchange. Regardless, the maxim that it is difficult for ordinary mortals to outsmart the markets remains a useful starting point for most investment analyses. Paraphrasing Yogi Berra, nobody can earn alpha in financial markets anymore because clever traders are already draining off all the easy profits.

Instead of the narrow econometric question of whether markets are efficient by some definition, I want to focus on the mechanism that forms the market's expectations, $E_m(p_{j,t} \mid \varphi^m_{t-1})$, in practice. In other words, if we rewrite this expectation as a functional mapping, $E_m(p_{j,t}) = f_m(\varphi^m_{t-1})$, what is the *process* for calculating f_m, given that the information set that it works on, φ^m, is enormously varied, dispersed, and nuanced? For many decades, we essentially relied on the coordinated and competing efforts of smart, ambitious, dedicated professionals armed with calculators and spreadsheets to solve the information puzzle, that is, $f_m(\varphi^m_{t-1})$. The basic availability of raw computational bandwidth was typically not a binding constraint. However, as the scale of the information-processing challenge continues to grow, the financial markets are gradually substituting big-data analytics and artificial intelligence (AI) for this traditional reliance on human analysis. In short, hardware and software are replacing wetware.

What does "big data" mean? The casual interpretation, unfortunately reinforced by the buzzword itself, is that bigness is a characteristic of the data set in question—that the data set is somehow "big" in an absolute sense. It is much more useful to define big data relative to the available data processing technologies, as a problem of scalability (Flood et al., 2016). In other words, big data does not simply mean lots of data. Rather, big data becomes an issue when a data set overwhelms the technologies available to process it.

Trading activity, for example, is growing at an increasing rate (Kirilenko and Lo, 2013). As a result, it is unsurprising that we observe occasional process bottlenecks that spiral into operational crises. Stiglitz, in his keynote, mentioned a very direct example of this: the robo-signing crisis that followed the mortgage meltdown as lenders foreclosed on home loans at a rate 10 times the routine level (Flood, et al., 2013). Few now recall that the U.S. Treasury itself pioneered robo-signing in the 1860s. As Civil War financing required increasing issues of notes of decreasing denominations, the number of official signatures needed expanded exponentially (Noll, 2009) because each note was signed individually. Before creation of the Bureau of Engraving and Printing in the 1870s, the U.S. Treasury building was largely a print shop, devoted to printing and mechanically signing newly issued Treasury securities. Operational bottlenecks may not be new, but we should expect them to occur more frequently now.

The accelerating expansion of increasingly precise data has other implications for finance. Derman's presentation (chapter 12) highlights a distinction between "models" and "theories" (see also Derman, 2011). His definitions of model and theory here are nonstandard but instructive. A model is a simplified emulation of reality, implying some approximation error; models are imperfect by definition. Per Derman, finance deals almost exclusively with models of reality, which can still be useful despite their limitations. The efficient markets hypothesis in equation (1) is a model in this sense. Typically, there is sufficient uncertainty present that several plausible models (or calibrations of a single model) are consistent with measured reality. Fama (1976), for example, emphasizes that any test of equation (1) must be a joint test of (1) itself, together with some model of equilibrium valuation. There are typically many such auxiliary models, which creates ambiguity in the interpretation of any test of (1).

A theory, in contrast, is the ideal achieved when a model's approximation error goes to zero. Derman argues that finance has no models in this sense because the space of possible future eventualities is too large to address everything precisely. One recent example (not raised by Derman) comes from Christian Jensen et al. (2017), who discuss the notion of "generalized recovery," a toolkit for inverting a pricing kernel to recover underlying behavioral parameters. The techniques are model-free, in the narrow sense that they require no assumptions regarding the probability distribution of state prices—prices become a sufficient statistic that permits recovery of risk preferences. However, this is the exception that proves the rule: Recovery is only feasible when the number of prices exceeds the number of possible states for the economy, which can be impossibly large. This is a big-data problem in the sense that we can only guarantee invertibility by expanding the dimensionality of the pricing kernel to complete the market. But we do not have the institutional infrastructure to trade (reliably) a range of securities that is as impossibly large as the state space itself. In short, the financial system is too large, intricate, and dynamic to be fully reducible to a finite collection of fundamental equations.

In his presentation, Noam (chapter 13; 2006) underscores an argument he first crafted for an analysis of the telecommunications sector. He argues that both industries are characterized by fundamental instability because the industrial organization of information-intensive sectors compels firms to grow large and grow quickly. On the supply side, information-based products typically have high fixed costs and low marginal costs. They are "expensive to create (produce) and cheap to reproduce, which means high economies of scale." On the demand side, there are networks effects. "The more people consume or use a product or a service, the more benefits each consumer gains from having it. This means that there are incentives both on the scaling, which is on the supply side, and on the network effects, which are on the demand side. There are benefits to being large, having a large market share, and being there early and to expand and possibly overexpand" (Noam, chapter 13). In finance, we see firms incurring the high fixed costs of setting up trading rooms and securitization pipelines, which are followed by the relatively low marginal costs of creating actual deals. The upshot is a sequence of winner-take-all tournaments that tend to produce a winner's curse of overcapacity: the firms that expand the fastest and most tend to overshoot in their capture of market share. Big data in this context is more a symptom of scalability pressures than their cause, but the ability of players in information-intensive sectors to manage big data is nonetheless critical to their success in these games of scaling.

One outcome of the big-data revolution in finance is that we are beginning to observe individuals' investment and consumption decisions with far greater precision and detail than ever before. Without venturing to assert that the modeling approximation error has gone to zero, it is still safe to say that big data should improve our ability to measure financial behavior. Whether measurement actually does improve is an empirical question, and academic and industry researchers are working on it. For example, one of the tenets of research in behavior finance is that human decision makers have attention constraints that can generate seemingly irrational behavior (Barberis and Thaler, 2003). As the overall information overload continues to increase, the hazards of limited attention grow in prominence as well. Assuming the bugs are worked out, one advantage an algorithm has over humans is its plodding consistency—algorithms do not tire, get distracted, or make fat-finger errors.

The crisis itself provides an example of the potential downside of limited attention. Larry Cordell et al. (2011) examined $641 billion (at issuance) of structured finance asset-backed securities collateralized debt obligations (SF ABS CDOs) issued between 1999 and 2007 (727 separate, publicly traded instruments). Their sample is effectively the universe of these complex securitization derivatives, dominated by residential subprime mortgage collateral, which played a central role in the 2007–2009 crisis. Exploiting the Intex records for these 727 publicly traded SF ABS CDOs, Cordell et al. are able to unpack the collateral details, subordination levels, and cash-flow waterfalls for each deal.

This was the first comprehensive study of its kind for the SF ABS CDOs, despite their central role in the crisis. The Federal Reserve system has now set up a big data stack—the Risk Assessment, Data Analysis, and Research data warehouse (RADAR)—to help with projects of this kind (Federal Reserve Bank of Philadelphia, 2010). A comprehensive analysis is critical because subprime (BBB-rated) bonds were widely cross-referenced into many CDOs, creating correlated exposures that are unobservable when considering a single CDO in isolation. In theory, it would have been possible for the market participants at the time to focus attention on this sort of analysis; all the data were available. But this imaginary exercise is an abstraction. In practice, scaling attention to meet the big-data challenge requires a significant commitment. It is clear in hindsight that the CDO underwriters themselves "were not fully aware of the risks in the CDOs, since the dealers that underwrote the worst-performing CDOs . . . all suffered large and debilitating losses from the 'super-senior' AAA bonds of the CDOs they underwrote and held" (Cordell et al., 2011, 24).

In this context, initiatives like the Open Source Risk Engine (ORE) are especially welcome. O'Halloran and Nowaczyk (chapter 14), and a companion paper (O'Halloran, et al., 2017), present the ORE and apply it to simulations of counterfactual regulatory policy sets applied to collateral and margining issues in interfirm exposure networks. In practice, even for a single market, these networks can have thousands of nodes and tens of thousands of contractual exposures. In considering the risks for these exposures, it is crucial that they not be treated in isolation. From the perspective of a given firm, a counterparty's creditworthiness can just as easily be impaired by external developments, such as the default of a third party elsewhere in the network, as by factors that affect the relationship directly. Yet, for the most part, market participants suffer from "endogenous myopia," in which they know their own positions but have very little visibility beyond that because trading firms guard their overall position information very carefully. This a big-data problem because the risks associated with each bilateral exposure can interact with various other bilateral exposures in the network, creating a combinatorial explosion of joint risks to consider.

The fact that the ORE is open source sharply reduces barriers to entry for researchers with limited funding, but it does not provide access to the actual data on counterparty network exposures. This, too, is changing, however. Since the crisis, regulators have gained access to a wealth of new network data sets, such as the credit-default swap (CDS) transaction and position data, opening a window into interactions that previously were largely the province of conjecture. Even industry participants have begun to explore ways to share network data—O'Halloran and Nowaczyk note the AcadiaSoft industry consortium—providing one more bit of evidence that the forces of big data are a permanent feature of the financial landscape.

References

Barberis, Nicholas, and Richard Thaler. 2003. "A Survey of Behavioral Finance." In *Handbook of the Economics of Finance*, ed. G. Constantinides, M. Harris, and R. Stulz, chap. 18. Amsterdam: Elsevier Science.

Cordell, Larry, Yilin Huang, and Meredith Williams. 2011. "Collateral Damage: Sizing and Assessing the Subprime CDO Crisis." Working Paper 11–30. Federal Reserve Bank of Philadelphia. August. https://doi.org/10.2139/ssrn.1907299.

Derman, Emanuel. 2011. "Metaphors, Models, and Theories." *Quarterly Journal of Finance* 1 (1): 109–26.

Fama, Eugene. 1976. *Foundations of Finance*. New York: Basic Books.

Federal Reserve Bank of Philadelphia. 2010. "Keeping Credit Markets on the RADAR Screen." *Annual Report*, 26–29.

Flood, Mark D., H. V. Jagadish, and Louiqa Raschid. 2016. "Big Data Challenges and Opportunities in Financial Stability Monitoring." *Financial Stability Review* 20, Banque de France,: 129–42.

——, Allan Mendelowitz, and William Nichols. 2013. "Monitoring Financial Stability in a Complex World." In *Financial Analysis and Risk Management: Data Governance, Analytics and Life Cycle Management*, ed. V. Lemieux, 15–46. New York: Springer.

Grossman, Sanford J., and Joseph E. Stiglitz. 1980. "On the Impossibility of Informationally Efficient Markets." *American Economic Review* 70, no. 3 (June): 393–408.

Jensen, Christian S., David Lando, and Lasse H. Pedersen. 2017. "Generalized Recovery." Working Paper. New York University. June. http://dx.doi.org/10.2139/ssrn.2674541.

Kirilenko, Andrei A., and Andrew W. Lo. 2013. "Moore's Law Versus Murphy's Law: Algorithmic Trading and Its Discontents." *Journal of Economic Perspectives* 27, no. 2 (Spring): 51–72.

Lo, Andrew W., and A. Craig MacKinlay. 2002. *A Non-Random Walk Down Wall Street*. Princeton, N.J.: Princeton University Press.

Noam, Eli M. 2006. "Fundamental Instability: Why Telecom Is Becoming a Cyclical and Oligopolistic Industry." *Information Economics and Policy* 18: 272–84.

Noll, Franklin. 2009. "Lincoln's Greenback Mill: Civil War Financing and the Start of the Bureau of Engraving and Printing, 1861–1863," *Federal History* 1: 25–31.

O'Halloran, Sharyn, Nikolai Nowaczyk, and Donal Gallagher. 2017. "Big Data and Graph Theoretic Models: Simulating the Impact of Collateralization on a Financial System." Proceedings of the 2017 IEEE/ACM International Conference on Advances in Social Networks Analysis and Mining, *ASONAM '17*: 1056–64.

Pedersen, Lasse H. 2015. *Efficiently Inefficient: How Smart Money Invests and Market Prices Are Determined*. Princeton, N.J.: Princeton University Press.

PART IV

REGULATING FOR THE NEXT CRISIS?

CHAPTER 15

RULES VERSUS PRINCIPLES IN FINANCIAL REGULATION FOLLOWING THE CRISIS

It All Depends on the Purpose

PAUL TUCKER

T his part of the book addresses some of the issues around whether regulatory reform has produced a sounder, healthier financial system without choking off economic growth and efficiency. By way of scene setting, in these introductory remarks, I locate a few of the deep questions about financial regulation that have not gone away. The exposition is intended to be suggestive rather than comprehensive, so I do not pin down each and every assertion or argument.[1]

Those questions include the perennial debate about the relative merits of rules versus discretion; whether conduct regulation and prudential supervision are similar endeavors; whether regulatory regimes should be in the hands of judges or administrative agencies; and whether an essentially common international reform program can coexist with serious diversity in institutional regulatory architecture across the main jurisdictions. As such, they bridge between the preoccupations and interests of, on one hand, policymakers and economists and, on the other hand, legal scholars and political scientists. Most of the examples are drawn from the United States and the United Kingdom because they occupy very different points on a spectrum of institutional reform following the 2007–2009 crisis.

Setting the Scene: The Core of the Reform Program

After the near collapse of the international financial system in late 2008 and its eventual stabilization in spring 2009, policymakers embarked upon the most significant reforms of finance in generations. The program was agreed upon internationally, mainly at the G20 and in Basel. Although there was some embellishment via local bells and whistles (such as the Volcker Rule in the United States and Vickers ring-fencing in the United Kingdom), the core reforms were intended to be shared—as they had to be in an era of liberalized capital flows and international finance.

In the words of the former key officials who now gather together as the Systemic Risk Council, the new regime has "five pillars":

1. mandating much higher common tangible equity in banking groups to reduce the probability of failure, with individual firms required to carry more equity capital, the greater the social and economic consequences of their failure;
2. requiring banking-type intermediaries to reduce materially their exposure to liquidity risk;
3. empowering regulators to adopt a system-wide view through which they can ensure the resilience of all intermediaries and market activities, whatever their formal type, that are materially relevant to the resilience of the system as a whole;
4. simplifying the network of exposures among intermediaries by mandating that, wherever possible, derivatives transactions be centrally cleared by central counterparties that are required to be extraordinarily resilient; and
5. establishing enhanced regimes for resolving financial intermediaries of any kind, size, or nationality so that, even in the midst of a crisis, essential services can be maintained to households and businesses without taxpayer solvency support—a system of bailing-in bondholders rather than of fiscal bailouts.[2]

That catalog of objectives makes the underlying objective clear enough. Although there was (and remains) some desire to dampen the macro-credit-asset price boom-and-bust "cycles" that have characterized financial capitalism since the nineteenth century and earlier, the dominant goal was to increase the *resilience of the financial system as a whole*. As part of that, there was a shift away from relying almost wholly on prophylactic regulation and supervision (i.e., trying to reduce the probability of distress and failure among financial intermediaries). Instead, almost equal billing was given to containing and mitigating the social costs of distress and failure when it occurs.

The Reliance on Rules

If that was a notable departure from half a century's substantive orthodoxy, in other respects—especially in the *form* of the reforms—it seemed to be business as usual. In particular, everywhere the new policies were implemented via new domestic regulations that were so voluminous—thousands of pages of them—that they seemed to ignore one of the deep flaws in the precrisis regime: that labyrinthine rule books are an open invitation to regulatory arbitrage that has the perverse effect of undermining the very systemic resilience they are designed to underpin.

Meanwhile, the scandals and detritus revealed as the financial tide went out raised questions about ethics and culture that could not obviously be fixed by more rules, vital though it was to remedy gaping holes in precrisis prohibitions.

Architectural Diversity: Common Policies Delegated Very Differently

If those puzzles are shared, the response to institutional design could hardly have been more different. In the United States, the multitude of financial regulators continued unscathed (almost).[3] A new Consumer Financial Protection Bureau (CFPB) was created, but the U.S. Securities and Exchange Commission (SEC), U.S. Commodity Futures Trading Commission (CFTC), and Federal Reserve retained most of their conduct-regulation responsibilities. In the United Kingdom, by contrast, prudential and conduct authorities were more clearly separated than ever before, with the precrisis Financial Services Authority being split into two parts—the Financial Conduct Authority (FCA) and Prudential Regulation Authority (PRA)—as the United Kingdom finally embraced the "twin peaks" idea promoted by some during the 1990s.

The two key international financial centers also took very different approaches to the challenge of delivering a joined-up stability policy. Whereas the United States established the Financial Stability Oversight Council (FSOC) as a multiagency committee with limited powers under the political leadership of the Treasury secretary, the United Kingdom delegated the lead in day-to-day stability policy to a new body within the central bank, the Bank of England's Financial Policy Committee.[4] Arguably, this was partly because the United States seemed to put more weight on (faith in) early-warning systems, creating a new Office of Financial Research with the Treasury, whereas the United Kingdom embraced the prospect of continuing policy evolution and action.

Nevertheless, there was one notable point of similarity, not only between the United States and the United Kingdom but more widely, including the euro area. This was the expanded responsibilities of central banks, nearly all of which accumulated new regulatory powers to sit alongside their monetary policy role and balance sheet powers. Having rediscovered that they were invariably at the scene of financial disasters, if only in their guise as lender of last resort, the fiction that monetary authorities were merely an adjunct to a macroeconomics PhD class was exposed as dangerous nonsense.

Even there, however, there were differences that amount to more than nuance. For example, as the Federal Reserve's lender of last resort powers were trimmed, the Bank of England's were, if anything, expanded.

A similarly subtle but important divergence was observable in resolution regimes. Just as the United Kingdom belatedly adopted U.S.-style special resolution regimes for financial intermediaries, first replicating the Federal Deposit Insurance Corporation's (FDIC) long-standing powers for small- and medium-sized banks and then leading the debate on bail-in and single-point-of-entry resolution for large and complex firms, the United States seemed to move away from its own orthodoxy. The Dodd-Frank Act (and, even more so, recent proposals from Treasury and the House) gives priority to bankruptcy procedures, which no other significant jurisdiction thinks can work to mitigate social costs.[5] In the background, and sometimes even in the foreground, was a belief that courts uphold the rule of law whereas administrative agencies such as the FDIC and the Fed do not.

With that sketch of the new world, we can turn to issues about the form of regulation and the division of regulatory labor among different unelected power holders.

Rules Versus Standards: The Demands of Rule-of-Law Values

Given the urgency that rightly gripped policymakers during the key reform years (broadly, 2010–2013), deep questions about rules versus principles (standards, as they are known to U.S. legal scholars) and about delegating to agencies instead of courts were not addressed head on, and at best only implicitly. Ten years on is not a bad moment to reopen them. In what follows, I conclude that, although rules are unavoidably central to the regulation of conduct, they cannot be the beginning and end of stability policy. Because that seems to challenge the regulatory orthodoxy of the past quarter century or more, I begin with why some of our deep values seem to demand rules-based policy.

Rules Versus Standards

The difference between rules and standards can be illustrated with an example from prudential policy for a stable financial system:

- *Rule*: "Licensed banks must maintain tangible common equity (as defined) of at least X percent of total assets (as defined)."
- *Standard*: "Licensed banks must manage their affairs prudently and maintain capital adequate to remain safe and sound in stressed states of the world."

The former could be thought of as a world in which the regulator monitors compliance with the letter of the law and punishes noncompliance: a world of enforcement. The latter is a world in which the regulator makes judgments about particular cases: its litmus test is adjudicatory fairness.

Regulatory policy was centered on the adjudicatory/standards model during the first half of the twentieth century in the United States, and even longer in Britain and other parts of Europe. By the 1960s, however, that approach was questioned in western Atlantic circles. Somewhat later, it became unsustainable in London too, after the so-called Big Bang reforms broke the clublike culture of Britain's domestic capital markets. And it was never a serious option when the European Union (EU) turned to forging common policies and practices across its member states.

The crucial point is that, over time, a series of adjudicatory decisions generates something like an implicit rule or general policy, but without the regulated community and the general public having the opportunity to comment or challenge it. In the early 1960s, some three decades after the New Deal regulatory initiatives, U.S. Judge Henry J. Friendly expressed concern that the standards applied via agencies' adjudicatory decisions were not "sufficiently definite to permit decisions to be fairly predictable and the reasons for them understood" and prescribed that "the case-by case method should . . . be supplemented by greater use of . . . policy statements and rulemaking."[6]

The judge was calling upon one of the central strands in the values of the rule of law (the other being procedural fairness). Perhaps most systematically expressed by late Harvard Law professor Lon Fuller, this requires law, whether statutory law or regulatory law, to have the following qualities: generality, being publicly announced, being prospective rather than retroactive, clarity, internal consistency, being reasonably stable over time rather than subject to unpredictable or capricious change, compliance being realistic, and the promulgated law actually being the law enforced and applied by the executive and courts.[7]

Although Fuller framed this in terms of law's morality, those formal rulelike qualities of law provide people with the (degree of) certainty and clarity useful for planning their affairs and for cooperative endeavors to be sustainable—distinctly instrumental welfarist considerations. Indeed, that is the classic liberal view of a law of rules, associated in modern times with Hayek:

> Rules fixed and announced beforehand—rules which make it possible to foresee with fair certainty how the authority will use its coercive powers in given circumstances and to plan one's individual affairs on the basis of this knowledge.[8]

The consequential preference for rules over (vague) standards is clear:

> When we obey laws, in the sense of general abstract rules laid down irrespec-
> tive of their application to us, we are not subject to another man's will and are
> therefore free. It is because the lawgiver does not know the particular cases to
> which his rules will apply, and it is because the judge [or administrative agency
> official] who applies them has no choice in drawing the conclusions that follow
> from the existing body of rules and the particular facts of the case, that it can be
> said that laws and not men rule.[9]

This inspires many on the liberal right today, who accordingly press for
rules-centered banking regulation (and instrument rules for monetary policy).

To eliminate discretion, however, the rules would have to be *mechanical*, in
the sense of everyone readily agreeing—indeed, finding obvious—how each
and every rule must be applied in every conceivable circumstance. Where the
law cannot be applied as a mechanical rule, as very often it cannot, it is subject
to both interpretation and judgment-based application.

Partly for that reason, on the other side of contemporary debates, standards (or a rule for an objective) are preferred by those who regard the state
of economic knowledge as insufficient for society to harness itself to a detailed
rule book, let alone a mechanical one, and who place weight on the avoidance
strategies likely to be adopted by regulated industries. Even though interpretation and discretionary judgment are then embraced, rule-of-law values
nevertheless push in the direction of those judgments being consistent over
time—in other words, principled (and so systematic); for any exceptions
being carefully explained; and for any change in the underlying principles
being signaled in advance. This is a world in which policymakers are expected
to furnish their choices with *reasons*, enabling challenge and incentivizing
consistency and clarity.

In the same spirit, formalist rule-of-law values mean that room for discretionary judgment should be constrained by laws that incorporate a *clear*
standard (or objective) and avoid unnecessary vagueness. As I say elsewhere,
Hayek might not get his mechanic, but he should be spared an artist.[10] This is
constrained discretion.

Why Does It Make a Difference?

It might reasonably be asked why any of this makes a difference. Surely the
distinction between rules and standards (principles) can be overdone. As we
have observed, regulatory rules require interpretation, and their application
involves judgment; and adjudicatory policy should be principled in order to

be consistent. Moreover, where agencies implement a statutory standard, they often publish guidelines on how they understand the standard along with fairly prescriptive internal manuals (quasi rule books) for their staff.

But, as lawyers would stress, different rules of the road apply to rules and adjudicatory decisions. In the United States, the agency is required by law to formally consult on draft rules via what is known as "notice and comment rulemaking," whereas no such process is imposed on general policy that emerges incrementally from the soft precedent created by a series of adjudicatory cases. In a similar spirit, an agency is bound by the rules it has issued, which it can amend only by reconsulting, whereas it is not bound by its guidance and internal manuals but only by the words of the statute. Incremental policymaking is, therefore, less onerous and less transparent—precisely the concern of the Hayekians.

So the question of rules versus standards does matter. Armed with that background, we can turn to the question about financial regulation.

The Role and Place of Rules in Financial Regulation: Distinguishing Conduct Regulation

Nearly every regulatory regime for financial intermediation has, in my view, ended up in a muddle about the role of rules. I assert three bold propositions and then go on to explain them.

1. Rules are central in the regulation of conduct.
2. Rules are ineffective in the preservation of stability.
3. The prevalence of rules in prudential policy has contributed to corrosive cynicism about rules in general and, therefore, about conduct rules.

Rules Are Needed for Market Conduct

When policies are framed in rules, and when firms are confident that the rules will be applied narrowly, to the letter, as it were, epidemics of regulatory arbitrage follow. That is so whether the rules are complex or simple.

In terms of how policymakers should respond, however, conduct regulation is quite different from stability policy. Conduct regulation is directed at preventing one private agent (service provider, counterparty, or customer) from cheating or reneging on promises to others; and, more generally, at laying down a framework of legitimate expectations in market transactions. Whether in wholesale or retail markets, it is vital that participants, customers, and counterparties know the rules of the game. If something goes badly wrong and it turns out that there was a gap in the rules, the rules need to be adjusted, but without retrospective effect. Breaches are to be punished, partly to deter bad conduct. All this is central to the rule of law in the ways outlined above.

For the reasons advanced in the next section, the same approach is much less compelling for stability policy, but it was the course taken in the main jurisdictions for more than a decade leading up to the 2007–2009 crisis. I suspect that an environment in which arbitrage around prudential rules was endemic—a normal part of life in financial firms—fostered cynicism toward regulatory rules in general, generating a culture in which the difference between "right" and "wrong" became blurred across large parts of the industry.

If that is correct, it was a high price to pay—on top of the crisis of instability—for the false turn taken by prudential supervision. Workers in firms need to grasp that the rules of a conduct regulator are not the same *kind* of thing as prudential and stability policies. They are not fair game.

This is easier when the institutional architecture separates the conduct regulator from the prudential supervisor. As described above, the UK's post-crisis twin peaks system is closer to delivering that than is the U.S. architecture. Creation of the CFPB introduces some specialism in the United States, but the responsibilities of the financial regulatory agencies continue to overlap much more there.

Architecture aside, those two jurisdictions (and many others) share a particular pathology: financial regulators working under multiple, vague objectives.[11] As a result, intermediaries and their customers cannot form clear expectations of the agencies' priorities or enforcement policy. As far as I can see, the postcrisis reforms did next to nothing to cure this.

Basing Conduct Regulation on Rules *Under* Binding Principles

One way of summing up the difference between prudential supervision and conduct regulation (as I shall go on to describe it) is that for the former it is the spirit that matters, whereas for conduct it is the letter of the rules that matters *at any particular time*. Although there is truth to that, conduct rules are always open to interpretation and are incomplete, driving those working in finance to search for legal loopholes.

In the United States, rule books have simply grown and grown. In the United Kingdom, over the past thirty years or so market-cum-conduct regulators have flip-flopped between rules- and principles-based regimes, but with a monotonic increase in reliance on rules.

This is a world of artful interpretations and creative loopholes, sowing the seeds of its own demise. It generates an industry of expert advisors who have a narrow commercial interest in lobbying to preserve this kind of regime as the status quo.

The truth, however, is that the spirit of the rules ought to matter in the conduct arena, too, because society expects it to: hence the renewed concern about ethics and culture prompted by the scandals that engulfed finance after the 2008 systemic collapse changed the weather.[12] Given the heterogeneity prevalent among financial intermediaries for three decades, it would be foolhardy to rely upon somehow recapturing the informal norms characteristic of thick community relations. International finance is almost unavoidably based on thin, rule-based morality.[13]

This seems to create a dilemma. On one hand, we cannot simply leave unelected regulators to construe their own rules in light of whatever they declare to be their policy's animating spirit. On the other hand, we should not sacrifice the reduction in uncertainty (and so inefficiency) that can be delivered by carefully crafted rules. What then should be done, or are we simply stuck?

One possible route would be to *combine statutory principles with detailed regulatory rules.* A set of principles would be enacted in primary legislation, together with a statutory provision—binding on the courts—that the detailed rules promulgated by the conduct regulator must be interpreted in light of those legislated principles. So far as I know, this legislative structure has not been attempted in a major jurisdiction. It does not give rise to the radical indeterminacy that afflicts nonstatutory principles because the rules reduce open-ended uncertainty. But the interpretation of those rules is tied to their social purpose, as instantiated in the statutory principles. Although leaving the courts as the final arbiter of how the principles should be construed, it would give elected legislators, not regulators, the responsibility of framing and specifying the principles that they judged best captured the political community's ethical standards.[14]

Stability Policy: Prudential Regulation of the System's Resilience

I argue that prudential regulation of the safety and soundness of the financial system as a whole is different. In essence, this is because neither enforcement nor compensation rises to the social costs imposed by systemic financial crises.

Enforcement Comes Too Late

What might be termed "regulatory avoidance," which can have very high social costs when it leads to instability and economic downturns, is not an offense.

Even if it were an offense, enforcement after the fact cannot undo those social and economic costs. The prudential endeavor is, in its essence, prophylactic, not retributive (see below).

The Infeasibility of Committing to Compensate for Financial Instability

In a similar spirit, legal rules (primary legislation or regulations) cannot offer a remedy by requiring improvident intermediaries to compensate the victims of a financial crisis. Very simply, in the event of a massive banking collapse pushing the economy onto a persistently lower path of output and employment, the losers are never going to be able to recover their costs from the "financial polluters" because the banks and other intermediaries are bust.

More broadly, if the hit to the economy is bad enough, society in aggregate is truly poorer, so it is impossible for transfers to restore all of the losers to the wealth (or well-being) they might reasonably have expected had the systemic crisis not occurred.

However well property rights had been designed and however fairly and efficiently the courts adjudicated conflicts over those rights, they could not be enforced. *Stability warrants state intervention to reduce the probability of crises and to contain the social costs when they occur.*

System Resilience as an Objective

That being so, intermediaries cannot be considered one by one. The financial system is just that, a *system*, its parts connected in myriad ways, including via the real economy and across countries. As George Blunden, the first chairman of the Basel Supervisors Committee, said over thirty years ago:

> [I]t is part of the [supervisor's] job to take [a] wider systemic view and sometimes to curb practices which even prudent banks might, if left to themselves, regard as safe.[15]

In consequence, it is difficult, although not impossible, to separate responsibility for system stability from micro-prudential supervision.[16] Further, unless society wills a zero-failures policy, which would be neither desirable nor feasible, the prudential regime, properly conceived, needs to embrace recovery planning and, even more important, resolution planning.

One obvious conclusion is that the standard micro-prudential statutory objective of ensuring the "safety and soundness" of individual intermediaries needs to be framed explicitly in terms of system resilience and stability.

The United States did not do that explicitly in its 2010 reforms. Two years later, perhaps benefiting from having more time to think and a legislative process less affected by negotiation to placate local interests, the United Kingdom did so. The safety and soundness objective of the Bank of England's micro-prudential supervisors is cast in terms of ensuring intermediaries carry on business in ways that avoid adverse effects on stability, and of minimizing the expected effect of their failure on stability.

Under this approach, policymakers need to determine the severity of shock that the system should be able to withstand. In principle, that would be driven by three things:

(a) A view of the underlying (stochastic) process generating the first-round losses from end borrowers that hit the system.
(b) A picture (or model) of the structure of the financial system through which those losses and other shocks are transmitted around the system.
(c) A tolerance for systemic crisis.

Although the first and second are properly objects of scientific inquiry by technocrats and researchers, the third is different, requiring political debate and decision to the extent that prosperity would (or might) be damaged by totally eliminating the risk-taking structures that can threaten periodic bouts of instability.[17]

In practice, politicians need to decide, or bless, a basic resilience requirement for core intermediaries (constraints on their balance sheets and interconnectedness). That cannot come from the sky but must reflect judgments on (a) and (b) above and also upon the effectiveness of other policies and instruments, including how far the provision of core services could be maintained by (i) resolving or transferring the functions of failed intermediaries (the domain of resolution policy) or (ii) replacement capacity entering the market (competition policy). The job of the financial authorities is, to use the usual language for the regulatory state, simply to police the resilience standard and the resolvability of individual firms. For reasons that go to the very heart of stability policy regimes, however, that turns out to need more than a detailed rule book constraining intermediaries' balance sheets and risk-management practices.

System Resilience as a Common Good Plagued by Hidden-Action Problems

The resilience of individual financial intermediaries is not akin to the resilience of individual airplanes. Some aircraft share common components, but each one is not invariably put in jeopardy by problems in other models. In the financial system, intermediaries are so interconnected that a serious problem almost anywhere can bring down the ceiling.

Both direct and indirect exposures and dependencies are almost impossible to avoid. As customers, we do not all use the same intermediary, so they have to meet on our behalf via settlement systems and the money markets through which an economy's financial transactions are effected and intermediaries' books are balanced. Smaller intermediaries depend on larger firms for what amount to infrastructure services, such as clearing, custody, and liquidity insurance. Efficiency is served through the competition that the interdependencies permit.

This means that the financial system's resilience can be thought of as a *common good*: the benefits accrue to everyone but can be eroded by individual members of the system. Each has incentives to take more risks than they would willingly incur if the system were not believed to be resilient. So, as long as they are not spotted, they will be undercharged for risk by their customers and market counterparties. Because firms seem to care about relatively short-term performance, it is hard for them to stay virtuous. If, however, many firms succumb, in aggregate some of the resilience of the system as a whole is eroded, invalidating the assumption upon which their private risk appetites were predicated. This is an example of the *problem of the commons*, where historically individuals would overuse the common grazing land, leaving everybody worse off.[18]

Unlike a local, physical commons, the erosion of the financial system's resilience creeps up on us because firms are able to disguise their true state via what economists call *hidden actions*. When the state writes rules to constrain intermediaries' balance sheet choices, *regulated firms* find ways of taking more risk than contemplated in the calibration of those rules. If the rules are complex, they take risk in forms that reduce, say, their regulatory capital requirements even when nothing material has changed economically. If the rules are simple, they take risk via routes that simply step around the constraint; say, via the composition of asset portfolios if they are subject to only a cap of their total assets/equity leverage.

Meanwhile, *unregulated intermediaries* have incentives to structure their activities in forms that replicate the economic substance of banking, insurance, or whatever but leave them outside the regulatory net. In other words, *finance is a shape-shifter*. Regulatory arbitrage is endemic, and the rule-writers end up chasing their tails.

By this way of thinking, the great financial crisis was waiting to happen. That it was triggered by the relatively small U.S. subprime mortgage market revealed that the system's resilience was wafer thin. It had been eaten away over the preceding years by the dynamics of the system itself.

At first blush, then, societies seem to face a clash between, on the one hand, the rule-of-law values of predictability and generality described earlier and, on the other hand, the welfare of the people. But it is not quite so straightforward. The value of predictability is thrown into doubt when rules (predictably) fail to achieve their public policy objective. As the Systemic Risk Council has put it:

> The resilience of national financial systems is a vital good, essential for citizens to live decent lives. It is necessary for individuals, families, businesses, and entrepreneurs to be able to plan for the future, transact with each other, and commit their savings to new ventures.[19]

Those are very much among the goods that drove Hayek's attachment to predictability and transparency.

Judgment-Based Prudential Supervision

Stability policy accordingly confronts the issue around rules versus standards in a particular way. To repeat, a compliance-based approach of identifying and punishing rule breaches after the financial system has imploded, creating economic havoc, does not exactly rise to the seriousness of the stability mission.

Where generalized rulelike quantity constraints are placed on intermediary balance sheets to induce them to internalize social costs or self-insure beyond their (perception of their) private interests, those requirements likely need tailoring to the specific cost and risk structures of each intermediary, and to their significance to the system being able to maintain the provision of core services in adverse circumstances. In the language of prudential supervisors, this would cover both Pillar 2 and "systemic surcharge" requirements. It is a form of regulation that requires deep knowledge of and judgments about each relevant intermediary. Further, the micro-supervisor has to be ready and able to make judgments of the following kind:

> Firm X is managed so imprudently that there is no reasonable prospect of its meeting the required standard of resilience in the states of the world it is likely to confront.

When that judgment is reached, the micro-supervisor needs to be ready (and legally empowered) to revoke the firm's license or to place constraints on its risk-taking. The basic criteria (*standards*) underpinning the supervisor's findings—for example, prudence, competent management—have to be established in statute. When applying them to individual firms, the micro-supervisor is called upon to comply with the canons of procedural fairness and reason that comprise the other central tenet of the rule of law.

More than that, we also want a micro-supervisor's judgments and actions to be fair in the sense of being *consistent across different cases and over time.*

This makes it important that the supervisor should articulate how it plans to apply the statutory criteria for authorization, consistent with the overriding standard for resilience.[20] I stress this because, as I hope will be clear by now, it is not the same as writing and enforcing legally binding rules for each and every dimension or facet of activities bearing on safety and soundness.

It is nothing short of tragic that this basic conception of prudential supervision was lost for a generation. That is precisely why, in the United Kingdom, when planning for the return of banking supervision to the Bank of England, the then top management stressed that the reform would entail a return to "judgment-based supervision" centered on statutory criteria for retaining authorization.

Making the Judgments: Stress Testing

It matters hugely to all of this that the postcrisis regulatory reforms have been accompanied by some major developments in the practice of prudential supervision, notably regular stress testing of key intermediaries and service providers. This has distinctly U.S. origins.

Since the spring of 2009, the Federal Reserve has led the world in seeking to undertake *credible* stress tests of banks' capital adequacy. As well as being forward-looking and focused on unlikely (tail) risks, they are conducted annually, concurrent for all firms above a certain size, systematic, and, by any previous standard of supervision, highly transparent.[21] They help supervisors to assess system resilience and, applying *statutory standards* for continued authorization, to make *adjudicatory judgments* on the safety and soundness of individual firms, taking into account correlated exposures across intermediaries.[22]

The Fed was followed by the European Central Bank (ECB) and the Bank of England when they took up their new prudential functions. At the level of high policy, this will help legislators think about the degree of resilience they want to require in the financial system, about how well the regime is working, where it needs reform, and where responsibilities should be rejigged.

Agencies Versus Courts

I hope it will be clear enough that this is not a regime that lends itself to courts applying a detailed legislative code. Why then the demands from some quarters in the United States, including the House of Representatives, that resolution policy be executed via the courts rather than by specialized resolution agencies?

Partly because, appealing to some of the rule-of-law values rehearsed earlier, there are concerns about the possibility of resolution agencies exercising powers to discriminate between creditors of the same class to preserve financial stability (or, more accurately, contain instability). But this ignores that courts exercise discretion; that the bankruptcy code does not give courts a priority of preserving stability; and, at a higher level, that it is a mistake to think that the rule of law is preserved by courts alone rather than by all senior state power holders.

The better point is that the authorities may well need to be more prescriptive about the structure of the creditor hierarchy of banks and other financial intermediaries in order to minimize the risk of stability being jeopardized (instability exacerbated) by treating equally ranked creditors exactly alike. This is a policy that would lend itself to the approach of "rules under binding principles" advocated above for conduct regulation. One such principle might be that purely financial liabilities should take losses before liabilities intrinsically connected with the provision or receipt of services.

With the exception of insured depositors being preferred creditors and certain bonds needing to be deeply subordinated, nothing of this kind has been attempted on either side of the Atlantic.

Beyond Banking to Market Resilience

If it was tragic that micro-supervision lost its stability-oriented roots in the run-up to the 2007–2009 crisis, it is no less disturbing that all too frequently stability policy does not face up to threats from beyond the perimeter of de jure banking.

Given that other parts of the financial system can deplete the common resource of system resilience and have equally powerful incentives to hide or camouflage their actions, it is vital that they too be supervised in the sense I have described: making judgments about whether the resilience standard is in jeopardy.

As the Systemic Risk Council put it in an open letter to G20 finance ministers and governors in February 2017:

> Policymakers should not doubt that with the formal banking sector required to be more resilient, there will be powerful forces pushing activity out of de jure banks into other types of firm, vehicle, or structure. Much of that could be for the good, adding to the vibrancy and depth of capital markets. But, to put it gently, it would be imprudent to disregard the likelihood that some banking activity will migrate to intermediaries or structures that replicate banking-like fragility through leverage and liquidity mismatches. If that happens, the executive and legislative branches will, later or sooner, face a choice between allowing socially costly distress or bailing out such nonbanks.
>
> The SRC wishes to repeat that relying on monitoring developments, which for the moment seems to be the default approach, is a recipe for failure given the obstacles to flexible, timely regulatory initiatives. That, more or less, was exactly the mistake of the early-2000s, as many people, including some SRC

members, could testify based on first-hand experiences. A clear substantive policy on shadow banking—focusing on liquidity mismatches and leverage, and so distinguishing between different asset-management activities and structures—is a glaring gap in the regimes of every major jurisdiction.[23]

Developing the same theme, a year later the SRC urged the U.S. Treasury Secretary to develop policies to ensure the resilience of market-based finance:

> The problem is not limited to specific non-banks becoming bank-like in their functions and significance. The SRC wants to suggest that the . . . authorities should be bothered about the resilience of markets themselves.
>
> In framing any such policy, it is important to distinguish: (i) between markets that serve end users and those on which intermediaries themselves depend; and (ii) between social costs that build over time and those that are severe and occur immediately when a market breaks down.
>
> For capital markets important to end users (businesses and households), the costs of closure depend in part on the availability of ready substitutes, including resorting to banks. The fewer the substitutes—and thus, among other things, the more constrained banks are—the more important it is that capital markets stay open. This is a matter of both *ex ante* design and *ex post* mitigants.
>
> In summary, the aim should be to identify what might be termed "systemically significant markets" that need to be especially resilient, and to pin down the particular vulnerabilities in any such markets that need to be addressed. Such vulnerabilities might lie in market structure, its physical or legal infrastructure, the underlying instruments, or the institutions acting as intermediaries.[24]

In the postcrisis years, no jurisdiction has risen to this challenge. At the level of supervision, we have barely seen rigorous stress testing extended to clearing houses and big asset management vehicles, let alone, as ECB Vice President Vitor Constancio has envisioned, *macro-prudential stress tests of the system as a whole.*[25] At the level of policy, with a few notable exceptions, including SEC policy on the liquidity of mutual funds, we seem to be stuck with a regime of monitor-and-play-catch-up-when-threats are obvious-and-hope-lobbying-power-isn't-too-great. It is a policy that, one day, will enrage the people.

Institutional Implications

Part of the problem is the failure of most jurisdictions to update their market regulators' statutory mandates in light of what was learned during the great financial crisis.

There can be no doubt that market regulators are absolutely vital to maintaining a resilient U.S. (and international) financial system. In the United States, the SEC is responsible for regulating and supervising dealers in securities, central counterparties that clear securities and repos, asset management vehicles, and disclosure requirements for securities of all kinds, including asset-backed securities. The CFTC is responsible for regulating and supervising swap execution facilities, derivatives-clearing organizations, designated contract markets, swap data repositories, swap dealers, futures commission merchants, commodity pool operations, and more. Between them, therefore, they cover many of the markets and structures through which shocks to the system are propagated, and they are the first line of defense in distinguishing healthy "market-based finance" from unhealthy forms of "shadow banking." Neither has an overt statutory objective for the stability of the financial system.[26]

Correcting that should be a priority in any legislative reform. At the very least, it is hard to see how the U.S. Financial Stability Oversight Council can be a long-term success when the agencies (as opposed to the individuals) around its table do not all have an unambiguous mandate from Congress to prioritize the resilience of the system.

In the United Kingdom, the powers of the Bank of England's Financial Policy Committee to issue formal recommendations and directions to the FCA helps. But the FCA's duty to prioritize stability has to be inferred from its statutory mandate: it is not clear.

Matters are clearer with the European Securities and Markets Authority, which was created in the aftermath of the crisis. Its statutory objective is to "protect the public interest by contributing to the short, medium and long-term stability and effectiveness of the financial system, for the Union economy, its citizens and businesses."[27]

Diverse Regulatory Architecture and the International Reform Program

This brings us to our final question: Can countries rely upon each other to preserve stability when their regulatory systems vary so much?

It seems that the rest of the world could reasonably be skeptical about whether U.S. market regulators will maintain interest and focus on the resilience of intermediaries and core infrastructure. That is one of the lessons of history; and as I write, we can see it in the reluctance to develop policies for ensuring the central counterparty clearing houses could be resolved in an orderly way if and when recovery plans do not suffice.

Meanwhile, Europe needs to persuade the world that its new ECB-centered system of banking supervision can rise above the problems of industry capture in member-state capitals and respond more decisively to banking system weakness.

This is a world in which it makes sense for the international soft-law standard setters to monitor the extent to which key jurisdictions are living up to their (nonbinding) commitments; in which central bankers need to work hard at their relationships with market regulators; and in which concerns about problems should be aired publicly rather than set aside in the interests of harmony during financial peacetime.

Summary and Conclusions

This introduction to Part IV has attempted to tee up discussion of a range of issues:

- Whether stability policy and conduct policy should differ in the weight they give to rules as opposed to principles (standards)
- Whether courts should have a bigger role
- Whether it matters that different jurisdictions approach the imperative of maintaining financial stability with very different regulatory structures

My overall conclusions include the following:

- ✓ Stability policy is different from conduct regulation, and in particular cannot safely be centered on legally binding detailed rule books enforced ex post by the courts.
    - In consequence, stability policy and prudential supervision require the continuous application of expert judgment.
    - But the degree of resilience demanded of the financial system as a whole should be decided by elected politicians.
- ✓ Much has been done to improve the resilience of the core banking system.
    - But there is room for a more prescriptive, rule-based approach to the creditor hierarchy of banks and other intermediaries to reduce the prospect of resolution agencies having to exercise discretion to contain instability when firms fail.
- ✓ Much less has been done to improve the resilience of the financial system beyond banking.
    - General policies enshrined in law are needed to address the threats to public welfare (and political stability) from intermediation that replicates the fragility of banking outside de jure banks.
    - More attention needs to be given to how markets (and so activities and the provision of services) can be made more resilient.

✓ Many jurisdictions have not done enough to reconfigure their regulatory architecture to deliver an enduringly resilient financial system.

- In particular, market regulators need to be given an explicit (and, perhaps, overriding) statutory objective to preserve system stability.
- Central banks need to work hard to establish cooperative relationships with market regulators.
- International standard setters should monitor whether agreed standards are being implemented around the world.

No jurisdiction has delivered all of this. Some might have regulatory architecture that is more fit for purpose than others. But the priority now should be to keep politicians and the public focused on the extraordinary costs of crises as memories of the implosion of a decade ago all too obviously begin to fade, even as its broader consequences continue to play out.

Notes

1. What follows draws on, and is expanded upon in, (1) Paul Tucker, *Unelected Power: The Quest for Legitimacy in Central Banking and the Regulatory State* (Princeton, N.J.: Princeton University Press, 2018), reprinted by permission; (2) Paul Tucker, "Banking Culture: Regulatory Arbitrage, Values, and Honest Conduct," in *Getting the Culture and the Ethics Right, Towards a New Age of Responsibility in Banking*, ed. Andreas Dombret and Patrick S. Kenadjian, 99–112 (Berlin: de Gruyter, 2016); and (3) Paul Tucker, *The Design and Governance of Financial Stability Regimes: A Common Resource Problem That Challenges Technical Know-How, Democratic Accountability and International Coordination* (Waterloo, Ontario: CIGI, 2016).
2. Systemic Risk Council, *Statement to the Finance Ministers, Governors, Chief Financial Regulators, and Legislative Committee Leaders of the G20 Countries*, February 27, 2017, http://4atmuz3ab8koglu2m35oem99-wpengine.netdna-ssl.com/wp-content/uploads /2017/02/Systemic-Risk-Council-Policy-Statement-to-G20-Leaders.pdf.
3. Only the small Office of Thrift Supervision was abolished.
4. Following reforms formally planned from 2010 and introduced into law in 2012, the Bank of England has separate statutory committees for macro-stability policy (Financial Policy Committee [FPC]) and micro-prudential supervision of banks and major dealers (Prudential Policy Committee [PRC], which had initially been set up as a subsidiary, following the French model). FPC is empowered to make formal recommendations to FCA and PRA and, in specific areas, may give the micro-regulators directions to act.
5. U.S. Department of the Treasury, *Report to the President of the United States: Orderly Liquidation Authority and Bankruptcy Reform*, February 21, 2018, https://home.treasury .gov/sites/default/files/2018-02/OLA_REPORT.pdf.
6. Henry J. Friendly, *The Federal Administrative Agencies: The Need for Better Definition of Standards* (Cambridge, Mass.: Harvard University Press, 1962), 5–6.
7. Lon L. Fuller, *The Morality of Law*, rev. ed. (New Haven, Conn.: Yale University Press, 1969).
8. F. A. Hayek, *The Road to Serfdom* (Chicago: University of Chicago Press, 1994), 80.

9. F. A. Hayek, *The Constitution of Liberty* (Chicago: University of Chicago Press, 1960), 153.

10. Tucker, *Unelected Power*, chap. 8.

11. In the paraphrase of its mission statement, the SEC is responsible for protecting investors; maintaining fair, orderly, and efficient markets; and facilitating capital formation. The Trump administration appointed a chair with the intention of shifting the emphasis to the last leg.

    Summarizing its statutory objectives, the CFPB is responsible for improving the quality and accessibility of information that consumers receive about consumer financial products; protecting consumers from unfair, deceptive, and abusive practices and from discrimination; maintaining transparent and efficient markets for consumer financial products; reducing unwarranted regulatory burdens; and ensuring that federal consumer financial law is enforced consistently.

    The UK's Financial Conduct Authority has a strategic objective of ensuring that financial markets function well, and three operational objectives: securing an appropriate degree of protection for consumers; protecting and enhancing the integrity of the UK financial system; and promoting effective competition in the interests of consumers. (The objectives of the old FSA, which was also the prudential supervisor of banks, were market confidence, public awareness, consumer protection, and reducing financial crime. It also had to have regard to the competitiveness of UK financial services, which some believe gave politicians a lever in pressing for "light touch" regulation. Safety and soundness were not mentioned.)

12. In the UK, this is being pursued by a new, nonstatutory body, the FICC Markets Standards Board (www.fmsb.com). Its aim is to establish global standards for wholesale fixed income, currency, and commodity markets, setting out how participants in the wholesale markets should behave in situations where conflicts of interest or ambiguity can lead to poor outcomes for market users. Its standards are designed to sit alongside formal regulation, perhaps addressing the space between high-level regulatory principles and detailed legally binding rule books. Although not formally pursuing an "ethical" or "cultural" mission, its output might provide guidance on "how to do business" and so might affect informal norms and culture.

13. On thick versus thin relations (or ethics versus morality), see Avishai Margolit, *On Betrayal* (Cambridge, Mass.: Harvard University Press, 2017).

14. I first encountered this thought in discussion at the Australian National University with John Braithwaite, who has canvassed it in the field of tax evasion versus avoidance. See John Braithwaite, *Markets in Vice, Markets in Virtue* (New York: Federation Press, 2005), especially chapter 10, "Reforming the Law"; John Braithwaite, "Making Tax Law More Certain: A Theory," Australian Business Law Review 31, no. 2 (2003): 72–80. For the initial and more general formulation that goes beyond tax, see John Braithwaite, "Rules and Principles: A Theory of Legal Certainty," Australian Journal of Legal Philosophy 27 (2002): 47–82, http://papers.ssrn.com/sol3/papers.cfm?abstract_id=329400.

15. George Blunden, "Supervision and Central Banking," *Bank of England Quarterly Bulletin* (August 1987).

16. Germany has an interesting system in which the Bundesbank makes micro-prudential inputs to the formal regulator (Bafin) and macro-prudential recommendations to the ministry without being formally responsible for decisions in either sphere. But it seems unlikely that this would be feasible in countries where accountability is a de facto as well as a de jure thing.

17. Romain Ranciere, Aaron Tornell, and Frank Westerman, "Systemic Crises and Growth," *The Quarterly Journal of Economics* 123, no. 1 (2008): 359–406.

18. Elinor Ostrom, *Governing the Commons: The Evolution of Institutions for Collective Action* (New York: Cambridge University Press, 1990).
19. Systemic Risk Council, *Statement to the Finance Ministers.*
20. In *Unelected Power* I call these "Operating Principles." They are, in my view, a vital part of any independent agency regime.
21. Transparency is not complete: notably, the regulator's own models are not published given the risk of gaming by the banks. Daniel K. Tarullo, "Departing Thoughts," Board of Governors of the Federal Reserve, April 4, 2017.
22. This is quite different from regarding stress testing as the enforcement of a rule, as argued by some U.S. scholars. See, Letter from the Committee on Capital Markets Regulation (CCMR) to Ann E. Misback, Secretary, Board of Governors of the Federal Reserve System, January 19, 2018; CCMR, *The Administrative Procedure Act and Federal Reserve Stress Tests: Enhancing Transparency*, September 2016, http://www.capmktsreg .org/wpcontent/uploads/2016/10/Final_APA_Fed_Stress_Test_Statement1.pdf. I regard that as utterly misconceived as a matter of policy if stress testing is to help protect citizens from stability-threatening risk (mis)management.
23. Systemic Risk Council, *Statement to the Finance Ministers.*
24. Systemic Risk Council, *Comment Letter on the U.S. Treasury Department Reports on Capital Markets and on Asset Management and Insurance*, February 23, 2018, https:// 4atmuz3ab8koglu2m35oem99-wpengine.netdna-ssl.com/wp-content/uploads/2018 /02/SRC-Comment-Letter-to-Treasury-Dept-2.23.18.pdf.
25. Vitor Constancio, "Macro-Prudential Stress Tests: A New Analytical Tool," *CEPR Policy Portal*, February 22, 2017.
26. In the case of the SEC, stability can be inferred as a statutory purpose from the SEC's key governing legislation. The preamble to the 1934 Act motivates the need for the agency very broadly, including the risk of sudden and unreasonable fluctuations in the prices of securities causing alternately unreasonable expansion and unreasonable contraction of the volume of credit supplied to the economy. That captures a good deal of modern thinking about why financial stability matters, but it is not fleshed out in the body of the legislation.
27. The legislation further stipulates that ESMA shall contribute to:
    (a) improving the functioning of the internal market, including in particular a sound, effective and consistent level of regulation and supervision,
    (b) ensuring the integrity, transparency, efficiency and orderly functioning of financial markets,
    (c) strengthening international supervisory coordination,
    (d) preventing regulatory arbitrage and promoting equal conditions of competition,
    (e) ensuring the taking of investment and other risks are appropriately regulated and supervised, and
    (f) enhancing customer protection.

    In the exercise of [its] tasks . . . , *the Authority shall pay particular attention to any systemic risk posed by financial market participants, the failure of which may impair the operation of the financial system or the real economy."* (emphasis added)

CHAPTER 16

HOW TO REGULATE IN TIMES OF CRISIS

STEPHEN M. CUTLER

I want to raise four cautionary notes about regulation in the aftermath of the financial crisis.

First, beware of extremes. Regulation, very much like an economy, can go through boom and bust cycles. Some people may remember when then governor Eliot Spitzer, fresh off a spate of enforcement actions against investment banks and mutual funds when he was the New York attorney general, convened a commission to consider whether our markets were overregulated and, in particular, to think about the merits of principles-based versus rules-based regulation. Animating that effort (the irony of which was not lost on a number of the targets of Mr. Spitzer's enforcement crackdown) was worry that New York was losing the competition with London for trading and banking activity, as well as for public company listings. As the United Kingdom was thinking about how to regulate in a kinder, gentler way, we were too. Once you find yourself in that place, you have to think about whether the pendulum has swung too far.

Some of what has happened over the last several years is at the other end of the pendulum. This is perhaps best reflected in what the government said in connection with the surcharge rule for U.S. Global Systemically Important Banks (G-SIBs). That is the rule that applies additional capital charges to the biggest financial institutions. In issuing the rule, the Federal Reserve Board specifically noted that cost-benefit analysis was not chosen as the primary calibration framework for the surcharge. Now I acknowledge that the weighing of costs and benefits is not directly within the mandate provided by the

Dodd-Frank Act, which instructs the Federal Reserve Board to mitigate risks to the financial stability of the United States. But once you start talking about regulation divorced from costs—remembering that financial regulation has dual objectives, growth and economic inclusion, as well as financial stability—you may want to consider whether the pendulum has swung too far in the other direction. That is not to say that I would let calls for regulatory reform become calls for wholesale deregulation. A lot of what has happened over the last decade has been critically important. Capital buffers, recovery and resolution planning, stress tests, and consumer protection are really good things, and we ought not to throw those babies out with the bathwater as we think about recalibrating.

Second, regulators have to step back and look at the whole of what they are doing rather than assessing each rule or regulation in a vacuum. I think about liquidity regulation, for example, and what has happened in that area over the last decade. Of course, liquidity regulation has been incredibly important to achieving stability in the financial system, but we now have the liquidity coverage ratio, the net stable funding ratio, and the short-term wholesale factor in the G-SIB surcharge. But wait, there is more! We have, within the regulation relating to total loss absorbing capacity, requirements around long-term funding and limitations on short-term funding, and we have the comprehensive liquidity assessment review (CLAR) process. We also have stress testing, which is contemplating the addition of liquidity shocks. All of those items may make sense individually, but if each one does not account for the others (and what compliance with the others will do), there is a danger of overregulation.

Third, beware of regulator overlap and duplication. We have seen this in the Volcker Rule, in the mortgage area, and in recovery and resolution—all examples of regulatory frameworks where we have more than one regulator at the table. This can create difficult situations, both for financial institutions and, ultimately, for the public, in how regulations are created and enforced. With respect to the Volcker Rule, we have five different regulators who have had to agree on what the statutory mandate means, how it should be enforced, and how it should be interpreted. In the mortgage area, at a firm like JPMorgan, on the order of seven different federal regulators, and a panoply of state regulators, are looking over the firm's shoulder every time it makes and services a home loan. For recovery and resolution, both the Federal Reserve and the Federal Deposit Insurance Corporation are involved. I do not think that is a recipe for good regulation. On the enforcement side, we have seen over the last decade a proliferation of multiple regulator actions every time someone does something wrong. I do not think that is particularly healthy either. I will give you another JPMorgan example, the so-called London Whale, involving trading losses by the firm's Chief Investment Office. That matter was investigated by five or six different regulatory agencies, each one of which determined that a monetary sanction was necessary—and figured out what that monetary sanction should be—without regard to what the others were doing. That sort of enforcement is not consonant with justice.

Finally, and perhaps relatedly, my fourth cautionary item is that enforcement can both complement and negatively undermine regulatory policy. Two examples illustrate this. The first is the use of the False Claims Act (FCA) with respect to a Federal Housing Administration (FHA) lending program. Many financial institutions paid massive FCA penalties for their FHA lending in connection with mistakes that were not intentional and in connection with mortgage lending practices on which the FHA and financial institutions had developed a course of conduct and understanding that was then completely ignored by U.S. attorneys' offices that brought False Claims Act cases against the financial institutions for those lending practices. The all-too-predictable result has been a reduction in large financial institution FHA lending. That is probably not the policy outcome the government wanted to achieve, but the manner in which government went about enforcing the rules has undoubtedly affected policy.

The second example that comes to mind relates to JPMorgan's $13 billion settlement with the government on mortgage-backed securities. The firm was penalized for what had happened at Bear Stearns prior to JPMorgan's acquisition of that entity. The firm was also required, as part of the same settlement, to give up an indemnity right the firm had bargained for and received in connection with its acquisition of the assets of WaMu. The Bear Stearns and WaMu transactions were transactions that the United States government favored (indeed, the government beseeched JPMorgan to do those transactions to help stabilize our financial system), and yet when it came to enforcers deciding what the appropriate sanctions or penalties were, they ignored the history behind those transactions. When JPMorgan complained to the Justice Department about the Bear Stearns component of the penalty and asked how it could make sense for the government to penalize the firm for preacquisition conduct by an entity that the government had *asked* the firm to acquire, the response of a very senior department official was, "That was the Department of Treasury. We are the Department of Justice." The next time we have a crisis and a financial institution is asked to acquire a company because it will help the economy and will help prevent a crisis, how do you think that company is going to react?

CHAPTER 17

THE ECONOMIC AND POLITICAL IMPLICATIONS OF THE DODD-FRANK ACT

BARNEY FRANK

T he topic I was assigned for this symposium, the economic and political implications of the Dodd-Frank Act, is a very significant change from the way in which I have been asked to address the subject until now. Understandably, for the first years after its passage in 2010, interest focused on how the Dodd-Frank Act would be implemented and the effect it would have on the way in which the financial industry performed its role in the broader economy. Then, as both the rules and their impact began to take shape, the election of Donald Trump shifted the focus to how much the law would be diminished, and if it would survive in any recognizable form.

Implicit in my now being asked to pass over these questions and move on to a discussion of what Dodd-Frank means for our economic and political systems are two very important points. One is the recognition that the law has become—albeit grudgingly in some quarters—an accepted part of the framework governing the operation of a major segment of the U.S. economy. The second is that this acceptance is explained by the fact that the law has worked well economically and remained very popular politically. The experience of the past eight years confirms what we hoped would be the case. Economically, we put in place a comprehensive, interrelated set of changes governing the conduct of financial institutions, which substantially reduce the likelihood of their engaging in excessively risky and therefore destabilizing behavior and better protect investors and consumers from unfair treatment. We were able to accomplish both goals without obstructing the sector's ability to perform its essential function of facilitating productive activity. Politically, not only were we able to use the outraged reaction to the crisis of 2007–2009 to pass the most important legislation on the subject since before World War II, over the vehement objection of some of the most influential segments of our society and the near unanimous support they received from congressional Republicans, but that success has largely survived the subsequent rightward shift in the mood of the electorate.

My basis for this positive assessment has two interrelated components. First, the functioning of the U.S. economy since Dodd-Frank took effect makes it very difficult to demonize the law that governs a piece of the economy as important as the financial sector. Although defenders of an unfettered free market, who most strongly opposed the bill, remain wholly unreconciled to its premise that government intervention in the operation of financial markets is a necessary protection for society, they have been unsuccessful in demonstrating the specific harmful effects of these interventions that would be necessary to win converts among the great majority of the public that does not share their ideological objections. To take the most prominent example of that effort, Donald Trump's early assertion that the law was preventing creditworthy businesses from receiving loans was so widely rebutted—including from people within the industry—that I cannot remember the last time anyone tried to make this point.

In the absence of any examples of the law having a destructive impact on economic activity, the attitude of most voters remains one of deep skepticism that they can trust the financial industry to serve the public interest without significant government supervision. The recognition of this prevailing opinion by the Republican congressional leadership forms the second component of my optimism that the continued existence of Dodd-Frank in essentially the form in which it was originally enacted is no longer in doubt for the foreseeable future.

There are two alternative tests that a major policy innovation can meet to be protected against repudiation. The obvious one is the continuation of power for those who enacted it. The other is when those who forcefully opposed its adoption come to power and leave it essentially unscathed. That is the status of the Dodd-Frank Act at the end of the first Republican-controlled Congress to serve with a Republican president since 2006. Listening to President Trump's denunciation of the law in January 2017, and looking at the near unanimous opposition of congressional Republicans to the bill in 2009 and 2010—of those from that time still serving, only Sen. Susan Collins voted in favor of the law— many people, myself included, expected the kind of battle that occurred over health care to occur over financial reform. It did not happen.

The House, dominated by free market true believers at the committee level, did pass a bill basically repealing the law in 2017, but it was widely seen as a manifesto rather than a serious attempt to legislate.

It is, of course, true that in 2017 the Senate did initiate a set of amendments loosening the restrictions it put on small- and medium-sized banks. At the time—and perhaps still—many defenders of the law treated this not merely as a major breach in the protective wall we had erected but as a harbinger of further damage. I was convinced that their fears were exaggerated, and my conviction on this point has been confirmed. Although I disagreed with two provisions of the package sufficiently strongly that I would have voted no, the fact that the Senate bill became law in exactly the form in which it passed that body is, counterintuitively and even paradoxically, both strong evidence that it will remain largely intact and an explanation of why this is the case.

At this point, a statement of personal interest is required. I was troubled during the debate over the Senate bill by the charge that I had not taken sufficient steps to make people aware of my membership on the board of directors of Signature Bank of New York, which benefited from the section raising the asset level at which a bank comes under the supervision of the Financial Stability Oversight Council. I thought that I had. For example, in the transcript of my remarks at the seminar out of which this volume grew, I verified that I did so in that discussion. I noted repeatedly that my advocacy for the amendments I supported came after they had been devised by the lead regulator in the Obama administration, former Federal Reserve Governor Daniel Tarullo, in 2013—two years before I had ever heard of Signature Bank.

However, I have added this preface to further discussion of the amendments because my confidence that I had adequately explained my role was apparently misplaced—probably as a hangover from my time in elected office when it seemed as if public notice was taken any time I did anything.

As to my argument that Dodd-Frank remains in force today in almost all important respects, the substantive point is that only one section of the amendment package in any way weakened the law's value as a protection against the recurrence of a crisis caused by the irresponsibility of financial institutions. That was the increase from $50 billion to $250 billion in the asset level defining the jurisdiction of the Financial Stability Oversight Council (FSOC). I argued for $125 billion—the amount to which the Obama administration would have agreed. Given that Lehman Brothers' asset value was approximately $750 billion when its failure triggered the crash in 2008, and that it is likely that more than one institution would fail in tough times, $250 billion seemed to me to be entering a potential danger zone. Even that amount is dwarfed by the largest institutions, and nothing in the Senate version weakened the restraints placed on those institutions.

The most important parts of the amendments were the exemptions they gave for community banks—those with less than $10 billion in assets. They were freed from proving that they were not engaging in derivative speculation with their own money—the Volcker Rule. Few if any of them ever did so, making this a paperwork requirement with no good justification. They were also allowed to make loans to borrowers with credit that did not meet the law's standards, but only if they were willing to keep them on their own books. That is, local banks can now make loans to local people with borderline credit, but only if they do not sell the loan and assume the responsibility for loss if it is not repaid.

Second, with regard to the fears expressed by many of my allies when the bill was debated, everything else in Dodd-Frank remains: strict rules requiring adequate financial backing for derivative trades; no securitizing of mortgages to people with poor credit; increased capital requirements for all banks; the orderly liquidation procedure prohibiting any public agency from bailing out troubled institutions at taxpayer expense, requiring instead that they be dissolved and that any taxpayer funds used to mitigate the negative effects be repaid by assessments on large institutions; and, very significantly, the Consumer Financial Protection Bureau, with its single administrator and protections against being savaged in the appropriations process. The survival of these critical elements of the interlocking set of protections we established was not the result of luck, parliamentary maneuvering, or a concession from the antiregulation faction who control the House Financial Services Committee.

In fact, they tried to use the Senate bill as leverage, threating to let it die unless it became much more of a vehicle for their repeal agenda. They failed because the Democratic senators who supported the package stayed true to their pledge that they would allow no further changes in the law, and their Republican senate colleagues agreed. Not only were the anti-Dodd-Frank House Republicans forced to acquiesce in passing a bill that they believed— accurately—did very little of what they sought, a subsequent effort to undercut the derivatives rules by exempting intrabank transactions from some of their provisions similarly failed, due to solid Senate Democratic opposition.

The firmness shown by the Senate Democrats who supported the changes that did occur and their success in fending off any changes beyond their agreement was based on the central political fact of the debate about financial regulation: the only group with the political influence able to overcome the continued general public support for tough regulation are local banks. By satisfying their main complaints about Dodd-Frank, the Senate Democrats who took the lead in this matter surgically removed from the ranks of Dodd-Frank's opponents the only ones who posed a threat to it. I will return to this point.

Analyzing the political and economic implications of Dodd-Frank prepares us to take the action necessary to adapt to the next paradigm shift in the conduct of financial business without the stimulus of a crisis. But that analysis must encompass not only the act itself but the events that both preceded and followed it: the crisis that led to its ultimate enactment and the angry political firestorm this provoked.

The justification for the longer exposition this entails is that greater length brings with it greater depth. The full story of the past, present, and immediate aftermath of Dodd-Frank is relevant, in some cases definitively so, to some of the most important questions in our current national debate. Affirming the good judgment of the editor in framing my assignment topic, they fall neatly into the division between economic and political issues. And again, to anticipate one of the main conclusions in this essay, this division is not simply between intellectual disciplines but between positive and negative effects. This effort must omit the history refuting the idea that it was too much government intervention rather than too little that brought on the crash. Here are my two sets of questions.

Economic

1. Does the central tenet of Ronald Reagan's view of regulation—"government is not the answer to our problems; government is the problem"—deserve the strong support it has been receiving from Republican policymakers over the past ten years?

2. As the most recent specific test of that statement, was the crash of 2008 caused primarily by liberals invoking government authority to force an economically unjustifiable increase in low-income home ownership; by the ability of private financial institutions to enhance their profits by employing resources and methods that postdated the adoption of the rules governing their activity; or by some combination of both, and if so, in what proportions?

3. When increased regulation of complex private business is the course chosen by the political process, as it was in the adoption of the Dodd-Frank Act, can it be appropriately sophisticated, avoiding the extremes of heavy-handed obstruction of important functions or easily evaded cosmetic treatment of harmful practices?

4. What does the passage and subsequent experience in practice of the Dodd-Frank Act say about the argument from some in the financial industry that it is sufficient for regulators to set down general principles to govern their behavior, or can the public interest be protected adequately only by promulgating specific binding rules?

Political

1. Who is responsible for the sharp increase in the disabling, harsh partisanship that now prevails in the country, and particularly in Congress?

2. To what extent does campaign spending by powerful companies and wealthy individuals outweigh the influence of the voters in the making of public policy in both the legislative and executive branches of the federal government?

3. Finally, there is a political analogue to the economic meta-question I have listed as number one. In this climate of activists dedicated to rendering government dysfunctional, rabid partisans motivated more by dislike of their opponents than by any positive goals, internet-fueled conspiracy theorists, and the ability of the overlapping members of these groups to instantly communicate with each other and their elected representatives, does our democracy retain the capacity to respond to difficult problems, especially when that response requires action in which the costs are immediately clear but in which the benefits not only take longer to occur but, most problematically, may be much harder to quantify, or even to document at all?

Things, even big things, can change very quickly. Taking my first economic question as an example, during George Bush's last year in office, debunking the argument that government is, as Ronald Reagan insisted, not the answer to our problems but rather their source would have invited the accusation that the debunker was assaulting a straw man. In the preceding few years, the Republican president led a Republican-controlled Congress to enact significant expansion of the federal role in public education (No Child Left Behind) and health care (prescription drug coverage under Medicare). In 2008, President Bush's chief economic advisors divided their time between deep interventions into the affairs of private financial institutions and urging Congress to enact legislation to systemize these efforts. Ron Paul had many who admired his integrity, myself included, but few allies in his allegiance to that Regan doctrine.

As to my first question on the political side, any commentator who chose that year to decry excessive partisanship in Washington would have seemed similarly distanced from reality. During our six years in the minority, Democrats gave President Bush strong support on domestic and foreign issues: majorities for No Child Left Behind and the war in Iraq, and near unanimity for the Afghan combat. Flashing forward to today, we have a Republican agenda that consists almost entirely of reducing the reach of government in every area of our lives except law enforcement, with the party's justly feared base voters greeting every repealed regulation like French spectators at the guillotine in 1792. This reversal is even shaper when considering partisanship. In an example to which I will return, there is no greater contrast on this point in our history than that between the cooperation Democrats extended to the Bush administration at the height of the 2008 election season and Sen. Mitch McConnell's fully redeemed pledge at the outset of President Obama's term to make defeating the president's reelection bid his major goal.

The fight over financial regulation, its cause, conduct, and outcome, was both part of the impetus for these drastic shifts and the consequences of them. Nowhere is this clearer than in the second economic question I posed: Does government or the private sector bear primary responsibility for the crash?

The case for the culpability of the latter begins with the enthusiasm, wholly uncoerced by government, with which profit-seeking financial institutions embraced the two developments that transformed their business. Each of these factors seemed wholly beneficial at the time, but they had a collective downside that escaped timely recognition. Working together, they offered financial institutions ways to evade the effective network of New Deal era rules that constrained irresponsibility.

For more than thirty years after World War II, almost all loans were made to recipients who directly repaid the institutions from which they received them. In addition to the strong incentive this gave lenders to avoid borrowers with poor credit, those loans made by regulated banks—the great majority, including almost all home mortgages—were further constrained by bank regulators charged with enforcing prudence. This last responsibility-enforcing factor eroded as vast amounts of money came into the United States from oil producing countries, Asian nations with large trade surpluses, and others. By the 1980s, large amounts of capital became available for loans outside the banking system.

Simultaneously, information technology was liberating both bank and non-bank lenders from the need to rely on the ability of their borrowers to repay. Instead, they were able to package large numbers of loans into securities, which could then be sold to the investing public. This meant that the lenders received their money back so quickly that it could be promptly re-lent, and also, more ominously, that the burden of nonpayment by borrowers fell on their lenders, not the buyers of the securities. By the 1990s, thanks to the ability to securitize, the focus of lenders shifted from the creditworthiness of individual borrowers to the ability to sell their loans in bulk. The quantity of loans made eclipsed the quality of individual loans as the key to lender profitability.

In addition, in a development entirely unforeseeable to the authors of the New Deal regulatory package, the subsidized loans themselves became financial instruments. Derivatives heretofore used largely by buyers and sellers of commodities to hedge against, or profit from, price volatility were becoming tradable instruments in their own right. Swaps of loan packages joined futures in the universe of complex finances, and they were attractive due to their ability to offer profits much larger than the money put up.

By the 1990s, the problematic aspects of these developments began to appear, along with the recognition that nothing in the existing regulatory scheme constrained them. Two efforts were made to adopt new rules that would preserve the undoubted benefits of the innovations while diminishing their potential for harm. Both were thwarted by the argument that there was no need for new rules, that the market was essentially sufficiently self-regulating. In one case, that of Brooksley Born's effort to tamp down the wild west activity of the derivatives market, the opposition was bipartisan. Brooksley Born was appointed by

President Clinton to head the Commodities Futures Trading Corporation, but her fellow Clinton appointees joined the financial industry, all congressional Republican, and some congressional Democrats in shutting her down.

The second effort to introduce rules governing the new process was very different. The conservative Republicans in power in Congress from 1995 to 2006, and in the Executive Branch from 2001 to 2008, blocked several efforts by liberal Democrats to adopt rules reducing mortgage loans to very low-income people in an effort to replace market incentive diluted by securitization. To directly answer the second economic question I posed, the reason for the flood of mortgages destined for foreclosure, the single biggest cause of the crash, was the self-interest of lenders in maximizing their profits. Protected by the antiregulatory stance of the Republican Party, not only were liberals not pressing banks into making these loans, Democrats made three unsuccessful efforts to prohibit them.

In 1994, Democrats last year in power until 2007, Democrats enacted the Home Owners Equity Protection Act to limit mortgage issuance to people who could not afford them. With no consumer protection agency in existence, the only place in which to lodge enforcement power was the Federal Reserve system. Dominated by Alan Greenspan's explicit view that subprime loans were good because, inter alia, they made people more likely to support capitalism, the Fed flatly refused to enforce this legislation:

> I was aware that the loosening of mortgage credit terms for subprime borrowers increased financial risk, and that subsidized home ownership initiatives distort market outcomes. But I believe then, as now, that the benefits of broadened home ownership are worth the risk. Protection of property rights, so critical to a market economy, requires a critical mass of owners to sustain political support. (2007, 233)

The next effort was to persuade states to adopt antipredatory rules. As that gained strength, the Bush administration used federal preemptive powers in 2004 to deny states any authority over nationally chartered banks. The final effort to do this not only established conclusively that the blame for the flood of toxic mortgages that ultimately brought down the system belongs to the antiregulatory conviction of conservative Republicans but also was the first indication of the imposition of strict party discipline with which Republican leaders would enforce their view.

When Democrats Brad Miller and Mel Watt responded to the preemption of state efforts by pushing for a federal bill to embody responsible lending standards, they began negotiating with Spencer Bacchus, Republican chair of the relevant subcommittee of the House Financial Services Committee. Bacchus expressed support for the concept, but the initiative came to a complete halt when House Majority Leader Tom Delay told Committee Chair Mike Oxley that Republicans did not impose restraints on the market, and that even if the committee produced a bipartisan compromise, it would never get to the House floor. To summarize, from the mid-1990s through 2006, conservatives succeeded in blocking three separate liberal initiatives to establish rules to govern the new reality.

Because this history so emphatically contradicts the government-is-the-problem philosophy at the center of current Republican ideology, the anti-regulators made a determined effort to provide a counternarrative. Reflecting their understanding that the unambiguous set of facts I have just recounted resist any explanation, they simply ignored it and argued instead that liberals, in our zeal to make homeowners out of the very poor, pressured the lenders into making bad loans by two instruments of public policy: the Community Reinvestment Act and the government-sponsored housing finance agencies, Fannie Mae and Freddie Mac. In fairness, it should be noted that only a few of the most passionate cite the Community Reinvestment Act.

The Community Reinvestment Act neither explicitly nor implicitly pushes banks into making imprudent loans. Its mandate is geographic, not economic. Enacted in 1977, it simply requires banks to conduct some of their activity in the geographical areas in which they are located. Not only is there no evidence that it has led to the issuance of mortgages to impoverished borrowers, but there is also authoritative testimony that it has not. Lawrence Lindsey, director of the National Economic Council under George H. W. Bush, in his capacity as the governor of the Federal Reserve overseeing the Community Reinvestment Act's effect, responded to an inquiry that the loans that counted for Community Reinvestment Act compliance were in no way inferior in quality to any others. It is also important to note that the Community Reinvestment Act applies only to banks, that is, federally insured deposit-tasking institutions. If the Community Reinvestment Act negatively influenced mortgage practices, banks would have had a much worse record than nonbanks, rather than the reverse, as is the case. One prominent conservative, Peter Wallison, insisted that the Community Reinvestment Act was part of the problem, but his three fellow Republicans appointed by the congressional leadership to the Financial Crisis Inquiry Commission explicitly rejected the idea—to his explicit dismay.

The case of Fannie Mae and Freddie Mac is more complicated. It does lend some support to the argument that public policy shares the blame for the crisis, but it fails in two ways to support the argument that liberal zeal for the poor was its major cause. First, in accordance with their charters, they never made loans of any kind or in any way forced lenders to do so. The role of Fannie and Freddie Mac was to buy loans that had been made by for-profit private institutions. They did contribute to the dimensions of the crisis by buying some of the imprudent loans, thereby providing funds for the lenders to increase their activity. They were, however, latecomers to this part of their business. They did succumb to the fever and began outsourcing loans that should never have been made, but not until years after private entities had created the securitization pipeline. The case was best summed up by *Financial Times* analyst Martin Wolf (2014) in his memoir *The Shifts and the Shocks*:

> The view that the GSEs played a central role in encouraging the private sector to enter into the subprime housing mania is false. Nobody forced sophisticated private financial institutions to enter into the transactions that made up the 'originate, securities, rate and distribute model . . . my conclusion then is that the role of regulation was principally one of omission. (140–41)

More than incidentally, because it was an important rebuttal to the charge that the government-sponsored enterprises (GSEs) were the liberal's major instruments of choice to force-feed unrepayable loans to the poor, if the lack of reform of Fannie Mae and Freddie Mac was to deserve blame for the crisis, this would add to the case against Republicans. Directly contrary to the Republican argument—a phrase I use often in this discussion—although the more energized version of the two GSEs was launched as a bipartisan collaboration between George H. W. Bush and a Democratic Congress in 1992, the various efforts to rein them in over the next fifteen years came with Republicans in the majority in Congress. To jump ahead in the chronology, it was not until I became chairman of the House Financial Services Committee in 2007 and my collaboration with President Bush's Treasury Secretary Hank Paulson—on whom much more later— that the House passed the reform bill that internal Republican divisions had prevented them from adopting since President George W. Bush first asked them to in 2002.

In my second disclaimer, I acknowledge that I was slow to see the need for the law, and in 2003, unwisely, I called for rolling the dice some more rather than tightening their reins. However, I was referring specifically to their multifamily inventory, which, in fact, never caused losses, and, more relevantly, I moved to support the law a year later.

The depths of the conservatives' need to pass the blame for allowing the mortgage crisis to worsen is best illustrated by Dick Cheney's bizarre assertion in his memoir:

> The problem here is that I was not the Chairman of the Committee in 2003—or 4 or 5 or 6 and even as the senior member of the minority, with Tom Delay ruling the House, I could not have blocked such as bill even if there had been one. The Republican majority never put forward legislation on the subject until 2005, and when it failed, Chairman Mike Oxley noting intra republican disputes said it failed because George Bush gave him the one-finger salute. (2012)

(I did note that Cheney's making a demonstrably false claim about my role in 2003 put me in the same category as Iraqi weapons of mass destruction.)

The Republicans did make one exception in this period to their firm antiregulatory stance, but it dealt not with the new aspects of financial activity but with an established one. Even for the Republicans in the Bush administration and the House, the Enron scandal was too big and ugly to ignore, and the result was a toughening of accounting standards in the Sarbanes-Oxley Act of 2002. However, this flirtation with government rules for condemning financial activity proved short-lived. By late 2006, conservatives had not only beaten back efforts to add rules to the New Deal package, they went on an antiregulatory offensive, affirming that no new rules were needed and, moreover, regretting that they had been pressured into adopting Sarbanes-Oxley and calling for its severe diminution.

I received the full measure of this let-my-bankers-go zeal as chairman-designate in December 2006, at a conference held by the Chamber of Commerce that focused on the need to avoid damage to our economy from the rules already on the books. Two prominent advocates, then mayor Michael Bloomberg and Harvard Law School Professor Hal Scott, issued reports to emphasize the point. Professor Scott explicitly described the financial industry as suffering from overregulation, and the prevailing opinion at the conference was that absent the cutting back of Sarbanes-Oxley and some regulations, America would get to host few if any IPOs going forward. Less than eighteen months before the failure of Bear Stearns and less than two years before the collapse of Lehman Brothers, America's business leaders passionately argued that the appropriate government response to the fundamental changes that had transformed the financial industry over the past decades was to give them more freedom to exploit their profit-making potential.

I cannot claim that those of us on the proregulatory side fully understood the problem at that stage. We saw specific important problems in the financial arena that required the government to take remedial action, but we did not yet link them in our minds to a systemic threat. Initially, our determination to curtail mortgage lending to people who had little chance of avoiding foreclosure was motivated primarily by our concern for these borrowers and for the negative effects foreclosures were having on lower-income neighborhoods. Similarly, we took the lead in restructuring Fannie Mae and Freddie Mac to diminish the possibility of their becoming a drain on the federal budget, and we worked to preserve their role in providing backup housing finance for creditworthy borrowers. Consumer protection was also the motivation for our passing a bill to protect credit card holders from abusive practices. Several items in this legislative record came to be a part of the Dodd-Frank story.

First, each of the three bills we passed in 2007 involved close relationships with the three most important financial regulators appointed by President

Bush: Treasury Secretary Hank Paulson on GSEs; Federal Deposit Insurance Corporation Chairman Sheila Bair on bad mortgage practices; and Federal Reserve Chair Ben Bernanke on credit cards. I realized that conservative objections to regulation notwithstanding, we were in a very different, more favorable universe for reform than we had been only a year before. A big part of that was the fact of a Democratic-controlled House. However, I was very pleasantly surprised to learn Paulson, Bair, and Bernanke did not share the antiregulatory position of their predecessors. They were pragmatists who believed in the market as a strong but imperfect engine that worked best in a framework of reasonable rules established by public policy.

Second, while we were still looking at these issues more as separate items than as parts of a systemic problem, the legislation we passed in each of the three cases fit very well into the overall reform package that we ultimately prepared. The mortgage bill was incorporated largely intact into Dodd-Frank. The credit card laws acquired an enforcer when the Consumer Financial Protection Bureau was established. Although the most conservative Republicans later complained when we did not further diminish the role of Fannie Mae and Freddie Mac as part of Dodd-Frank, in the eight years since its passage—years in which Republicans held the House majority—they have taken no further action, reflecting the consensus that even though there could be better-designed housing finance mechanisms, the GSEs were not a contributor to financial instability when the Senate joined us in enacting the new law in 2008.

These two aspects of our work in 2007 prefigured 2009, but the last early indicator of what lay ahead was very negative, both contemporaneously and as the harbinger of worse to come. It is not just significant in its prefiguring of the debate climate for consideration of Dodd-Frank; it is part of the answer to my fifth question: When and at whose initiative did hyperpartisanship begin to be the single dominant aspect of congressional deliberations?

As noted above, Spencer Bacchus agreed that the subprime lending situation called for protection for vulnerable borrowers. Understandably, he believed he had more freedom to act on this conviction in 2007 as the ranking Republican minority member than he had exercised as a subcommittee chairman in 2004. With Tom Delay's power over the House agenda having passed to Nancy Pelosi, Bacchus led a significant minority of House Republicans to support our bill when it passed late in 2007. He soon learned that the transformation of a Republican majority—with mainstream Republican Mike Oxley as a committee chair comfortable with bipartisanship (see, for example, his coauthorship with Democratic Senator Paul Sarbanes of the Sarbanes-Oxley Act)—into a minority increasingly dominated by dedicated advocates of an unrestrained free market, simultaneously transformed his support for legislative restrictions on subprime lending from a difference on a particular issue with the majority of his colleagues into an act of treason twice over. He helped the new Democratic majority look effective; and he did so in violation of what had become by that time the fiercely held Republican doctrine that the market must be left to its own devices.

Bacchus did have a powerful warning of how deep the divide between him and Republican orthodoxy had become when the single most influential advocate of that viewpoint vigorously debunked the idea that loans to people with weak credit was a fit subject for regulation.

> As early as today, Mr. Frank plans to hold a committee vote on his Mortgage Reform and Anti-Predatory Lending Act of 2007. . . .
>
> For the first time, banks that securitize mortgages would be made "explicitly liable for violations of lending laws." The reselling of mortgages has been a boon both to housing liquidity and risk diversification. So, to the extent the Frank bill adds a new risk element to securitizing subprime loans—and it surely will—the main losers will be subprime borrowers who will pay higher rates if they can get a loan at all. . . .
>
> Most of these new homeowners are low-income families, often minorities, who would otherwise not have qualified for a mortgage. In the name of consumer protection, Mr. Frank's legislation will ensure that far fewer of these loans are issued in the future. ("A Sarbox for Housing," 2007)

For those of us who admired Bacchus's break with his colleagues to support what we believed was very reasonable regulation, this became an example of a good deed that did not go unpunished. The less senior Republican committee members complained of his role to House Speaker John Boehner and pressed for his removal as ranking minority member. Bacchus fought back but held on to the position only at the cost of having representatives from Boehner's office on the committee staff to monitor him and control his work. At one point, when I complained to Bacchus about blatant misrepresentations in a statement in his name criticizing our committee's work, he told me, sadly, that it was not his doing. He held his job, but not, it seemed to me, his convictions. We received no cooperation from him on any issue during the next three years of Democratic control, not even in late 2008, when it came to working with the Bush administration to cope with the crisis.

Paradoxically, as the last traces of bipartisanship in the House were being obliterated by the increasingly militant conservatism of the Republicans, the cooperation between congressional Democrats, especially in the House, and the Republican president's economic appointees was flourishing.

Our work with Paulson, Bair, and Bernanke on specific issues in 2007 was broadening into a mutually supportive collaboration on what was becoming an increasing concern: the stability of the financial system. They shared with me their growing apprehension that there were structural weaknesses in the operation of our financial industry and that existing law did not provide them with adequate tools to avoid a crisis or to mitigate its effects if it occurred. I was not taken completely by surprise in March 2008, therefore, by the impending collapse of Bear Stearns and their aggressive invocation of what federal power existed to limit its harmful effect. The events that followed are the clearest possible rebuttal to the "plague on both your houses" approach of those who blame both sides equally for the death of cross-party cooperation and its replacement with the most virulent congressional partisanship since the Civil War.

The conservatives who succeeded in severely curtailing Spencer Bacchus's role of Republican leader of the committee had by then established their control of the Republican position on financial regulation. They not only denounced the Paulson-Bernanke engineered takeover of Bear Stearns by JPMorgan Chase, they asked me to convene committee hearings on the subject, in which they could confront Paulson, Bair, and Bernanke, and they criticized me when I declined. I believed then, as I do now, that providing a platform for members of Congress to demonize a transaction, which I was persuaded was the best available response to a potential crisis, would have exacerbated the problem. Nothing stopped them from voicing their complaints in the coming months when the officials would be testifying before us on one issue or another, but the very act of calling a special session in the heat of the moment solely for that purpose would have meant promoting turmoil when we least needed it.

I do not consider bipartisanship to be among the highest political values, and I cite my appreciation of it here not as a sign of my virtue but to note that absolute refusal by the opposition party in Congress to lend support to a president of the opposite party, even on critical national issues, began with the Republicans treatment of President Obama in 2009, and this was in sharp contrast to Democrats working with George Bush's team in 2008.

Even before the Bear Sterns episode, Bernanke and Paulson had stressed in our conversations one crucial gap in our ability to deal with the possible failures of large financial institutions. In the case of a large institution owing much more than it could repay, lenders had made it clear that they had only two choices. They could let it fail, triggering a downward economic spiral as creditors were forced in turn to default on their own debts. Alternatively, they could use federal money to pay what the bankrupt entity owed, preventing the knock-on depressive effect, but using taxpayer dollars for private benefit and incurring the moral hazard of telling potential creditors that the creditworthiness of their institutional partner was not a major concern.

This discussion went from theoretical to very real in September 2008. There is an ongoing debate over whether Paulson could have advised Lehman Brothers, but was deterred from doing so by strong Republican congressional opposition he knew that might produce, or, as I believe, he tried very hard to replicate the Bear Stearns example but found no possible partner. His last hope was Barclays, which said it was willing to do the deal but was prohibited from doing so by British regulators; the result was an economic collapse. Its severity led them to use the Feds' authority to pay AIG's debts in full two days later. Our conversations with Paulson and Bernanke on how to respond to the impending failure of a systemically important institution was thus interrupted by our need to deal with the crisis produced by the absence of such a procedure.

The history of the Troubled Assets Relief Program (TARP) is well told in many of the excellent commentaries on the subject. My focus here is on two parts of the story that have received less attention and are particularly relevant to the theme of this essay: the effect of the deliberations on Dodd-Frank and their role in exacerbating the toxic political climate, which remains today the major reason for my uncertainty over our capacity to respond effectively to a future crisis.

In one dimension, the House vote on the TARP was a high watermark for bipartisanship in recent history. House Democratic leaders literally pleaded with our own members to vote for a package initiated by the Bush administration, even though we knew it was unpopular with their voters. In a much more troubling, and accurate, foretaste of the virulent increased partisanship that has dominated the conduct of House business ever since, the rightward movement of most House Republicans was proceeding so intently that their leadership refused to participate in negotiations for a bill. After a bill was written, they then argued strongly for an alternative the Bush administration officials considered wholly unrealistic, and they ended by voting in a majority against the final version—even on the crucial second vote that came after the first defeat caused one of the largest one-day stock market drops in history. If that was all the help their own president could get from the House Republicans on what he described as one of the most important votes he had ever asked them to cast, my already-lowered expectations for some Republican support of the reform bill that was now our number one priority dropped lower than the stock of Lehman Brothers.

Although this Republican solidarity against updated rules was an obstacle to the passage of Dodd-Frank, it was one we were able to overcome. Much more damaging in both the depth and the length of its toxic effect is a major failing in our otherwise effective crisis response: the failure, then and since, to provide any significant foreclosure relief to borrowers who had been misled into taking loans they could not afford or had seen the value of their homes get dragged down by the crisis to levels that trapped them in underwater mortgages or, in many cases, both.

This absence of any help to the lower- and middle-class homeowners who suffered serious losses was a major contributor to the deep, enduring anger that was one result of our crisis response. The argument that we had subsidized the banks and left their victims unaided was a powerful driver of unhappiness on the left. In fact, both insurgent movements that arose from the crash were, in substantial part, responses to the issue of aid to homeowners unable to repay their loans. On the right, the Tea Party excitedly rose from anger that, as its members saw it, irresponsible people were getting out of their mortgage obligations while the responsible citizens had to pay in full. Occupy adherents, on the other hand, could cite the paucity of such aid in contrast to the hundreds of billions in assistance to banks as a sign of the system's unfairness. The fact that assistance to banks was repaid to the government at a profit did nothing to alleviate this.

A number of individuals bear varying degrees of blame for the fact that the TARP will be seen historically as one of the most substantially successful but politically unpopular things the federal government ever did. On this particular point, culpability belongs more to the United States Constitution than to any other entity.

As lead Housie negotiator with Secretary Paulson on the terms of the TARP, I stressed two elements both morally compelling and essential to getting the votes to pass it—especially as Republican defections meant that Democratic voters would have to carry the burden. One was restrictions on compensation to the executives of recipient banks, to which he reluctantly agreed, fearing that some executives would forego preadoption of the program rather than accept limits on their very generous pay. Then and now, I thought that this was one of the most negative assessments of the moral fiber of top financial executives I had ever encountered, and it did turn out to be exaggerated. On the other hand—and one of the few points on which Paulson and I disagreed—his enforcement of this was unenthusiastic, so compliance was not a heavy lift for them.

Our major disagreement was with his refusal to use any of the first $350 billion of TARP resources for homeowner assistance out of an undoubtedly sincere objection that he needed all of it to stanch the bleeding. When I angrily reminded him that Maxine Waters and I had asked for Democratic votes to pass the bill based in part on this pledge of foreclosure assistance, he agreed to use much of the second $350 billion for this purpose, if it was made available. However, this is where our constitutional system became a problem: specifically, the months' long transition between the election of a president and he or she taking office. Much has been written about the Hoover-Roosevelt deadlock in 1932–33, which delayed action to deal with the Great Depression. The result of this was the constitutional amendment moving inauguration day forward from March 4 to January 20. Nevertheless, for the first time in seventy-five years, even that was too long to avoid a serious problem.

Paulson had the authority to ask for the release of the second $350 billion tranche and promised to use it as we asked. But as the lame-duck secretary of an outgoing administration, he would not make the request unless the president-elect agreed. Following the precedent of not dictating official policy before taking office, President Obama declined to do so. Knowing how unfair the outcome would be to low- and middle-income victims of shady lending practices, fearing the long-term negative consequences to our political climate, and feeling guilty that I had some votes from my democratic colleagues on what was about to be an empty promise, I reacted angrily. My response to President Obama's explaining that "we only have one president at a time" was that, sadly, for people in legitimate need of government assistance, he had badly overstated the number of presidents available to help.

This was the setting in which the House took up the subject of financial regulatory reform early in 2009. Anyone interested in the legislative history of Dodd-Frank will find it very well described and analyzed in Robert Kaiser's (2013) *Act of Congress*. I focus here on aspects of that process that are relevant to the theme of this essay. Specifically, the economics of the job were both easier than the politics and more positive in their implications for our future. From the substantive economic standpoint, the controlling fact was the near unanimity that existed among other relevant officials of both the Bush and Obama administrations on the need for four major policy initiatives:

1. Significant tightening of the rules governing home mortgage loans, particularly to people with weak credit ratings.
2. Increasing the supervision of banks, with special emphasis on raising the amount and quality of their capital.
3. Substantially reforming the derivatives market, requiring that commitments be backed up by greater capital, the posting of adequate margin, and transparency.
4. Special supervision of those financial institutions capable of incurring a level of indebtedness that, if unpaid, would jeopardize economic stability, along with a method of dealing with that debt without either burdening taxpayers or suffering the resulting turmoil.

Other important provisions were added during the legislative process, including authority for regulators to impose risk retention requirements on securitized loan packages; the Volcker Rule limiting banks' derivative trading; and the independent Consumer Financial Protection Bureau. Differences inevitably existed about which agencies should perform these functions and in what way. Nonetheless, I was struck by the extent to which all of those who had held, or were to assume, financial regulatory duties under presidents Bush and Obama agreed on these provisions, which formed the basic framework of the new rules governing financial activity. No similar example of continuity between an outgoing administration and its opposite party's successor on the substance of a major change in economic policy comes to mind. But neither can I think of a comparably sharp discontinuity between the cooperation

Democrats extended to the Bush administration on this subject and the militant opposition President Obama encountered from Republicans.

The break between the support of the Bush administration's economic team for increased regulation and House Republican's repudiation of that concept was now complete. Their growing ideological opposition to government intervention in the workings of the market had been tempered somewhat by the pressure to support their party's president. With his replacement by a Democrat, this factor now had the opposite effect. Some hoped that, as with the TARP, Senate Republicans would be more reflective of the Bush administration's approach than were their House colleagues. Senate Committee Chair Christopher Dodd was a very talented legislator who had maintained good relations with Republican colleagues, and he was committed to making interparty cooperation work. Sen. Mitch McConnell's surprisingly explicit declaration soon after the inauguration that for the next four years he would be focused not on any legislative objective but on preventing President Obama's reelection proved, unfortunately, to be an accurate description of his party's legislative strategy. In quiz show terms, McConnell's declaration of all-out political war on President Obama is the final answer to the question I posed above about the cause of our current level of harsh partisanship—the decision of the Republican Party that their response to the Obama administration would be total, unrelenting opposition. There are answers to two more of the questions posed to be gleaned from the politics of Dodd-Frank and its aftermath.

Much of what I have written takes an unavoidably pessimistic view of our current political situation. I am happy to note, however, that both the original passage of the act and the one subsequent amendment to it demonstrate that, as much as campaign contributions distort the course of public policy, when citizens are energized, either as a sufficiently large segment or as the public as a whole, their votes will outweigh even the largest contributions.

Passage of Dodd-Frank came over the strenuous, well-financed objections of almost all the largest, wealthiest, and generally most influential banks, securities firms, investment companies, and hedge funds in the country. Not only was widespread public anger at the financial irresponsibly that had caused a deep recession sufficient to pass the bill in the heart of the crisis, it has remained strong enough, as I noted above, to sustain the essentials of the law even after the election of a Republican president rigorously committed to undoing it.

Also, as I previously pointed out, in the lobbying of Congress on the specifics of the bills' provisions, there was a near-perfect inverse relationship between the financial resources of the institutions seeking influence and the impact they had. The large banks, securities firms, and other mega-institutions lost out to the network of community banks on each issue where their interests clashed. No contributions, no matter how lavish, from a trillion-dollar institution located hundreds or more miles from a House district in which none of its employees live, outweighed the impact of opinion expressed by the hundreds of local bank employees who did live there. In sum, as cynics should be reminded, when the public gets engaged on an issue, when it comes to influencing the votes of members of Congress, votes beat money.

The answer to the least cosmic of my questions, but one of great relevance to the particulars of future reforms, is found in our experience with the law in operation, especially under the Trump administration. How specific should the rules be? The last rhetorical refuge of financial executives who understand that more increased regulation is unavoidable is to argue that it should be general. Legislate principles, not rules, they advise; do not put us in a legalistic strait-jacket but give us the flexibility to adopt the most economically efficient way to comply. It is, of course, true that some general statements of expected behavior are essential, lest the law be an invitation to loop-holing and because future innovations are unknowable. But where particular patterns of bad behavior have manifested themselves, and continue to temper, outlawing them very specifically is important for two reasons.

First, given the core requirement of due process that no one should be criminally prosecuted if the meaning of the prohibitory section was not clear, keeping the statute at the level of principle guarantees that the chance of prosecutions for financial dishonesty will go from slim to none. In addition, even in civil cases, the defense that a particular financial maneuver may well have been ethically challenged but is nowhere banned by any explicit rule is common in administrative proceedings. Beyond its invocation instances, the argument that what is not specifically outlawed is therefore permissible has been a major part of the Trump administration's assault on the Consumer Financial Protection Bureau. In an impressive display of forget-what-I-said politics, Republicans who tried unsuccessfully to amend the section of the Consumer Financial Protection Bureau law giving it federal power to combat fraudulent, deceptive, and unfair acts now insist that relying on these general mandates to restrict or penalize practices that are not specifically named exceeds its statutory authority.

I end essentially where I started, but with some optimism that things may improve. The substantive success of Dodd-Frank is that it is helping produce a financial industry that is prosperous, less risky, and performing its various functions in a way that ensures the broader economy has been insulated from major assault, even as its ideological enemies took power. But that success has done little to persuade a skeptical public that government can play an administratively constructive role in other sectors. It is, unfortunately, seen much more as an exception to Reagan's belief that government can do no good than as an example that he was wrong. Yet, if the political climate does shift—for example if the election of 2020 produces a Democratic administration—the fact that Dodd-Frank will remain, with its powers almost fully intact, could make of it an argument for trying to achieve similar public policy success in the future.

References

Cheney, Dick. 2012. *In My Time: A Personal and Political Memoir*. New York: Threshold Editions.
Greenspan, Alan. 2007. *The Age of Turbulence*. New York: Penguin Press.
Kaiser, Robert G. 2013. *Act of Congress: How America's Essential Institution Works, and How It Doesn't*. New York: Alfred Knoph.
"A Sarbox for Housing." *Wall Street Journal*, November 6, 2007.
Wolf, Martin. 2014. *The Shifts and the Shocks: What We've Learned—and Have Still to Learn—from the Financial Crisis*. New York: Penguin Books.

CHAPTER 18

THE REGULATORY SINE CURVE

*What Explains the Retreat from Systemic Risk Regulation
(and Why It Was Predictable)*

JOHN C. COFFEE JR.

T he tenth anniversary of anything (even a financial crisis) usually
presents an opportunity for celebration. Regulators will recall how
they redesigned policies to foil the "bad guys," to protect victims,
and to prevent future crises. Enforcement victories will be recalled (with more
than a hint of self-satisfaction), and legislators will proclaim their courageous
opposition to "special interests." The problem with such a self-congratulatory
retelling of the decade since the financial crisis of 2008 is that it would be largely
fictional. Yes, to be sure, there was a prompt response in the United States,
and the Dodd-Frank Act of 2010 did address most of the critical gaps in U.S.
financial regulation.[1] Even if it was imperfect (as human efforts usually are),
it contained important reforms, such as the Volcker Rule, curbs on incentive
compensation, special rules for "systemically important financial institutions"
(SIFIs), and the Consumer Financial Protection Board (CFPB).[2]

Unfortunately, one cannot stop the story at this point. Since 2012 and
the passage of the JOBS Act, regulatory and legislative movement has been
almost entirely in the direction of deregulation. So far, this has involved repeal
of some provisions of the Dodd-Frank Act, the relaxation of many rules
adopted by federal regulators (including the Volcker Rule), the dismantling
or muting of some agencies (most notably the CFPB), and a sharp reduction in enforcement directed at public companies by the U.S. Securities and
Exchange Commission (SEC). The old practices that caused or contributed
to the 2008 crisis are resurfacing: complex securitizations are reappearing;
the repo market is heating up; "interest only" mortgage loans (on which no

amortization of principal is charged) have returned; and banks are actively trading securities-based swaps through unregulated offshore subsidiaries.[3]

Although one can decry this retreat ("How soon they forget!"), it was also predictable. Why? A recurrent cycle has characterized most major financial crises and the reaction to them. The cycle begins (at least in democracies) with a swift (and often punitive) political reaction,[4] and significant reform legislation is enacted. Only at such moments can democratic majorities, enraged and demanding action, overcome the entrenched financial establishment. This tendency can be traced back to the South Seas Bubble, which crashed in 1720 and caused an infuriated Parliament to overreact and prohibit the private chartering of corporations.[5] But at some later point, the second phase of this cycle begins. Once the crisis cools and the public's attention turns elsewhere, powerful institutions quietly lobby to unwind much of the regulation to which they have been subjected. Sometimes, this may take a substantial period. For example, Parliament's ban enacted after the South Seas Bubble on privately chartered corporations (which are universal today) lasted (in both the United Kingdom and the United States) until the advent of the industrial revolution and the appearance of the railroads (which needed to raise capital on a massive scale and whose promoters wanted to utilize limited liability to do so). Similarly, the federal securities laws and the Glass-Steagall Act in the United States were a direct response to the 1929 stock market crash, and they lasted (largely untouched) until the 1980s when deregulation gradually pruned away many of their original (and arguably outdated) provisions.[6] All that is different and unique in the case of the Dodd-Frank Act is the speed with which it has been eclipsed. The federal securities laws and Glass-Steagall remained impregnable for a half century at least, but Dodd-Frank has enjoyed at most a window of a few years (and more trimming may yet come).

I have previously termed this phenomenon the "Regulatory Sine Curve,"[7] but what explains its much faster pace in the case of the Dodd-Frank Act? First and most obvious, the public does not understand financial regulation, which is complex and arcane. Of course, that was true with respect to the federal securities laws as well (and they survived much longer without serious change). Possibly, the public did understand that Glass-Steagall was intended to keep banks small (and liked that). Put differently, the public (and Congress) had no more than a dim idea of who the villain was in the case of the 2008 crisis. At best, systemic risk regulation is an abstract concept, focused less on fraud than on requiring lenders to be prudent on the obvious grounds that a large bank's collapse can set off a domino-like wave of failures. Still, such a goal requires prophylactic and seemingly rigid rules.

Second, Dodd-Frank challenged very entrenched practices (such as incentive compensation), and the financial industry was strongly motivated to challenge it. Third, virtually everyone—both on the left and the right—likes easy money. Thus quasi-public lenders, such as Fannie Mae and Freddie Mac, were able to escape potential death sentences, despite very culpable behavior on their part, because the vast majority in Congress wanted to assure the easy availability of mortgage funds. Hence the industry had a powerful argument that they did not have after 1929: deregulation will mean more and easier lending.

To be sure, the public does know what it does not like—most notably, "bailouts." Unfortunately, the bailout of a large financial institution may be the soundest way to prevent its failure from triggering a financial contagion (think for a moment about what might have happened if the Federal Reserve and the Treasury had not bailed out AIG). In contrast, the exact point at which a large bank should be classified as a SIFI or the precise leverage ratio to which it should be subjected triggers no emotional or intuitive response from the public. To put this a different way, after a vivid scandal, such as Bernie Madoff's Ponzi scheme, no one could conceivably seek the repeal of mutual fund regulation, but the financial industry could easily (and did) lobby for the redefinition of "SIFI" and a loosening of "proprietary trading" restrictions under the Volcker Rule, arguing that their reforms would create jobs and ease credit. The crash of 1929 both produced more vivid villains and ones that better aligned with the needed reforms; thus the laws engendered by that crash may have lasted longer.

Beyond these observations, there is a larger generalization about the asymmetry between the contending forces that explains why financial reforms tend to be watered down over time. It was first offered in an integrated fashion by Mancur Olson in his classic book, *The Logic of Collective Action: Public Goods and the Theory of Groups*.[8] Olson's central idea is that smaller, better-organized, and naturally cohesive groups will predictably outperform larger, citizen-based "latent" groups. Self-funded business lobbies—for example, the U.S. Chamber of Commerce or the Business Roundtable—will thus dominate broader, but less well-funded groups seeking to represent diffuse groups, such as investors, bank depositors, or the general public. Once the public's indignation subsides (as it eventually does), banks and other "inside" players will out lobby a broader, but loose-knit aggregation, such as the public. That is now happening.

These comments do not deny that necessarily rushed legislation can result in overregulation. For example, the Sarbanes-Oxley Act in 2002 indirectly created an obligation under its Section 404(b) to verify a reporting company's internal controls, and this proved unduly costly for smaller companies.[9] Not surprisingly, this provision was quickly cut back by both legislative and regulatory action.[10] Similarly, the Dodd-Frank Act set the level at $50 billion at which a financial institution became a closely regulated SIFI. In retrospect, this level was probably too low[11] (whereas the new legislatively set level of $250 billion may be too high). This recognition of the potential for hasty overregulation reveals the problematic side to the Regulatory Sine Curve on which this article focuses. Simply put, it is never easy to identify the "Goldilocks point" at which the temperature is neither too hot nor too cold, but just right. In this light, this article briefly surveys, in deliberately nontechnical prose, five areas where deregulation may have gone past the point of sensible adjustment. Its specific conclusions may be debatable, but not its central point about the accuracy of Mancur Olson's prediction that better organized groups will win most regulatory contests. That, in turn, frames the final question: How, if at all, can we adjust or respond to the inevitable tendency of collective action to favor the better organized minority?

What Problems and Regulatory Gaps Have Re-emerged Postcrisis?

If one contemporaneous statement made during the 2008 crisis should survive and be remembered, it is the comment of Charles Prince, the then CEO of Citigroup, who was asked in 2007 what would happen now that securitizations were encountering resistance and recognition was growing that financial institutions were overleveraged. He responded, with a seemingly resigned shrug:

As long as the music is playing, you've got to get up and dance![12]

In short, even if problems are evident, one has to keep on closing deals. Ignore that they may later explode, producing litigation and bankruptcy. That is someone else's problem.

Behind this attitude lie two powerful forces: (i) financial competition, as banks dare not fall behind their rivals, for fear that their shareholders will revolt; and (ii) incentive competition, as financial executives have come to be compensated under incentive formulas that give them both a short-term and risk-tolerant orientation. Ironically, the Dodd-Frank Act actually aggravated the first factor by authorizing "proxy access," a procedure that gave activist shareholders increased leverage over corporate managements.[13] But the Business Roundtable sued and invalidated the SEC's rule adopted to implement proxy access,[14] thus both ending this threat and again demonstrating the power of a well-organized group.

Not surprisingly, the Dodd-Frank Act specifically addressed incentive compensation and sought to limit its influence. But of all the areas in which Dodd-Frank has been cut back, this is the clearest (and most extreme) example because, despite elaborate draft rules, nothing was ever adopted. The problem of incentive compensation has now been deemed a nonproblem.

The 2008 crisis also demonstrated beyond argument that major banks were "too big to fail." Given also that Congress chose to limit the Federal Reserve's authority to bail out a major bank, it was blindingly obvious that banks had to be regulated so they did not fail. The Dodd-Frank Act attempted to accomplish this in several ways, and for our purposes it will be sufficient to examine two such efforts: (1) the Volcker Rule and (2) new controls on capital and leverage. In both cases, strong rules were imposed but have already (as of mid-2018) been substantially cut back. The rules that remain in place are clearly an improvement over the pre-Dodd-Frank regulatory environment, but it is reasonable to conclude that they fall somewhere short of the Goldilocks point at which the level of regulation is "just right."

Next, the Dodd-Frank Act created a new body to protect consumers in the financial sector: the Consumer Financial Protection Bureau (CFPB).[15] Its core priorities, according to its first director, Richard Cordray, were mortgages, credit cards, and student loans.[16] To this end, the CFPB promulgated rules seeking to reform mortgage lending, including by specifying income ratios for "qualified mortgages"—an obvious response to the decline in mortgage lending standards prior to the 2008 crisis.

Since its outset, the CFPB has been the subject of legal and legislative challenges. In 2018, Congress passed, and President Trump signed into law, legislation (i) repealing CFPB's automobile lending regulations and (ii) exempting smaller banks that had been subject to its regulations.[17] Here the banking industry has clearly counterattacked vigorously and effectively and left the CFPB today a weak and muted agency.

Finally, what has happened to financial enforcement? Here the most active enforcer is the SEC, and as will be seen, the SEC has shifted its focus to the retail level and sued few public companies under President Trump. This is a major shift from the Obama administration, which in its final years compelled the largest banks to pay massive settlements for their role in the 2008 crisis.

Each of these examples needs a fuller (but still brief) examination.

Incentive Compensation

A long list of authorities can be cited for the proposition that incentive compensation (and particularly stock options) induces corporate managers to accept increased risk.[18] Some studies show that this incentive also may incline executives to engage in financial misreporting.[19] Historically, executive compensation has shifted dramatically, beginning in the 1980s. Figure 18.1 shows the sudden acceleration in the median compensation of CEOs and other top officers from 1939–2005.[20]

Clearly there is a major inflection point in the 1990s. What caused it? Figure 18.2 shows that a shift from crash to equity compensation bears the principal causal responsibility.[21] As of 2015, Equilar has reported that the share of total CEO compensation deriving from equity was 60 percent for companies in the S&P 500.[22]

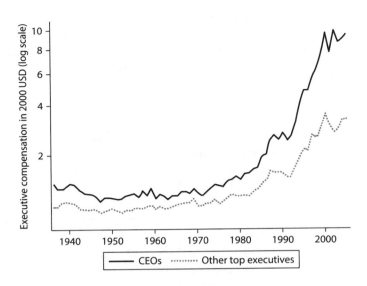

Figure 18.1 Median compensation of CEOs and other top officers, 1936–2005

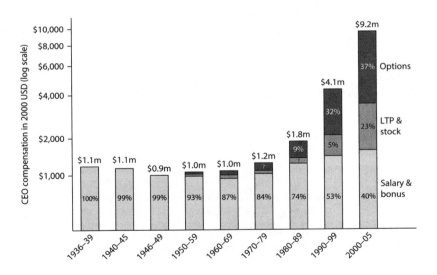

Figure 18.2 The shifting structure of CEO compensation

The dangers of incentive compensation are particularly acute in the world of investment banking.[23] Suppose a bank realizes that securitizations have become toxic and the mortgages it has assembled into portfolios are likely to default. Should it halt their sale? If senior bank officials handling these deals stand to make bonuses of $10 to $20 million when these deals close this year, those officers will push back hard at any such suggestion. Some will leave for other jobs, and an executive revolt is predictable. Arguably, the bank just had to keep dancing "while the music was playing."

Table 18.1 shows just how endemic such bonuses were at the major banks specializing in mortgage-backed securitizations. As table 18.1 shows, the major banks lost billions ($27.7 billion in the case of Citigroup) but still created enormous bonus pools even while heading toward insolvency ($5.33 billion at Citigroup in this worst year on record).[24] Citigroup paid bonuses of over $3 million to 124 persons (and other similar banks paid such bonuses to over 200 persons). These bonuses ensured that the bankers would be closing deals to earn them even at the brink of insolvency.

The drafters of the Dodd-Frank Act understood this problem and designed §956 to enable regulators to discourage inappropriate risk-taking at "covered financial institutions." In terms of its substantive commands, Section 956 did essentially three things: (i) it authorized financial regulators to prohibit "excessive compensation"; (ii) instructed them to discourage incentive compensation which, even if not "excessive," could lead to "material financial loss"; and (iii) required most "covered financial institutions" to disclose to their respective regulator "the structure of all incentive-based compensation" paid to officers, directors, and employees, to enable the regulator to regulate compensation "that could lead to material financial loss to the covered financial institution."[25]

TABLE **18.1** Selected TARP Recipients 2008 Bonus Compensation

Institution	Earnings/ (Losses)	Bonus Pool	No. of Employees Receiving Bonus >$3 million	No. of Employees Receiving Bonus >$1 million
Bank of America	$4 billion	$3.3 billion	28	172
Citigroup, Inc.	$(27.7 billion)	$5.3 billion	124	738
Goldman, Sachs Group	$2.322 billion	$4.823 billion	212	953
JPMorgan Chase & Co.	$5.6 billion	$8.693 billion	> 200	1,626
Merrill Lynch	$(27.6 billion)	$3.6 billion	149	696
Morgan Stanley	$1,707 billion	$4.475 billion	101	428

This was vague, but it seemingly allowed regulators to request at least what was disclosed in Table 18.1 (which was disclosed by then New York State Attorney General Andrew Cuomo after an investigation of these banks).

Nothing like Table 18.1 was ever disclosed (or even required in draft regulations to be disclosed). The various regulators (including the Federal Reserve, the SEC, and the FDIC) were simply faced down in negotiations by the banking community. In terms of disclosure, the regulators were convinced to accept only a generalized narrative description of the structure of executive compensation. This would have produced a largely formalized boilerplate of limited value. Still, in the case of the larger banks in Levels 1 and 2 (i.e., those with assets over $50 billion), the draft regulations did require more, including disclosure of specific details as to incentive compensation arrangements. More important, in these cases, the regulations proposed substantive requirements to mitigate the impact of incentive compensation, including deferrals of up to 60 percent of incentive compensation for up to four years (depending on the institution's size) plus clawbacks.[26]

These were meaningful reforms, but they did not apply to many of the persons most likely to injure their institutions in pursuit of incentive compensation. Although the Dodd-Frank Act recognized that employees other than senior executives (whom it termed "significant risk-takers") might similarly cause material losses, it did not specify how persons in this latter category should be defined or identified. Logic and experience suggested that most traders can easily cause such a loss, possibly through unauthorized trading (Barings Bank had failed from such an experience, and Societe Generale had had a very recent similar experience).[27] Although this expanded coverage was logical, it threatened banks and caused them to push back. If banks had to disclose their compensation levels for traders and then design rules that restricted or delayed their incentive compensation, these traders might migrate *en masse* to unregulated hedge funds (and indeed many did). Thus the banking industry wanted a different standard under which the board (or a committee thereof) of each large bank would determine who could cause it a "material financial loss." Only these identified individuals would then be subjected to restrictive policies (such as clawbacks). Obviously, banks had an incentive under this standard to underidentify those who could harm it.

Based on this weak compromise, the Obama administration in 2011 proposed to implement Section 956 to require only (i) a lengthy narrative on covered banks' executive compensation policies; (ii) in the case of banks with assets over $50 billion, more specific rules on disclosure with respect to executive officers and those persons, if any, identified by the board as being capable of causing a "material loss;" and (iii) deferral and clawback rules for the executive officers and other persons so identified.[28] In short, each major bank could largely decide for itself to whom Section 956 would apply.

This was extreme deference to the industry, but it was only the beginning. The rules proposed in 2011 and published in the *Federal Register* were never adopted. Even these were resisted by the industry. By the end of the Obama administration in 2016, new rules—tougher in some respects and softer in other respects—were widely circulated, but these too were never adopted.[29] Then came the Trump administration, and the entire project was quickly shelved. No rules are currently under consideration, and Section 956 has been quietly abandoned.

To sum up, the 2008 crisis was caused at least in substantial part by excessive risk-taking motivated in the view of most observers by excessive incentive compensation. Congress passed a broad grant of authority (Section 956) to curb excessive incentive compensation, but the entire project collapsed (in stages) in the face of industry opposition. To be sure, many major banks today do have clawback policies, but examples are few and far between in which compensation has been recovered pursuant to them.[30] If this shows anything beyond political cowardice in Washington, it is that Mancur Olson was onto something important.

Who Is a SIFI?

Recognizing that major banks (and other financial institutions) were "too big to fail," the Dodd-Frank Act subjected them to additional oversights and imposed higher capital and more restrictive leverage requirements. At the time, this was relatively uncontroversial because Lehman and AIG were very visible cases in point of poorly managed financial institutions (and they were not the only firms rendered insolvent in 2008). But when the Regulatory Sine Curve turns downward, lobbyists pursue deregulation incrementally. A first target was the level at which a bank must become a SIFI. Under the Dodd-Frank Act, this level was set at $50 billion. Almost everyone today concedes that that level was probably set too low. The "Economic Growth, Regulatory Relief and Consumer Protection Act," enacted by Congress and signed by President Trump in 2018, raised this level (in stages) to $250 billion.[31] Is this level too high? Here one can quickly generate a spirited debate. Probably around two dozen banks were exempted from SIFI status by this change. It is unlikely that the failure of any one of these banks would have the same impact as Lehman's failure in 2008 (although Lehman's failure may have shocked the market because it showed that the market did not properly understand the vulnerability and exposure that financial institutions had, both in the "repo" market and in terms of the illiquidity of their holdings).

Still, even if the impact of raising the level of SIFI-hood is indeterminate, one example bears special emphasis. The 2008 crisis started in the market for residential mortgage-backed securities. Here one villain does stand out:

Countrywide Financial Corporation, the largest U.S. lender in subprime mortgages. By most accounts it was a "freewheeling mortgage machine" that led a general relaxation in mortgage lending standards through such techniques as "exploding interest rates" and "interest only" mortgages.[32] On the brink of insolvency, Countrywide was acquired (probably unwisely) by Bank of America, which has been forced to absorb billions in liabilities attributable to Countrywide's behavior. The relevant point here is that Countrywide (at the time of its acquisition) fell in the zone between $50 billion and $250 billion that has now been deregulated. Had Dodd-Frank existed in 2006, Countrywide would have been subject to leverage ratios, capital levels, and stress tests that might have identified it as a dangerously exposed bank at an earlier stage. Countrywide's example suggests that more supervision is needed over banks in this range, particularly because stress tests would reveal weaknesses that can later destabilize the market.[33]

In addition to the Economic Growth, Regulatory Relief, and Consumer Protection Act, the Federal Reserve is currently rewriting and lowering its leverage-ratio rule (which requires U.S. banks to maintain a minimum level of capital defined in terms of their total assets). Essentially, this reduction will be down to a level required by the Basel Committee on Banking Regulation; thus it is unlikely to be a game-changing reduction. Nonetheless, this reduction should be measured against a contemporaneous marked change in banking behavior. In 2018, for the first time since 2008, U.S. banks will pay out in dividends and stock buybacks more capital than they are earning from their operations.[34] In effect, capital is flowing out, just as deregulation is reducing the mandatory standards. If this trend continues, banks could return to their position in the pre-Bubble era.

The Volcker Rule

If major banks are "too big to fail" and if Congress insists that bailouts are impermissible, then banks must be regulated so they do not fail by barring them from risky activities. The Volcker Rule is a means to this end.[35] To be sure, the activities barred by the Volcker Rule did not cause the 2008 crash. But this concession means little because all crashes come from the blind side. Restricting the risks that banks can run, therefore, makes sense.

In its core provision, the Volcker Rule barred banks from engaging in "proprietary trading" on the obvious premise that banks (which have thin equity) should not be able to bet on securities, effectively, with their depositors' money. But the term *proprietary trading* is not self-defining, and thus an important provision in the rule was its presumption that any position in a security held for less than sixty days was to be deemed a "proprietary" trade. That presumption would now be abandoned. In addition, the Volcker Rule contained exemptions for trading done as a part of hedging, market-making, or underwriting activities by the bank. These exemptions will now be expanded, and the documentation necessary to justify them will be greatly relaxed. As others have phrased it, the result is to turn the Volcker Rule into "a 'we'll-take-your-word-for it' kind of a rule."[36] Depending on how the Volcker Rule is enforced, these changes will downsize it somewhere between moderately and greatly.

In all likelihood, the level of speculative trading by banks in securities will not return to pre-2008 levels, largely because high-paid traders have migrated to hedge funds. This migration was partly caused by expected controls on incentive compensation at banks, but those rules were never adopted. Thus, over the long-run, it is unclear whether traders will return to banks, so that banks could again become major players in speculative trading.

To sum up, the Volcker Rule has not been abolished, but compliance with it is likely to vary significantly across banks, and ultimately this could produce a standard race to the bottom.

The Consumer Financial Protection Bureau

This agency, created by Dodd-Frank based on a 2007 proposal by now Senator (but then Professor) Elizabeth Warren, has always been controversial.[37] Essentially, Dodd-Frank concentrated the consumer protection responsibilities of several federal agencies in the CFPB. From its outset, the CFPB made clear that its high-priority concerns were with mortgage lending, credit cards, and student loans.[38]

Correspondingly, from its outset, the Trump administration made clear its hostility to the agency, and the CFPB director initially appointed by President Trump, Mick Mulvaney, once called the agency a "sick, sad joke."[39] In 2018, legislation supported by the Trump administration was twice enacted, in the first case, exempting smaller banks from the CFPB's jurisdiction, and in the second case, repealing the CFPB's rules on automobile lending.[40] Mulvaney also summarily dismissed the CFPB's Advisory Committee after they had criticized his failure to meet with them.

In short, in contrast to the more moderate reforms relating to SIFI status, the Volcker Rule, or leverage ratios, the CFPB has been effectively placed in a deep freeze and rendered inactive. The impact of such a move on systemic risk regulation is, however, less clear. Although rules restricting "interest only" mortgages and overly liberal lending might have a salutary effect on systemic risk, this was never the CFPB's mission or priority. No agency in Washington is prepared to stand between borrowers and easy money. And that is one way to state the dilemma surrounding systemic risk regulation.

Financial Enforcement

Legal realism tells us that rules do not work unless they are enforced. Yet enforcement with respect to financial regulations (including antifraud rules) appears to be on the wane. A 2018 study by Cornerstone Research and the NYU Pollack Center finds that SEC enforcement actions against public companies declined to the lowest level in five years, with only fifteen new actions being filed in the first half of 2018.[41] This was a 67 percent decrease from the corresponding period in 2017. Of course, the SEC is only one agency, but it has the largest enforcement resources and capacity of any federal administrative agency and has traditionally been the leader. Add to this picture the forced muting of the CFPB and the extent to which revised rules (such as the revised Volcker Rule) depend on voluntary compliance, and the prospect for undetected misbehavior looms large.

An Initial Summary

This tour has been brief and incomplete. One could alternatively have examined recent developments in swaps and derivative trading, or at money market funds, or at clearing and credit rating agencies. But the same picture would likely emerge: some deregulation may seem justifiable; other deregulatory efforts are harder to evaluate; and finally, some deregulation seems unjustifiable, leaving us with a half-built regulatory fortress lacking a wall on at least one side. This does not mean that another financial crash is predictable in the short run; indeed, realists should recognize that the banking industry is now at the top of its business cycle, and banks' stock prices have never been higher. The point is rather that the business cycle eventually turns downward,[42] and our defenses against systemic risk remain incomplete and inadequate.

How to Moderate the Regulatory Sine Curve

To this point, this article has emphasized two themes: (i) incentive compensation and competitive pressure will continue to fuel excessive risk-taking in the financial sector; and (ii) the forces favoring deregulation are better organized, better funded, and better able to fight longer and harder than the temporary coalitions that assemble to seek reform after a financial crisis. In response, one can imagine ways in which Congress could write more mandatory legislation on incentive compensation, but the real problem is that more rigid rules are even more likely to be repealed or watered down by a later Congress.

For example, the central idea adopted by the original designers of Dodd-Frank's incentive compensation rules was to delay incentive compensation (or at least 50 percent of it) for a period of years to permit bonuses and options to be clawed back if the transaction justifying the bonus later soured. Conceptually, this seems sound, but its impact will be minimal if the clawback period is not long enough or if the "covered persons" do not include all those who could cause material loss to the company (such as "star" traders). Realistically, the Obama administration's proposed rules (at least the 2011 version) were full of loopholes and inconsistencies. For example, the proposed holdback would have senselessly applied to the company's General Counsel (who is an "executive officer," but seldom a key financial decision maker) but not to its star traders. The statutory language in Section 936 was adequate, but the proposed rules were too compromised to be effective.

This example illustrates that the deeper problem here is how to minimize postcrisis backsliding when the lobbyists begin to pressure the regulator. Predictably, those doing this lobbying will be former regulators themselves, and their approach will be friendly, helpful, and well informed. Nor will there be any organized group, ready, able and well-funded enough to counter their efforts.

In that light, this article makes two modest proposals: the first contemplates a special watchdog for systemic risk, and the second seeks to enlist existing gatekeepers to focus on systemic risk.

Creating a Watchdog for Systemic Risk

Financial reform legislation needs to create its own guardian. This guardian could not be part of the administration itself because shifting political tides would cause it to be staffed by the president and party in power. Rather, a permanent body, with an Inspector General-like authority, needs to be created whose views would have to be solicited and which would publicly provide its evaluation. Its initial members would be persons with expertise in the field of systemic risk who would be presidential appointees. Ideally, they would be appointed at (or immediately after) the time of the legislation's passage,[43] but these initial members would appoint their own successors by majority vote. This self-perpetuating feature is intended to assure greater continuity and less political pressure. Suppose, for example, that the Dodd-Frank Act had required such a body, and President Obama had appointed to it persons such as Paul Volcker and Barney Frank. By now, some initial appointees might have retired, but to the extent their successors would have been appointed by the rest of this board, greater stability and consistency of outlook seems likely.

What powers would it have? First, rules and regulations (such as the Volcker Rule) adopted pursuant to the statute (and any amendments thereto) would have to be presented to it for its review and public comment. Possibly, this body could even require a delay (conceivably of up to a year) if it felt the proposed rules or regulations were inadequate or misguided.[44] Of course, this body would be constrained by the knowledge that Congress could at any time abolish it (or change its powers), and its members would be removable by the president for cause and could serve no more than a specified term of years. Its real power would lie in its prestige, as its criticism should embarrass the agencies it criticized. Essentially, the proposal is to create a counterweight to lobbying pressure, and this would be a small, cohesive, well-informed (and well-paid) body.

Besides commenting on proposed rules, this body could also be asked to comment on proposed plans submitted pursuant to the statute by covered institutions. For example, if a bank were required to submit its executive compensation and clawback policies to the Federal Reserve, they would be passed onto this body for its public evaluation. It would not necessarily have the power to modify or delay, but its comments could help the regulator negotiate a stronger compromise (as the regulator could point to this body as insisting on a stronger policy). Often regulators are being pushed only from one side, and the proposal here is to ensure that there is counterpressure when needed.

How powerful is prestige in a political world dominated by sound bites, twenty-four-hour news cycles, and "alternative facts"? Skeptics can question this premise that prestige still counts, but this body's members would be nationally known, either for their expertise (think, Paul Volcker) or their commitment to the goals of the legislation (think, Barney Frank). The regulator—whether the Federal Reserve, the Federal Deposit Insurance Corporation (FDIC), or the SEC—would not want to be in a public quarrel with it. Power also comes from financial resources, and this body could also be funded through industry assessments (much as FINRA or the FDIC are today), which all covered financial institutions would be required to pay. Thus it would have adequate funding. This differentiates it from private groups. To be sure, private advocacy groups seeking strong systemic risk regulation are desirable and have arisen,[45] but they have neither the prestige nor the funding of this proposed body. Is this a panacea? By no means will such a body fully counter the power and impact of lobbyists, but it is a counterweight that could partially compensate.

Enlisting the Gatekeepers

The landscape of contemporary corporate governance is populated by a number of "gatekeepers" who are essentially reputational intermediaries who pledge their reputational capital to give credibility to their assessments to investors.[46] Auditors verify past earnings; securities analysts predict future earnings; and credit rating agencies assess the company's creditworthiness. But no gatekeeper evaluates a large financial institution's vulnerability to systemic risk. That omission can and should be rectified.

One means to this end would begin by recognizing that a large financial institution's internal controls should focus on the financial institution's exposure to systemic risk. Today these controls focus on the accuracy of its financial statements and its exposure to fraud and misappropriation. Since the Sarbanes-Oxley Act in 2002, public companies (with some modest exceptions for smaller companies) are required by Section 404 of that Act to report on the adequacy of their internal controls, and Section 404(b), as interpreted by the Public Company Accounting Oversight Board (PCAOB), requires the auditor to audit these controls, reporting on their adequacy.[47]

The next step is the key one. A financial institution's internal controls should guard it, not only from the overstatement of earnings or the misappropriation of assets but from a systemic risk crisis. What would such internal controls look like? They might include constraints on "excessive compensation" and incentive compensation that could lead to "material losses"—just as Section 956 of the Dodd-Frank Act mandated. Although Section 956 has been ignored, a body such as the PCAOB could require the auditor to express its view on whether the financial institution had adequate policies and procedures to address systemic risk. To be sure, this will not happen during the Trump administration, but our vision has to extend beyond that point. If the concept of internal controls is to make sense and be relevant, it has to encompass not only protections against small errors in financial reporting but also major inadequacies (such as exposure to a systemic risk) that could ignite a major financial crisis. Ideally, future legislation could instruct the SEC and the PCAOB to insist that certain issuers (i.e., largely major financial institutions) design their internal controls to address this issue and that auditors assess and report on the adequacy of these controls. Even in the absence of new legislation, however, a future PCAOB could focus auditors on this issue.

Conclusion

The last decade has seen the Regulatory Sine Curve follow its customary path, but more quickly than usual. This speed may be partially attributable to the appearance of Donald Trump—clearly a disruptive personality eager to junk existing law and favoring massive deregulation. But it overstates to accord him a primary role in the recent retreat from strong systemic risk regulation. The Economic Growth, Regulatory Relief and Consumer Protection Act, enacted by Congress in 2018,[48] was designed in Congress with little direct involvement by the president. Nor does that statute repeal the Dodd-Frank

Act (or take other severe action of the kind that President Trump usually favors). At most, it represents the beginning of a death by one thousand cuts, which is the classic pattern.

The most important defeat for systemic risk regulation came before President Trump's election: the failure to implement Section 956 of the Dodd-Frank Act and curb incentive compensation at major financial institutions. Absent such a reform, everything else may amount to little more than rearranging the deck chairs on the *Titanic*. So long as financial executives are incentivized by the jet fuel of high incentive compensation, they will focus on the short-run tactics that maximize that compensation. That best explains the 2008 crisis, and it eventually will likely explain the next crisis.

Notes

1. Technically, the act is more properly identified as the Wall Street Reform and Consumer Protection Act, Pub. L. No. 111–203, 124 Stat. 1376 (2010). For purposes of this nontechnical article, I will shorten this title to the "Dodd-Frank Act."

2. For an overview of the Dodd-Frank Act and the pushback that it generated from the outset, see John C. Coffee Jr., "The Political Economy of Dodd-Frank: Why Financial Reform Tends to Be Frustrated and Systemic Risk Perpetuated," *Cornell Law Review* 97, no. 5 (2012): 1019–82. Beyond the subparts of the Dodd-Frank Act noted in the text, its provision on stress testing may have proved the most useful (and it predictably has been rolled back, as discussed later).

3. Some of the Dodd-Frank Act's rules appear to have been evaded simply by moving transactions offshore. See Charles Levinson, "Vanishing Act: U.S. Banks Moved Billions of Dollars in Trades Beyond Washington's Reach," *Reuters Investigates*, August 21, 2015, https://www.reuters.com/investigates/special-report/usa-swaps/. Essentially, if U.S. banks trade through foreign subsidiaries and the parent bank does not guarantee the transaction, the Commodities Futures Trading Commission takes the position that these transactions are beyond its jurisdiction. More generally, with respect to the reappearance of risky securitizations and overly leveraged lending, the Bank of England has just "sounded the alarm," focusing particularly on the U.S. market. See Jason Douglas, "U.K. Central Bank Warns on Debt Risk," *The Wall Street Journal*, June 28, 2018. For fuller details, see infra at note 42.

4. For a fuller description of this cycle, see Coffee, "The Political Economy of Dodd-Frank," 1020–21; Stuart Banner, "What Causes New Securities Regulation? 300 Years of Evidence," *Washington University Law Quarterly* 75 (1997): 849–51; Anthony Downs, "Up and Down with Ecology—The Issue 'Attention' Cycle," *Public Interest* 28 (1972): 38–41, arguing that legislative inertia and interest group veto power can only be overcome after a crisis that captivates the public's attention. Others argue that the same phenomena apply to the passage of environmental laws. See Christopher H. Schroeder, "Rational Choice Versus the Republican Moment—Explanations for Environmental Laws, 1969–1973," *Duke Environmental Law & Policy Forum* 9 (Fall 1998): 29–60, at 33–36.

5. The South Seas Company was a British joint-stock company, founded in 1711 as a public-private partnership to consolidate and reduce the national debt; it was granted a

monopoly to trade with South America and nearby islands (which at the time remained under Spanish control). Because the South Seas Company had no access to South America, trading of government debt became its principal activity, and its stock price rose precipitously, before crashing in 1720. The scandal deepened when some members of the Royal Family were found to have engaged in significant self-dealing relating to the South Seas Company. In reaction, Parliament enacted The Bubble Act 1720 (6 Geo. I, c. 18), which prohibited the creation of joint stock companies without a royal charter. Ironically, this act was supported by the South Seas Company itself, which wanted to eliminate competition.

6. The Glass-Steagall Act, passed in 1933, denied commercial banks the ability to underwrite securities, thus eliminating a source of both risk and conflicts of interest for banks. It was not formally repealed until the Gramm-Leach-Bliley Financial Modernization Act was enacted in 1999. But well before that point, the Federal Reserve Board had gradually loosened many of Glass-Steagall's prohibitions during the 1980s. Similarly, although the Securities Act of 1933 has never been repealed (nor is it likely to be), many of its restrictions were relaxed in the 1980s, with the introduction of integrated disclosure, shelf registration, and eased requirements for private placements (including both Regulation D and Rule 144).

7. For a fuller description of this term, see Coffee, "The Political Economy of Dodd-Frank," 1029–31.

8. See Mancur Olson, *The Logic of Collective Action: Public Groups and the Theory of Groups*, 2nd ed. (Cambridge, Mass: Harvard University Press,1992). A number of important scholars have followed in Olson's wake. See Russell Hardin, *Collective Action* (Baltimore, Md.: Johns Hopkins University Press, 1982); and Todd Sandler, *Collective Action: Theory and Application* (Ann Arbor: University of Michigan Press, 1992). For an application of Olson's ideas to the world of corporate governance, see Robert A. Prentice and David B. Spence, "Sarbanes-Oxley as Quack Corporate Governance: How Wise Is the Received Wisdom?", *Georgetown Law Journal* 95 (2007): 1843–92, at 1847–49.

9. Section 404(b) of Sarbanes-Oxley Act did not actually require the auditor to "audit" the company's internal controls, only to "attest to and report on" management's assessment of its internal controls (which assessment was required by Section 404(a)). However, the Public Company Accounting Oversight Board (PCAOB) adopted its Auditing Standard No. 2 in 2004, which required a full-scale audit of the issuer's internal controls, and industry reaction was swift and hostile. For the fuller statutory language, see note 47.

10. This audit requirement was costly, particularly for smaller companies, and the JOBS Act in 2012 exempted "emerging growth companies" from this requirement. Even earlier, in 2006, the PCAOB also relaxed its rule for smaller companies. See Auditing Standard No. 5. See Coffee, "The Political Economy of Dodd-Frank," 1037–39.

11. For example, I have heard Congressman Barney Frank concede that the $50 billion level was, in retrospect, probably set too low.

12. See Dealbook, "Citi Chief on Buyouts: 'We're Still Dancing,'" *New York Times*, July 10, 2007.

13. Pursuant to authority granted by the Dodd-Frank Act, the SEC adopted Rule 14a-11, which would have permitted a specified level of shareholders under defined circumstances to nominate candidates for the issuer's board of directors and include them on the corporation's own proxy statement (thereby allowing dissident shareholders to economize on the costs of a proxy solicitation).

14. In a controversial decision, this rule was struck down by the D.C. Circuit Court of Appeals for failure to conduct an adequate cost-benefit analysis. See Business Roundtable v. S.E.C., 647 F. 3d 114 (D.C. Cir. 2011).

15. The CFPB is most easily defined as the federal agency charged by the Dodd-Frank Act with overseeing consumer protection in the financial sector. Much of its power was reallocated from other federal agencies, including the Federal Reserve Board, which was thought to have underperformed in this area. Technically, it is housed within the Federal Reserve System, but it is independent of the Federal Reserve Board. The CFPB remains the subject of litigation challenging its constitutionality. The CFPB was clearly the brainchild of Senator Elizabeth Warren, who authored a law review article in 2007, calling for its creation. For her original conception, see Elizabeth Warren, "Unsafe at Any Rate: If It's Good Enough for Microwaves, It's Good Enough for Mortgages," *Democracy* (Summer 2007): 8.

16. See Jean Eaglesham, "Warning Shot on Financial Protection," *The Wall Street Journal*, February 9, 2011 (quoting Richard Cordray, the CFPB's first director).

17. See Zachary Warmbrodt, "Trump Signs Bill Blocking Consumer Bureau Auto-Lending Measure," *Politico*, May 21, 2018; Erik Sherman, "Scaling Back Dodd-Frank Is Just the Beginning in Trump's Run on Deregulation," *NBC News*, May 24, 2018.

18. For an overview, see Jeffrey Coles, Naveen D. Daniel, and Lalitha Nayeen, "Managerial Incentives and Risk-Taking," *Journal of Financial Economics* 79 (2006): 431–68; David Larcker, Gaizka Ormazabal, Brian Tayan, and Daniel J. Taylor, "Follow the Money: Compensation, Risk and the Financial Crisis," *Stanford Closer Look Series*, September 8, 2014.

19. See Christopher S. Armstrong, David Larcker, Gaizka Ormazabal, and Daniel J. Taylor, "The Relation between Equity Incentives and Misreporting: The Role of Risk-Taking Incentives," *Journal of Financial Economics* 100 (2013): 327–50.

20. See Carola Frydman and Dirk Jenter, "CEO Compensation," *Annual Review of Financial Economics* 2 (2010):75–102.

21. Frydman and Jenter, "CEO Compensation,"

22. See Equilar, *2015 CEO Pay Strategies*, 2016, at 90.

23. Lucian A. Bebchuk and Holger Spamann, "Regulating Bankers' Pay," *Georgetown Law Review* 98 (2010): 247–87, at 255–74; Lucian A. Bebchuk et al., "The Wages of Failure: Executive Compensation at Bear Stearns and Lehman 2000–2008," *Yale Journal on Regulation* 27 (2010): 257–82, at 273–76, arguing that incentive compensation created moral hazard problems.

24. See Andrew M. Cuomo, *No Rhyme or Reason: The "Heads I Win, Tails You Lose" Bank Bonus Culture*, 2009, at 5; see also Coffee, "The Political Economy of Dodd-Frank," 1068.

25. Section 956 was codified at 12 U.S.C. §5641. Still, it is the rules under Section 956 that are crucial. From early on in the implementation of the Dodd-Frank Act, it was contemplated that there would be three levels of "covered financial institutions": Level 1 would cover institutions with total consolidated assets of $250 billion or more; Level 2 would cover institutions with total consolidated assets between $50 billion and $250 billion; and Level 3 would cover institutions in the range of $1 billion to $50 billion in total consolidated assets. Institutions in Levels 2 and 3 were required to impose deferrals of payment, downward adjustments, and clawback provisions on senior executive officers and certain other employees engaged in risk-taking to reduce their incentives to enter transactions that could result in material losses. But institutions in all three levels were required (with some small exceptions) to comply with Section 956's disclosure provisions.

26. Senior executive officers at Level 1 financial institutions were, under the proposed rules, to be subject to deferral of 60 percent of incentive compensation for four years (and significant risk-takers at Level 1 institutions, who were not such executives, would face a deferral of 50 percent of such compensation for four years). Thus traders, if covered at a Level 1 bank, would not receive half of their bonuses or other incentive payment for four years.

27. For example, Jerome Kerviel lost $7.2 billion for Societe Generale in 2008 through unauthorized trading as a relatively junior trader. See Kim Iskyan, "Here's the Story of How a Guy Making $66,000 a Year Lost $7.2 Billion for One of Europe's Biggest Banks," *Business Insider*, May 8, 2016. Ultimately, Mr. Kerveil was criminally convicted by a French court, but whether he was a "rogue trader" (as his employer characterized him) or only a fallible trader who responded to excessive incentives remains debatable.

28. See "Incentive-Based Compensation Arrangements," Exchange Act Release No. 64, 140, 76 Fed. Reg. 21,120, April 14, 2011.

29. No single proposed regulation was jointly released by all six agencies (the Federal Reserve Board, the Federal Housing Finance Agency, the Office of the Controller of the Currency, the Federal Deposit Insurance Corporation, the Securities and Exchange Commission, and the National Credit Union Administrator); nor were these rules filed in the *Federal Register*. Major law firms, however, wrote detailed memos to their clients about these changes. See Latham & Watkins, "Client Alert: Revised Rules on Dodd-Frank Incentive Compensation Requirements for Financial Institutions Proposed," May 4, 2016, no. 1963. One important change was to define "significant risk-taker" to include only people at Level 1 and 2 institutions who received at least one-third of their compensation in the form of incentive compensation *and* were "among the top 5 percent (for Level 1 covered institutions) or top 2 percent (for Level 2 covered institutions) of highest compensated covered persons" *and* had "authority to commit or expose 0.5 percent or more of the capitals of the covered institution." "Incentive-Based Compensation Arrangements," 6. Such a definition would likely exclude most traders at most institutions. But at least this provision would have ended total reliance on the board's (or committee's) identification of "significant risk-takers."

30. To my knowledge, as of mid-2018, the only significant use of clawbacks subsequent to the 2008 crisis has been at Wells Fargo Bank, where the board clawed back $75 million from two executives (Chairman John G. Stumpf and Executive Vice President Carrie L. Tolstedt) in the wake of a scandal there that was unrelated to the 2008 crisis. See Stacy Cowley and A. Kingson, "Dealbook: Wells Fargo to Claw Back $75 million from 2 Former Executives," *New York Times*, April 10, 2017.

31. This legislation, sponsored by Senator Michael Crapo of Idaho and known as S.2155, passed Congress in late May 2018 when the House adopted the Senate bill. In both the House and the Senate, there was relatively bipartisan support for the legislation. Clearly, this legislation did not repeal the Dodd-Frank Act (and the House version, which would have repealed the Volcker Rule, did not pass the Senate, although S.2155 does exempt banks with less than $10 billion in assets from that rule). Title IV of S.2155 raises the SIFI threshold from $50 billion to $250 billion (but permits the Federal Reserve Board to determine that specific banks with assets greater than $100 billion should be subject to the same standards as a SIFI). Title IV further ends "company run" stress tests for banks with under $250 billion in assets. "Periodic" supervisory stress tests are still permitted for banks with assets from $100 billion to $250 billion.

32. See Gretchen Morgenson, "Fair Game: Countrywide Mortgage Devastation Lingers on as Ex-Chief Moves On," *New York Times*, June 26, 2016.

33. It should be added that even under the 2018 legislation, the Federal Reserve can still order banks with assets over $100 billion to undergo stress tests, but such authority is likely to be used by the Fed only sparingly.

34. See Alistair Gray and Ben McLannahan, "U.S. Banks Poised to Hand Out $170 bn," *Financial Times*, June 18, 2018.

35. Essentially, the Volcker Rule bars commercial banks from "proprietary trading" or owning or sponsoring a hedge fund. Section 619 of the Dodd-Frank Act, which has been codified at 12 U.S.C. §1851, expresses this prohibition. The rules implementing the Volcker Rule were delayed as the result of lobbying and did not go into effect until July 21, 2015.

36. See Chris Arnold, "Fed Proposes Changes in Volcker Rule," *NPR*, May 21, 2018. Smaller banks with assets under $10 billion are now exempted from the Volcker Rule. See supra note 31.

37. For the article by then Professor Warren, see supra note 15.

38. See supra note 16 (quoting CFPB's first director, Richard Cordray).

39. See Katy O'Donnell, "Mick Mulvaney Isn't Blowing Up the CFPB; It's More Like a Death by a Thousand Cuts, Critics Say," *Politico*, April 30, 2018.

40. See sources cited supra note 17.

41. See "SEC Enforcement Activity: Public Companies and Subsidiaries, Midyear FY 2018 Update," Cornerstone Research, https://www.cornerstone.com/Publications/Reports/SEC-Enforcement-Activity-Public-Companies-and-Subsidiaries-Midyear-FY-2018-Update.

42. Despite a healthy, even booming, stock market, there are already warning signals flashing of a crisis in global debt markets. In June 2018, the Bank of England released a highly critical report on global debt markets that (in the words of *The Wall Street Journal*) "voiced particular concern about the U.S., where corporate borrowing has ballooned to 290 percent of first quarter earnings, according to BOE calculations" and has been "accompanied by looser lending standards, leading to a surge in high-risk lending . . . , a large share of which is being parceled into securitized assets sold to investors worldwide." See Douglas, "U.K. Central Bank Warns on Debt Risk." This sounds like 2007 all over again.

43. No position is here taken on whether senatorial confirmation should be necessary for the initial appointees. Obviously, many agencies have advisory boards whose members are not confirmed by the Senate. But this body would have power to delay the effectiveness of proposed agency rules, and this might point to the need for Senate confirmation. Also, a requirement of Senate confirmation might give this body greater prestige and visibility. To the extent that this body has any power, removal of its members for cause by the president (or perhaps the Federal Reserve Board) is probably constitutionally required. See Free Enterprise Fund v. Pub. Co. Accounting Oversight Bd, 561 U.S. 477 (2010).

44. In this light, the members of this body would have to be subject to some conflict of interest rules.

45. One such example is Better Markets, a nonprofit organization founded after the 2008 crisis "to promote the public interest in the financial markets."

46. For an overview of gatekeepers in corporate governance, see John C. Coffee Jr., *Gatekeepers: The Professions and Corporate Governance* (Oxford, UK: Oxford University Press, 2006).

47. Under Section 404(a) of the Sarbanes-Oxley Act, management must first provide an "internal control report" as part of the company's Annual Report on Form 10-K, which must contain "an assessment of the effectiveness of the internal control structure and procedures of the issuer for financial reporting." Then, under Section 404(b), the auditor "shall attest to, and report on, the assessment made by the management of the issuer." Section 404(b) further provides that this assessment shall be "made in accordance with standards for attestation engagements issued by the" PCAOB (which required a full audit for this assessment). Section 404 of Sarbanes-Oxley has been codified at 15 U.S.C. Section 7262.

48. See text and supra note 31.

CHAPTER 19

ROUNDTABLE

It's Not Too Much or Too Little Regulation; It's Getting It Right

JOHN C. COFFEE JR., STEPHEN M. CUTLER, BARNEY FRANK, AND KATHRYN JUDGE

Kathryn Judge: I'm going to keep the introductions brief because I have the great pleasure of introducing three esteemed individuals from different areas who are leading voices in their respective areas. For anybody who doesn't know them, they have longer bios in the program. First, let me introduce Stephen Cutler, who is Vice Chairman for JPMorgan. He was previously General Counsel there and had been a partner at WilmerHale, and a director of the SEC's Division of Enforcement. Barney Frank spent thirty-two years serving in the House of Representatives and, of course, is the "Frank" of the Dodd-Frank Act, so he'll have quite a bit to share with us over the congressional dynamics of financial regulation. To my left, Jack Coffee is the Adolf Berle Professor of Law at Columbia Law School, as well as a director of the Center for Corporate Governance at the Law School. He has been listed more times than I can count on the "100 Most Influential Lawyers in America," and he will provide the academic perspective. So, today, we have experts from industry, government, and academia, as I host an incredibly rich conversation focused not only on the quantity of regulations, which, I think, too often dominates the headlines, but the deeper question of how we go about structuring the nature of regulation to be responsive to the problems we're seeking to address, where we are right now, and what's going to happen in the coming years.

How to Regulate in Times of Crisis

Stephen Cutler: First of all, I should say that it's really an honor to be here with these two gentlemen. The gentleman immediately to my right (Congressman

Barney Frank) changed my life over the last decade, and as for the gentleman two over (Professor Jack Coffee), he doesn't know this, but when I was at the SEC I always used to read what Professor Coffee would say, and I'd say to myself, "That's incredibly annoying, but you know, he's right." So I am delighted to be here with you in the audience today and here with these two gentlemen, in particular.

I think the way I want to talk about how to regulate in times of crisis is to talk about four cautionary items. This feels a little presumptuous and I probably should let these gentlemen do it, but I'm going to take a crack at it. They're idiosyncratic and we could choose lots of ways to talk about regulation, but these are at the forefront of my mind, particularly [. . .] today. First, beware of extremes. Regulation goes through boom and bust cycles just as economies do. It was only a dozen years ago that we were talking about deregulation or lighter-touch regulation . . . some people may remember that Eliot Spitzer convened a commission to think about principles-based versus rules-based regulation. What was that about? That was about competing with the UK for listings. As the UK was thinking about how to regulate in a kinder, gentler way, we were too. Once you're in that place, you have to consider whether the pendulum has swung too far. You can think about some of what's happened over the last several years at the other end of the pendulum. And maybe most reflective of this is what the government said recently in connection with the issuance of the United States G-SIB surcharge rule—this is the rule that applies additional capital charges to the biggest financial institutions. So what the government said is that cost benefit analysis was not chosen as the primary calibration framework for the G-SIB surcharge. It is not directly related to the mandate provided by the Dodd-Frank Act, which instructs the Federal Reserve Board to mitigate risks to the financial stability of the United States. I think once you start talking about financial regulation divorced from costs, divorced from the dual objectives, especially in this space—one is financial stability, but on the other side is growth and economic inclusion— I think once you ignore one of those you may have gone too far on the other side of the pendulum. Finally, I would say today, sitting where we are, I wouldn't let calls for regulatory reform become calls for wholesale deregulation. A lot of what's happened over the last decade has been so important: capital buffers, recovery and resolution planning, stress tests, and creation of a regulator whose mission is the protection of consumers. All those are really good things, and we ought not, as we think about recalibrating, throw out those babies with the bathwater.

Second, regulators have to step back and look at the whole of what they're doing. They can't get siloed even within their own agencies; they have to think about the full landscape of what they're doing. I think about something like liquidity regulation and what's happened in that area over the last decade. [. . .] Liquidity regulation has been incredibly important to achieving financial stability in the system, but we now have the liquidity coverage ratio, the net stable funding ratio, and the short-term wholesale factor in the G-SIB surcharge. Within the total loss absorbing capacity requirements, we have requirements around long-term funding and limitations on short-term funding. We have CLAR, which is the comprehensive liquidity and assessment review process, and we have stress testing, which is contemplating the addition of liquidity shocks. All of those may make sense individually, but if they're not accounting for the other, if they're not assuming compliance with the other, I think there's a danger of overregulation.

Third, I would say beware of multiregulator overlap and duplication. That can create, I think, some very difficult situations, both for financial institutions and, ultimately, for the public in how regulations are both created and enforced. In connection with the Volcker Rule, for example, we've got five different regulators who've had to agree on what the rule means, how it should be enforced, and how it should be interpreted. In the mortgage area, to give you a second example, JPMorgan is subject to, I think, seven different federal regulators and a panoply of state regulations every time we issue and service mortgages. In a third example, the requirement that banks develop recovery and resolution plans [. . .], you have not only the Fed but also the FDIC involved. I don't think that's a recipe for good regulation.

Echoing this on the enforcement side, we have got and we have seen a proliferation over the last decade of multiregulator actions every time someone does something wrong. I don't think that's particularly healthy either. So I'll give a JPMorgan example, again, our London Whale situation. We were dealing with five and six different regulatory enforcement arms, each one of whom decided on a monetary sanction without regard to what the others were doing. That's not good regulation, that's not good enforcement.

Finally, my fourth idiosyncratic point is that enforcement can both complement and it can negatively undermine regulatory policy. Two examples: One, FHA and the use of the False Claims Act. Lots of financial institutions paid massive penalties in connection with the FHA lending that they did, as a result of what I would tell you were non-scienter-based, unintentional mistakes in connection with mortgage lending practices that, over the course of time, the FHA and financial institutions had developed an understanding were okay. That course of conduct was completely ignored once a U.S. Attorney's Office decided that they were going to bring False Claims Act cases. What has that done? That's essentially taken big financial institutions way down in FHA lending. That's probably not a policy the government hoped to achieve. The way the government went about enforcing the rules has very much affected policy. Two, I'll give you yet another JPMorgan example: In connection with one of our settlements with the government we were penalized for what happened at Bear Stearns. We were also required to give up an indemnity right in connection with our acquisition of the assets of WaMu. Those are transactions the United States Government wanted JPMorgan to do, and yet when it came time for enforcers to decide what the appropriate sanctions or penalties were, they dealt with those acquisitions in very different ways. When we complained to the Justice Department about a penalty related to Bear Stearns and said "Look, the United States asked us to take over Bear Stearns. Why would you want to penalize us for preacquisition conduct by Bear Stearns?" The response we got was, "That was the Department of Treasury, we're the Department of Justice." How do you think, the next time we have a crisis, a financial institution that is asked, "You should think about acquiring this company because it'll help the economy, it'll help prevent a crisis," that company is going to react?

I'll turn the floor over to Congressman Frank.

More or Less Regulation Isn't the Question; It's Getting It Right

Barney Frank: I'll begin by saying that I said exactly that publicly with regard to Bear Stearns. In fact, you understated the case. You weren't asked to take over Bear Stearns, you were pressured by the Bush administration, specifically Hank Paulson and Ben Bernanke, to take over Bear Stearns. I was there, I was chairman of the committee, I understand that, and I thought it was, exactly for the reasons you said, a terrible mistake. It was both unfair and counterproductive for the future. Also, you can differentiate. Bank of America faced the same situation with regard to being held accountable for the previous mistakes of Merrill Lynch and also of Countrywide. Now Countrywide they eagerly went out and sought, and they deserved everything they got for Countrywide. I was asked what I thought at the time about Bank of America taking over Countrywide, and I said, "Look, I'd be happy if Syria took over Countrywide." It was an outrageous, irresponsible institution. But in the Merrill case, which was very similar to the Bear case, the federal government was wrong, and I was very disappointed that they did not intervene or object to that.

On the other hand, I'm much less sympathetic to the complaint about the London Whale because JPMorgan Chase brought that on itself, not simply in the mistakes, which will happen, but in the resistance to any regulation whatsoever. And if you take a position that there should be no regulation, that makes it harder to work with us to get the right kind of regulation. When the London Whale hit, a bill was on its way through the Republican-controlled Congress, with JPMorgan's great enthusiasm, to say that the U.S. regulators would have no jurisdiction whatsoever over the derivative activities of foreign subsidiaries of U.S. banks. So the position that JPMorgan Chase had was that it should be none of America's business what happened with the London Whale. Now I will acknowledge . . .

Stephen Cutler: By the way, Congressman, I don't think that was our position at all. But . . .

Barney Frank: I was there. Excuse me, I was on the committee. But you go ahead, tell me how—what was your position with regard to . . . Was it not JPMorgan Chase's position that the U.S. regulator should have no jurisdiction over the derivative activities of the subsidiaries in England on the basis that they were being regulated over there?

Stephen Cutler: Well let me put it this way . . .

Barney Frank: Could you answer the question?

Stephen Cutler: The regulations on which enforcement actions were brought in the United States existed prior to Dodd-Frank and we were completely fine with [them]. And by the way, we acknowledged that we made . . .

Barney Frank: You haven't answered my question. You were pushing a bill through the committee. The bill went through the committee, you guys were for it, which would've said that the CFTC and the SEC had no jurisdiction over the activities of the London-based subsidiary. So whatever regulations had been there they would've gone through; you would've been free of any regulation. And that's what happened, and, by the way, it's the same with mortgages. The fact is that up until the crash, the financial industry as a whole resisted any regulation, and it would've been better if we could have been able to work together on some of them. The frustration originally came from Hank Paulson and Ben Bernanke. Much of the structure of the bill really came out of their notions of what to do, and that was particularly the case in mortgages. There was great resistance. I don't hold you accountable for this, but on November 6, 2007, our first year back in power, when we were putting a bill through for the first time to restrict subprime mortgages being given to people who were unlikely to pay them back, I was attacked on that in an editorial, which said I was keeping low-income minorities from becoming homeowners. It was in the *Wall Street Journal*, they said we were creating the SarBox for housing. Interestingly, they boasted, they celebrated the fact that about 80 percent of the loans were being repaid on time, not previously in my judgment a great statistic about the reliability of loans. So I agree, there were problems. The second thing I would agree on is the proliferation of regulatory activities, it's a political problem, two problems. People wonder why we haven't simplified. The stupidest public policy in America in this area is to have a separate Securities and Exchange Commission and Commodity Futures Trading Commission.

It is a total mess, and you can't figure out who did what; and we tried hard to separate them out.

John C. Coffee Jr.: And it's Congress's fault.

Barney Frank: Who do you think I'm blaming?

John C. Coffee Jr.: Oh, wow, what a brilliant point.

Barney Frank: What a brilliant point. By the way, it's not Congress's fault alone, it's the American people's fault. There was this great mistake in analysis that assumes that what goes on in Washington is in a kind of bubble. No, the public has a major impact. The two major duplications in our regulatory system come from political pressure. The Commodity Futures Trading Commission is seen by the agricultural interests as their baby, and the SEC they see as the tool of east coast and west coast, increasingly, interests. And there would simply have been no way to get a bill through and merge them.

Now, I would say this. You can only do so many things at once in a political context. Passing the substance of regulations in the face of a great deal of resistance from the financial community made it hard to rationalize the organizational structure as well. Going forward, I think there may be a chance to rationalize the organizational structure when that's the only thing you are working on. I was aware of the problem, we were trying to sort out the jurisdictions. I proposed at one point that the CFTC be given jurisdiction over everything edible, that would be the best way to rationalize it, but there was just too much political resistance. The other major duplication is, and this is something people lose track of, we have, unlike I believe all other counties, certainly most, the dual banking system of state- and federal-chartered banks. Chris Dodd, in particular, wanted to put all bank regulation into the Comptroller of the Currency, taking some of that away from the Fed, and the state chartered banks objected and said, "No, you can't throw us in there with the big guys because it'll be one size fits all." So that's another reason, again, and it's the electorate. Yes, Congress made the final decision, but responding to electoral pressures.

The other thing I did want to say with regard to the rollback [. . .] there is virtually no rollback coming legislatively, and I take that frankly as sort of an indication, as a sign that things are working reasonably well. There are tweaks that need to be done, but you will not see any significant legislative change in the bill that we adopted in 2010. The House did pass a bill that would've essentially abolished it. Nobody other than the people on that committee paid any attention to it. That had the same impact as those repeated repeals of the health care bill back when they knew it was going to be vetoed, so the House passed that bill knowing that the Senate would not take it up. The Senate was totally ignoring it. What you have now going through the Senate is what was alluded to, relaxing the rules for banks under $10 billion in assets. And one mistake we made was that $50 billion was too low for people to be put into the FSOC. I thought it should be $100 billion. They talk about $250 billion.; $250 billion worries me a little bit because Lehman was $700-something billion and you get to a couple of $250s billions and you could have some kind of problem. But those are the only substantive changes that are going to be made. There will be administrative changes, the worst of which, from my standpoint, is the effective shutdown of the Consumer Financial Protection Bureau. And I think that people in the financial community who may be cheering for that may be making a mistake because it's going to build up a lot of anger, the kind of anger that, frankly, made it harder for us to legislate in some ways, that's one of the issues we had. The Volcker Rule is in part a response to beat up the banks. The Volcker Rule is not in the bill that passed the House. We gave the regulators the power, institution by institution, to do things like the Volcker Rule, to insist on some divestments, but you had this kind of anger. That's also, by the way, when you talk about the penalty for Bear Stearns, there was this public demand and public anger that more people weren't beaten up. Unfortunately, that, I think, is what was reflected by the administration when they did go after them. The Justice Department in particular was getting criticized for not prosecuting anybody. And whatever the merits of that were, I have to say some of my liberal friends seemed to have forgotten about due process and the rule that you don't criminally prosecute someone unless it was very clear that the behavior was criminal, and that you don't bring prosecutions unlikely to succeed just to have some emotional satisfaction. But I think that was the Justice Department, in part trying to deal with the fact that they were being criticized for not doing enough in the criminal area, and, as I said, I think it was a mistake. But to go back, I take the fact that there is no significant demand for any legislative change as an indication things have worked out reasonably well; that is, I think we have more stability and no noticeable drag on economic growth.

What we were trying to do, and I think it should be clear, we regarded what we were doing in 2009–2010 as basically pro-market. What happens is regulation lags behind innovation. Inevitably the private sector is much more dynamic. And I think the problem that culminated in 2008 was that regulation had lagged too far behind innovation, and the framework that came out of the New Deal had been outmoded by a lot of money coming into the system from nonregulated entities and, most important, by information technology. None of it could have happened if you had to do it all without information technology. But our view was that the financial community with the innovations and with the competitive pressures had substantially diminished the responsibility for taking risks that went bad, that you could make loans that weren't going to be repaid without having to worry about it because they were securitized, and you could make these derivatives bets without having any backup. The key revelation for us was when AIG told Ben Bernanke that they needed $85 billion because they couldn't pay off on their credit default swaps. A week later he was telling us how much money they needed for the TARP, and he and Paulson had said, "I want $85 billion for AIG," and we said, "No, you told us that last week," and he said, "No, no, that's another $85 billion." AIG was, in fact, $170 billion in debt and didn't know it and had no idea of the magnitude. But I do think we have achieved a reasonable balance. The law does allow the regulators to moderate and some of what is going on, and I think that's fine. Even in the Consumer Financial Protection Bureau, while it will be rendered virtually nonfunctional for a while, depending on what the judge says, there'll be no substantive legislative changes. The powers will remain, and they'll just be there to be resumed.

So I think what we've done has held up reasonably well, in fact, I think, very well. It continues to be very popular, and that's why there's a big difference in the approach of the Trump administration to the health care bill and the financial reform bill. There was an all-out effort to repeal, in effect, the health care bill, but from the Trump administration almost no proposals to legislatively change the financial reform bill. And in yesterday's *Wall Street Journal* I noticed a lament from Peter Wallison complaining that the Trump administration was being more aggressive in enforcement, particularly going after money market funds. So as I said, there is no rollback. There will be a less aggressive forfeit, and I'm not terribly troubled by that because I think what it means is that the current regulators will be more sanguine about what institutions will be doing. They are less inclined to think that the institutions needs cosupervision. But the powers for them to act well in advance of any real problem developing will remain undiminished, so I don't have any kind of systemic fears about that.

I want to go back to my first point that part of the problem was that we were operating in a situation . . . and much of the financial community was resistant to any regulation at all. I became the chairman-designate after the elections of 2006, and in December 2006 I was told, and we heard reference to, to regulate by principle and not by rule, which I have never been able to translate into anything meaningful. I remember at the time they were saying you could be like England, and the chief regulator at the time in England said, "Oh yes, we have a 900-page rule book." But what you got were two reports that came out in 2006 complaining that the financial industry was substantially overregulated. One came from Hal Scott of the Committee on Capital Markets Regulation at Harvard Law School, complaining that we were overregulating them and predicting that unless, in this case, we substantially lessened Sarbanes-Oxley there would almost never be an IPO again in the United States. And then a report came out of McKinsey, charted by Mayor Bloomberg, which also said we were overregulating to the point where we would be at a financial disadvantage. So that's the atmosphere in which we start, and then you also had this great public anger. Given all that, I believe we successfully did what we were trying to do, which was to increase the extent to which financial institutions taking risks had to bear some responsibility if the risks went bad and [that the financial institutions] had the financial capacity to deal with that if they went bad. That's essentially what we tried to do and I think that framework has held up.

Global Financial Crises and Regulatory Cycles

John C. Coffee Jr.: As was correctly observed, I am incredibly annoying, and I want to continue some of that. To be fair, I think everything Steve Cutler said is very reasonable. I disagree with some of his reasonable observations, I agree with some. And the Congressman, of course, is a hero to me, and I agree that the legislative proposals that are now going through the Senate, which are a bipartisan bill, will only affect the regional banks and the community banks and something called custody banks; it won't affect the major banks. But that does show one of the points I'm going to make.

What have we learned over the last ten years? Systemic risk reform has very few long-term allies, and many, many enemies. In fact, I would say the safest generalization about how we move forward with financial reform is this: Financial reform regulation is passed only in the aftermath of a major scandal. I can talk about the South Sea bubble, I don't want to give you the history lesson there, but the British Parliament responded by barring any companies from privately incorporating; instead, they had to get an Act of Parliament, which was overly prophylactic. I think Steve could make a valid criticism that barring all corporations from incorporating may have been too much, although at the time it seemed like a nice punitive response. And, of course, we know about the '29 crash, we know that Enron and WorldCom precipitated SOX, and the 2008 Great Recession gives us Dodd-Frank, and you could see the same thing going on around the world. But after each crash the financial industry begins to dismantle the legislation, pointing out that there are areas where it probably did overly regulate. But the problem here is there's often a very easy, natural coalition—the liberals on the left want to restore easy credit for the poor and minority groups in the mortgage market, and conservatives on the right want to downsize all regulation—and what you get is a very significant rollback that leaves lots of stuff that was working dismantled. Thus I'll go through an annoying survey of where I think systemic risk reform has not gone quite far enough.

What's happened that may make us a little bit more risky than we think we are right now? First of all, the Federal Reserve is no longer the lender of last resort as it is in most other countries where the central bank is the lender of last resort. And that means that, in a new crisis, it's not going to be clear how the Federal Reserve can structure a quick bailout. They may find evasions of the provisions in Dodd-Frank, which said no more lending to specific banks, but we don't know, it's uncertain. Next, what's happened [is that] non-bank SIFIs have largely escaped the reach of regulators.; insurance companies, AIG and all—all of those people are likely to escape. Regional banks will escape most of Dodd-Frank once the Senate bipartisan bill passes. Stress testing has been eased for all banks below the largest banks. I'm not saying this is wrong, I'm just saying that we're seeing significant movements in the direction of deregulation. The Volcker Rule is going to be amended in a number of ways, but it may be that all the regional banks and community banks will be exempted from the Volcker Rule. I'm not really sure why small . . .

Barney Frank: Not the regional banks, community banks, not the regional banks. The Volcker Rule is only for the under $10 billion.

John C. Coffee Jr.: We're going to see much of the bill eliminate the Volcker Rule by legislation. The rest of it is going to come from the White House, and . . .

Barney Frank: That's different.

John C. Coffee Jr.: I don't care if it's administrative or legislative, we're going to see much downsizing of the Volcker Rule. When you say that the smaller banks can engage in proprietary trading, I'm not sure that's what the regulators really want smaller banks to do. In any event, that's the Volcker Rule side of this.

Attempts to implement Section 956 of Dodd-Frank, which restricts incentive compensation, and it had strong prophylactic language, have been totally abandoned. I'm going to focus on that because basically I think they are the two biggest missing sides of the barn. We have a very strong barn with regard to the large banks. There is increased capital, there is increased stress testing, all good. But financial crises always come from the blind side, and the blind side now involves things like the money market funds and the moral hazard problems that are inherent in not having any regulation dealing with incentive compensation.

We have resolution authority, which was a tradeoff. The idea was we no longer had the central bank be the lender of last resort, but we'll intervene earlier through resolution authority. I have great doubts that in a political world the president and the secretary of Treasury will ever intervene early to put a large bank into receivership if there is the slightest chance that it might survive if everything turned and became more rosy. As a result, the incentives for any president of either administration would be to kick the can down the road and let the crisis get worse, and only put a company into receivership on the very doorsteps of bankruptcy. And that wasn't the original idea. The original idea is that there would be earlier intervention.

Next, I thought one of the better things done by the Dodd-Frank Act was to greatly strengthen the FSOC. Give us a real thinking research capability in the federal branch. The FSOC has been abandoned, and its research side has been largely laid off, so we no longer have the brain capacity in the Federal Reserve to spot crises in advance.

Okay, that's just a quick overview. Now let me turn to scenarios for a panic. Scenarios for a panic. It's always a panic that drives the crisis; that is the real problem. There is a cultural and a cognitive side to all this. There's good news and there's bad news, but where is the risk of financial collapse greatest? Well, the good news: I think large banks are much better capitalized, and stress testing does work and has desirable consequences. I think the unregulated shadow banks of 2008 have all moved over and become bank holding companies. The shadow banks that are left are really boutique investment banks that don't have a great deal of consequence. OTC derivatives, which is, of course, the AIG problem, have been substantially changed and now significantly trade through clearing houses; that is, they trade through clearing houses most of the time, but there are a lot of exceptions for end users and the like. Okay.

Now the bad news. The largest bailout commitment in 2008 was the government's guarantee of money market funds. That could happen again. As you'll recall, the Reserve Fund broke the buck, there was a crisis, and the government simply guaranteed to all of America's retail investors that their money market funds would be safe and guaranteed by the government. That's an extraordinary bailout, and I think the industry, the money market industry, wants the same relationship for the future. Because there has not been significant reform. The FSOC did propose increased capital requirements, and they were rebuffed. The industry faced them down, and the SEC was fairly equivocal on this. The SEC put in place some, what I'll call, tinkering reforms, rearranging the deck chairs on the *Titanic* by giving us more floating valuations, but it's an uncertain question whether those floating valuations will increase or reduce the risk of crisis and panic if there is stress on the money market funds.

Now, more generally, asset-backed securitizations are popular again. Synthetic collateralized debt obligations have returned in volume, and low documentation and interest-only mortgages are once again being included in securitization portfolios. That's eerie to me that we're once again seeing low credit, interest-only mortgage loans go into securitization portfolios. Everybody has forgotten a lot there quickly.

Lending by U.S. money market funds, which is the body that I think is most likely to be the subject of a future crisis, has grown in the repo market. You remember problems in the repo market from , but lending in it rose significantly from $0.6 trillion through all of 2016 to over $1 trillion now in 2017. That's a 60 percent increase in just one year. And on Monday, bitcoin futures start trading on the CME, and it won't be long after that before the CBOE starts trading options on bitcoin.

What does this mean to me? I'm not saying the crisis is imminent, I'm saying that the appetite for risk-taking has returned and there are sides to the financial barn that have no protection, particularly the side dealing with money market funds. And then I want to come to the other little topic I want to focus on, which is moral hazard and executive compensation.

Given the strong perception that incentive compensation produced short-termism and moral hazard, Dodd-Frank quite properly took two divergent and maybe somewhat contradictory steps, but one of them I really approve of. First, it federalized some aspects of corporate governance in order to give shareholders greater power. I have some doubts about that. But then second, in Section 956, it authorized regulators to prohibit executive incentive-based compensation—specifically, excessive incentive-based compensation at covered financial institutions where "it could lead to a material financial loss." Now what's happened here? There was much evidence then and now—I'm referring here largely to the work of Rene Stulz—that the more closely the alignment between the interests of shareholders and bank senior executives, the worse the bank fared during the 2008 crisis. That is, banks with shareholder-friendly corporate governance fared much worse than banks that had only old-fashioned unfriendly corporate governance. Why? The interests of shareholders and the interests of systemic risk reform are very much in opposition. Indeed, the worst thing that could happen for the future, in my view, would be that hedge funds decided to become much more active in investing in large too-big-to-fail banks. Bottom line, I don't think empowering shareholders was a great idea. The Dodd-Frank Act did this, but, rightly or wrongly, the D.C. Circuit struck it down. The Proxy Access Rules produced a lawsuit. The Business Roundtable and Chamber of Commerce sued, and they won in a very dubious decision. [Although] the decision is dubious, I think proxy access for large financial institutions was a dangerous idea. Anyway, for better or worse, it's disappeared. The SEC has not sought to propose any replacement or reform rule.

More important, however, was what the act did in terms of its paternalistic prong. Let me see if I can move us on. Section 956, which I think was exactly the right step that had to be taken, said that federal regulators had to jointly prescribe regulations requiring covered financial institutions to disclose the structure of all incentive-based compensation arrangements covering executives, and to bar those kinds of incentive-compensation that could lead to excessive risk-taking. I won't give you the exact statutory language. What was going to be done? Well, the first thing you could do is look at what the total structure of incentive compensation was. And here I want to go back to a document that was much disclosed in 2008 and hasn't been seen since. This is then Attorney General Andrew Cuomo's listing of the incentive compensation paid at the largest banks in 2008. What we're seeing here is the really large too-big-to-fail-banks, and by the way JPMorgan is the hero of this group, it has very [few] problems compared to the others. But let's take a look at Citigroup. They managed to lose $27.7 billion, and for that success they had a bonus pool of $5.33 billion. I've occasionally observed, somewhat cynically, that if you want to lose $27 billion much more cheaply, I could do it for under $100 million. Just put me in charge, and I won't charge anything like that price for losing $27 billion. But we see it at Citigroup and we see the same thing at Merrill Lynch, $27 billion loss and a $3.6 billion bonus pool. Even at firms that did relatively well, like JPMorgan, the bonus pool exceeded the total profits for that year. That's the size of the bonus pool. My point is only [that] the bonus culture has very deep roots on Wall Street. This is the area where I think reform was needed. The most famous line of the era was the CEO of Citigroup, Chuck Prince, saying that, well, he knew there were problems with these securitizations, but "you can't stop dancing until the music stops." What does that mean? It means probably that because of the high incentive compensation being paid, most of the executives wanted their securitization deals to close no matter what. "We've got to get it done by year-end even if it's adding to our total liability and a bigger explosion down the road." And there was a bigger explosion down the road, but they got their incentive compensation. So Section 956 said you should do a number of things.

What happened in Section 956? Let me give you a very short history because time is running out. Very elaborate rules were proposed in 2011, the year after Dodd-Frank was adopted, and this was a topic they went to right away because it's a very important topic that involves real causation. Those rules sat for five years, and in 2016 a much murkier set of rules came out that no longer required the same level of deferrals—it applied only to senior executives and totally exempted traders. Now my view is that traders are the real danger at banks, not the senior executives. The general counsel, as important as he is, is probably not the person who's going to cause a systemic risk crisis; the trader might be that person. But they were exempted. Anyway, all those rules and the strange tradeoffs in 2016 are totally irrelevant. It came out in August 2017 that all of the financial regulators have now moved the topic of incentive compensation reform from the short-term to the long-term study; that is, none of the financial regulators is seeking to do anything with incentive compensation, even though the act instructed all the financial regulators to impose such controls on incentive compensation. Instead it's been moved everywhere to the long-term study and out of the short-term reform. We've seen nothing in this area. So I've left you with these two comments. I'm going to go down to my final page so I can finish in time.

I think boards today probably are more cautious about incentive compensation. Certainly they understand the need for greater capital. I don't think the real problems are with our major banks at the moment. But I think we have a new attitude toward accepting increased risk-taking, and risk-taking by institutions that have no protection, such as the money market funds. I also noticed that with respect to incentive compensation the attitude has changed. Last Friday the lead headline in the *Financial Times* was "UBS Chief Says Drive to Curb Bankers Pay Fueled by Envy." And now we're back to the wonderful world of the food fight. You are doing this to me because you have deep envy. I still think that if you have unrestricted incentive compensation you're going to have some very short-term moral hazard decisions made.

We're now in a constantly rising stock market with tax relaxation, at least tax relaxation for the rich, about to appear, and concern about systemic risk is becoming dated. People are no longer talking about it. Crises always come from the blind side, but the vulnerability of money market funds and the possibility that incentive compensation will give us extreme risk-taking is still very much there. This is not the fault of Dodd-Frank. You put the stuff in the legislation, and no one has followed up on that. The FSOC started out trying to do something about money market funds, but they were clearly rebuffed by the powers that be. And I think thus we have a financial barn with a couple of sides that have nothing more than paper and no substance. Therefore I'm going to tell you again—I told you, I can be incredibly annoying—the problem of systemic risk is still very much with us. It will come from a different blind side, but there's always that pattern that it comes from the blind side, and we have several blind sides where the vulnerability of these institutions is clear, and sooner or later they're likely to be tested. Thank you.

Barney Frank: Obviously, I agree with much of what Professor Coffee says in specific because he was defending the bill, but I have to say that I think that, as is often the case outside of the strict mathematical field, that the whole was smaller than the sum of the parts. I agreed with many of the points. I think you exaggerate the systemic risk in a couple of ways. First of all, this one I know well because I'm confident in my political expertise, I think you misread badly the political pressures that would come on a president if a large institution was in trouble. Even in the current atmosphere, the insistence would be that they shoot people, not that they bail them out. The notion that . . .

John C. Coffee Jr.: Afterwards, afterwards.

Barney Frank: No, the notion that there would be great pressure, first of all because there are some inconsistencies, which is one of the things I gather you lamented, was that we restricted the ability of the Federal Reserve simply on its own hook to put that money in there, which, of course, they do without the president, that would be irrelevant to the president. What they did get instead was the ability to lend as long as it is to more than one institution if they can say that it's illiquid and not insolvent. And here I've got to say, you talk about who does this. The American people are not going to tolerate a return to the legal framework that existed in 2008; this is something Tim Geithner has argued for. The American people will not tolerate a restoration to the Federal Reserve of an unblinkered discretion to put money into any institution it wants to whenever it wants to, which is what Section 13.3 said. And the reason for that, by the way, it was a very specific time, it's when it came out that AIG, which was the main culprit, had paid bonuses to the people who had incurred $170 billion beyond what they could pay off. But on the other side, in terms of intervening, the political pressure would still be against helping one of the big banks, and the notion that a president would be constrained, or the secretary of the Treasury, from inter-vening if a big institution got in trouble I think just gets it wrong. Second, with regard to mortgages, yes, some interest-only are coming, and I agreed with your point that I was dismayed when some of my liberal friends joined with some of the banks to basically get rid of the risk retention rule for most mortgages. But the worst mortgages and the mortgages that were most the cause are still illegal, nobody can make them, except some of the smallest banks, and they can only make them in that case if they keep them in portfolio. So the ability to make those kinds of loans that caused the most problem and securitize them is just not there anymore for any institution.

John C. Coffee Jr.: Well, we have an empirical question here, and we'll see in the future. You can have a difference in perspective on whether presidents will put a bank that's in trouble, but not yet known to be clearly failing, into receivership. I see the opposition party in such a case immediately saying, "The president caused the failure. It happened on his watch." I think every president doesn't want a major bank to fail on his watch.

Barney Frank: No, even more now, given the recent political history, and this is why you don't see even the Republicans in Congress seriously trying to undercut any of that ability. Even more now, the president is still afraid of being too favor-able to that kind of institution. Bailout is still a bad word. One of the frustrations I have is that we Democrats get blamed for the bailouts when all five of the bail-outs were started by George W. Bush. That one I think you misread politically. But on the more specifics, the worst mortgages are still illegal and can't be made. Similarly with regard to the banks under $10 billion, I am not worried about . . .

John C. Coffee Jr.: I wasn't challenging that. I understand that's a reasonable thing to do.

Barney Frank: No, I understand that. But what you said was you can still have the securitization on interest-only mortgages. And I agree with that, but what

I'm saying is the worst kind of mortgages are not going to be in securitization because they can't be made.

Kathryn Judge: All right, this is a lively debate that I want us to continue. This being an academic conference, my role was shifted from moderator to discussant. So part of what I want to spend just a minute doing is trying to focus on a theme that I think actually cuts across all three of these presentations and that motivates some of our discussion over the challenges we're facing and where we're likely to go. And one of the things that I noticed was a common theme in all three were these concerns about complexity. So I just want to, in a few pictures, look at where we are today. So really quickly, this is work by some economists using techniques that are used in computer science to evaluate the U.S. Code. And what they're trying to figure out is how well structured is this code: Will it achieve what it's meant to achieve versus lead to breakdowns? And what they found is Title XII, which is the title of the deals with banks and financial institutions, is second only to the Internal Revenue Code in terms of its complexity. Moreover, this looks nothing like what it's supposed to look like. We have a few nice red dots in the middle and blue dots all along the periphery, so we have this incredibly complex and, therefore, prone to breakdown structure of the U.S. legal code. That code, as we all know, is then put into place by a bunch of regulators. This is a nice chart put out by JPMorgan, admittedly at a point in time where, as pointed out earlier, they were trying to push back very strongly against . . .

Stephen Cutler: This was after it had happened.

Kathryn Judge: This was after it happened.

Stephen Cutler: This was a reflection, so this probably cost us a few billion dollars because regulators got so mad at us for publishing this.

Barney Frank: I doubt that very sincerely.

Kathryn Judge: And they were constrained by reality.

Barney Frank: What regulators are you accusing of acting out of pique and what punishment did those . . . I think that's irresponsible.

Stephen Cutler: No regulator would ever do that.

Barney Frank: I don't want to drop that. I think that's an outrageous charge, particularly from one of the banks that made some of the mistakes. Tell me what regulator you think penalized you and to what extent because they got politically mad at you.

Stephen Cutler: Regulators are human beings too.

Barney Frank: You never answer questions. I feel like I'm back in the House and you guys are testifying. Let me just say that's an outrageous, irresponsible thing to say, and the fact that you can't back it up . . .

Stephen Cutler: I don't think it is, but . . .

Barney Frank: Back it up then.

Stephen Cutler: I can't actually tell you where it happened. I suspect it happened.

Barney Frank: Oh, you suspect it happened.

Kathryn Judge: And the Congressman admitted earlier that this has been an ongoing challenge.

Stephen Cutler: But this was postadoption of, I think, a regulatory scheme, which is actually very fair. One of the things, and you talked about it, Congressman, one of the areas where I think we could've done better is simplifying the regulatory scheme.

Barney Frank: No question.

Stephen Cutler: And there is a multiplicity of regulators all looking at the same areas. That's not great regulation, right? Things could be . . .

Barney Frank: I agree, but here's a problem. You get vested interests in existing institutions. Consolidating, i.e., abolishing—we did abolish one institution, we abolished the Office of Thrift Supervision, which was a duplicate of the Office of Comptroller of the Currency. I was determined to get rid of that because when institutions want to do dishonest things, or irresponsible things, they got a thrift charter, and I was determined either to abolish that or change its name to the Office of Fig Leaf Dispensation. But we were able to abolish it. The other problem is all those other institutions had vested interests. Here was a problem. Given the political fight we had to get the substantive regulations done, we wouldn't have had the votes to do both. I do think going forward—and I'll finish with this— I do think the fact is we now have President Trump and a Republican Congress and essentially there is no legislative effort to change things. That's relevant only in the sense that it doesn't even survive for a future administration. Given that there now appears to be a consensus on the major outlines of the substantive regulations, now I do think you could ask people to put the political effort into simplifying and there would be a unity with the financial institutions. So I agree, SEC, CFTC, rationalizing banks among OCC and the Fed and the FDIC, that ought to be the next agenda item with, I think, more consensus. The precondition for that was agreement on the substantive regulation, which I think essentially we have.

Kathryn Judge: And since we had Steve Cutler jumping in, understandably, on the complexity of the regulatory regime, I just had to jump ahead to my slides on the complexity of financial institutions. So this is work being done by Carmassi and Herring and what they're looking at is both the size, but also the complexity. The proxy they're using for complexity is the number of subsidiaries, and what we see is a dramatic increase over time. We also see it in the breakdown of the different types of subsidiaries they have. And again, regulators will say postcrisis things like stress tests have been used to try to bring about simplification. What we are still seeing on the whole, though, is large financial institutions with well over 1,000 one thousand different subsidiaries working across different areas, which, of course, maps onto the challenges mapped out earlier regarding the different regulatory bodies that they're subject to. And then going back to alongside the banking system, as was already discussed, we have, of course, the rise of the shadow banking system, which is alive and well. You look at mortgages, and a great majority of the mortgages are shifting outside of the banking sector into the nonregulated sector, and that's where they're being originated. So this was an effort by the New York Fed to map what is sometimes called shadow banking, sometimes market-based intermediation, and the idea is simple: We have liquidity transformation, and we have maturity transformation happening outside the banking sector through disaggregated entities in ways that we didn't even realize were a source of fragility prior to the crisis. We've tried to address it. This is the complexity of the system on the whole where, again, you have money market mutual funds, through a whole variety of different entities, eventually providing the capital for things like home loans and, of course, this is within those securitization structures. We have heterogeneity of different assets that are bundled together and ways of creating massive informational challenges. So again, for all three of you, this reads as some incredibly interesting issues. So I'm going to turn it over to Congressman Frank.

Barney Frank: Let me just say with regard to the mortgages that any mortgage is regulated. You can't issue prohibitive mortgages outside of banks. The problem is . . . that there are institutions now that provide money for people to buy homes without regulatory oversight. The Consumer Financial Protection Bureau was looking into that. It wasn't technically a mortgage, so it evaded the restrictions on these kinds of mortgages that applied to everybody, bank or nonbank. The CFPB was beginning to go after those products from the consumer protection standpoint, and that now will be shut down by Mulvaney, and so you will have that problem with those kind of alternatives.

John C. Coffee Jr.: I wanted to extend the Congressman's point. He picked on the SEC and the CFTC, and that's usually the example, but it's only one example. We have something like seventeen different financial regulators. We have a special regulator for credit unions, we have a special regulator for Fannie Mae and Freddie Mac, and when you have that many, small regulators are probably more easily captured than very large regulators.

Barney Frank: There is another problem with the OCC, FDIC, and the Fed, I mentioned that one as well.

John C. Coffee Jr.: We have seventeen different regulators for different categories of financial institutions. And I think the problem with that is that you can have the industry better capture a very small invisible regulator. Now, look around the globe, what do you see? Countries deviate between a single peak or a dual peak structure of financial regulation. The United States has a Himalayas of small peaks, not a Himalayas, a Catskills of small peaks, little bumps. And I think you need broader consolidation so you could have better political accountability. So I'm agreeing with your point, but I want to go beyond . . .

Barney Frank: I would say this, and I would say this to Steve, I'm serious, this is my frustration. We tried to consolidate and ran into the fun with the dual banking system. That's why we have more bank regulators than most countries, and the state chartered banks had a lot of power and were able to resist. But now, it does seem to me now, at the end of this year, that if the Senate passes the bill that it's going to pass, I believe, it will—by the way, the other thing I would say about derivatives is even though there won't be a Volcker Rule for banks with less than $10 billion in assets, all derivatives are still subject to those restrictions that you mention, which make it better, although the end user piece they connive to getting out from under. But I think there is enough of a consensus now that there's not going to be any effort at a major weakening of the basic legislative structure. I would hope at this point that people in the industry and those of us who wanted regulation in general should be able to come together on a scheme for administrative consolidation, because there's now a common interest. Instead of fighting about whether we have the substance or not, I think there is a common interest among a lot of entities, now, who are interested in an efficient and effective regulation in rationalizing the structure. And I'm going to propose that that be kind of a joint effort that people undertake.

Stephen Cutler: I'm saying less than what I think than you are, Congressman, that the political will is there—you're the expert on political will—to do things like consolidate agencies, and we're doing it around the margins a little bit, so you can see . . .

Barney Frank: Let me repeat: The problem before was that until this year the Senate bill means two—and it's very important, it means two things. First, the under $10 billions get some relief, and the regionals don't go into the FSOC, although they're still subject to all the other regulations. What that bill means is that there's no change to anything else, there is an acceptance of everything else. So I think now . . . there is a new situation where there is essentially a consensus on the outlines, the major outlines, of the legislation, even on Section 956—obviously that broke my heart, but it's there for the future, although the Obama administration, as you pointed out, lagged on that one—they were no great shakes. By the way, the corporate governance thing, I'll give you it politically—that came from CalPERS. The reason for the corporate governance, the proxy access, that was at the insistence of the two major California retirement funds, transmitted through a person of great legislative influence and California-ness.

Stephen Cutler: Proxy access has actually happened without . . .

John C. Coffee Jr.: A different kind, a much more aggressive hedge fund activism has happened.

Stephen Cutler: Well, no, proxy access has happened. If you look, the vast majority of public companies have adopted a form of proxy access because, frankly, the market has demanded it.

Barney Frank: And even on compensation . . .

Stephen Cutler: . . . a wave of that without the SEC actually having to do it. The SEC rule did get scuttled, but essentially the market has replaced that. That may or may not be a good thing, but I think on balance I'm a little bit more optimistic about . . .

John C. Coffee Jr.: I'm not surprised about that.

Barney Frank: I would say this. Yes, the market is doing it, but if we hadn't told the SEC to start it, I don't think . . . The other point I would make, and this is—

I get this from being on a bank board—an influence, whether good or bad, but an influence constraining at least to some extent compensation for now; the powerful influence is from the proxy advisory services. They are a major input that boards have to take into account.

John C. Coffee Jr.: Say on pay has done something, I agree.

Stephen Cutler: Say on pay has done something. I would also say, and you mentioned this, Professor Coffee, when it comes to the big financial institutions, you've got a combination of disclosure and you've got regulatory oversight, notwithstanding the absence of an expressed rule. And so if you look at what big financial institutions have done in terms of compensation of senior management, it's got very serious clawbacks, it's got very serious deferrals, it's got a lot of compensation that is subject to a board saying, "You know what? We had a year, or we had several years, in which we didn't perform, and you're not going to get paid." And you've seen that. Just look at what's happened to compensation at Deutsche Bank, just look at what's happened to compensation at Credit Suisse. And you can argue that notwithstanding the absence of some of the regulatory mechanisms that you were talking about it's happened.

John C. Coffee Jr.: Well, again, just so we understand what I am saying, we have a financial barn that has strong walls on three sides, and we have no wall at all with respect to money market funds. We may have some practice that's better with regard to incentive compensation at the largest banks with boards that are probably the most professional, but it's not law, it's practice, and practice can change as the climate for risk-taking becomes more aggressive.

Barney Frank: John, I'm on the board of a midsize bank, and I have learned two things. People ask me what I've learned on the board. By the way, one of the things I've learned on the board is that very little of it is my fault. The major pain in the ass for the medium banks and some of the others has got nothing to do with the bill I cosponsored, it has to do with money laundering and bank secrecy and the Patriot Act. The Know Your Customer Rule that people complain about was not in our legislation. There's a lot of punks going elsewhere. But the other one is [that] the proxy advisory services have a major impact on compensation.

Kathryn Judge: Following up on this question of complexity, because I think it does cut through what each of you is talking about, Article I clearly authorized Congress to engage in lawmaking. Looking at the complexity of the legal scheme that we have, you did a great job, but how did you confront the informational challenges that you were facing and, in particular, the anti-bailout rhetoric that was so powerful—and they couldn't understand the liquidity mismatch and the reasons we want to have this. Steve Cutler, you mentioned earlier the London Whale, and you were talking about the frustration of having to deal with five or six different regulators. That might be an understandable frustration, but again how does having, I think, at this point, thirteen hundred subsidiaries in terms of the corporate structure potentially increase the possibility of those types of things arising? Even if not challenges to the system, there are going to be losses that are going to be harder to detect. Professor Coffee you did a great job summarizing some of the challenges this creates for regulators, but could you talk a little bit more about whether the SEC is going to stand strong when they are working against banks where they can't, they really can't, understand the internal working and how the incentives are going to break down inside those institutions?

Stephen Cutler: I'll start by saying that first of all, we brought the number of subsidiaries way down, and I think one of the helpful things about the recovery and resolution process is that it has forced banks to look inward at how they are structured. Having said that, there are probably fifty subsidiaries that actually matter at JPMorgan, and so a lot of them are set up for one-transaction vehicles. And I would also say none of that, none of the structural number of subsidiaries, maybe it's a proxy for something, but none of it's the cause of the crisis. And so we ought to be careful about sort of pointing to something and saying, "Aha, that suggests that these firms were way too complex and that caused the crisis." It really didn't. There is not a nexus between number of subsidiaries and problems that we had in 2007–2008.

Kathryn Judge: I'll turn to the Congressman, but I do want to add to that one of the key challenges was not the overall losses—we've talked a lot about risk-taking here—but the fact that nobody knew how those losses were allocated. If we look at the actual value of wealth that was wiped out, it was by no means all that significant given the size of the financial system, but there was incredible difficulty within institutions and within the market as a whole for regulators to understand how those losses were allocated. And I think a lot of work has been done to suggest that the degree of market dysfunction would far outweigh the losses is at least in part a byproduct of the fact that people just didn't know whether their counterparties were healthy.

Barney Frank: Well, yes, even worse—and again talk about the opacity at AIG. They literally had no idea how much money they owed. They told Ben Bernanke one week in September that they owed $85 billion and a week later they said, "Whoops, it's $170 billion." I mean this isn't a marginal error, this is like no idea. As to the question about which one . . .

Kathryn Judge: What does it mean for Congress right now? As we are in this incredibly complex world dealing with these complex structures, how does that shape the challenge that you're facing?

Barney Frank: Remember, there's no such thing as Congress in this issue. There's a Democratic Congress and a Republican Congress. I wish that weren't the case. What I will go back to saying is I think we have a basis for going toward the administrative stuff [because] the Republicans in Congress who wanted to substantially diminish the legislative structure have now acknowledged that they don't have the votes for that, in part because it is popular. People running for reelection don't want to re-deregulate derivatives. But where you are in Congress now is at a kind of a stalemate because you have a president and House that wants to cut way back. Hear the filibusterers, you can't do this by reconciliation. Of the forty-eight Democrats, none are ready to reduce the regulation, and you have Senator Collins who voted for it and a few others who don't want to deal with it. I would hope people might take up the other.

But with regard to your other question, How do we deal with this? We paid a lot of attention to the Executive, but people forget whatever happened to bipartisanship. Well, I will tell you what happened to bipartisanship is that Obama got elected and Mitch McConnell went on strike, and I will document that. Read the books by Hank Paulson, Ben Bernanke, and Sheila Bair, the three top financial regulators appointed by George W. Bush, and they're all about how much cooperation they got from us on the Democratic side, much more than they got from their Republican colleagues. And beginning in 2007–2008, we worked closely with Ben Bernanke and Hank Paulson. And I will give George W. Bush credit on this, by the way. Knowing that the great bulk of his party hated a lot of this effort, he gave Paulson and Bernanke full backup. But we spent a lot of effort with them, and then we, of course, had it with the Obama people as well. We also had consumer groups and others who were relevant, academics, and then some from the financial industry. As it became clearer that we were going to go ahead, then we were able to work with people in the financial industry about how to do it. I had particular relations with the Bank of America people, their political people based in Boston. Once people were willing to accept [that] this is what we're going to do, we listened to some of that. But the single biggest source of information was the two administrations, Bush and Obama.

John C. Coffee Jr.: Well, I think the Congressman has raised an interesting idea, that now that it's clear that Dodd-Frank will not be dismantled and just minor edge changes, we should be thinking about reorganization of financial regulation for systemic risk purposes. Now, what should be done in that light? I think we should recognize first, and I have told you I'm very annoying, that some agencies are better at some things than others. The SEC is a good disclosure agency, a good consumer protection agency, not nearly so good about systemic risk. One of the unknowable questions is whether, if the Federal Reserve was supervising Bear Stearns and Lehman Brothers, they might have intervened a little bit earlier than the SEC, which I don't think was aware of what was going on.

Barney Frank: They wouldn't have been given the right to set their own capital standards.

John C. Coffee Jr.: You're suggesting that I might be right, that there might have been closer regulation. We don't know what would have happened.

Barney Frank: Are you annoyed if I say you're not annoying?

John C. Coffee Jr.: It would be so hard to prove that thesis.

Barney Frank: I'm just saying that's a specific example, I think, of where the Fed would've . . .

John C. Coffee Jr.: Well, the SEC may not be perfect at everything it does, but it's very used to its own dogma and its own status quo. Next, if we're going to do anything for the future, the FSOC has been given a lobotomy by the current administration. We need to put some brains back into the FSOC to have someone direct it. And third, we are much too obsessed with saying, "What caused the 2008 crisis?" I fully agree the proprietary trading did not cause the 2008 crisis, but if too-big-to-fail banks are too big to fail, which I think is definitional, you've got to restrict their risk-taking. And things like the Volcker Rule are important. We can't let you engage in every kind of risk-taking where you see potential for profit. Banks have to be treated a little bit differently, and I think things like the Volcker Rule should be maintained as part of the heart of the current system.

Barney Frank: The impetus for the Volcker Rule [was] kind of to deal with people who want to break them up and Glass-Stegall. The Volcker Rule reduced both their size and complexity, and it could've been any of a number of things. And that was why, when it was first proposed, it became widely accepted.

Questions and Answers

Audience member 1: I hate to interrupt this amazing debate between Barney and John, but I will. I want to address this to Barney and John. In terms of Jamie

Dimon saying there will be another hit in the market and John saying the barn door is wide open to the problems to come, I go back to the previous problem where Eric Holder and company decided that bankers were too big to jail and the anger of the American public that nobody was held accountable for taking down the global financial system. And I think the book that you've probably both read, *The Chicken Shit Club*, starring Eric Holder, is worthy of . . .

Barney Frank: I was waiting for the movie.

Audience member 1: . . . was worthy of some note. So let me ask you both what can we do to prevent the hit that Jamie says is coming?

Barney Frank: Well, first, I am sorry that more people weren't prosecuted, but a couple of things. Again, a number of my liberal friends have forgotten our belief in due process. A central element of due process is that you should not be criminally prosecuted if you could not have known that your behavior was criminal to a reasonable degree. That doesn't mean ignorance of the law. If you didn't know the law, that's not the issue; the issue was if you did know the law could you have figured that out? And the other thing to say in fairness to them, part of the problem once again is the American people. Look at what's happened— I don't think there is a worse example of acquittals, if you're looking at the scorecard for the prosecutors, than we've seen in the financial field recently, where they have tried to bring some of these cases. It's kind of hard to get the jurors to think about this as criminal. So I also believe that they—then again, it's, I think, partly why they were so tough, unfairly tough, on JPMorgan Chase and Bank of America with regard to liability for institutions that they were pressed to take over, on things that had happened before they took them over. As to the future hit, I don't know exactly what Jamie Dimon said it's going to be, so I can't predict. I don't know what specifically he said. Steve, do you know what he was talking about?

Stephen Cutler: Well, look, we're going to have failures. I think what has happened over the last ten years is that we have gotten ourselves to a place where if any one big bank fails it's not going to be systemic, that we've so capitalized the system, we've created so much liquidity, that we can actually see a bank, a big bank, fail without the kind of systemic impact that we . . .

Barney Frank: Without bringing down everybody with it.

Stephen Cutler: Correct. So let me just actually say one word about prosecutors and where their heads are, because I've been on that side of the table. There is nothing that a prosecutor would want more than to bring a case against an executive of a big financial institution. So it's not for want of trying, believe me, it's not for want of will that those cases didn't get brought. But as Congressman Frank said, we do live in America. We are a system where you don't bring cases unless actually someone did something that's provable and wrong.

Barney Frank: Remember, we did pass a law. Some of the things that were outrageous weren't illegal. We have made a few more of them illegal.

John C. Coffee Jr.: If I can get a comment in here because I sort of specialize in white collar crime. Whether or not Holder really said "banks are too big to jail" is a debate I don't want to get into. But there seemed to be a passive approach. That changed at the end of the Obama administration with something called the Yates Memorandum, which said if you are going to prosecute a corporation, don't give them a deferred prosecution agreement until you force them to cooperate fully and identify who was responsible. Yes, the prosecutors didn't have the evidence to go against individuals, partly because they didn't pressure the entity enough to give them that evidence. If the entity says, "we are either going to get fined a very high excessive fine in our , or we're going to turn over the responsible officers," you will see some change in behavior. So I think that the Yates Memorandum took the right tack, not that we're going to send CEOs to prison, they're too remote, I'm not arguing for vicarious liability, but you can find intermediate senior executives who knew enough to be criminally liable if the entity is under great pressure to identify them. Is that going to happen? Well, the Yates Memorandum was the end of the Obama administration. Attorney General Sessions has just announced that they are going to greatly increase and have a new policy toward the Foreign Corrupt Practices Act, which is basically about foreign bribery, and they are going to have a policy under which you can always turn yourself in, possibly at the last moment, identify some of the facts that happened, and get a complete pass, complete guaranteed immunity. That's a big shift, and I think we're going to see some problems from that. I'm not saying that you shouldn't sometimes give companies a pass if they turn themselves in, but they should turn in the officers as well before they get this kind of pass. Someone was responsible, and not everyone deserves that kind of immunity. So this is sort of beneath the area that's yet hit the headlines. But there is a new policy toward the Foreign Corrupt Practices Act, and it a very deregulatory policy in the criminal law field.

Barney Frank: Part of the problem there again, I wish they'd been a little more aggressive, and you're right, it would have been impossible to get the CEOs, it was just hard to make a criminal case. If you got too far down the chain, then people stopped and said, "Oh, you're letting the big guys off the hook." By the way, I'm sure most people recognized it. The Yates in question is the Yates that Donald Trump fired early in the administration.

Audience member 2: Thank you very much. I have quick question for Congressman Frank and also a follow-up for Mr. Cutler. I'm a graduate of Columbia Business School. I also worked for Senator Lugar on the Senate Foreign Relations Committee during the financial crisis and was brought over to the Ag Committee as far as working on legislation, the oversight of the CFTC. I would like to correct a little bit of the record there. And one of the things that has been repealed in the Dodd-Frank language is the Cardin-Lugar Amendment, which was a bipartisan amendment to give sunshine, specifically, Mr. Coffee, what you were talking about, was the extractive industries, especially with oil, with forcing companies to disclose in their financials payments that they were making overseas. The Europeans and the Canadians have also gone along with that. That's been repealed by this administration. Specifically, I'm coming back to thinking about the underlying problems with the original crisis, and that was home ownership. Congressman Frank, you've always been a great supporter of home ownership and personal home ownership.

Barney Frank: I think we've overdone it a bit.

Audience member 2: My question is, What role do you think the government should play in home ownership, and is there an optimal level, if you do think there is?

Barney Frank: Two things. First of all, thank you for bringing that up. By the way, the Cardin-Lugar Amendment—I don't know if you know Senator Lugar and Senator Cardin, they may seem unlikely people to you to have channeled Bono—but the amendment in question was called "Publish What You Pay," and its major champion was Bono, the entertainer, and it was a very important point, which said that any American corporation that is paying to extract any resource from a foreign country—it didn't ban anything—they simply had to make public what they paid, both in bribes or in taxes or anything else because you have the substantial problem of countries not getting any of the benefit from that. Unfortunately, by the time they got around to promulgating that regulation, they could not have repealed it because they couldn't have gotten sixty votes in the Senate. But they were able to repeal it under this sixty-day rule, this provision whereby any regulation that hadn't been in effect for sixty days could be repealed by a simple majority of both houses and signed by the president. And you're right, . . . we got the European Union to do it. In fact, I was at a meeting in Davos with the European Union and Bono, and we got it done.

As far as home ownership, I think it is a great mistake. My single biggest cause during my time in Congress—well, obviously my rights as a gay man took a certain amount of my attention—was rental housing. We should be doing a lot more for rental housing. And I was generally, even with regard to Fannie Mae, my biggest thing that I was pushing there was their multifamily portfolio, which, by the way, was never in trouble, that one was good. I think we have made a great mistake on the home ownership issue. In fact, one of the things that I got through that's been a victim of the transition was legislation that would take some of the profit from Fannie Mae and Freddie Mac and fund a low-income housing fund to build affordable rental housing. No, there is no number, but I think in general this notion that it devalues lower income people, it overvalues— . . . In the *New York Times* you had a series about what a terrible thing it was for these neighborhoods when these renters were moving in. So I think it's a great social problem that we underfinance affordable rental housing and overly subsidize home ownership. That's some part of the Trump tax bill with which I have some sympathy.

Audience member 3: Picking up on your comment about sympathy for the Trump tax bill, I was curious if there is any other aspect of it which you support or has merits.

Barney Frank: No.

Audience member 3: And if the ship has left the port, if there's anything that can be done?

Barney Frank: I do think the limits on the home mortgage interest deduction—I mean if I was making a new country, you wouldn't have the home mortgage interest deduction, but you've got vested interest here. But limiting it to a great extent makes a lot of sense. And the argument from realtors that you should not raise the standard deduction because that will diminish the value of the home mortgage interest deduction makes me crazy. But beyond that, no, I think it's unlikely to be stopped. First of all, the precondition for stopping it would be the election of Doug Jones in Alabama, because I don't see them getting three Republicans, two maybe, maybe Senator Collins. There is a lot of kickback over the limitation on state and local, but most of the states there have no Republican senator, so that doesn't affect them. Senator Collins could have problems with that in Maine. So I think that the political impulse to get that done is so important for the Republican Party, and you have this other problem which is—and this again affects Senator Collins—you're in a legislative body, you're a member of a party, there are limits to the extent to which you can just tell them to go screw. Having killed health care, it's very hard for a senator who wants to continue to be a Republican and operate in that atmosphere to say no on both health care and taxes. You know, Corker can do it because he's going anyway. You might have thought Flake might do it, but I think Flake's a faker, so I do not expect him to ever . . . Apparently his major objection to Donald Trump is that he has hurt his feelings and he will [be] critical back, but he will never vote in any way other than what Donald Trump wants.

PART V

THE ORIGINS OF THE NEXT FINANCIAL CRISIS

CHAPTER 20

INTERVIEW

Striking the Right Balance Between Markets and Regulation

WILLIAM T. WINTERS INTERVIEWED BY AILSA RÖELL

Ailsa Röell: In the United States we are seeing a major backlash against the regulations put in place after the global financial crisis, with major rollbacks proposed daily. How do you view this swing of the pendulum and the ability of the current regulatory regime to address the risks arising in the financial sector? And what is the situation in Europe and East Asia in this regard?

William Winters: The premise of your question is that we are in the midst of a major rollback in the United States. I don't see that happening actually. I see some fine-tuning. We'll see how it develops, but certainly the "deregulation proposals" that I've seen so far represent a very small proportion of the progress made in reforming the regulatory framework since the financial crisis.

In 2010 and 2011, I was a member of the Independent Commission on Banking, which was set up by the UK government to develop policy recommendations to increase the resilience of the banking sector. The commission was chaired by Sir John Vickers. We had a discussion at the time about how likely it was that we would overshoot in our recommendations, and my view was that it was a dead certainty that we collectively, the body of regulators, were going to do this. To give you an example, back then the Basel Committee on Banking Supervision had proposed a minimum global regulatory capital standard, referred to as the Common Equity Tier 1 ratio, of 7 percent, which very few banks satisfied at the time. The Vickers Commission made a recommendation, which became law in the UK, that banks that undertake certain core banking activities, including taking retail and SME (small and medium-sized enterprise) deposits, would need to ring-fence such activities in a separate legal entity and maintain a minimum capital ratio of 10 percent. We thought we were being extraordinarily adherent to where the Basel Committee was likely to end up with its proposed global standard, and that's the way it was received by banks at the time. They saw it as an overreaction in response to the financial crisis. Today we can expect the ring-fenced banks to have capital ratios of 13 to 15 percent by the time new requirements are implemented in 2019, so 30 to 50 percent more than what we thought was reasonably draconian back in 2011. And I think that's where it will stick. I don't see any rollback of that capital standard. Why are we going from what seemed like, at least to the Basel Committee, a reasonable target back then of 7 percent to a substantially higher target of 15 percent? I think there was just a really hard look at banks' underlying business models and the amount of capital needed to ensure their resilience in future crises. There's also been a significant shift in the thinking about the role of nonequity capital in bank resolution, in particular the form of various types of bail-in bonds.

What I see in the United States right now is a fine-tuning of the regulatory regime for smaller banks that probably weren't intended to be caught up in the systemic nets in the first place, and a relative fine-tuning of the transparency around the stress testing process. As you know, in the United States the Comprehensive Capital Analysis and Review stress testing regime, or CCAR, is the binding capital constraint on most large banks, not the Basel rules or other risk-weighted asset or leverage ratio rules. The big complaint from banks has been that CCAR is a nontransparent process and therefore very difficult to plan around, which is a valid complaint. I think we'll see the new Fed regime putting some incremental transparency in place, not to make it predictable or gameable, but rather just to make it a bit easier for banks to actually run their businesses and make long-term investments with a greater feeling of security.

I think we'll probably see some revision of the Dodd-Frank rules, in particular around the Volcker Rule. As somebody who has had to deal with the Volcker Rule on the receiving side, I will say upfront that I, along with my Vickers Commission colleagues, never thought the Volcker Rule was a good idea; it's part of the reason there is no Volcker type structure in the UK. As a policy, it was always going to be extremely complicated to implement and monitor. This has proven to be the case, and those rules are being simplified, but I do not consider this to be a major rollback of the postcrisis reforms. We won't see capital ratios in the United States falling from 11 to 14 percent back down to 4 to 6 percent, but we'll see a little fine-tuning, including in Europe.

It's been interesting to see how the Basel III-IV process has played out. It would appear that, from the consultation phase to the final policy development phase, there was a substantial rollback of what was going to be a very significant increase in capital requirements for European banks, probably a 60 to

70 percent rollback compared to the initial consultation. However, the initial proposals saw an almost doubling of the capital requirements for many internationally active banks. Some would say that is necessary in certain European jurisdictions. Any rollback in the final Basel rules recognizes that the starting point proposed in 2014 was extreme, particularly given that the objective of the Basel Committee was not to significantly increase the overall amount of capital held by banks.

Ailsa Röell: With Standard Chartered having substantial business in Asia, can you give us a picture of what's happening there on the regulatory front?

William Winters: It's been really interesting to watch how the regulators in Asia have responded to the regulatory changes in the United States and Europe, typically through the Basel Committee's work. It's very clear to me that Singapore and Hong Kong intend to match the most stringent forms of U.S. and European regulation in order to be credible as international financial hubs, but in a more pragmatic way. These are much smaller economies, dramatically smaller, managing far fewer banks as primary regulators, but also overseeing the local operations of international banks, like Standard Chartered. What we have found is that Singapore and Hong Kong follow the United States and Europe very closely in their rulemaking to maintain consistent international standards, but on the other hand apply a level of pragmatism, for example, in the implementation of new banking risk models. Despite the general tightening up in Basel III-IV standards, risk models will still be used. Whilst Asia may be behind in the use of risk models in their local banking sectors, with their local banks not using sophisticated internal risk-based (IRB) models that have been common in the United States and Europe, they are catching up quickly. So I think we'll see a great convergence.

The idiosyncrasies of India and China, just to pick the two major markets in that part of that world, are very pronounced. We know that in India half of the banking system is state-owned and undercapitalized. The government has launched plans in the last couple of months for ways in which they can address the capitalization issue in India. Once these plans are implemented, India's banking system will be better placed to support the broader economy and help foster even stronger economic growth.

China is very different. In China the big banks have been effectively an arm of policymakers. And there's a great deal of speculation about the percentage of loans on Chinese banks' balance sheets that are nonperforming. And I think we could all agree that if the economy in China went through a U.S. or European style postindustrial transition the way we experienced in the 1970s, 1980s, and into the 1990s, that would be very challenging for Chinese banks. But we also know that's a very unlikely scenario in China, given that both the banks and the companies that are being transitioned are owned by the government to a substantial degree. So we should expect a much smoother transition. It almost makes the banking regulatory framework in China less relevant.

Ailsa Röell: Turning back to Europe and the United States, how do you view the overall shift of activities into the shadow banking sector, and what do regulators need to be aware of to ensure that risks do not get out of hand?

William Winters: I've always seen the shadow banking sector through two lenses. During the period between my running of JP Morgan's investment bank and starting at Standard Chartered, I ran a shadow bank. It was not in the shadows, it was a direct lender, a marketplace lender. We didn't borrow money from banks, we took equity that we used to finance loans to clients. So no matter how big we got, I would make the argument that there was no systemic risk. Some would argue that with the proliferation of equity-funded marketplace lenders, the price of credit is going to be mispriced over time. I find it a little hard to understand why an equity-funded lender would be more inclined to misprice credit than a bank would be, but some people make that argument. I don't buy it. So I don't see any systemic risk in loans moving off bank balance sheets and going into the nonbank sector, whether it's the public transparent capital markets or the private nontransparent capital markets.

Where systemic risk might arise is where there's a connection between the still highly leveraged banking market and the shadow banking market, or the nonbank market. That happens when banks lend money to other lenders. Obviously, a big part of the genesis of the financial crisis was the banking sector's exposure to the nonbanking sector, most obviously through SIVs (structured investment vehicles) and other structured credit products that took the losses that would otherwise have been borne by equity. Once the equity in these structures had been depleted, the remaining losses flowed straight back into the banking sector, and we all know what the consequences were. But that's not really happening today. The regulatory framework has developed in such a way that banks are highly disincentivized from extending credit to other nonbank financial institutions. It's a significant capital drag. It would be cheaper to access that funding from nonbank sources. Equity capital for those vehicle types is relatively cheap today. So we've got a reasonably healthy collateralized debt obligations market. There's plenty of leverage in those structures, but the investors behind those leveraged investments are equity investors, not leveraged debt investors, and the equity holders are not connected back to the banking system.

The big exception is China. In China, wealth management products, as they're known, are about 60 percent originated from banks. People talk a lot about the nonbank market in China and how that's going to be the genesis of the next major crisis. I don't really think so. If you took all of the wealth management products that have been initiated by banks, and consolidated them all back onto the banks' balance sheets, you would reduce their Common Equity Tier 1 ratios by about 2 percent, from somewhere around 11.5 to 12 percent to around 9.5 to 10 percent, so not a particularly high level of capital, but nowhere near a crisis level in an economy that's still growing strongly. Having said that, there is a big block of off-balance-sheet credit in China with a connection back to the banking system. And that certainly is one to watch. I am sure that the Chinese banking regulators are watching that very closely.

There's also the 40 percent of wealth management products in China not originated by banks, but by insurance companies or free agents that have setup vehicles that typically offer low-quality loans, often with some embedded leverage, marketing investments in these vehicles to retail or less sophisticated investors. That could be a real shock to the financial system, but probably not to the banking system because it doesn't bear the residual exposure.

Ailsa Röell: Do you think anything needs to be done about FinTech and cryptocurrencies to bring regulation up to date? I'm thinking of the inherent risks and investor protection challenges such as the quite alarming bitcoin bubble, the dangers of identity and password theft, the diversion of seigniorage profit away from government into private sector hands, and the opportunities offered for money laundering. In 2015, you formed a cyberdefense alliance with three other large European banks to address cybersecurity issues. As an international bank that's seeking proactively to fight financial crime, what are the lessons you have learned so far?

William Winters: Well, I think these are lessons that we'll be learning for years to come. We're extremely preoccupied with cybersecurity. I see this as a really separate issue to cryptocurrencies. I'm not an expert in cryptocurrencies. I have been observing the bubble, and it's a bit scary, but it doesn't appear to be systemic in the sense that there seems to be little connection as yet between the mainstream banking payment system and those who are investing in bitcoin or other cryptocurrencies. Again, not being an expert, my view isn't too relevant, but it's hard for me to see what the underlying usefulness of cryptocurrencies really is, certainly if they are to merit anything like the value that's being attached to them, other than for the facilitation of crime. But that's just my view.

Cybersecurity is a critical issue for us, and it comes on a couple of fronts. One is obviously our exposure to being an unwilling party in making payments to people we don't want to make payments to, or theft. And the second is the way in which criminals are using the banking networks of the world to launder money, pay bribes, or evade sanctions. I would say that we are at the forefront of all of those things as one of the largest trade and payments banks in the world. We're the largest clearer of U.S. dollars that isn't an American bank, seventh largest overall. We're the second largest trade bank in Asia. A significant portion of the renminbi that goes in or out of China, or in and out of Africa, is transacted through Standard Chartered Bank, the second largest after the Bank of China in fact. So we're heavily involved in the flow of payments, which puts us in the flow of would-be financial criminals. If I can be very simplistic about it, we've got two generic approaches. One is to go it alone, looking at reams and reams of data, trying to understand what a suspicious transaction might be, and then, when it hits a particular level of concern in terms of indicators of possible criminal activity, we file a suspicious activity report. That's extremely cumbersome and time-intensive, and although we don't know the precise value of the information that we provide to the law enforcement agencies, we can only assume that much of it is not very valuable and that only a tiny fraction of what we identify as suspicious is either actually related to criminal activity or may be investigated by law enforcement. The other approach is collaboration. For criminals, this is international business—arguably the most profitable in the world. The most sophisticated money launderers use multiple institutions for their activity, so any one bank or government agency may only see a fragment of the story. That's why the new information-sharing partnerships on financial crime that are being set up around the world are so important. The breakthroughs they're producing would have been impossible only a few years ago. We're taking a lead on this, working together with governments, regulators, and other global banks to forge new models for combating financial crime. A true tipping point will only be reached when all major financial centers adopt legislation that allows financial information sharing to happen at scale and speed with appropriate safeguards, so it's paramount that governments prioritize these types of meaningful partnerships.

Ailsa Röell: Continuing on the theme of cybersecurity, what is your view on the problems we've seen with SWIFT, in Bangladesh, for example?

William Winters: SWIFT is, as I think most people know, the interbank payment system, and it has recently demonstrated a level of vulnerability. But the Bangladesh situation was rather different. It wasn't the SWIFT system that was compromised, it was the system that the Central Bank of Bangladesh uses to access the SWIFT system that was compromised. That system was used by about fifteen central banks around the world, so presumably they had some of the same vulnerabilities, but one would assume these were quickly patched after the issues in Bangladesh came to light. Of course, you can get a false sense of security, as there are lots of ways to access the SWIFT system, and even the promoters and managers of SWIFT wouldn't suggest that they are impenetrable, because I don't think anyone should assume that they are. The question is how quickly can the vulnerability be tackled once it's been identified, and how much money would be lost in the meantime? As we know, in the Bangladesh case, the savior was a "typo" in one of the payment instructions coming from the perpetrators who were wiring the money out, rather than some structural defence mechanism that was put in place either by SWIFT or by the Central Bank of Bangladesh, or, for that matter, by the Federal Reserve Bank who was the one receiving the instruction. Fortunately, the typo was spotted by the Fed, which stopped what was a bad outcome from becoming really awful.

There's another way around this—another thing I didn't mention—which is the use of distributed ledger technology. At Standard Chartered we deal in a number of markets where the settlement mechanism is very long-term. So, for example, consider the transfer mechanism between Singapore and India; if you're doing a Singapore dollar versus Indian rupee transaction, it's typically four days to settle. During that four-day period, the players on either side of that trade are exposed to each other's credit, and given that Singapore-India is a reasonably active trade corridor, with a large expat community going both ways, that's a lot of capital to be tied up, and a significant risk exposure for the various counterparties. So we worked with a blockchain company called Ripple, which we have invested in, to set up a prototype distributed ledger technology and settlement platform for Singapore dollars and Indian rupees. We intend to roll this out to all currency pairs over time. The settlement time on a distributed ledger technology platform for an agreed trade is T+0; it's real-time, there's no settlement risk, and it obviously doesn't go through Swift. We didn't do this to dis-intermediate SWIFT, although it does have that effect; we did it to reduce the friction costs of trading in Singapore dollars and Indian rupees. We will do that over and over again, and the market will do that over and over again, and eventually, by reducing the settlement risks, we will also be reducing a potential vulnerability to cyberattacks. The obvious question is: Does this technology cyberattack proof itself? I don't think it's possible to predict today that the distributed ledger technology platforms that underpin bitcoin are impenetrable. Now, we know for sure that you can penetrate the bitcoin vaults and exchanges, although these are not built using distributed ledger technology. Nevertheless, I think we can safely say that the cyberprotections of a distributed ledger technology platform are vastly superior to the cyberprotections of any conventional payment system.

One final observation I would make: it's hard for me to imagine governments allowing distributed ledger technology to proliferate without governments having a back door look-in. Once they have a back door look-in, it's no longer secure.

Ailsa Röell: Finally, turning to Brexit, many of your peer banks in London have started moving personnel to Frankfurt, Amsterdam, Paris. I take it your bank is less involved on the continental European scene. But how do you see Brexit affecting London's position as a financial center and investment banking in Europe more generally?

William Winters: Well, we are involved in the European banking sector. We're a big clearer of euros, so in the same way that we clear U.S. dollars out of New York, we clear euros out of Frankfurt today. We do this through a branch of Standard Chartered Bank, which we have done for years. We employ a few hundred people in Frankfurt to do that. We're a major G10 currency trader, as well as providing our clients with interest rate derivatives and other financial instruments to help them manage their financial risks. So we've got a meaningful European business and about 2,000 people covering European clients. We're nowhere as big in Europe as a JP Morgan or Barclays or Deutsche Bank, but nevertheless meaningful. We were one of the first banks to announce our post-Brexit plan to convert our branch in Frankfurt to a subsidiary, which will be an EU-licensed bank. The remainder of our European business will be passported out of the Frankfurt subsidiary.

The consequences for us are rather modest. Current estimates are that it will cost tens of millions of dollars to establish the new subsidiary, we will need to employ between five and fifty more staff in Frankfurt, and we'll have to deploy regulatory capital into the subsidiary that isn't in the branch today. We don't know how much capital will be required; that'll be subject to discussion with the regulator in Germany, but it will be material and may lead to capital inefficiencies. The setting up of the subsidiary will be inconvenient, quite expensive, but manageable. At the end of the day, it's just one of those things that businesses will need to contend with.

When you look at the other banks that have gone through exactly the same exercise that we have, probably two-thirds are going to Germany, maybe 10 percent or 15 percent are going to Ireland—which was our second choice because we actually have a subsidiary in Ireland today—a handful will go to Amsterdam, and a handful will go to Paris. There are likely to be tens of thousands of jobs that will leave the UK banking sector. And that's too bad, it's an own goal, as you would say in soccer.

CHAPTER 21

MONEY MARKET FUNDS AFTER THE ONSET OF THE CRISIS

VIKTORIA BAKLANOVA AND JOSEPH TANEGA

Money market funds are a type of mutual fund developed in the 1970s as a more profitable alternative to bank savings accounts.[1] Since the 1990s, institutional investors have used money market funds as a professional cash management option.[2] Like all mutual fund shares, shares of money market funds are redeemable on demand. This means that investors can generally sell their shares back to a money market fund on any business day at the net asset value. When investors come to redeem their shares, a portfolio manager may have to raise cash by liquidating the fund's investments in a fire-sale manner, potentially at a loss. Massive withdrawals of investments accompanied by liquidations of portfolio assets are referred to as a run on a fund.

The run on U.S. prime money market funds in September 2008 was a defining moment of the financial crisis. Prior to the crisis, investors paid little attention to these funds, which were perceived as a safe, conservative investment option, and they served this function well for nearly forty years.

The importance of money market funds to capital markets is apparent from the size of the industry. In the United States, these funds had assets under management in excess of $3 trillion in early 2008. Globally, money market fund assets reached an all-time high of $5.8 trillion in the first quarter of 2009 and currently stand at $5.3 trillion.[3] Since the crisis, a substantial body of literature has developed explaining the importance of money market funds as providers of funding and market liquidity.[4] Money market funds facilitate household savings and serve as a source of funding for financial institutions and nonfinancial firms worldwide.

On September 16, 2008, the Reserve Primary Fund, a large prime fund, announced that it could no longer maintain a stable $1.00 transaction price (or "broke-the-buck") due to the write-off of its investments in Lehman Brothers' debt.[5] Following this announcement, investors withdrew hundreds of billions of dollars from other similar funds. The run on these funds contributed to strains in the U.S. dollar short-term funding markets and led to a systemwide liquidity freeze.[6]

Unprecedented action by government and regulators stabilized the short-term funding markets.[7] These emergency actions included the Treasury Department's share price guarantee program for eligible money market funds and the Federal Reserve's liquidity facility for asset-backed commercial paper held by money market funds.[8] Less than two years after these events, the Treasury Department issued a proposal for the new regulatory framework that was intended to make the money market fund industry more resilient. The blueprint urged the U.S. Securities and Exchange Commission (SEC) to

> strengthen the regulatory framework around money market funds to reduce the credit and liquidity risk profile of individual money market funds and to make the money market fund industry as a whole less susceptible to runs.[9]

At the international level, the Financial Stability Board (FSB) and the International Organization of Securities Commissions (IOSCO) have developed their own recommendations for structural changes in the global money market fund industry.[10] A call for a harmonized global approach was, in part, motivated by the similar liquidity problems experienced by European funds during the crisis.[11]

In this chapter, we discuss how far money market fund regulation has come in the decade since the onset of the crisis and where we need to go. The discussion has three parts. In the first part, we describe the postcrisis framework under which money market funds operate. In the second part, we outline the availability of data on money market funds. In the third part, we consider whether the right tools are now available to manage the remaining industry vulnerabilities and mitigate potential spillovers.

New Foundation: Postcrisis Regulatory Framework

In the United States

In the United States, Rule 2a-7 under the Investment Company Act of 1940 is the most applicable regulatory construct, although, depending on the question considered, a plethora of other rules and regulations may apply.[12] Rules and regulations under the Investment Company Act constitute a comprehensive regulatory framework that covers not only money market funds but also mutual funds more generally.[13] The framework includes provisions for fund governance, the safekeeping of fund assets, and contractual arrangements presenting conflicts of interest. There are several other broad categories of regulation under the statute: (a) the so-called affiliated transaction provisions; (b) regulation of mutual fund capital structure; (c) regulations relating to certain fund investments and activities; and (d) regulations relating to the issuance and redemption of shares.

The regulations relating to the issuance and redemption of shares as well as the pricing of fund shares and the valuation of fund assets are the two topics central to Rule 2a-7 and the money market fund reforms that were implemented after the financial crisis. When Rule 2a-7 was first adopted in 1983, at its core was an exemption permitting money market funds to use special valuation methods in the sale and redemption of their shares to facilitate the maintenance of a stable price per share, generally of $1.00.[14]

Over the years, Rule 2a-7 has been amended several times, mostly in connection with market events that reflected money market funds' vulnerabilities and threatened their ability to maintain a stable price per share. In the decade since the crisis, the SEC has adopted two rounds of Rule 2a-7 reforms, the first in 2010 and the second in 2014.[15] The reforms adopted in 2010 were intended to strengthen the liquidity and credit risk profile of money market funds and enhance reporting requirements.[16] As a result of the crisis, the need for appropriate liquidity assumed heightened importance. The 2010 amendments to Rule 2a-7 included liquidity requirements, which were based on a qualitative assessment of the fund shareholders' potential liquidity needs as well as specific quantitative limits on fund investments.[17] Money market funds were required to maintain liquidity buffers in the form of daily and weekly liquid assets.[18] These liquidity buffers were intended to provide a source of internal liquidity and to help funds withstand high levels of redemptions during times of market illiquidity.

The 2010 amendments to Rule 2a-7 imposed, for the first time, requirements that money market funds provide monthly disclosure of their portfolio holdings on their websites. The goal was to provide more transparent portfolio information to money market fund investors. This information must be posted on the fund's website no more than five business days after month-end and must show the current portfolio information as of the last day of the month.[19] It was anticipated that investors equipped with the knowledge of portfolio holdings would take actions to influence the levels of fund risk-taking.

Furthermore, the 2010 amendments adopted a new rule requiring money market funds to provide the SEC with monthly electronic filings of portfolio holdings information on Form N-MFP.[20] The form was required to be filed within five business days of the month-end in a specific machine-readable format through EDGAR, the SEC's filing system. The purpose of Form N-MFP filing was to permit the SEC to create a central database for money market fund portfolio holdings, thus enhancing the SEC's ability to respond to market events.[21]

Information filed on Form N-MFP was made available to the broad investment public on the SEC's website. To limit the potentially competitive or destabilizing effects of disclosure, particularly with respect to the disclosure of market-based value information, the public availability of Form N-MFP was required to be delayed by sixty days from the end of the month to which the information pertains. The SEC anticipated that

> many investors, as well as academic researchers, financial analysts, and economic research firms, will use this information to study money market fund holdings and evaluate their risk. Their analyses may help other investors and regulators better understand risks in money market fund portfolios.[22]

The 2014 reforms provided for structural changes that were intended to address run risk.[23] The most notable of these reforms was the requirement that institutional nongovernment money market funds transact at a floating net asset value and that all nongovernment money market funds had the ability to impose a liquidity fee or a temporary redemption gate if their level of weekly liquid assets falls below a specified level.[24]

The floating net asset value requirement was intended to reduce the first mover advantage inherent in a stable transaction price.[25] Liquidity fees and redemption gates were intended to address runs on funds and limit the potential stress on the financial system if a run occurs.[26] In the adopting release, the SEC acknowledged that, on its own, a floating net asset value feature does not eliminate the incentive to redeem fund shares in the pursuit of higher quality or greater liquidity options should the portfolio credit quality deteriorate or the fund liquidity be depleted.[27] The risk associated with these incentives—the risk of run—was addressed by the addition of fees and gates.

The compliance deadline for the 2014 reforms was October 2016. The reforms had a significant effect on the U.S. money market fund industry. In the nine months leading to the compliance deadline, assets in prime funds declined by more than $1 trillion (or 64 percent) to $562 billion, and those in government funds increased by a similar magnitude.[28] U.S. money market funds' total assets under management have been stable at around $3 trillion, but the allocation between nongovernment and government funds has changed dramatically. However, the transition was orderly and showed the ability of the financial system to undergo significant shifts in an orderly manner if given sufficient warning time and planning.[29]

In Europe

Since its origin in the early 1970s, the U.S. money market fund industry has standardized products to a considerable degree. The great majority of U.S. funds were offered at a stable $1.00 price per share where fund portfolios were run in similar manners and their service was perceived as a commodity. In contrast, European money market funds have always offered varied risk profiles.[30] The concept of a constant share price, so favored by U.S. money market fund investors, did not take hold in most European countries. For example, French money market funds, which account for approximately 30 percent of European money market fund assets, have always transacted at variable net asset values.[31] In contrast, money market funds registered in Ireland resembled those in the United States by offering a stable net asset value per share.[32] Irish money market funds currently account for about 37 percent of the European total.[33]

During the early stages of the financial crisis, European money market funds experienced a run stemming from investments in securities, the credit quality and market values of which declined. In the late summer of 2007, bouts of outsized redemptions affected money market funds in France, Germany, and Luxemburg, to mention but a few.[34] The liquidity of European money markets deteriorated, and the European Central Bank took steps to ease funding conditions by injecting billions into the euro money market.[35] These developments highlighted a link between European and U.S. money market fund industries despite differences in fund structure and regulation. Because of apparent market interconnectedness, postcrisis regulatory considerations tend to focus on similarities in the economic functioning of U.S. and European money market funds, resulting in calls for regulatory harmonization.

The European regulatory framework for money market funds developed over the past decade.[36] Prior to the crisis, the majority, though not all, of European money market funds were registered as Undertakings for Collective Investment in Transferable Securities (UCITS) and had to comply with the provisions of the UCITS Directive, which defines rules in respect of eligible assets, leverage, diversification, and counterparty risk.[37] The UCITS Directive does not target money market funds specifically, but it serves as a primary source for harmonized rules at the European Community level, applicable to the funds registered under the UCITS brand. There are, however, two general limitations of the UCITS regulatory framework. First, generic investment parameters established under the UCITS regime are too broad and, per se, do not satisfy the spirit of the low-risk investment product that money market funds are intended to be. Second, a UCITS authorization is not compulsory.

To level the playing field, the Committee of European Securities Regulators, predecessor of the European Securities and Markets Authority (ESMA), published guidelines of a harmonized definition of European money market funds in May 2010.[38] According to these guidelines, European money market funds can be standard or short-term. Portfolio requirements such as maximum asset maturity are stricter for short-term funds than for standard funds. Short-term funds can be sold and redeemed at a stable net asset value per share, whereas standard money market funds must feature floating (or variable) net asset value.[39] ESMA guidelines stipulated a specific disclosure, drawing attention to the difference between a money market fund and a bank deposit, but no obligations to disclose the fund's holdings were included.[40]

In the summer of 2017, almost four years after the European Commission proposed new rules to regulate money market funds at a pan-European level, the regulation was published.[41] Existing money market funds had until January 21, 2019, to comply, whereas new funds created after July 21, 2018, must comply from inception. These new rules apply to all European money market funds, whether they are UCITS or alternative investment funds (AIFs).[42] The new European money market fund regulation permits four types of funds:

1. Public debt constant net asset value money market funds, which must invest at least 99.5 percent of their assets in government securities;
2. Low volatility net asset value money market funds, which may invest in non-government money market securities within certain parameters;
3. Short-term variable net asset value money market funds, which may invest in nongovernment money market securities and have a broader risk profile relative to the low volatility funds;
4. Standard variable net asset value money market funds, which may invest in assets with relatively long maturities to short-term variable net asset value money market funds.[43]

It seems that by virtue of regulatory fine-tuning, the European money market fund industry will likely become incredibly complex. The availability of high-quality, granular data on portfolio holdings is, more than ever, essential for investor monitoring of risk-taking by portfolio managers and for regulatory oversight and enforcement.

Availability of Data About Money Market Funds

As described in the previous section, in the years since the crisis, regulators in the United States and Europe have taken steps to change the structure of the money market fund industry. The main goal of regulatory changes was to improve the ability of money market funds in the United States and the EU to withstand stressful market conditions and make the funds more resilient to runs, while preserving benefits for investors and capital markets. However, we also learned that gaps in data and understanding of the market microstructure contributed to the crisis and hampered efforts to contain it. For this reason, improving market transparency was a substantial part of the U.S. money market fund reform.

In the United States

In 2010, the SEC adopted a new rule requiring money market funds to provide disclosure of portfolio holdings and certain fund statistics on the fund websites, as outlined previously. Moreover, funds were required to file electronic reports of detailed portfolio holdings information on a monthly basis.[44]

The reforms of 2014 represented another significant step toward improved information transparency around money market funds. The new rules provided for more frequent and more substantial website disclosures. First, money market funds are now required to show on their websites the percentage of the fund's total assets invested in daily and weekly liquid assets, as of the end of each business day during the preceding six months.[45] The SEC staff believed that

> having daily information in times of market stress can reduce uncertainty, providing investors assurance that a money market fund has sufficient liquidity to withstand the potential for heavy redemptions.[46]

Public comments regarding the new website disclosure provision revealed expectations that daily disclosure will improve market discipline, thereby reducing the likelihood of heavy redemptions.[47]

Second, money market funds are required to disclose on their websites daily net inflows or outflows, as of the close of the previous business day during the preceding six months.[48] Last, funds are required to disclose on a daily basis the current market-based net asset value per share, rounded to the fourth decimal place in the case of a fund with a $1.0000 share price or an equivalent level of accuracy for funds with a different share price, as of the close of the previous business day during the preceding six months.[49] These daily disclosures must be accompanied by a schedule, chart, graph, or other depiction on the money market fund website showing historical information during the preceding six months.[50] These depictions are intended to make the historical information more easily understood by investors with limited analytical resources.

The 2014 reforms also enhanced Form N-MFP, introduced under the 2010 reforms. Data filed on Form N-MFP were harmonized with the new website disclosures, and certain other modifications were made with the goal of providing investors with more precise information on portfolio holdings.[51] The SEC continued to evaluate the efficacy of portfolio information filed on Form N-MFP, and it used the information to monitor money market funds and inform SEC examination and regulatory programs.[52] To make the portfolio information more timely for investors, the SEC eliminated the sixty-day delay on public availability of Form N-MFP data.[53]

When the rule was adopted, the SEC expected to use this information to create a central database of money market fund portfolio holdings, which would enhance the oversight of money market funds and regulators' ability to respond to market events.[54] Since the autumn of 2014, the SEC has provided monthly summaries of money market fund industry statistics on its website.[55] These summaries are useful in monitoring industry trends and developments, but they do not display any of the granular data at the individual fund level that are available in actual filings. Presumably, individual investors can access these data through the SEC filing database or on the fund websites.

Although fund filings are publicly available, a complex structure and the substantial volume of data are, in effect, obstacles for an average investor to quickly obtain actionable information. Using these new data, the Office of Financial Research (OFR) has developed an interactive U.S. Money Market Fund Monitor and made it publicly available.[56] Investors, fund managers themselves, and policymakers can use it to explore and display fund investments on a granular basis.

The monitor has six charts. Three charts allow users to track money market fund investments by individual fund (drilling down to an individual fund's exposures to specific securities), by fund category (drilling down to aggregate money market fund industry holdings of specific securities), and by prime funds (drilling down to specific a fund manager's exposures to securities issuers). Three charts focus on money market fund activities in the market for repurchase agreements, or repos.[57] The structure of the monitor was motivated by the most frequently asked questions on money market funds during the crisis. For brevity, we limit our explanation of the utility of the monitor to two examples.[58]

Example 1. Normally, individual investors and supervisory agencies would like to be able to track detailed portfolio holdings of a specific fund. The first chart of the OFR Money Market Fund Monitor makes this information readily available.[59] Prime money market funds, in particular, were in the crosshairs of policymakers during the financial crisis. During the events of the European sovereign debt crisis in 2011, these funds rose to the top of the regulatory agenda once again.[60]

Example 2. Historically, U.S. prime money market funds served as important sources of wholesale USD funding for non-U.S. banks.[61] In 2011, when the credit quality of non-U.S. banks came into question in connection with their investments in nonperforming debt of peripheral European countries, the funds ceased the supply of credit. Affected banks struggled to replace this source of USD funding. Government had to step in to ease USD funding conditions.[62] The OFR Money Market Fund Monitor's third chart provides a view of the amount of investments that individual institutions have from prime money market funds.

These examples demonstrate that detailed data on fund portfolios can aid rational decision making by investors and regulators. When data are presented in an accessible, visual format, the universe of users expands to include those with fewer analytical resources. Indeed, portfolio managers believe that "this transparency goes a long way toward educating Chief Financial Officers and treasurers (who are institutional investors) about what the funds do own. Additionally, we believe that the funds are now better prepared to withstand runs with respect to any uncertainty.[63]

This view by a manager of a large money market fund complex confirms that, aside from the needs of the regulatory community, greater transparency helps to align incentives in the right way. Portfolio managers adjust their risk appetites to meet the objectives of their investors and limit excessive risk-taking. Transparency enforces market discipline and promotes the correct pricing of risk. All these factors matter to fund investors and to the industry stakeholders. The alignment of incentives enabled by portfolio transparency serves, ultimately, to reduce the run risk and improve systemic stability.

In Europe

In November 2017, over ten years after the run on European money market funds wreaked havoc on investors, portfolio managers, and regulators alike, ESMA has published a final report explaining the implementation of the new EU regulation covering money market funds. The final report contains the implementation of technical standards, guidelines on stress test scenarios carried out by money market fund managers, and the key requirements related to asset liquidity and credit quality. Most relevant to our discussion, the ESMA Technical Advice provides a quarterly reporting template and states that the first reports should be furnished to the funds' national competent authorities in October or November 2019.[64]

It is our understanding that European national authorities will collect these filings from money market funds registered in their respective jurisdictions. To our knowledge, no central depository of these data has been envisioned. Furthermore, the filings are not expected to be made available to the public. We anticipate a number of issues, which, if not corrected, would substantially reduce the value of this enhanced reporting.

First, a centralized depositary of money market fund filings should be established to enable policymakers to monitor the industry as a whole. National authorities with access to data for only those funds registered in their jurisdictions are likely to overlook potentially troublesome developments at the industry level. Second, more frequent filings should be made. At present, the ESMA Technical Advice requires quarterly filings. Money market fund portfolios, due to their short average maturities, have substantial securities turnover. Quarterly filings will provide stale, less useful information. The filings should be required with at least monthly frequency. Third, the data from the filings must be made available to the public to improve market discipline. Last, a cross-border data sharing arrangement with U.S. authorities should be put in place.

Potentially, the OFR Money Market Fund Monitor could be enhanced with data on portfolio holdings by European funds. Such a powerful tool would greatly improve the ability of policymakers to monitor trends and developments properly in the money market fund industry on both sides of the Atlantic. If warranted, it will enable them to track emerging vulnerabilities and craft a coordinated policy response.

Money Market Funds and Financial Stability

This section builds on the above discussion of regulatory changes around money market funds and debates whether the right tools are now available to manage remaining industry vulnerabilities and mitigate potential spillovers.

Remaining Challenges

Among the features of money market funds that contributed to the financial crisis are liquidity transformation and interconnectedness. The run on prime institutional money market funds in September 2008, and a subsequent systemwide liquidity freeze, offer a powerful example. Adopting 2014 reforms, SEC Chair Mary Jo White stated that

> [the reforms] will reduce the risk of runs in money market funds and provide important new tools that will help further protect investors and the financial system in a crisis . . . [the] strong reform package will make our financial system more resilient and enhance the transparency and fairness of these products for America's investors.[65]

As discussed above, the 2014 reforms provided fund boards with new tools to manage liquidity risk: liquidity fees and gates. These tools are, however, untested. Furthermore, a study conducted by the Federal Bank of New York suggests that these tools can be counterproductive and may lead to preemptive runs. This means that the ability of funds to restrict redemptions when liquidity falls short may threaten financial stability.[66]

Addressing this concern, the SEC highlighted a number of features associated with the actual implementation of fees and gates that would greatly reduce the likelihood of a preemptive run.[67] Specifically, a fund board has discretion in the decision of when to impose fees or gates, if at all. Given this discretion, it would be impossible for any shareholder to foresee the exact moment when it is optimal to run preemptively. In addition, the new daily disclosures help keep shareholders informed about their fund's weekly liquid assets. The disclosures would help shareholders understand if their fund's liquidity is at risk and thus a fee or gate more likely. Transparency should lessen the likelihood of contagion stemming from shareholders' indiscriminate redemption in response to another fund imposing a fee or gate.[68]

This discussion by the SEC reveals a lack of consensus among policymakers over the ultimate effect of certain features of the postcrisis money market fund reforms. In its 2017 annual report, the Financial Stability Oversight Council recommended continued monitoring of the impact of the reforms on other markets and institutions.[69] In addition, we have identified three important challenges:

- Because of the postcrisis structural changes in capital markets outside the money market fund industry, transmission of financial shocks is difficult to assess;
- Different priorities among policymakers still stymie the adoption of the best practices, especially in terms of transparency and data availability;
- With respect to cross-border coordination, more work needs to be done to level the playing field while preserving the benefits to local investors.

Limiting Transmission of Shocks

In 2009, the Money Market Working Group, convened by the Investment Company Institute, studied the events of the financial crisis in connection with the run on money market funds in September 2008 and recommended specific changes in regulation designed to make money market funds more resilient in the face of extreme market conditions.[70] One of the recommendations was a requirement for fund managers to conduct regular stress testing.[71] The working group studied the experience of other non-U.S. regulatory regimes and found evidence of the successful use of stress testing by investment funds in Europe under the UCITS regime.[72]

In 2010, the SEC adopted a new stress testing requirement. The amended rule provided that a fund must periodically test its ability to maintain a stable net asset value per share based upon certain hypothetical events, including an increase in short-term interest rates, an increase in shareholder redemptions, a downgrade of or default on portfolio securities, and widening or narrowing of spreads between yields on an appropriate benchmark.[73] The 2014 reforms amended the stress testing requirements. The new stress testing provisions required that funds periodically

> test their ability to maintain weekly liquid assets of at least 10 percent and to minimize principal volatility in response to specified hypothetical events that include (i) increases in the level of short-term interest rates, (ii) the downgrade or default of particular portfolio security positions, each representing various exposures in a fund's portfolio, and (iii) the widening of spreads in various sectors to which the fund's portfolio is exposed, each in combination with various increases in shareholder redemptions.[74]

In the case of government and retail money market funds, this still includes "the fund's ability to maintain the stable price per share."[75]

We believe that stress testing has enormous potential as a risk management and risk communication tool. The SEC requires that the results of the stress testing be reported to the money market fund boards at their regularly scheduled meetings. This ensures that board members better understand the potential risks to each fund and are equipped with the information necessary to manage those risks.

In its recent report on the core principles for regulating the U.S. financial system, the U.S. Department of the Treasury supported stress testing for money market funds. The report cited the success of the initial supervisory stress test exercise, led by the Federal Reserve for the largest bank holding companies in the midst of the financial crisis.[76] Bank supervisors consider stress testing to be an important contribution to financial stability.[77] Furthermore, the results of the stress tests for banks were made available to the public because

> the Federal Reserve believes that disclosure of stress test results provides valuable information to market participants and the public, enhances transparency, and promotes market discipline.[78]

As a result of public scrutiny, stress testing methodology for banks has consistently improved since the crisis. In contrast, the results of stress tests for money market funds are not publicly available, and we see this as a weakness. Market discipline is not at work. These funds are missing an opportunity to enhance their stress tests through a public dialogue and peer comparison.

Indeed, the SEC stated that through examinations of money market fund stress testing procedures, they

> have observed disparities in the quality and comprehensiveness of stress tests, the types of hypothetical circumstances tested, and the effectiveness of materials produced by fund managers to explain the stress testing results to boards. For example, some funds test for combinations of events, as well as for correlations between events and between portfolio holdings, whereas others do not.[79]

Given the lack of public disclosure of the results of stress testing, policymakers are unable to fully ascertain the benefits of this information for the industry stakeholders. In fact, after noting the benefits of bank stress testing, the U.S. Department of the Treasury made a recommendation to eliminate the stress testing requirement for investment advisors and investment companies, which was codified through the passage of the Dodd-Frank Wall Street Reform and Consumer Protection Act (Dodd-Frank).[80] Under Dodd-Frank, stress testing is required for registered investment companies and registered investment advisors having more than $10 billion in consolidated assets.[81] The SEC also considered ways to implement the Dodd-Frank requirements for annual stress testing, but no rule has been proposed by the SEC to date.[82]

In our view, stakeholders in the asset management industry would benefit from appropriately tailored stress testing. With regard to money market funds, where the stress testing has been implemented through the 2010 reform, appropriate disclosure of the stress testing results would also benefit all stakeholders. It would enable market discipline and allow for continuing improvements of the stress testing process via input from market participants and academia. With respect to improving systemic stability, stress tests would help assess potential shocks to the rest of the financial system and contribute to the development of appropriate policy tools to limit potential contagion.

Implementing Best Practices for Transparency

Given the global nature of the financial industry, it would make sense to have a common set of parameters around data availability. As described in the previous section, the OFR has developed a monitoring tool that provides granular information on U.S. money market funds in an easily accessible visual format. The financial industry participants, and regulators globally, would benefit from a similar tool if the data from other counties were to be added. The recently adopted European Money Market Fund Regulation 2017/1131 did not include such a mechanism but directed the ESMA to adopt reporting requirements.[83] In November 2017, the ESMA issued technical advice that requires European money market funds to file portfolio information with their national authorities, beginning in October or November of 2019.[84]

Through these filings, European authorities will, for first time, gain access to regular data on portfolio holdings of the funds they oversee. These data, however, will not be available to the public. This lack of public disclosure will significantly reduce the usefulness of the data filed under the requirements of the ESMA Technical Advice. The OFR U.S. Money Market Fund Monitor demonstrates that even complex information could be made easily accessible and, therefore, provide significant utility to market participants and policymakers. By adopting a similar approach—making information on money market fund portfolios publicly available—European regulators would have paved a way for the development of data tools accessible to all stakeholders. Better information on money market funds, which are important providers of funding and market liquidity, would in turn encourage market development and improve systemic stability.

Weighting Regulatory Harmonization Against Preserving Benefits to Local Markets

The run on prime institutional money market funds in the United States during the financial crisis was the main motivation for substantial regulatory reforms of money market funds in the United States and across the globe. As shown earlier in this chapter, U.S. money market fund reforms changed the structure of the industry, and a new set of rules at the pan-European level has emerged in the EU. Regulations on both sides of the Atlantic were the result of multiyear work, including consultations with industry and academic studies.

A treasure-trove of information is available on U.S. money market funds. This information has been used to conduct multiple studies, on the basis of which regulatory changes have been made.[85] In contrast, relatively little is known about money market funds in other countries, aside from fund flows and assets under management statistics collected by trade associations.[86] Given the lack of local data, much of the debate around new money market fund regulation in Europe was based on information derived from data about funds in the United States. We are concerned that little attention was paid to the needs of local investors, local market microstructure, and the supply of assets required to be held by money market funds. For example, we are not aware of any substantive studies on how European local markets may react to potential changes in asset supply-demand resulting from European money market fund reform.

It appears that European regulators were focused primarily on replicating the industry structure created in the United States, but some tradeoffs were made to accommodate local market participants. These compromises resulted in a relatively complex, four-tiered construct described in the first section. We suspect investors will have difficulties navigating the new regime. A lack of detailed information about portfolio holdings in the public domain will impede the production of potentially useful academic studies and industry research.

Conclusion

We have come a long way since the onset of the financial crisis, but there is still work to be done and challenges remain. In this chapter, we identified three important challenges related to (1) the adequacy of regulatory tools to manage potential spillovers if a run on funds develops; (2) a lack of data on money market funds outside the United States; and (3) untested results of harmonization in money market fund regulation.

We argue that these challenges could be addressed by improving data availability, by making data accessible for all industry stakeholders, and by sharing data among regulators globally. Better data would improve market analytics, investor education, and regulatory policy, and result in a more resilient financial system.

Notes

We are immensely grateful to Thomas Groll, Geraldine McAllister, and Sharyn O'Halloran for making this project a reality, and for their encouragement and support. We also thank Shyam Sunder and other participants of the conference "Ten Years After the Financial Crisis" organized by the Columbia University for their helpful input. The views expressed in this chapter are ours and do not necessarily reflect those of the OFR, or the U.S. Department of the Treasury. All errors and omissions are ours.

1. Matthew P. Fink, *The Rise of Mutual Funds. An Insider's View* (Oxford: Oxford University Press, 2008).
2. Viktoria Baklanova and Joseph Tanega, eds., *Money Market Funds in the EU and the US: Regulation and Practice* (Oxford: Oxford University Press, 2014), 7.
3. Investment Company Institute, Worldwide Market Statistics as of the second quarter of 2018, https://www.ici.org/research/stats/worldwide.
4. Baklanova and Tanega, eds., *Money Market Funds in the EU and the US*, chap.1.14.
5. On September 16, 2008, the Board of Trustees of the Reserve Fund wrote off $785 million in Lehman Brothers' debt securities held by the Primary Fund. As a result, the net asset value of the Primary Fund dropped from $1.00 to $0.97. See http://www.primary-yieldplus-inliquidation.com/pdf/PressRelease2008_0916.pdf.
6. Treasury Secretary Geithner: "some of the largest companies in the world and the United States [were] losing the capacity to fund and access those commercial paper markets": Financial Crisis Inquiry Committee, *Financial Crisis Inquiry Report*, January 2011, 358, https://www.gpo.gov/fdsys/pkg/GPO-FCIC/pdf/GPO-FCIC.pdf. The President's Working Group on Financial Markets (PWG) noted that the run on prime funds "contributed to severe dislocations in short-term credit markets and strains on the businesses

and institutions that obtain funding in those markets": PWG, "Money Market Fund Reform Options," October 2010, https://www.treasury.gov/press-center/pressreleases /Documents/10.21%20PWG%20Report%20Final.pdf. See also, Naohiko Baba, Robert N. McCauley, and Srichander Ramaswamy, *US Dollar Money Market Funds and Non-US Banks*, March 2009, http://www.bis.org/publ/qtrpdf/r_qt0903g.pdf.

7. For the summary of the policy response to the financial crisis, see Board of Governors of the Federal Reserve System, "The Federal Reserve's Response to the Financial Crisis and Actions to Foster Maximum Employment and Price Stability," undated February 23, 2017, https://www.federalreserve.gov/monetarypolicy/bst_crisisresponse.htm.

8. U.S. Department of the Treasury, "Treasury Announces Temporary Guarantee Program for Money Market Funds," Press Release, September 29, 2008, https://www.treasury.gov /press-center/press-releases/Pages/hp1161.aspx. For additional information on emergency lending facilities established by the Federal Reserve, see https://www.federalreserve .gov/monetarypolicy/bst_lendingother.htm.

9. U.S. Department of the Treasury, "Financial Regulatory Reform. A New Foundation— Rebuilding Financial Supervision and Regulation," June 2009, 12, https://www.treasury .gov/initiatives/wsr/Documents/FinalReport_web.pdf.

10. International Organization of Securities Commission, "Policy Recommendations for Money Market Funds," October 9, 2012, https://www.iosco.org/news/pdf/IOSCONEWS255 .pdf.

11. Julie Ansidei, Elias Bengtsson, Daniele Frison, and Giles Ward, *Money Market Funds in Europe and Financial Stability*, European Systemic Risk Board Occasional Paper Series No.1, June 2012, https://www.esrb.europa.eu/pub/pdf/occasional/20120622_occasional _paper_1.pdf.

12. 17 CFR § 270.2a-7. Extensive discussion of U.S. money market fund regulations can be found in Baklanova and Tanega, eds., *Money Market Funds in the EU and the US*, chap. 5.

13. Those requirements are voluminous and need not be discussed here in detail. See, e.g., Tamar Frankel and Clifford E. Kirsch, *Investment Management Regulation*, 3rd ed. (Anchorage, AK: Fathom, 2005); and Thomas P. Lemke, T. Gerald Lins, and Thomas A. Smith III, *Regulation of Investment Companies* (Albany, NY: Matthew Bender, 1995, updated October 2012).

14. Mutual funds that were not registered under Rule 2a-7 were generally required to sell or redeem their shares at a price based on the current net asset value of the fund's holdings.

15. See SEC Press Releases, "SEC Approves Money Market Fund Reforms to Better Protect Investors," 2010, https://www.sec.gov/news/press/2010/2010-14.htm; and "SEC Adopts Money Market Fund Reform," 2014, https://www.sec.gov/news/press-release/2014-143.

16. Money Market Fund Reform, Investment Company Act Release No. 29132 (February 23, 2010) [75 FR 10060 (March 4, 2010)].

17. See Baklanova and Tanega, eds., *Money Market Funds in the EU and the US*, 139–41.

18. 17 CFR § 270.2a-7(d)(4).

19. 17 CFR § 270.2a-7(h)(10).

20. 17 CFR § 270.30b1-7.

21. Money Market Fund Reform, Investment Company Act Release No. 29132, Section II.E.2.

22. Money Market Fund Reform, Investment Company Act Release No. 29132, 82.

23. See Money Market Fund Reform; Amendments to Form PF, Investment Company Act Release No. 31166 (Jul. 23, 2014) [79 FR 47736 (Aug. 14, 2014)].

24. Money Market Fund Reform; Amendments to Form PF, Investment Company Act Release No. 31166, 39–135.

25. Money Market Fund Reform; Amendments to Form PF, Investment Company Act Release No. 31166, 138.

26. Money Market Fund Reform; Amendments to Form PF, Investment Company Act Release No. 31166, 135–202.

27. Money Market Fund Reform; Amendments to Form PF, Investment Company Act Release No. 31166, 145.

28. For the period January 2016 through October 2016, SEC Form N-MFP. For a more in-depth discussion of the effects of the reforms, see Kenechukwu Anadu and Viktoria Baklanova, *The Intersection of U.S. Money Market Mutual Fund Reforms, Bank Liquidity Requirements, and the Federal Home Loan Bank System*, OFR Working Paper No. 17–05, October 31, 2017, https://www.financialresearch.gov/working-papers/files/OFRwp-17-05 _MMF-Reforms_Liquidity_FHLBs.pdf.

29. Marty Burns, *For Money Market Funds, Massive Preparation Has Paid Off in Smooth Transition*, Investment Company Institute, September 26, 2016, https://www.ici.org /viewpoints/ci.view_16_mmf_transition_1.print.

30. Baklanova and Tanega, eds., *Money Market Funds in the EU and the US*, chap. 2.

31. Investment Company Institute, Worldwide Market Statistics, https://www.ici.org /research/stats/worldwide.

32. Baklanova and Tanega, eds., *Money Market Funds in the EU and the US*, chap. 2.

33. Investment Company Institute, Worldwide Market Statistics as of the second quarter of 2018, https://www.ici.org/research/stats/worldwide.

34. Elias Bengtsson, "Shadow Banking and Financial Stability: European Money Market Funds in the Global Financial Crisis," *Journal of International Money and Finance* 32 (2013): 579–94.

35. European Central Bank, "Supplementary Longer-Term Refinancing Operation," Press Release, August 22, 2007, https://www.ecb.europa.eu/press/pr/date/2007/html/pr070822 .en.html.

36. Baklanova and Tanega, eds., *Money Market Funds in the EU and the US*, chap. 3.

37. Council Directive 85/611/EEC, December 20, 1985, on the coordination of laws, regulations, and administrative provisions relating to undertakings for collective investment in transferable securities (UCITS). This directive is no longer in force; it was repealed by Directive 2009/65/EC of the European Parliament and of the Council and the four implementing acts—Commission Regulation (EU) No 583/2010 and Commission Regulation (EU) No 584/2010, Commission Directive 2010/42/EU, Commission Directive 2010/43/EU, and Directive 2007/16/EC under Directive 2009/65/EC.

38. European Securities and Markets Authority, *CESR's Guidelines on a Common Definition of European Money Market Funds*, Ref. CESR/10-049, May 19, 2010, https://www.esma .europa.eu/sites/default/files/library/2015/11/10-049_cesr_guidelines_mmfs_with _disclaimer.pdf.

39. Baklanova and Tanega, eds., *Money Market Funds in the EU and the US*, chap. 3.

40. European Securities and Markets Authority, *CESR's Guidelines on a Common Definition of European Money Market Funds*, 3.

41. Regulation (EU) 2017/1131 of the European Parliament and of the Council, June 14, 2017, on Money Market Funds, OJ L 169, 30.6.2017, 8–45.

42. The wide range of investment funds that are not registered under the UCITS Directive are referred to as "alternative investment funds." These funds are governed by Directive 2011/61/EU of the European Parliament and of the Council, June 8, 2011, on Alternative Investment Fund Managers, OJ L 174, 1.7.2011, p. 1–73.

43. Regulation (EU) 2017/1131 of the European Parliament, OJ L 169/19.

44. Money Market Fund Reform, Investment Company Act Release No. 29132, 77. A new Rule 30b1-7 required money market funds to report portfolio information on new Form N-MFP.

45. Money Market Fund Reform; Amendments to Form PF, Investment Company Act Release No. 31166, 335.

46. Money Market Fund Reform; Amendments to Form PF, Investment Company Act Release No. 31166, 336.

47. Money Market Fund Reform; Amendments to Form PF, Investment Company Act Release No. 31166, 338.

48. Money Market Fund Reform; Amendments to Form PF, Investment Company Act Release No. 31166, 339–40.

49. Money Market Fund Reform; Amendments to Form PF, Investment Company Act Release No. 31166, 341–42.

50. 17 CFR § 270.2a-7(h)(10)(ii) and (iii).

51. Money Market Fund Reform; Amendments to Form PF, Investment Company Act Release No. 31166, 348.

52. Money Market Fund Reform; Amendments to Form PF, Investment Company Act Release No. 31166, 435.

53. Money Market Fund Reform; Amendments to Form PF, Investment Company Act Release No. 31166, 436.

54. Prior to adoption of Rule 30b1-7, information on money market portfolio holdings was limited to quarterly reports filed with the SEC. Portfolio holdings information available through these reports has quickly become outdated due to the high turnover rate of portfolio securities.

55. Securities and Exchange Commission, *Money Market Fund Statistics*, https://www.sec.gov/divisions/investment/mmf-statistics.shtml.

56. Office of Financial Research, *U.S. Money Market Fund Monitor*, https://www.financialresearch.gov/money-market-funds/.

57. Repos are financial contracts in which one party sells a security to another with the promise to repurchase it at a later date for a previously specified price. Money market funds use repos as an investment that is secured by collateral.

58. For more details, see Viktoria Baklanova and Daniel Stemp, *Reference Guide to the OFR's U.S. Money Market Fund Monitor*, OFR Brief Series 16–07, July 20, 2016, https://financialresearch.gov/briefs/files/OFRbr_2016-07_Money-Market-Fund-Monitor.pdf.

59. Baklanova and Tanega, eds., *Money Market Funds in the EU and the US*, 50.

60. Sergey Chernenko and Adi Sunderam, *The Quiet Run of 2011: Money Market Funds and the European Debt Crisis*, Ohio State University Working Paper Series 2012–04, March 2012, https://fisher.osu.edu/supplements/10/12092/mmmf_2012-03-31.pdf.

61. Baklanova and Tanega, eds., *Money Market Funds in the EU and the US*, chap. 1.22.

62. Board of Governors of the Federal Reserve System, "Federal Reserve and Other Central Banks Announce an Extension of the Existing Temporary U.S. Dollar Liquidity Swap Arrangements Through August 1, 2012," Press Release, June 29, 2011, https://www.federalreserve.gov/newsevents/pressreleases/monetary20110629a.htm.

63. Securities and Exchange Commission, "Roundtable on Money Market Funds and Systemic Risk," quote by Robert P. Brown, Fidelity Management & Research Company, May 10, 2011, https://www.sec.gov/spotlight/mmf-risk/mmf-risk-transcript-051011.htm.

64. European Securities and Markets Authority, "Technical Advice, Draft Implementing Technical Standards and Guidelines under the MMF Regulation," Final Report, Reference ESMA 34-49-103, November 13, 2017, 5, https://www.esma.europa.eu/sites/default/files/library/esma34-49-103_final_report_on_mmf_cp.pdf.

65. Mary Jo White, "Statement at SEC Open Meeting on Money Market Fund Reform," July 23, 2014, https://www.sec.gov/news/public-statement/2014-07-23-open-meeting-statment-mjw.
66. Marco Cipriani, Antoine Martin, Patrick McCabe, and Bruno M. Parigi, "Gates, Fees, and Preemptive Runs," Federal Reserve Board Finance and Economics Discussion Series No. 2014-30, April 3, 2014, https://www.federalreserve.gov/pubs/feds/2014/201430/201430pap.pdf.
67. Money Market Fund Reform; Amendments to Form PF, Investment Company Act Release No. 31166, 63–66.
68. Money Market Fund Reform; Amendments to Form PF, Investment Company Act Release No. 31166, 66.
69. Financial Stability Oversight Council, *2017 Annual Report*, December 14, 2017, https://www.treasury.gov/initiatives/fsoc/studies-reports/Documents/FSOC_2017_Annual_Report.pdf.
70. Investment Company Institute, *Report of the Money Market Working Group Submitted to the Board of Governors of the Investment Company Institute*, March 17, 2009, https://www.ici.org/pdf/ppr_09_mmwg.pdf.
71. Investment Company Institute, *Report of the Money Market Working Group*, 75.
72. Investment Company Institute, *Report of the Money Market Working Group*, 185.
73. Money Market Fund Reform, Investment Company Act Release No. 29132, 67–70.
74. Money Market Fund Reform; Amendments to Form PF, Investment Company Act Release No. 31166, 552–553.
75. 17 CFR § 270.2a-7(g)(8)(i).
76. U.S. Department of the Treasury, "A Financial System That Creates Economic Opportunities: Asset Management and Insurance," Press Release, October 2017, https://www.treasury.gov/press-center/press-releases/Documents/A-Financial-System-That-Creates-Economic-Opportunities-Asset_Management-Insurance.pdf.
77. Governor Daniel K. Tarullo, "Stress Testing After Five Years," June 25, 2014, https://www.federalreserve.gov/newsevents/speech/tarullo20140625a.htm.
78. Board of Governors of the Federal Reserve System, "The Dodd-Frank Act Stress Test 2013: Supervisory Stress Test Methodology and Results," https://www.federalreserve.gov/bankinforeg/stress-tests/executive-summary.htm.
79. Money Market Fund Reform; Amendments to Form PF, Investment Company Act Release No. 31166, 554.
80. Board of Governors of the Federal Reserve System, "The Dodd-Frank Act Stress Test 2013," 41.
81. Dodd-Frank § 165(i)(2) (codified at 12 U.S.C. § 5365).
82. Chair Mary Jo White, "Enhancing Risk Monitoring and Regulatory Safeguards for the Asset Management Industry," December 11, 2014, https://www.sec.gov/news/speech/2014-spch121114mjw.
83. Regulation (EU) 2017/1131 of the European Parliament, OJ L 169/16.
84. European Securities and Markets Authority, "Technical Advice," 5.
85. Money Market Fund Reform; Amendments to Form PF, Investment Company Act Release No. 31166 contains many pages of the SEC staff's discussions of various relevant studies, including a study by the SEC's Division of Risk, Strategy, and Financial Innovation, "Response to Questions Posed by Commissioners Aguilar, Paredes, and Gallagher," November 30, 2012, https://www.sec.gov/files/money-market-funds-memo-2012.pdf.
86. Investment Company Institute, Worldwide Market Statistics, https://www.ici.org/research/stats/worldwide.

CHAPTER 22

THE 2017 TAX ACT'S POTENTIAL IMPACT ON BANK SAFETY AND CAPITALIZATION

MARK J. ROE AND MICHAEL TRÖGE

A key but underappreciated reason for banks' recurring excessive risk-taking is the structure of corporate taxation. Current tax rules penalize equity and boost debt, thereby undermining the capital adequacy efforts that have been central to the postcrisis reform agenda. This tax-based distortion incentivizes financial firms to undermine regulators' capital adequacy rules, either transactionally or by lobbying for their repeal. The resulting debt-heavy structure not only renders banks fragile but also pushes them further toward excessively risky strategies.

In a related paper,[1] we analyze how to fix this pro-debt bias via a revenue-neutral corporate tax reform for banks that should improve bank stability and safety at a magnitude approximating that achieved by the totality of post-2009 crisis capital regulation. Here we apply that analysis to understand the likely impact of the 2017 Tax Act on bank stability: positive but limited. We also estimate its likely impact on bank equity capitalization.

The pro-debt bias in the tax code arises because the cost of debt is deductible from the corporate tax bill, whereas the cost of equity is not, as is well known.[2] Firms consequently can reduce their tax-adjusted average cost of finance by using more debt and less equity. These costs and benefits affect firms' capital structure choices. A firm will generally choose its debt level by trading off the positive and negative effects of leverage. If the tax savings from debt were not in the mix of tradeoffs, then the chance of failure would weigh more strongly in the bank's mix of pluses and minuses, incentivizing them to adopt safer capital structures.[3] Hence, all else equal, the current corporate tax system pushes firms to take on more debt.

The effect of taxation on the financing structures of nonfinancial firms is well understood, but it is often assumed that bank capital structure is principally determined jointly by regulation and by the business of banking, such as the banking system's basic functions of maturity transformation, by which it turns short-term debt in deposits into long-term loans. Hence, it is thought that bank capitalization is less sensitive to the tax advantage of debt or indeed is impervious to the tax impact.

This turns out not to be true. Banks' actual capital exceeds regulatory requirements and the size of this equity cushion responds to tax changes. In the next section of this paper, we review substantial empirical work that clearly documents this relationship between tax rules and bank equity levels: Whenever tax rules change in favor of debt, bank equity levels fall significantly and, conversely, tax reforms favoring equity lead to an increase in equity levels. The magnitude of the impact on banks approximates that on nonfinancial firms. The latter start out, though, with a higher level of equity.

There are reasons to believe that the effect of taxes on capital structure for both banks and nonfinancial firms can be quite strong. A bank's principal "raw material" is not steel or electricity but funding. Because equity carries a tax penalty, an increase in equity levels adversely affects banks' marginal costs, which diminishes their competitiveness. Given the narrow interest margins for banks, even a small tax increase in their marginal funding costs—a fraction of a percent—can sharply alter their behavior. It will not only affect banks' ability to compete with more highly leveraged banks but also affect their ability to compete with the newer nontaxed financial intermediaries that are proliferating in the so-called shadow banking sector.[4]

The 2017 Tax Act lowered the basic corporate tax rate—which applies to banks as well as to nonfinancial corporations—from 35 percent to 21 percent and thereby changes the banks' tradeoff between debt and equity.[5] That 21 percent rate still provides considerable incentive to banks to use too much debt in their capital structure, but less than the prior 35 percent rate did. We extrapolate from existing studies on the impact on leverage of different corporate tax rates, estimating that the change incentivizes banks to increase their capitalization from the low regulatory 4 percent rate before the crisis to about 6.5 percent to 10 percent, with the former falling just below current capital levels and the latter just above. A full-scale and successful effort at tax neutrality should, we estimate, lead to bank capital levels between 10 percent and 20 percent—the former being somewhat more than the current level of bank equity, and the latter being far higher than what is on even an aggressive reformer's regulatory agenda.

Multiple negative features of the 2017 Tax Act have been brought forward, with which we agree—its negative impact on long-term budget deficits, its inappropriate timing when the economy is improving, and its potential to exacerbate inequality. But the act's impact on bank safety and capitalization, albeit modest, is an undiscussed benefit.

The Tax Code's Impact on Bank Safety

In this section, we show the basic tax bias toward debt embedded in today's tax code and then outline how the change in the corporate tax rate from 35 percent to 21 percent reduces that bias.

The Basic Pro-Debt Bias Stated

The basic tax bias toward debt arises from the U.S. corporation tax, which allows corporations to deduct their interest expense on debt from their gross profits, while there is no equivalent advantage for the cost of common equity, such as the dividends and capital gains that stockholders expect.[6]

Consider two operationally identical firms, with one raising its funding before the 2017 tax rate change only via equity and the other raising its funding via significant borrowing. Both earned $50 million from operations. At the then-prevailing 35 percent tax rate, the unlevered, all-equity firm paid 35 percent of its $50 million of income in taxes and had a $32.5 million return to its owners. The first column of figures in table 22.1 illustrates this.

The highly leveraged second firm borrowed heavily to fund itself and paid $40 million in interest, the deductibility of which lowered its tax bill. By paying taxes on the net income of $10 million at a 35 percent tax rate, it returned

TABLE **22.1** Corporate Tax Impact in an All-Equity vs. a Highly Leveraged Firm Under the 35 Percent Corporate Tax Rate

	All-Equity Firm	**Highly Leveraged Firm**
Earnings from operations	$50 million	$50 million
Deductible interest	0	(40 million)
Income before corporate taxes	50 million	10 million
Corporate income tax	(17.5 million)	(3.5 million)
Income to shareholders	32.5 million	6.5 million
Income to creditors	0	40 million
Total investor income	**$32.5 million**	**$46.5 million**

$46.5 million to its investors ($40 million to its creditors and $6.5 million to its stockholders, from $10 million in pretax income, minus $3.5 million in corporate income tax), yielding $14 million more to its investors than the non-leveraged firm. Hence, unless this rather large difference of $14 million had been fully offset by the increased risk of failure, financial stress, or operational degradation, the total value to investors of the second, indebted firm was much higher than that of the first firm. The second column shows the higher after-tax returns to investors in the highly leveraged firm.

To emphasize this result (which is standard in financial analysis): the total value that these firms create for private investors came from the sum of all monies returned to investors. The all-equity operation returned $14 million less to its private investors than did the leveraged firm. Ordinarily the leveraged firm would be worth much more to its total investor pool than the all-equity firm, solely due to the tax deductibility of interest paid.

One might mistakenly think that the equity investors in the leveraged firm suffered compared to the investors in the all-equity firm. Stockholders of the highly leveraged firm received $6.5 million after taxes, whereas the all-equity stockholders get $32.5 million. But such a view is wrong because the leveraged firm needed, and had obtained, less investment from stockholders. The key feature to know is which firm could return more dollars to the totality of its investors. Clearly, it's the leveraged firm.

Real-life situations are more complicated than the simple example given here. In particular, in the above calculations, we neglected the taxes investors pay. To some extent, these taxes offset the strong tax advantage of debt at the corporate level, as interest income from an investment in debt is typically taxed at higher rates than the dividends and capital gains received by an equity investor. Balancing out these pluses and minuses yields a more nuanced picture with the overall tax advantage, depending on the precise income tax rate paid by an investor. However, when all factors are added up, the tax system is biased toward debt. For the large majority of investors, the taxation of debt at the individual investor level does not fully compensate for the tax advantage on the corporate level.[7] Important pro-debt biases have been increasing over time as individual income tax rates have come down and an increasing fraction of investments are held in tax exempt retirement accounts or are otherwise tax advantaged.[8]

The 2017 Tax Reform

This analysis of how the corporate tax makes the corporate system more prone to use debt persists with the new corporate tax rate of 21 percent. But the incentive is not as strong. Table 22.2 illustrates this.

TABLE **22.2** Corporate Tax Impact in an All-Equity vs. a Highly Leveraged Firm Under the New 21 Percent Corporate Tax Rate

	All-Equity Firm	**Highly Leveraged Firm**
Earnings from operations	$50 million	$50 million
Deductible interest	0	(40 million)
Income before corporate taxes	50 million	10 million
Corporate income tax	~~(17.5 million)~~* (**10.5 million**)[†]	~~(3.5 million)~~* (**2.1 million**)[†]
Income to shareholders	~~32.5 million~~* **39.5 million**[†]	~~6.5 million~~* **7.9 million**[†]
Income to creditors	**0**	**40 million**
Total investor income	~~$32.5 million~~* **39.5 million**[†]	~~$46.5 million~~* **47.9 million**[†]

*Items with a line through them represent the values when the tax rate was 35 percent.
[†]Boldfaced entries show the shift in value when the tax rate is 21 percent, as it is now.

Before the 2017 tax reform, the after-tax gap in income provided to investors between the all-equity and the leveraged firm was $14 million; after the tax reform, it is $8.4 million. That $8.4 million in tax saved on $50 million of income is considerable, but not as considerable as $14 million. Table 22.2 shows how to derive these differences. (Again, this analysis neglects the taxation of investment income, which the 2017 tax reform also changed. A more precise analysis would include other, sometimes offsetting effects.[9])

Estimating the 2017 Tax Act's Impact

Is a change in tax rates from 35 percent to 21 percent likely to have a large impact? We can build on the existing studies on the impact of tax reforms on bank capital structure to try to answer this question. We report and discuss this empirical evidence in the following sections.

The Overall Evidence: Tax Incentives Change Banks' Capital Structure

Table 22.3 summarizes all studies since 2010 that examine the effect of taxes on bank capital structure.[10] The methodologies used and the types of tax changes

TABLE 22.3 Impact of Debt to Equity Tax Neutrality on Bank Equity Levels

Study	Methodology	Key Result	Extrapolated Impact (in Percentage of Assets in Added Equity)	Scope of Sample and Added Results	Extrapolated Impact Under a 35% Corporate Tax Rate
Worldwide banks subsidiaries					
1. Gu, de Mooij and Poghosyan, 2015	Leverage reaction to changes in corporate tax rate	Equity increases 3% when tax rate decreases 10%	10.5%	60 countries, 1998–2011 Debt shifts to subsidiaries in high tax countries	10.5%
Worldwide commercial banks					
2. de Mooij and Keen, 2016	Leverage ratio reaction to changes in corporate tax rate	Long-run 2.7% equity increase for 10% decrease in corporate tax rate	9.5%	82 countries, 2001–2009 Banks with small equity buffers and larger banks less sensitive	6.4%
3. Hemmelgarn and Teichmann, 2014	Leverage ratio reaction to changes in the corporate tax rate	A 10% increase in the statutory tax rate increases leverage by 0.98%	3.4%	87 countries, 1997–2011 Lower taxes reduce dividend payout	
U.S. bank holding companies and commercial banks					
4. Milonas, 2016	Commercial banks	Equity increases by 0.15% when tax rate decreased by 1%	5.3%	Effect is symmetric for tax increases and decreases, 1995–2012	8.4%
5. Schandlbauer, 2017	Reaction of nondepositary debt to increase in U.S. state taxes	Tax increase of 1% increases nondepositary debt ratio by 0.60%	11.6%	Tax increases have an effect, decreases do not, 1998–2011	

Belgian banks					
6. Schepens, 2016	Change in relative equity in Belgian and European banks after Belgium ACE	Previously taxed at 34%; after 2 years, Belgian banks' equity levels rise 1.03% more	1.1%	2002–2007 Interrupted by the crisis and Belgian cutbacks in ACE	1.0%
7. Célérier et al., 2017	Change in equity growth rates after ACE introduced	Equity increases by 1% for a tax reduction of 34%	1.0%	1997 Positive effect on market share of Belgian banks in Germany	
Italian mutual banks					
8. Bond et al., 2016	Exogenous regional and time variation of value added tax	Equity increases by 0.3% for each 1% reduction in the value added tax	11.1%	1998–2011 Muted when banks are closer to the regulatory constraint	8.2%
9. Gambacorta et al., 2016	Exogenous regional and time variation of value added tax	Equity increases by 0.15% for each 1% reduction in the value added tax	5.3%	1998–2011 Measured impact is of reduced nondeposit liabilities	
Italian banks					
10. Martin-Flores and Moussu, 2017	Introduction of partial ACE	Equity increases by 0.44% for a tax reduction of 18%	0.9%	2000 and 2002 Impact of ACE removal stronger than its introduction	1.4%
11. Célérier et al., 2017	Change in equity growth rates after removal of partial ACE	Equity increases by 1% for a tax reduction of 18%	1.9%	2002 Negative effect on market share of Italian banks in Germany	
Average impact on equity for banks from neutral tax					6%

Source: Mark J. Roe and Michael Tröge, "Containing Systemic Risk by Taxing Banks Properly," *Yale Journal on Regulation* 35, no. 1 (2018): 181–231, which provides further detail on the location of each study used in this table.

analyzed differ. Most studies observe the debt to equity reaction following a change in corporate tax rates, but some studies also measure the impact of introducing other special taxes that have a pro-debt bias. Three studies examine the effect in Belgium and Italy of their allowance for corporate equity (usually abbreviated as ACE), whereby the firms are able to deduct an imputed cost of equity from their corporate taxes. The majority of the studies focus on a single nation, but some examine large panels with several countries that can be used to exploit cross-country differences in tax laws.

All studies confirm that banks' capital structure choices include a tradeoff of tax benefits for other costs. In every study, banks' capital structure changes in the direction predicted by theory.

In the fourth column of table 22.3 we provide a linear extrapolation of the effect identified by each study to estimate the change in equity levels if the tax benefit generated by the U.S. corporate tax had been fully removed. In the last column, we group studies analyzing the same tax change and provide the average effect of this tax change. Finally, we average these extrapolations to estimate how equity levels are likely to change if the tax benefit of debt were fully removed. Based on these calculations from the bank studies, we would predict a 6 percent increase in total equity. This is not negligible. A bank whose equity was 4 percent of its assets would, by extrapolation, have equity at 10 percent of assets, according to these studies.

The impact of taxes on capital structure is not necessarily linear. But in the absence of added information or better theory, it is the most plausible unbiased estimator here. We also estimated the tax impact of the corporate tax on nonfinancial firms, using the same averaging and extrapolation method.[11] This points to the 35 percent corporate tax boosting debt levels by 14.8 percent (compared to no corporate tax), somewhat more than but similar to the averaged, extrapolated impact revealed in the bank studies.

Extrapolating the Proposal's Impact on U.S. Banks

Thus the estimated impact of removing the tax incentive entirely would lead to about a 6 percent increase in equity—somewhat more than the entire increase from the precrisis 4 percent. However, the 2017 tax reform does not eliminate the tax benefit of equity. It just reduces it. We can adapt the simple linear extrapolation to estimate the impact of a partial removal of tax incentives for leverage.

A rough estimate for the impact of the tax reduction would be 14/35 of the impact of a total elimination of the tax incentive for debt. (The 14 percent comes by subtracting the new 21 percent rate from old 35 percent rate, yielding 14 percent. If the impact is linear, the impact of reducing the 35 percent rate by

14 percent would be 14/35 of the impact of eliminating the tax bias altogether.) Given that we expect a 6 percent increase in equity if the tax advantage were fully removed, we should see equity levels rise by 14/35*6 percent = 2.4 percent for the rate reduction from 35 percent to 21 percent. For nonfinancial firms, we expect a similar but slightly stronger effect with equity levels increasing by 5.9 percent (from 14/35*14.8 percent).

Obviously, when making this estimate, we have assumed that a tax change will have the same effect on capital structure changes, independently of what the preexisting levels of capital are. This assumption is not innocuous. Command-and-control safety regulation since the financial crisis (and banks' assessment of their own safety) has increased capitalization from about 4 or 5 percent to about 8 or 9 percent. Given that most of the studies listed in Table 22.3 were done on banks that had substantially lower equity levels, the base should probably rather be the precrisis capital level, not the forced postcrisis level. In this case, the incentives from the corporate tax decrease would lead to bank capital levels of about 7 or 8 percent—approximately where we are today.

Still, one should not dismiss the safety benefits of even this change in incentives. Banks are now seeking to reduce their capital levels and have stated that they would not have the current levels of equity if not required to be there. Even if the tax change does not lead to further equity increases, the change in incentives due to the tax rate change will reduce banks' incentives to decapitalize sharply from where they are now, either transactionally or by lobbying for weakening of capital regulation.

Conclusion

The next regulatory frontier for making finance safer should be to restructure the corporate taxation of financial firms. Interest should no longer be taxed favorably, at least at the margin, while equity is taxed unfavorably. Evening up the two will create better incentives for safety in finance. The tax change would incentivize banks to use more equity and less debt.

The simple change in tax rates of the 2017 tax reform will have a positive impact on bank safety and decrease banks' incentives to leverage up. In our estimation—extrapolated from the existing studies on bank leverage sensitivity to tax rates—the impact will be on the order of an additional 2.4 percent of equity compared to precrisis levels of around 4 percent. This might not incentivize banks to add equity beyond the levels already achieved since the crisis, but it should still be felt in banks not as aggressively seeking to roll back current capital capitalization.

The 2017 reform is a step in the right direction, but much more could have been achieved by specifically targeting the banks' capital structure incentives with a simple tax reform. Elsewhere we argue that the best way to do this would be to allow banks a deduction for the cost of their equity using some variant of the "Allowance for Corporate Equity" system that Belgium and Italy have partially used.[12] That deduction would make additional bank equity as tax-attractive as debt. This fix best combines safety enhancement, minimal disruption to the extant tax system, and political viability. Tax revenue losses from this reform would be substantially smaller than the decreases in tax revenue generated by the 2017 reduction in tax rates and could be further reduced by only applying the deduction to the portion of equity that the bank has above the regulatory required level. Moreover, to the extent that the new equity substitutes for tax deductible debt, the revenue impact would be neutral. To the extent that it is not, offsetting taxes not based on corporate income should lead to tax revenue neutrality and enhanced financial safety.

Finally, fundamental stability-enhancing tax reform should not stop at solving the pro-debt bias for banks but should also address the larger problem of other tax incentives for debt that pervade the economy. For households, the deductibility of interest on personal debt, such as mortgages, has long had the same systemically detrimental effect of encouraging excessive levels of debt. For the industrial sector, the deductibility of interest artificially boosted the demand for debt from the financial sector. Both enlarged the size of the financial sector, which is detrimental for financial stability. Fully fixing the corporate and household debt bias would contribute to financial stability by shrinking an unnaturally large financial intermediation sector.[13] The new 21 percent rate is a small step in the right direction, but given the size of the problem, much more needs to be done.

Notes

Mark J. Roe and Michael Tröge are professors at Harvard Law School and ESCP-Europe, respectively.

1. Mark J. Roe and Michael Tröge, "Containing Systemic Risk by Taxing Banks Properly," *Yale Journal on Regulation* 35, no. 1 (2018): 181–231.

2. See Franco Modigliani and Merton H. Miller, "Corporate Income Taxes and the Cost of Capital: A Correction," *American Economic Review* 53 (1963): 433–43; see also "Ending the Debt Addiction: A Senseless Subsidy," *The Economist* (May 16, 2015), http://www.economist.com/news/briefing/21651220-most-western-economies-sweeten-cost-borrowing-bad-idea-senseless-subsidy [http://perma.cc/L7MA-KXN3]; Mark J. Roe and Michael Tröge, "How to Use a Bank Tax to Make the Financial System Safer," *Financial Times*, March 24, 2014, http://www.ft.com/content/468a9fe2-b2ce-11e3-8038-00144feabdc0 [http://perma.cc/387W-RPT5].

3. See Alan Kraus and Robert H. Litzenberger, "A State-Preference Model of Optimal Financial Leverage," *Journal of Finance* 28 (1973): 911–22; James H. Scott Jr., "A Theory of Optimal Capital Structure," *The Bell Journal of Economics* 7 (1976): 33–54.

4. See Jeremy C. Stein, "Comment," *Brookings Papers on Economic Activity* (Spring 2010): 50, 52; George Pennacchi, "Banks, Taxes and Nonbank Competition," *Journal of Financial Services Research* 52 (May 2017). See Claire Celerier, Thomas K. Kick, and Steven Ongena, "Changes in the Cost of Bank Equity and the Supply of Bank Credit," Working Paper, 2017, http://papers.ssrn.com/abstract2829326 [http://perma.cc/7XW7-T3KE], demonstrating that changes in the tax cost of equity in Italy and Belgium strongly affect banks' competitiveness.

5. Tax Cuts and Job Act, Pub. L. No. 115–97, 131 Stat. 2054 (2017).

6. Sven Langedijk, Gaëtan Nicodeme, Andrea Pagano, and Alessandro Rossi, "Debt Bias in Corporate Taxation and the Costs of Banking Crises in the EU," European Commission Taxation Papers, Working Paper No. 50–2014, 2014, http://ec.europa.eu/taxation_customs /sites/taxation/files/resources/documents/taxation/gen_info/economic_analysis/tax _papers/taxation_paper_50.pdf [http://perma.cc/AS77-2WZ4].

7. Richard A. Brealey, Stewart C. Myers, and Franklin Allen, *Principles of Corporate Finance*, 11th ed. (New York: McGraw-Hill, 2014), 441–43; John R. Graham, "How Big Are the Tax Benefits of Debt?", *Journal of Finance* 55 (2000): 1901–41.

8. "[T]he share of U.S. corporate stock held in taxable accounts fell more than two-thirds over the past 50 years, from 83.6 percent in 1965 to 24.2 percent in 2015": Steven M. Rosenthal and Lydia S. Austin, "The Dwindling Taxable Share of U.S. Corporate Stock," *Tax Notes* 151 (2016): 923.

9. *Tax Loophole from 1960s Could Let Wealthy Tap 21 Percent Corporate Rate*, Bloomberg, June 11, 2018, www.bloomberg.com/news/articles/2018-07-11/tax-loophole -from-1960s-could-let-wealthy-tap-21-corporate-rate.

10. Roe and Tröge, "Containing Systemic Risk by Taxing Banks Properly," 209–10. Table 23.3 is reproduced from this paper.

11. Roe and Tröge, "Containing Systemic Risk by Taxing Banks Properly," 215.

12. Roe and Tröge, "Containing Systemic Risk by Taxing Banks Properly," 199–205.

13. Shawn Donnan, "Financial Sector in Advanced Economies Is Too Big, Says IMF," *Financial Times*, May 12, 2015, http://www.ft.com/content/4b70ee3a-f88c-11e4-8e16 -00144feab7de [http://perma.cc/LXJ5-VLUG].

CHAPTER 23

DERIVATIVE CLEARINGHOUSES

Collateral Management and Policy Implications

AGOSTINO CAPPONI

Regulatory reforms enacted after the global 2007–2009 financial crisis, most prominently the European Market Infrastructure Regulation (EMIR) and the Dodd-Frank Wall Street Reform and Consumer Protection Act in the United States, require standardized derivative contracts to be executed through the central counterparty (CCP) clearinghouse. The clearinghouse acts as the centralized counterparty to all trades and aids the efficient management of counterparty credit risk. The functioning mechanism is as follows. Dealers that trade derivative contracts, such as interest rates and credit default swaps, become clearing members of a clearinghouse. They post collateral resources to it, and in return the clearinghouse guarantees the fulfillment of clearing member contractual positions, effectively insulating each member from the default risk of its trading counterparties. In addition to mitigating counterparty risk, central clearing also increases trade transparency, legal and operational efficiency, and default management. Clearing members provide services to smaller clearing participants, which can access the cleared market by becoming customers of a clearing member. A clearing member thus holds both proprietary and customer positions. Refer to Pirrong (2011) for a comprehensive survey.

The vast majority of derivative clearinghouses are publicly traded, for-profit corporations. For example, the Chicago Mercantile Exchange (CME) group is a publicly traded company that manages both exchanges and clearinghouses. Clearing members are heavily involved in clearing operations, but they do not directly own the clearinghouse. The current clearing landscape, especially in the United States, is rather monopolistic. ICE Clear Credit covers more than 60 percent of the cleared credit default swap (CDS) contracts, LCH clears more than 50 percent of all over-the-counter (OTC) interest rate swaps globally, and more than 95 percent of the overall cleared OTC interest rate swap market.

In the United States, CCP clearinghouses are principally governed by the U.S. Commodity Futures Trading Commission (CFTC). Major clearinghouses are required to report confidential trade data to CFTC on a daily basis. Those data include the traded portfolios of their clearing members and the corresponding amount of demanded and posted collateral resources. Clearinghouses are also monitored and subject to periodic stress tests from the CFTC's Division of Clearing and Risk (CFTC, 2016). Clearinghouses are considered systemically important institutions, and their defaults may severely harm the stability of financial markets due to the liquidation of large positions and the collateral that they manage. Historically, defaults of clearinghouses have been rare and include the French Caisse de Liquidation (CLAM) in 1974, the Kuala Lumpur Commodity Clearing House in 1983, and the Hong Kong Futures Exchange Clearing Corporation (HKFE) in 1987. These clearinghouses did not use the modern default waterfall structure, but were relying on default funds provided by third parties and thus did not have assessment rights. Modern clearinghouse failures occur when the clearinghouse fails to obtain sufficient resources to fulfill obligations toward their clearing members, in which case resolution procedures are triggered. These procedures are discussed in detail in ISDA (2013).

In this paper, I provide an overview of the clearinghouse functioning mechanism. I review existing works dealing with the clearinghouse's choice of collateral resources and focus on the incentives behind the determination of various layers of loss-absorbing capital, also referred to as the default waterfall. This stock of loss-absorbing assets typically consists of initial margins, prefunded default fund contributions, and the capital contributed by the clearinghouse. I discuss empirical studies on clearinghouse collateral requirements and members' composition. I also highlight policy implications.

Clearinghouse Default Waterfalls

Clearinghouses demand that their participating clearing members post daily variation margins. When the mark-to-market value of a portfolio changes value, either because of price fluctuations or new positions added, a payment needs to be made to the member in the form of variation margins. This guarantees that the net obligation of the clearinghouse to the member (and vice versa) at day's end is kept at zero. In addition to variation margin payments, clearinghouses require their members to post initial margins to cover losses that would be incurred when the portfolio of a defaulted member needs to be liquidated.

When a clearing member defaults, the clearinghouse inherits the member's positions and is required to offload them to return to a balanced book. Because the portfolio value may deteriorate during this liquidation period, the clearinghouse is exposed to liquidation losses. These losses are allocated among the surviving members according to a default waterfall.

The first line of defense against default losses is the defaulting member's initial margins. When margins are exhausted, losses accrue to the member's contribution to the default fund. If losses exceed the defaulting member's contribution, they are absorbed by the capital of the clearinghouse first, and any residual loss is absorbed by default funds contributed by other clearing members. There are two prevailing loss allocation mechanisms. The first allocates losses proportionally to the size of members' contributions to the default fund. Such a rule is followed by Ice Clear Credit, the largest CDS clearinghouse that allocates losses to members on a pro rata basis based on the uncollateralized losses of each individual member's fund under a stressed scenario. The second loss attribution mechanism is based on auctions. Each clearing member submits a bid to the clearinghouse, and the clearinghouse determines the winning bid. For each short bidder (that is, for each member who bids less than the winning bid), the clearinghouse computes the ratio between the distance of the member's bid from the winning bid over the variance of the short bidders. Losses are then proportionally allocated following this criterion. The auction based loss allocation scheme is followed by LCH, the largest clearinghouse for interest rate swaps (LCH Clearnet, 2014b). If all these collateral resources are exhausted, clearinghouses reserve the right to call for additional member contributions to the default fund, typically capped at a multiple of the original default fund contribution.

Initial Margin Requirements

Initial margins constitute the junior layer of the default waterfall structure. Posted margin is overwhelmingly in the form of cash or close cash substitutes (e.g., Treasuries). An early theoretical study of initial margin requirements was done by Duffie and Zhu (2011). They show that exposures (and thus margin requirements) are lower when institutions trade bilaterally rather than through a clearinghouse only if all asset classes are simultaneously cleared through a single central counterparty. They show, however, that if exposures are netted for each asset class separately, then bilateral exposures between dealers may increase because of reduced netting opportunities. Duffie and Zhu (2011) define the aggregate exposure as the CCP risk measure because this quantifies the losses that would be incurred by the clearinghouse if its members were to default. Menkveld (2015) uses a similar measure to measure the effects of crowded trades on losses. He argues that crowdedness present significant risks to the CCP and should be incorporated in member-by-member margin methodologies. The intuition is that losses in members' portfolios become more correlated if their trades are concentrated on a single security or are exposed to similar risk factors. If a large shock hits this factor, then large variation margin calls would take place simultaneously. In this case, if the layers of loss absorbing collateral posted by the members are not sufficient, the CCP would need to make up for losses affecting several portfolios at the same time.

Capponi and Cheng (2018) introduce a model that balances the trade-off between initial margins and clearing fees in the clearinghouse's profit-maximization process. Their work highlights the clearinghouse's fundamental trade-off: high initial margins help reduce the clearinghouse losses and high fees increase its revenue from operating the clearing business, but both reduce trading activity because they impose larger opportunity costs on traders. The model proposed by Capponi and Cheng (2018) consists of a continuous mass of traders, each characterized by his own type, which describes income the member can generate from trades. Each trader's type is private information and known only to the trader, but not to the clearinghouse, which only knows the distribution of types. Traders' types directly impact the clearinghouse's profit because they determine both their trading motives and default probabilities. More specifically, traders extract profit both from fundamental value and default protection. Because the fee lowers traders' overall surplus, and margins lower the value of their default options, the fee and margin requirements affect traders' incentives differently.

The analysis of Capponi and Cheng (2018) shows that margins arising in equilibrium depend on the riskiness of the traded contract, the average fundamental value that traders can generate from trading, and the cost of trading. The latter is of the cost of funding the clearinghouse fee and the initial margin requirements. They show that margins are not determined only by contract risk characteristics, such as price volatility, but also depend on market variables such as the contract volatility and the funding costs. The conclusions of their analysis are consistent with Hedegaard (2014), who provides empirical evidence that margins increase with volatility. This study offers an explanation of the "term-structure" of margins. For instance, the model contributes to partly explaining why back month futures contracts have lower margin requirements. This is likely due to participating traders being mostly hedgers, which in this model correspond to traders with high incomes who trade mostly to capture fundamental value, as opposed to speculators who trade to take advantage of their limited liability.

Biais et al. (2016) use an optimal contracting approach for the determination of margins. Their paper studies the moral hazard problem arising in derivatives hedging, which is caused by the lack of exerting effort in risk management by protection sellers of credit default swap insurance. Their analysis shows that margin calls are a tool for mitigating such a moral hazard problem.

Default Fund Requirements

Clearing members are mandated to contribute to a loss-mutualizing default fund. Current regulations require members to post default funds sufficient to cover the liquidation costs of the two largest members, in extreme yet plausible market conditions; see also the CPSS-IOSCO regulatory guidelines. Such a Cover II rule is adopted by major derivative clearinghouses, including ICE Clear Credit, CME Clearing, ICE Clear, and LCH Clearnet (Armakola and Laurent, 2017).

Whereas initial margins follow a defaulter-pays principle in that the clearinghouse relies on the margins provided by the defaulting party to cover potential losses, default funds are consistent with a survivors-pay principle. In case of a member's default, CCP then relies on a prefunded collective default fund of surviving members to cover losses. There is, at present, considerable debate on the optimal design of such a clearing arrangement.

In a recent study, Capponi et al. (2018c) studied the optimal size of default fund contributions. Their model economy consists of risk-neutral protection sellers who are clearing members of the CCP, risk-averse protection buyers, and a regulator. Protection sellers decide on the riskiness of their projects, which models in reduced form their risk management efforts or engagement in risky investments. Their analysis considers two different market scenarios. In the first scenario, protection sellers do not join the clearinghouse as clearing members and always choose the risky project. In this case, protection buyers are not insured against the defaults of protection sellers. In the second scenario, protection sellers join the clearinghouse and contribute a default fund amount to loss mutualization. Protection buyers are then insured against losses, and thus willing to compensate the protection sellers for joining the clearinghouse by paying a premium. Their study characterizes the premium as the certainty equivalent that the buyer is willing to give up for eliminating counterparty risk; that is, this premium leaves the buyer indifferent between trading bilaterally with the seller or through the CCP.

They show that if the default fund is sufficiently low, members take excessive risk to earn potentially higher returns, imposing a negative externality on the other members. This may result in an inefficient clearing, which is directly related to the size of default fund contributions, whereas a higher default fund imposes higher funding costs to the members and mitigates the negative externalities by incentivizing members to choose safer projects. In their game theoretical model, a regulator (leader) faces a trade-off when he decides the default fund contributions to collect from the clearing members (followers). On one hand, he wants to charge a high default fund to prevent members from excessive risk-taking, and on the other hand, he does not want members incur too high a funding cost because this results in lost investment opportunities for the protection sellers.

Their analysis warns against the use of Cover K rules, guaranteeing against the default of a fixed number K of members. Rather, they find that the socially optimal default fund should be determined to cover a fixed fraction of the default costs, provided that funding costs are not too high. This eliminates the member's incentives to free-ride on the shared pool of default fund resources. Their findings are also supported by Murphy and Nahai-Williamson (2014), who argue that the Cover II standard is not prudent enough and higher levels of financial resources should be considered. Legal studies are supportive of these predictions, for example Yadav (2013) argues that clearing members face risk-taking incentives that can encourage them to pursue risky payoffs at the expense of the clearinghouse.

Clearinghouse Equity

The clearinghouse equity, also referred to as skin in the game, is the capital contributed by the clearinghouse in the default waterfall. It is used to absorb losses in excess of initial margins and default fund contributions posted by the defaulting members, before using the default funds posted by other clearinghouse members. The problem of how to determine the skin in the game for a clearinghouse has long been debated by regulators and was actively discussed during the Global Markets Advisory Committee Meeting held on May 14, 2015, by the CFTC. Clearing members have argued for larger contributions from clearinghouses to align clearinghouse incentives with those of their members. Although major clearinghouses generally agreed that their incentives should be aligned with those of other participating members, they have argued against their skin in the game being a major source of loss absorption (LCH Clearnet, 2014a; CME Group, 2015). Although the contribution of CCP capital to the default waterfall is an important loss absorber, Duffie (2015) argues that at the moment it is not that significant and provides only a means of giving the clearinghouse the incentive to design and manage the clearing network safely.

A study by Capponi et al. (2018b) explores the interplay between the clearinghouse equity and its clearing members' default funds. Their analysis identifies an important trade-off faced by the clearinghouse and its potential clearing members. On one hand, funding large default fund requirements is costly for the members and decreases the amount of risk they can transfer to the clearinghouse; on the other hand, default funds shield against losses arising when other members default and thus reduce the losses that need to be borne by the clearinghouse. Large equity capital from the clearinghouse raises the profits of clearing members because it provides an additional layer of protection before their collateral resources need to be used. As a consequence, it attracts the participation of more members and increases the clearinghouse's revenue. At the same time, this increases the expected losses of the clearinghouse that now has a higher amount of capital at stake. Capponi et al. (2018b) show that the economic roles of default funds and clearinghouse equity are complementary to that of initial margins: they incentivize safe members to participate rather than deterring risky ones from not participating. The main intuition behind their results follows from two key insights: (i) the loss mutualization mechanism implicitly transfers wealth from safe to risky members, and (ii) the monopolistic clearinghouse commits equity to absorb losses only if doing so increases its profits. Their study shows that risky members always gain from sharing their risk with safe ones regardless of the default fund requirement because of the higher value of their default option. The clearinghouse's equity commitment is more effective at incentivizing safe members to participate relative to the default fund requirement. This is because this layer of collateral is posted by the clearinghouse and does not require any additional contribution from the safe members. Their analysis shows that more risk-sharing increases the default fund requirement and thus raises the funding costs of the participating members, but it also leads to a safer outcome because the expected losses are lower. However, the clearinghouse needs to reduce the default fund and equity commitments if funding costs are higher, which in turn may raise systemic risk because it reduces protection from defaults.

The End of the Waterfall

Losses may be so large that they exceed all layers of loss-absorbing collateral described in the earlier sections. If this happens, then the end of the waterfall is reached. There are, at present, two main procedures to deal with default resolution under these extreme circumstances. The first procedure is called variation margin gains haircutting. Under this approach, the CCP reduces any variation margin payments that it was supposed to make to its clearing members, and at the same time it collects in its entirety the variation margin payments due from its members. The CCP would then use savings coming from forgiven variation margin payments to absorb excess losses. Clearing members who suffer losses coming from the lack of received variation margin payments are typically given claims that can be exercised after the CCP has recovered, or they are compensated with equity issued by the CCP. According to ISDA (2013), this "winner-pays" procedure is robust and typically sufficient to stop liquidation losses.

A second contractual restructuring approach is called tear-up. The CCP closes either in full, or in part (partially tearing up), its outstanding positions with the clearing members. For example, if a complete tear-up of its cleared contracts is implemented, a clearinghouse would remain solvent and be operationally ready to continue clearing activities without any need to recapitalize the clearinghouse entity.

Both contract tear-ups and variation margin gains haircutting impose uncertainty on the nondefaulting members of a clearinghouse. The uncertainty regarding the magnitude of these cuts and whether or not the clearinghouse will resort to these measures is costly for members. To avoid these costs, the member may have an incentive to exit the clearinghouse prematurely if he anticipates the occurrence of distress, and this could endanger the clearinghouse. If a member decides to remain because he has a high exposure to the clearinghouse, then he may be negatively affected by these haircuts and enter into financial distress. Hence, regulators who design end-of-the-waterfall resolution policies should account for the reactive behavior of clearinghouse members.

Empirical Studies

There is, at present, little empirical study on the determinant of clearinghouse collateral requirements. Many clearinghouses suggest that their margins are broadly set to cover five days of adverse price/credit spread movements for the portfolio positions with a confidence level of 99 percent (Ivanov and Underwood, 2011), a rule that is commonly referred to as a five-day 99 percent Value-at-Risk (VaR) margining rule. The VaR rule, however, represents a simplified description of the actual margining rules because clearinghouses typically add scenario-specific add-ons to produce the final margin requirement; see, for instance, CME Group (2010) or ICE Clear US (2015). For example, the largest clearinghouse in the credit default swaps market, ICE Clear Credit (ICC), uses: (i) a jump-to-default charge to account for the large payouts that a protection seller would need to make at the occurrence of the credit event, (ii) a spread response charge to reflect changes in the counterparty credit qualities, (iii) an interest risk charge, (iv) a concentration charge to penalize large positions held by clearinghouse members, and (iv) a bid-ask spread charge to capture the basis risk due to the different behavior of an index and its constituents. There are, however, parameters that are discretionarily chosen by the clearinghouse (e.g., the threshold above which the clearinghouse applies a concentration charge).

Capponi et al. (2018a) analyze the main determinants of clearinghouse collateral requirements, focusing on the cleared credit default swap market. They pin down the portfolio and market variables that best explain the collateral requirements set by ICC. Their analysis rejects the long-standing assumption that margins are based on value at risk and instead show that margins are more conservatively set than what was prescribed by a VaR rule. They find that more extreme measures of risk, such as the maximum shortfall, are able to better explain the collateral requirements in this market. They also find that the inclusion of market-based variables such as the CBOE Volatility Index, measuring market volatility, and the Overnight Index Swap spread, proxying the costs of funding, help explain cross-sectional variation of initial margins. The emphasis on tail risk as a determinant of margin requirements is also stressed in the margining model proposed by Duffie et al. (2015). In their study, initial margins are based on a mix of maximum shortfall and short notional, where the latter measure captures the fact that CDS short positions have large downside risks because of the jump-to-default risk. Using a data set of CDS bilateral exposures covering a large fraction of the global single name CDS market, they confirm the findings in the theoretical study by Duffie and Zhu (2011). They find that the introduction of central clearing lowers collateral demand unless a large proliferation of CCPs specializing in different asset classes emerges.

Jones and Perignon (2013) study the default risk of clearing members using a data set including variation margins of all clearing members of the Chicago Mercantile Exchange's CCP. They distinguish between house and customer accounts and find that the primary source of clearing member default risk is proprietary trading. They show that extreme losses of systemically important institutions cluster over time. Even more, they find evidence of a negative correlation between variation margins posted for house and customer positions. Cruz Lopez et al. (2017) introduce a margining methodology called CoMargin, which accounts for the interdependence of profits and losses of clearing members. They define CoMargin as the profit and loss VaR of a clearing member's portfolio, conditional on one or several other members being in financial distress. Their analysis shows that CoMargin enhances the resilience of a CCP and outperforms other unconditional measures that do not condition on the occurrence of extreme events.

The empirical study of Armakola and Laurent (2017) suggests that the credit quality of members who are part of European CCPs is significantly lower than those who belong to U.S. CCPs. This increases the risk that clearing members in European clearinghouses would not be able to fulfill margin calls, hence reducing the short-term liquidity that can be raised to absorb losses. Moreover, risky members would have incentives to free-ride on the services provided by the small proportion of high-quality members. They conclude that default fund contributions should take into account the credit quality of clearinghouse members, and that Cover II charges may not be conservative enough and lead to inefficiencies if market conditions deteriorate.

Policy Implications

The pros and cons of central clearing relative to bilateral trading are still the subjects of investigation. Ghamami and Glasserman (2016) use exposures data from five of the largest U.S. banks on five major asset classes (interest rate derivatives, credit derivatives, commodity derivatives, equity derivatives, and foreign exchange derivatives). They reject the hypothesis that OTC derivatives reforms create a cost incentive for central clearing. Rather, they find that bilateral trading may result in lower capital and collateral costs. Their results contrast with those documented in BCBS (2014a, 2014b), which finds that capital and collateral costs favor central clearing.

The Cover II requirement is still being debated among clearinghouse supervising authorities, especially with regard to clearing of cross-border transactions. U.S. rules include both a Cover I and a Cover II requirement, whereas the European Union primarily uses a Cover II model.[1] However, international and systemic U.S. clearinghouses need to comply with a Cover II model.[2]

Each clearing member may have several accounts with the clearinghouse. U.S. rules require clearinghouses to demand margins on a gross basis for customer accounts, whereas EU margin requirements are calculated on a net basis for omnibus client accounts. This requirement for margins to be posted on a gross, rather than net, basis provides a thicker layer of loss-absorbing collateral to U.S. clearinghouses and delays the need to access default fund resources within the default waterfall relative to their EU counterparts. It is likely that these higher costs of margining and clearing may provide incentives to firms for taking bigger risks through the clearinghouse. As a result, how different regulators choose the types of assets needed to fulfill margin requirements would influence the decomposition of the default waterfall and the extent to which members would take risks through the clearinghouse.

A consideration made by clearing members is whether they should put all trades in a single account held at one clearinghouse or, instead, split the trade across multiple clearers. An obvious advantage of maintaining a single account is that risk is better offset and the overall margins paid to the clearinghouse are lower. If instead the portfolio is split across multiple clearers, then the member loses the diversification benefits arising from consolidating the position into a particular clearinghouse and would need to pay higher initial margins. From the clearinghouse perspective, it would be easier to move small transactions in the case of a default (multiple clearers) rather than a large transaction held a specific clearinghouse. These portability considerations are important when a larger number of transactions become centrally cleared; not only the portability of positions but also the collateral resources associated with them should be taken into account.

A major benefit of central clearing is transparency. A critical feature of bilateral trading in OTC markets is opacity. For example, in a CDS transaction, the protection buyer does not have complete information on the credit quality of the seller. It is shown in Acharya and Bisin (2014) that the lack of monitoring leads the protection seller to take excessive leverage, short-selling many contracts to earn premium upfront and then default on their obligations. Their analysis shows that these inefficiencies can be remedied by a centralized clearing mechanism, because all trades executed through the clearinghouse are registered in a data repository that provides full transparency. Contracts can then be designed based on the protection sellers' positions, hence reducing their incentive to take excessive leverage through short positions because the term of the contracts would then be adapted to reflect this behavior.

The most significant source of systemic risk is the failure of a clearinghouse. LCH Clearnet handled the resolution of the extensive interest rate swaps portfolio held by Lehman at the clearinghouse. As pointed out in Allen (2012), LCH did not need to access its Default Fund during the crisis. Approximately 35 percent of Lehman's initial margin was required to hedge the risk and auction Lehman's house portfolio, hence permitting LCH to return a significant amount to the administrators of Lehman's bankruptcy. In this circumstance, LCH forced the defaulter, instead of the survivors, to pay for the default and insured all market participants from systemic risk consequences that could have followed this unprecedented default. The effective management of Lehman's default by LCH should be interpreted with care and in light of the fact that LCH had developed sophisticated risk management procedures over its twenty years of existence prior to Lehman's default. As the class of cleared products increase, new clearinghouses will enter the market, and their lack of expertise may lead to insolvency during distressed market periods. If a major derivative clearinghouse were close to default, the only option for regulators would be to bail out the clearinghouse or to risk a bankruptcy, with devastating consequences for social welfare.

Notes

The research of A. Capponi is supported by a NSF-CMMI CAREER 1752326 grant.

1. In the United States, clearinghouses must abide by a cover-one system at a minimum; see https://www.law.cornell.edu/uscode/text/7/7a-1, Financial Resources for details.
2. See https://www.law.cornell.edu/cfr/text/17/39.33. They are subject to a more rigorous regulatory regime under Subpart C of the DCO Clearing Standards (Derivatives Clearing Organizations and International Standards, 78 Fed. Reg. 72476 (Dec. 2, 2013)). The CFTC designates a clearinghouse as needing to follow Subpart C if it is deemed to be sufficiently complex, international, and systemic.

References

Acharya, Viral, and Alberto Bisin. 2014. "Counterparty Risk Externality: Centralized Versus Over-the-Counter Markets." *Journal of Economic Theory* 149: 153–82.

Allen, Julia. 2012. "The Problematic Case of Clearinghouses in Complex Markets." *Stanford Law Review* 64: 1079–1108.

Armakola, Angela, and Jean-Paul Laurent. 2017. "CCP Resilience and Clearing Membership." Working Paper, PRISM, Université de Paris 1, Panthéon-Sorbonne.

BCBS. 2014a. "Capital Requirements for Bank Exposures to Central Counterparties." Bank for International Settlements, Basel, Switzerland.

——. 2014b. "The Standardized Approach for Measuring Counterparty Credit Risk Exposures." Bank for International Settlements, Basel, Switzerland.

Biais, Bruno, Florian Heider, and Marie Hoerova. 2016. "Risk-Sharing or Risk-Taking? Counterparty Risk, Incentives and Margins." *Journal of Finance* 71(4): 1669–98.

Capponi, Agostino, and Wan-Schwin Allen Cheng. 2018. "Clearinghouse Margin Requirements." *Operations Research* 66(6), 1542–58.

Capponi, Agostino, Wan-Schwin Allen Cheng, Stefano Giglio, and Richard Haynes. 2018a. "The Collateral Rule: An Empirical Analysis of the CDS Market." Working Paper, Columbia University.

Capponi, Agostino, Wan-Schwin Allen Cheng, and Jay Sethuraman. 2018b. "Clearinghouse Default Waterfalls: Risk-Sharing, Incentives, and Systemic Risk." Working Paper, Columbia University.

Capponi, Agostino, Jessie Wang, and Hongzhong Zhang. 2018c. "Central Clearing and Default Fund Sizing." Working Paper, Columbia University, (1).

CTFC. 2016. "Supervisory Stress Test of Clearinghouses." Technical report, U.S. Commodity Futures Trading Commission.

CME Group. 2010. *CME SPAN: Standard Portfolio Analysis of Risk.* http://www.cmegroup .com/clearing/files/span-methodology.pdf.

——. 2015. "Clearing–Balancing CCP and Member Contributions with Exposures." CME Group White Paper.

Cruz Lopez, Jorge A., Jeffrey H. Harris, Christophe Hurline, and Cristophe Pérignon. 2017. "CoMargin." *Journal of Financial and Quantitative Analysis* 52 (1): 2183–2215.

Duffie, Darrell. 2015. "Resolution of Failing Central Counterparties." In *Making Failure Feasible: How Bankruptcy Reform Can End Too Big to Fail*, ed. Thomas H. Jackson, Kenneth E. Scott, and John B. Taylor, chap. 4. Stanford, CA: Hoover Institution Press.

Duffie, Darrell, Martin Scheicher, and Guillaume Vuillemey. 2015. "Central Clearing and Collateral Demand." *Journal of Financial Economics* 116 (2): 237–56.

Duffie, Darrell, and Haoxiang Zhu. 2011. "Does a Central Clearing Counterparty Reduce Counterparty Risk?" *Review of Asset Pricing Studies* 1 (1): 74–95.

Ghamami, Samim, and Paul Glasserman. 2016. "Does OTC Derivatives Reform Incentivize Central Clearing?" *Journal of Financial Intermediation* 32: 76–87.

Hedegaard, Esben. 2014. "Causes and Consequences of Margin Levels in Futures Markets." Arizona State University Working Paper.

ICE Clear US. 2015. *Span Margin System.* https://www.theice.com/publicdocs/clear_us /SPAN_Explanation.pdf.

ISDA. 2013. "CCP Loss Allocation at the End of the Waterfall." International Swaps and Derivatives Association White Paper.

Ivanov, Stan, and Lee Underwood. 2011. "CDS Clearing at ICE: A Unique Methodology." *Futures Industry Magazine*, 31–33..

Jones, Robert, and Christophe Pérignon. 2013. "Derivatives Clearing, Default Risk and Insurance." *Journal of Risk and Insurance* 80: 373–400.

LCH Clearnet. 2014a. "CCP Risk Management Recovery & Resolution." LCH.Clearnet White Paper.

——. 2014b. "LCH.Clearnet Limited Default Rules."

Menkveld, Albert J. 2017. "Crowded Positions: An Overlooked Systemic Risk for Central Clearing Parties." The Review of Asset Pricing Studies 7(2), 209–42./

Murphy, David, and Paul Nahai-Williamson. 2014. "Dear Prudence, Won't You Come Out to Play? Approaches to the Analysis of CCP Default Fund Adequacy." Bank of England Financial Stability Paper 30, Bank of England.

Pirrong, Craig. 2011. "The Economics of Central Clearing: Theory and Practice." International Swaps and Derivatives Association.

Yadav, Yesha. 2013. "The Problematic Case of Clearinghouses in Complex Markets." *Georgetown Law Journal* 101: 387–444.

CONCLUDING REMARKS

SHARYN O'HALLORAN AND THOMAS GROLL

Ten years after the financial crisis, the U.S. economy has come full circle. As the economy improves and the housing market is once again on an upward swing, the debate has returned to whether and how financial markets should be regulated. Has the pendulum swung too far? Have capital requirements, countercyclical buffers, surcharges, and other rules governing the financial sector overshot their mark? Moreover, does the resultant risk mitigation offset the costs of lending and the accompanying loss of liquidity to the economy?

These are fair questions. What the chapters in this compilation remind us is that we cannot regulate away the risk inherent in financial transactions. Legal contracts can transfer risk from one party to another or from one geographic location to another. Financial instruments can transform the timing of when risks are realized or the concentration of risk throughout the financial system. But the total sum of risk does not change.

Governments can enact regulations that reduce the cost of resolution when things go awry, such as initial margin requirements or deposit insurance. Regulations also can align incentives so firms and individuals do not take risky bets in the first place, such as risk-weighted capital requirements and compensation based on multiyear results. Regulators can similarly limit predatory lending practices by requiring financial institutions to disclose accurate information to consumers and charge reasonable interest rates. But once a financial transaction is undertaken, regulations alone cannot ameliorate risk.

Moreover, rules and procedures that either ban transactions or impose prohibitively high costs spawn unintended consequences. In the postcrisis era, for example, financial institutions have shifted their riskier activities to tax havens and the shadow banking sector to escape the regulatory umbrella. Indeed, in chapter 8, Vincent Bouvatier, Gunther Capelle-Blancard, and Anne-Laure Delatte show that it is some of the largest, most globally connected banks that funnel the greatest percentage of their global activity through tax havens. In chapter 22, Mark Roe and Michael Tröge emphasize the relationships between corporate taxation and financial market activities and argue that the next step in making financial markets safer is to restructure the corporate taxation of financial firms. Similarly, as the cost of doing business in the financial sector has increased, many small and medium-sized banks have exited the market or merged with larger national or regional banks to benefit from economies of scale. Perversely, this trend has increased market concentration in the financial sector and created even bigger banks that may be *much too big to fail.* In chapter 5, Pierre-Charles Pradier finds similar results for the EU financial sector: after regulatory reforms, the insurance industry underwent significant consolidation.

Although we remain circumspect in overstating generalizations, we do believe the contributions in this retrospective of *After the Crash* provide salient insights. Our first remark is to note that given the interconnectedness of capital markets, financial crises are no longer local or even regional events. Rather, they are global events that require global responses. The 2007–2009 financial crisis exemplifies this point. To stabilize global capital markets, demand for goods and services, supply chains, and currency exchanges required coordinated, global efforts. A crisis that began in U.S. financial markets quickly spilled over to trading partners in the European Union, Japan, and other economies. Moreover, the road back has been long and slow. Despite monetary and fiscal policies oriented toward supporting a recovery of financial markets and economic expansion, it took eight years to bring the U.S. unemployment rate to a level consistent with the Federal Reserve's employment objective. In southern Europe, other economies still struggle with instabilities in their banking sectors and with high unemployment.

Second, we observe that mitigating risk at the individual firm level does not eliminate risk at the systemic level. The regulatory changes in response to the financial crisis were necessary to shore up the safety and soundness of large financial institutions. Higher capital requirements, stress test simulations, and greater accountability for banks have stabilized U.S. financial institutions. Moreover, given the results of public stress tests, the banks seem more robust and resilient than a decade ago (and as compared to European banks). As Paul Tucker points out in chapter 16, although much has been done, some regulatory challenges still have not been fully addressed. Before memories fade and we are once more lulled into complacency, Tucker emphasizes that it is essential to remind politicians and the public about the extraordinary costs of the financial crisis and to continue to uphold regulatory reforms as safeguards against future crises.

The other side of the coin of banks holding significantly more capital is a reduction in lending and thus liquidity in the overall economy. Current regulatory uncertainties create a dilemma: how to provide liquidity to borrowers and at the same time manage systemic risk when restrictive capital and legal requirements limit lenders ability to make loans. In response, companies and individuals have migrated financial activities toward alternative sources of funding and payments. Many of these new banking methods lie outside traditional financial exchanges and beyond the regulatory ambit (crowdfunding and cryptocurrencies such as bitcoin, for instance). As a result, it is unclear whether systemic risk, that is, the risk in the financial system as a whole, is ultimately reduced or simply shifted to other financial products or parts of the market.

Regulators focusing on compliance at the bank level may thereby miss the risks that lurk throughout the financial system. Coordinated action among bank regulators would account for both a bank's risk exposure to international capital markets and how much risk a bank exports to the rest of the financial system. Not recognizing both effects implies that many risks will go undetected until an adverse event triggers a downturn. The experiences of both AIG and Lehman Brothers demand a rethinking of how risk exposures are measured and their interaction at the individual bank and systemic levels. The microprudential regulations that make perfect sense at the individual firm level can, in the aggregate, create systemic risk.

Third, we emphasize what Emanuel Derman (chapter 11) and several other contributors have pointed out: industry participants and regulators alike need to incorporate better tools, modeling techniques, and data analytics to make better decisions. Ad hoc policy measures that stabilize financial markets and economies took a severe toll on monetary and fiscal policy instruments. As Antoine Parent observed in chapter 4, the policies adopted during the recent financial crisis were different to the responses (or lack of responses) to the Great Depression. Central bank interest rates have been low for many years, creating hardships for savers and retirement accounts; quantitative easing has provided more liquidity to markets but increased central banks' balance sheets tremendously; government stimulus packages and increased social spending have caused public budgets and debt levels to soar. These efforts helped the U.S. economy come full circle. Looking ahead, however, there is little firepower remaining to stabilize markets should another economic crisis arise anytime soon. To avoid further domestic economic hardships and adverse effects on the global economy, it will take time to restore these policy instruments—interest rates, reducing balance sheets, and fiscal retrenchment. These daunting scenarios suggest that it is even more important that financial market regulation succeed in preventing another financial crisis, or at least dampen its effects, and provide the necessary time to recoup these important fiscal and monetary policy levers crucial to stabilizing economic business cycles.

To manage financial crises, regulators cannot rely on the same antiquated tools and models and expect a different outcome. Complex global markets require tools that are transparent, collaborative, and developed not in silos but that incorporate the insights from industry, regulators, and academics. New data science technologies enable regulators to simulate the impact of various regulations *before* they are implemented. Sharyn O'Halloran and Nikolai Nowaczyk introduce a *systemic risk engine* in chapter 13 that offers a method to evaluate the impact of alternative regulations, such as collateralization, on the financial system before the policy is law. Centralized data depositories, such as the one for money market funds proposed by Viktoria Baklanova and Joseph Tanega in chapter 21, can enhance rulemaking and reduce market uncertainty. Similarly, in chapter 23, Agostino Capponi analyzes clearinghouses that require members to post assets as collateral to design a default waterfall structure and offers policy recommendations to mitigate default risks and enhance centralized clearing. Cooperative efforts between banks can improve transparency in pricing and reduce uncertainty in setting initial margins when entering into over-the-counter derivatives trades. These tools and data depositories enable decision makers to identify, evaluate, and manage systemic risk before the next crisis happens.

Fourth, how governments regulate matters. As we highlight in chapter 3, the structure of decision making, the amount of discretion afforded to agencies, the incentives given to market participants and regulators, and the role of political oversight all affect the performance of financial markets. Yet regulations that seek only to eliminate harmful actions miss an opportunity—the upside of risk mitigation. Regulations also can encourage banks to take actions that promote growth and foster economic prosperity.

In chapter 9, Jeffrey Gordon observes that the set of regulatory rules and actions are not necessarily subject to a static framework. Financial products and transactions continuously change; a right-fit regulatory approach must therefore follow one of "dynamic precaution." Furthermore, financial markets are not only evolving in products but also are becoming more interconnected. Regulators, however, cannot simply shift governance from the local to the global sphere. Instead, solutions must be integrative. By way of an example, in chapter 11 Eli Noam examines how new information technologies pose a significant challenge for the regulation of financial markets, especially when restrictions limit the development of technology that will likely be key drivers of future economic growth.

Along these lines, in chapter 20 William Winters rightly notes that it is not only how much regulation but how you regulate that matters: who regulates whom, how transparent are the rules, and ultimately what do they mean for profitability and market innovation. U.S. financial laws are a patchwork of statutes and rules; no single framework guides regulations and regulatory authority. The number of U.S. regulators is large, implemented rules and expectations can be unclear, and at times coordination among regulators is insufficient for the task at hand. In chapter 2, Glenn Hubbard recognizes that one implication of this regulatory design was that market participants, regulators, and governments were ill prepared for the 2007–2009 financial crisis.

As our recounting in chapter 1 of the demise of Bear Stearns illustrates, decision makers implemented policies, regulatory actions, and stabilization measures hastily—often with the logic of "too big to fail" and disrupting "chains of events and vicious cycles"—to provide market liquidity and to absorb large investment risks incurred by the private sector and contain systemic risk and protect consumer and labor markets. In chapter 7, former Treasury Secretary Jacob Lew recognizes that these ad hoc policy levers and stopgap measures—public "bailouts," economic stimulus packages, monetary policies with "zero bound"-interest rates, quantitative easing, et cetera—were necessary evils to prevent further economic spillovers, stop pessimistic expectations, and prevent the risks of deflation. Obviously, the dilemma with such unforeseen economic shocks—systemic risk in finance and banking resulting from a lack of transparency in asset portfolios and short-term managerial incentives—is that optimal policies and interventions to avoid further economic adversity may cause responses that are insufficient or too restrictive.

The questions is not just whether policy interventions into financial markets were too limiting but did the financial sector bear its fair share of the costs, especially as unemployment and home disclosure rates skyrocketed? Our contributors have offered many answers to the first question of effective regulation—capital requirements, transparency, risk management, and principles and rules, for example. As Jacob Lew further asserts, if done right, these sound and forward-looking policies will prevent other crises and protect people from economic hardships in the future.

In chapter 19, Barney Frank, Stephen Cutler, John C. Coffee Jr., and Kathleen Judge echoed these insights. As the Trump administration seeks to roll back many of the postcrisis reforms and "tailor" financial regulations to specific industry needs, we must remind ourselves why these regulations were necessary in the first place. What has worked, what has not? Arbitrarily setting policies without thought for possible consequences led to the 2000 deregulation of financial derivatives and credit default swaps. As they say, the rest is history.

We end where we began. Financial crises have different distributional effects on different segments of the economy and workforce. Regulators and regulations that focus only on ensuring the smooth functioning of the financial system may lose sight of why financial institutions are important: intermediation of wealth. Right-sizing regulation therefore requires that risk be appropriately distributed, information be readily available, and those least able to bear the burden of risk not be forced to carry the most risk.

To illustrate the importance of this volume's contributions and increase pressure on the financial sector and policymakers alike, in chapter 10 Joseph Stiglitz reminds us that financial crises and the fiscal and monetary policy actions stabilizing them also have distributional consequences. The origins of the financial crisis and the controversial policy responses contributed significantly to economic inequalities and subsequent political turmoil in the aftermath of the crisis. The growth of populism, protectionism, and nationalism can be partially attributed to the economic hardships and perceived unfairness of policies after the 2007–2009 financial crisis and Great Recession. We may have mastered stabilization and recovery of financial markets and economies. Unfortunately, the remaining economic inequalities and political uncertainties continue to affect policy discussions and pose a long-term threat to the global economy and, perhaps, to democracy itself.

CONTRIBUTORS

Viktoria Baklanova, CFA, PRM, is acting associate director for Current Analysis, at the Office of Financial Research. Baklanova joined the OFR in 2014, after almost fifteen years in the financial services industry. She has an extensive background in short-term funding markets and asset management. Baklanova has authored OFR briefs and working papers and has contributed to the agency's annual reports. She led the interagency bilateral repo and securities lending data collection projects and currently represents the U.S. Treasury on the Financial Stability Board's Data Experts Group. Previously, Baklanova worked at Fitch Ratings, Moody's Investors Service, and Landor Capital Management LLC. She coauthored *Money Market Funds in the EU and the US: Regulation and Practice* (Oxford University Press, 2014) and has published numerous articles in law and financial journals. She received her doctorate in finance law from the University of Westminster and certificate in financial engineering from Columbia University.

Gunther Capelle-Blancard is professor at the University of Paris 1 Panthéon-Sorbonne, deputy dean of the Sorbonne School of Economics, and research associate at Labex ReFi. From 2007 to 2009, Capelle-Blancard served as a scientific advisor to the French Council of Economic Analysis, an independent, nonpartisan advisory body, reporting to the prime minister. From 2009 to 2013, he was deputy director of CEPII, a research center in international economics. His research interests include financial markets, financial regulation and taxation, ethics, and corporate social responsibility. His research has been published in international peer-reviewed journals including *The Review of Finance, The European Financial Management Journal, Business Ethics, The Journal of Environmental Economics*

and Management, and *The Journal of Investing.* He received his PhD from the
University of Paris 1, for which he was awarded the Euronext Best Thesis in
Finance Prize from the French Finance Association.

Vincent Bouvatier is professor of economics at the University Paris Est Créteil,
research fellow at ERUDITE, and research associate at CEPII. Bouvatier holds a
professorial thesis from the University of Paris Nanterre and a PhD in economics
from the University of Paris 1. From 2008 to 2017, he was associate professor at
the University of Paris Nanterre and a research fellow at Economix. His research
focuses primarily on empirical banking, particularly issues relating to banking
activities and prudential regulation.

Agostino Capponi is associate professor in the Industrial Engineering and Operations
Research Department at Columbia, where his research interests are in systemic
risk and financial stability, clearinghouses, and market microstructure.
Capponi serves as an external consultant to the U.S. Commodity Futures
Trading Commission in the Office of the Chief Economist on topics related to
clearinghouse collateral requirements. Capponi serves on the editorial boards
of Mathematical Finance, Applied Mathematical Finance, SIAM Journal on
Financial Mathematics, Mathematics and Financial Economics, Operations
Research, Operations Research Letters, Stochastic Systems, and the American
Institute of Mathematical Sciences Journal of Dynamic and Games. He also serves
as a Co-Editor of the Finance Department of Management Science. Agostino is
a recipient of the NSF CAREER award, and the JP Morgan AI Faculty Research
award. Agostino's research on clearinghouses, joint with the Department of
Treasury's Office of Financial Research, has received attention by various media
outlets, including Bloomberg, Thomson Reuters, and the American Banker.

John C. Coffee Jr. is the Adolf A. Berle Professor of Law and director of the Center on
Corporate Governance at Columbia Law School. He is a fellow at the American
Academy of Arts & Sciences and has been repeatedly listed by the *National Law
Journal* as among its "100 Most Influential Lawyers in America." Coffee has served
as a reporter to the American Law Institute for its Corporate Governance Project,
has served on the Legal Advisory Board to the New York Stock Exchange, and as
a member of the SEC's advisory committee on capital formation and regulatory
processes. Coffee is the author or editor of several widely used casebooks on
corporations and securities regulation, including *Securities Regulation: Cases
and Materials* (Foundation Press, 2015) with Hillary Sale; *Cases and Materials
on Corporations* (Aspen, 2013) with Jesse H. Choper and Ronald J. Gilson; and
Business Organizations and Finance (Foundation Press, 2010) with William Klein
and Frank Partnoy. According to a recent survey of law review citations, Coffee is
the most cited law professor in law reviews over the last ten years in the combined
corporate, commercial, and business law field. In 2015, *Lawdragon* included him
on its one-hundred-member "Hall of Fame" list of influential lawyers in the
United States.

Stephen M. Cutler is a litigation partner at the law firm of Simpson Thacher & Barlett LLP in New York. Previously, he was vice chairman at JPMorgan Chase & Co., following eight years as the company's General Counsel, including during the financial crisis. Cutler serves on the boards of the Legal Action Center, the National Women's Law Center, and the Metropolitan Museum of Art. He previously served on the board of the Financial Industry Regulatory Authority. Before joining JPMorgan Chase, Culter served for nearly four years as director of the U.S Securities and Exchange Commission's Division of Enforcement, where he oversaw the commision's invesitgations of Enron and WorldCom. Cutler is a 1982 graduate (summa cum laude) of Yale University and a 1985 graduate of Yale Law School.

Anne-Laure Delatte is deputy director of CEPII, a French government-funded research center in international economics. Delatte is a tenured researcher at CNRS (French Institute for Scientific Research), CEPR research affiliate, also a member of Conseil d'Analyse Economique (Council of Economic Analysis, an independent, nonpartisan advisory body reporting to the French prime minister), and a member of the Scientific Committee of Fondation Banque de France. From 2014 to 2017, she was a visiting scholar at Princeton University. Delatte's research focuses on financial economics and international macroeconomics with an empirical approach, applied to several areas including the euro crisis, cross-border banking, tax havens, exchange rates, forex reserves in emerging countries, and commodity prices.

Emanuel Derman is a professor at Columbia University, where he directs the program in financial engineering. Born in South Africa, Derman has lived in Manhattan for the majority of his professional life. He began his career as a theoretical physicist, doing research on unified theories of elementary particle interactions. In the 1980s, he developed programming languages for business modeling at AT&T Bell Laboratories. From 1985 to 2002, he worked on Wall Street, where he codeveloped the Black-Derman-Toy interest rate model and the local volatility model. Derman is the coauthor of *The Volatility Smile* (Wiley, 2016) and author of *Models. Behaving. Badly.* (Free Press, 2011), one of *Business Week*'s top ten books of 2011. He is also the author of *My Life as a Quant* (Wiley, 2004), also a *Business Week* top ten books of 2004, in which he introduced the quant world to a wide audience.

Mark D. Flood is currently a visiting assistant professor of finance at the University of Maryland, and a senior visiting research scholar to the Center for Financial Policy in the R. H. Smith School of Business there. Previously, he was a research principal in the research and analysis center of the Office of Financial Research in the U. S. Department of the Treasury. Flood joined the office in 2011, soon after it was established. He has taught finance and business at universities in the United States and Canada and worked as a financial economist on issues of regulatory policy and risk management at the Federal Reserve Bank of St. Louis, the Office of Thrift Supervision, the Federal Housing Finance Board, and the Federal Housing Finance

Agency. Flood was a founding member of the Committee to Establish a National Institute of Finance. His research focuses on financial data and risk analysis and has appeared in a number of leading scholarly and policy journals, and in the two-volume *Handbook of Financial Data and Risk Information*. Flood received his doctorate in finance from the University of North Carolina, Chapel Hill, and bachelor's degrees in finance, German, and economics from Indiana University, Bloomington.

Barney Frank is a former member of the U.S. House of Representatives from Massachusetts and currently sits on the Board of Directors for Signature Bank. From 2007 to 2011, Frank served as chairman of the House Financial Services Committee and was a cosponsor of the Dodd-Frank Wall Street Reform and Consumer Protection Act, an extensive reform of the U.S. financial industry. He was elected to the House of Representatives in 1980 and reelected every term thereafter, serving in the ninety-seventh to one hundred eleventh Congresses. During his thirty-two-year career as a member of the U.S Congress, Frank became well known for his involvement in the House Financial Services Committee and in mortgage foreclosure bailout issues, in particular. Frank began his education at Harvard College and later graduated from Harvard Law School. He has published numerous articles on politics and public affairs, including *Speaking Frankly* (Random House, 1992), an essay that discusses the role the Democratic Party should play in the 1990s.

Jeffrey N. Gordon is the Richard Paul Richman Professor of Law at Columbia Law School, visiting professor in the Law Faculty of Oxford University, and a fellow of the European Corporate Governance Institute. He is codirector of Columbia Law School's Millstein Center for Global Markets and Corporate Ownership as well as codirector of the Richman Center for Business, Law and Public Policy. He is currently a participating researcher in The Future of the Corporation project of the British Academy, on the topic "Is Corporate Governance a First Order Cause of the Current Malaise?" Gordon teaches and writes extensively on corporate governance, mergers and acquisitions, comparative corporate governance, and, more recently, the regulation of finance institutions. He is coauthor of *Principles of Financial Regulation* (Oxford University Press, 2016) and coeditor of *The Oxford Handbook on Corporate Law and Governance* (Oxford University Press, 2018). Recent articles relevant to current debates include "The Agency Costs of Agency Capitalism: Activist Investors and the Re-valuation of Governance Rights," *Columbia Law Review* 113 (2013): 863 (with Ronald Gilson); "Systemic Harms and Shareholder Value," *Journal of Legal Analysis* 6 (2014): 35 (with John Armour); and "Bank Resolution in the European Banking Union: An American Perspective on What It Would Take," *Columbia Law Review* 115 (2015): 1297 (with Georg Ringe).

Thomas Groll is lecturer in International and Public Affairs at Columbia University's School of International and Public Affairs. Groll's research interests include industrial organization, political economy, and public economics. His current research focuses on lobbying activities, how they are organized and undertaken, and their effects on policymaking and regulatory outcomes. Groll teaches the core master's course "Macroeconomics for International and Public Affairs." He earned his PhD in economics from the University of Oregon and his diploma/master's in economics from the University of Konstanz, Germany.

Glenn Hubbard is dean and Russell L. Carson Professor of Finance and Economics at Columbia Business School. From 2001 to 2003, he was chairman of the U.S. Council of Economic Advisers. Hubbard is cochair of the Committee on Capital Markets Regulation; he is a past chair of the Economic Club of New York and a past cochair of the Study Group on Corporate Boards. In the corporate sector, he is on the boards of ADP, BlackRock Fixed Income Funds, and MetLife, where he is chairman. In addition to writing more than one hundred scholarly articles in economics and finance, Hubbard is the author of three popular textbooks as well as coauthor of The Aid Trap: Hard Truths About Ending Poverty (Columbia University Press, 2009) with William Duggan; Balance: The Economics of Great Powers from Ancient Rome to Modern America (Simon & Schuster, 2013) with Tim Kane; and Healthy, Wealthy, and Wise: 5 Steps to a Better Health Care System (Hoover Institution Press, 2011) with John Cogan and Daniel Kessler. His commentaries appear in numerous publications, as well as on television and radio. Hubbard received his BA and BS degrees (summa cum laude) from the University of Central Florida and holds a PhD in economics from Harvard University.

Kathryn Judge is a professor of law at Columbia Law School. Judge is an editor of the *Journal of Financial Regulation*, a research member of the European Corporate Governance Institute, and a member of the Financial Research Advisory Council of the Office of Financial Research. She is an expert on financial markets and regulation, including banking, the 2008 financial crisis, regulatory architecture, central bank governance, and regulatory accountability. She has had two articles selected by peers as among the top business law articles of the year, and her scholarship has been published in numerous leading journals, including the *Stanford Law Review, Harvard Law Review, The University of Chicago Law Review, Virginia Law Review*, and *Columbia Law Review*. Prior to joining the Law School, Judge clerked for Judge Richard Posner of the Seventh Circuit Court of Appeals and Justice Stephen Breyer of the Supreme Court. She also worked as a corporate associate with Latham & Watkins. She is a graduate of Stanford Law School, where she earned the Urban A. Sontheimer Honor (second in class), and Wesleyan University.

Jacob (Jack) J. Lew served as the 76th Secretary of the Treasury from 2013 to 2017. He also served as White House Chief of Staff to President Barack Obama and Director of the Office of Management and Budget in both the Obama and Clinton Administrations. Previously, he was principal domestic policy advisor to House Speaker Thomas P. O'Neill, Jr, and has held a variety of private sector and nonprofit roles. Jack is currently a partner at Lindsay Goldberg and on the faculty at the School of International and Public Affairs at Columbia University. Lew graduated (magna cum laude) from Harvard University and received his JD from Georgetown University Law Center.

David Madigan served as the ninth executive vice president for the Arts and Sciences and dean of the Faculty of Arts and Sciences, Columbia University from 2013 to 2018. He is professor of Statistics at Columbia University and served as department chair from 2007 to 2013. Before coming to Columbia in 2007, Madigan was dean of Physical and Mathematical Sciences at Rutgers University. He is a fellow of the American Statistical Association, the Institute of Mathematical Statistics, and the American Association for the Advancement of Science. He received a BA degree in mathematical sciences and a PhD in statistics, both from Trinity College Dublin. Madigan has previously worked for AT&T Inc., Soliloquy Inc., the University of Washington, Rutgers University, and SkillSoft, Inc. He has over 170 publications in such areas as Bayesian statistics, text mining, Monte Carlo methods, pharmacovigilance, and probabilistic graphical models.

Geraldine McAllister is director of the Columbia University Senate. Prior to joining Columbia, McAllister worked in business development in Russia, East Central Europe, and the Middle East and has contributed to and coedited a number of volumes on foreign direct investment. She holds a master's degree in international affairs from Columbia University.

Nolan McCarty is the Susan Dod Brown Professor of Politics and Public Affairs at the Woodrow Wilson School of Public and International Affairs at Princeton University. McCarty was formerly associate dean at the Woodrow Wilson School of Public and International Affairs and chair of the Politics Department. His research interests include U.S. politics, democratic political institutions, and political game theory. He is the recipient of the Robert Eckles Swain National Fellowship from the Hoover Institution and the John M. Olin Fellowship in Political Economy. He has coauthored three books: *Political Game Theory* (Cambridge University Press, 2006) with Adam Meirowitz; *Polarized America: The Dance of Ideology and Unequal Riches* (MIT Press, 2006) with Keith Poole and Howard Rosenthal; and *Political Bubbles: Financial Crises and the Failure of American Democracy* (Princeton University Press, 2013) with Keith Poole and Howard Rosenthal. In 2010, McCarty was elected a fellow of the American Academy of Arts and Sciences. He earned his AB from the University of Chicago and his PhD from Carnegie Mellon University.

Eli Noam is the Paul Garrett Professor of Public Policy and Business Responsibility at Columbia Business School and director of the Columbia Institute for Tele-Information. Noam is the former commissioner for Public Services of New York State. His thirty books include *Who Owns the World's Media* (Oxford University Press, 2016); *Managing Media* (forthcoming); *Cloud-TV* (forthcoming); *Broadband Networks and Smart Grids* (Springer, 2013); *Media Ownership and*

Concentration in America (Oxford University Press, 2009); and *Peer to Peer Video* (Springer, 2008). Noam received his BA, MA, PhD (economics) and JD from Harvard University, and he has received honorary doctorates from the University of Munich (2006) and the University of Marseilles Aix-la-Provence (2008).

Nikolai Nowaczyk is senior consultant at Quaternion Risk Management and works with large investment banks to develop, implement, and validate models that help to comprehend the risks in derivative trades. Nowaczyk's fields of research are finance, mathematics, and data science. His current research studies new topics in financial regulation, in particular forecasting initial margin requirements and their impact on counterparty credit and systemic risk. He received his degree in mathematics from the University of Bonn, Germany, his PhD in mathematics from the University of Regensburg, Germany, and has been an academic visitor at Imperial College London. Nowaczyk collaborates with Sharyn O'Halloran in the Columbia University FinTech Lab.

Sharyn O'Halloran is the George Blumenthal Professor of Political Economy and Professor of International and Public Affairs and serves as the senior vice dean and chief academic officer at the School of Professional Studies at Columbia University. A political scientist and economist by training, O'Halloran has written extensively on issues related to the political economy of international trade and finance, regulation and institutional reform, economic growth and democratic transitions, and the political representation of minorities. O'Halloran received her MA and PhD from the University of California San Diego. Her work focuses on formal and quantitative methods and their application to politics, economics, and public policy.

Antoine Parent is professor of economics at Sciences Po Lyon, a member of the Laboratoire Aménagement Economie Transports (LAET CNRS), and affiliate researcher at OFCE (Observatoire Français des Conjonctures Economiques). Parent's fields of research are cliometrics, market finance, monetary economics, economic history, history of economic thought, and complexity. He has published in *The Journal of Economic History, Explorations in Economic History, The Journal of the History of Economic Thought, The Journal of Institutional Economics, Journal of Evolutionary Economics, Economic Modelling, Journal of Economic Dynamics and Control, Macroeconomic Dynamics*, and *Mathematical Social Sciences*. Parent is the founding director of Team "Cliometrics and Complexity" (CAC), launched in 2014 and hosted by the Complex Systems Institute of the Ecole Normale Supérieure de Lyon. With the creation of Team CAC, he aims to foster interdisciplinary collaboration in the modeling of historical macroeconomic and financial data and to stimulate new approaches to economic history by drawing inspiration from other disciplines, most notably complex systems modeling in physics, econophysics, mathematics, signal processing, and data analytics.

Pierre-Charles Pradier is a lecturer at Paris 1 Panthéon Sorbonne University and joint chief academic officer of Labex ReFi (Laboratory for Excellence for Financial Regulation). Pradier served as dean of the Economics Department at Paris 1 from 2004 to 2010, as vice provost until 2012, and as dean of the CNAM National School of Insurance until 2014. His research interests include economics of risk, insurance, financial regulation, and history. Pradier was awarded the *Risques* prize for his book on the economics of risk (La Découverte, 2007). His latest book, *Financial Regulation in the EU: from Resilience to Growth*, coauthored with Raphaël Douady and Clément Goulet, has been published recently by Palgrave.

Mark J. Roe is the David Berg Professor of Law at Harvard Law School where he teaches corporate law and corporate bankruptcy. Roe wrote *Strong Managers, Weak Owners: The Political Roots of American Corporate Finance* (Princeton University Press, 1994), *Political Determinants of Corporate Governance* (Oxford University Press, 2003), and a casebook, *Bankruptcy and Corporate Reorganization*. His most recent academic articles include "Stock Market Short-Termism's Impact," *University of Pennsylvania Law Review* (forthcoming, 2018); "Three Ages of Bankruptcy," *Harvard Business Law Review* 7 (2017): 1877; "Containing Systemic Risk by Taxing Banks Properly," *Yale Journal of Regulation* 35 (2017): 181 (with Michael Tröge); "Corporate Structural Degradation Due to Too-Big-to-Fail," *University of Pennsylvania Law Review* 162 (2014): 1419; "Breaking Bankruptcy Priority: How Rent-Seeking Upends the Creditors' Bargain," *Virginia Law Review* 99 (2013):1235 (with Fred Tung); and "The Derivatives Market's Payments Priorities as Financial Crisis Accelerator," *Stanford Law Review* 63 (2011): 539.

Ailsa Röell is professor of international and public affairs at Columbia University. Her academic specialty is financial economics and the regulation of financial markets. Röell's research and teaching spans securities markets, corporate finance, and corporate governance. She has published extensively in the area of stock market microstructure, with empirical and theoretical papers on market trading architecture and its impact on liquidity and price formation; a coauthored textbook on the subject, *Market Liquidity*, appeared in 2013. Her research also focuses on corporate governance, with work on topics ranging from corporate governance in banks to the history of concentration of control, shareholder rights and takeover defense mechanisms in the Netherlands, and theoretical and empirical analyses of compensation, earnings manipulation, and class action litigation in the United States. Röell received a PhD in political economy from Johns Hopkins University and an MSc in economics from the University of Groningen. Previously, she was a senior research scholar at Princeton University's Bendheim Center for Finance, following a career on the faculty of the London School of Economics, Université Libre de Bruxelles, and Tilburg University.

Joseph E. Stiglitz was born in Gary, Indiana, in 1943. A graduate of Amherst College, he received his PhD from MIT in 1967, became a full professor at Yale in 1970, and in 1979 was awarded the John Bates Clark Award, given biennially by the American

Economic Association to the economist under forty who has made the most significant contribution to the field. Stiglitz has taught at Princeton, Stanford, MIT, and was the Drummond Professor and a Fellow of All Souls College, Oxford. He is now University Professor at Columbia University in New York. He is also the founder and president of the Initiative for Policy Dialogue at Columbia and chief economist of the Roosevelt Institute. In 2001, he was awarded the Nobel Prize in Economics for his analyses of markets with asymmetric information, and he was a lead author of the 1995 "Report of the Intergovernmental Panel on Climate Change," which shared the 2007 Nobel Peace Prize. In 2011, *Time* named Stiglitz one of the one hundred most influential people in the world. Known for his pioneering work on asymmetric information, Stiglitz's work focuses on income distribution, risk, corporate governance, public policy, macroeconomics, and globalization. He is the author of numerous books, and several bestsellers. His most recent titles are *The Great Divide* (Norton, 2015), *The Euro* (Norton, 2016), *Rewriting the Rules of the American Economy* (Norton, 2016), *Globalization and Its Discontents Revisited* (Norton, 2018, 2002), and *People, Power, and Profits* (Norton, 2019).

Joseph Tanega is professor of law, Vrije Universiteit Brussel (VUB), visiting professor of the University of Bologna, and professor of law at King Abdulaziz University (KAU), Jeddah. Tanega is the author and editor of sixteen volumes and over sixty chapters and articles on securities and capital markets law, and he has published articles in *NYU Journal of Law and Business, Oxford Capital Markets Law Journal*, and *Columbia European Law Journal*. He is the author of *Securitisation Law, EU* and *US Disclosure Regulations* (LexisNexis Butterworths, 2009, 2015) and coeditor and coauthor of *Money Market Funds, EU and US Regulation and Practice* (Oxford University Press, 2014). Tanega is the founder and former course leader of the LL.M. Corporate Finance Law Program in Corporate Finance Law at Westminster Law School.

Michael Tröge is professor at ESCP Europe. Prior to joining ESCP Europe, he was research associate at the Wissenschaftszentrum Berlin (WZB), a government-sponsored think tank, and visiting scholar at J.L. Kellogg Graduate School of Management at Northwestern University. Tröge's research focuses on game theory and commercial banking and, in particular, the competitive interaction of banks in credit markets. His work has been published in numerous academic and practitioner-oriented journals, including the *Journal of Mathematical Economics, Games and Economic Behaviour, Journal of Economics, European Journal of Finance, International Journal of Industrial Economics, Annales d'Economie et de Statistiques*, and *EC Competition Policy Newsletter*. In addition to his academic research, Tröge has served as an expert on the European Commission's Sector Inquiry in Retail Banking and regularly serves as a consultant specializing in the intersection of antitrust and finance. Tröge received a master's in mathematics from the Ludwig Maximilians Universität

München, a DESS in finance from the Institut d'Etudes Politiques, and a PhD from Humboldt University Berlin.

Sir Paul Tucker is chair of the Systemic Risk Council, a fellow at Harvard Kennedy School, and author of *Unelected Power: The Quest for Legitimacy in Central Banking and the Regulatory State* (Princeton University Press, 2018). His other activities include being a director at Swiss Re, a senior fellow at the Harvard Center for European Studies, a member of the Advisory Board of the Yale Program on Financial Stability, president of the UK's National Institute for Economic and Social Research, and a governor of the Ditchley Foundation. Previously, a central banker for over thirty years, he was deputy governor at the Bank of England, sitting on its monetary policy, financial stability, and prudential policy committees. Internationally, he was a member of the G20 Financial Stability Board, chairing its group on too big to fail; and a director of the Bank for International Settlements, chairing its Committee on Payment and Settlement Systems.

William T. (Bill) Winters was appointed to the Board of Standard Chartered PLC as group chief executive on June, 10, 2015. Winters spent twenty-six years with JPMorgan in diverse leadership roles, becoming co-CEO of the investment bank in 2004 until 2009. He was a member of the Independent Commission on Banking, established by the UK government in 2010. Subsequently, he served as advisor to the Parliamentary Commission on Banking Standards and was asked by the Court of the Bank of England to complete an independent review of the bank's liquidity operations. Winters was chairman and CEO of Renshaw Bay, the hedge fund company he founded in 2011, until his appointment to the Standard Chartered PLC Board. Winters is an iNED of Novartis International AG and was a nonexecutive director of Pension Insurance Corporation PLC. He received a bachelor's degree in international relations from Colgate University and an MBA from the Wharton School at the University of Pennsylvania.

INDEX